Community, Self, and Identity

World Anthropology

General Editor

SOL TAX

Patrons

CLAUDE LÉVI-STRAUSS
MARGARET MEAD
LAILA SHUKRY EL HAMAMSY
M. N. SRINIVAS

MOUTON PUBLISHERS · THE HAGUE · PARIS
DISTRIBUTED IN THE USA AND CANADA BY ALDINE, CHICAGO

Community, Self, and Identity

Editors
BHABAGRAHI MISRA
JAMES PRESTON

MOUTON PUBLISHERS · THE HAGUE · PARIS
DISTRIBUTED IN THE USA AND CANADA BY ALDINE, CHICAGO

Copyright © 1978 by Mouton Publishers. All rights reserved.
No part of this publication may be reproduced,
stored in a retrieval system, or transmitted,
in any form or by any means, electronic, mechanical,
photocopying, recording or otherwise without the
written permission of Mouton Publishers, The Hague
Distributed in the United States of America and Canada
by Aldine Publishing Company, Chicago, Illinois
ISBN 90-279-7650-3 (Mouton)
0-202-90072-X (Aldine)
Jacket photo by James Preston
Cover and jacket design by Jurriaan Schrofer
Indexes by Society of Indexers, Great Britain
Printed in Great Britain

General Editor's Preface

Anthropology began with the study of the nature and history of human culture as a singular phenomenon, then it moved quickly to the dynamics of the cultures of particular societies, and then to studies of the societies themselves as cultural phenomena. The present book moves in turn to the new "intentional" — often ephemeral — communities which form themselves in response to an increasingly anonymous large society. As usual in anthropology, it places these communities in a comparative framework by providing descriptions of a worldwide array of other, longer lasting societies, which also vary from the traditional anthropological specimens. Religion emerges as important both in the formation and in the maintenance of almost all such societies, hardly less so than in the historic "natural" human communities in which individuals also — but less manifestly — found protection. It is not surprising that a book emphasizing problems of community and identity should be a product of a Congress of scholars from the widest variety of the world's cultures.

Like most contemporary sciences, anthropology is a product of the European tradition. Some argue that it is a product of colonialism, with one small and self-interested part of the species dominating the study of the whole. If we are to understand the species, our science needs substantial input from scholars who represent a variety of the world's cultures. It was a deliberate purpose of the IXth International Congress of Anthropological and Ethnological Sciences to provide impetus in this direction. The *World Anthropology* volumes, therefore, offer a first glimpse of a human science in which members from all societies have played an active role. Each of the books is designed to be self-contained; each is an attempt to update its particular sector of scientific knowledge and is written by specialists from all parts of the world. Each volume should be read and reviewed individually as a separate volume on its own given subject. The set as a whole will indicate what changes are in store for anthropology as scholars from the developing countries join in studying the species of which we are all a part.

The IXth Congress was planned from the beginning not only to include as many of the scholars from every part of the world as possible, but also with a view toward the eventual publication of the papers in high-quality volumes. At previous Congresses scholars were invited to bring papers which were then read out loud. They were necessarily limited in length; many were only summarized; there was little time for discussion; and the sparse discussion could only be in one language. The IXth Congress was an experiment aimed at changing this. Papers were written with the intention of exchanging them before the Congress, particularly in extensive pre-Congress sessions; they were not intended to be read aloud at the Congress, that time being devoted to discussions — discussions which were simultaneously and professionally translated into five languages. The method for eliciting the papers was structured to make as representative a sample as was allowable when scholarly creativity — hence self-selection — was critically important. Scholars were asked both to propose papers of their own and to suggest topics for sessions of the Congress which they might edit into volumes. All were then informed of the suggestions and encouraged to rethink their own papers and the topics. The process, therefore, was a continuous one of feedback and exchange and it has continued to be so even after the Congress. The some two thousand papers comprising *World Anthropology* certainly then offer a substantial sample of world anthropology. It has been said that anthropology is at a turning point; if this is so, these volumes will be the historical direction-markers.

As might have been foreseen in the first post-colonial generation, the large majority of the Congress papers (82 percent) are the work of scholars identified with the industrialized world which fathered our traditional discipline and the institution of the Congress itself: Eastern Europe (15 percent); Western Europe (16 percent); North America (47 percent); Japan, South Africa, Australia, and New Zealand (4 percent). Only 18 percent of the papers are from developing areas: Africa (4 percent); Asia-Oceania (9 percent); Latin America (5 percent). Aside from the substantial representation from the U.S.S.R. and the nations of Eastern Europe, a significant difference between this corpus of written material and that of other Congresses is the addition of the large proportion of contributions from Africa, Asia, and Latin America. "Only 18 percent" is two to four times as great a proportion as that of other Congresses; moreover, 18 percent of 2,000 papers is 360 papers, 10 times the number of "Third World" papers presented at previous Congresses. In fact, these 360 papers are more than the total of *all* papers published after the last International Congress of Anthropological and Ethnological Sciences which was held in the United States (Philadelphia, 1956).

Among other books in this series which will interest the reader of the present volume are those on psychological anthropology, on education, socialization and youth, on religion and ritual, and on traditional cultures and the effects of urbanization and social change in many parts of the world.

Chicago, Illinois   SOL TAX
May 16, 1978

Table of Contents

General Editor's Preface — v

Introduction — 1
   by *Bhabagrahi Misra* and *James J. Preston*

SECTION ONE: COMMUNITY IN SOUTH ASIAN CULTURES

Gods, Kings, and the Caste System in India — 7
   by *L. K. Mahapatra*

Commercial Economy of an Urban Temple in India: A Shift from Inheritance to Consignment Rights — 27
   by *James J. Preston*

The Indian Caste Community as a Social System — 37
   by *M. K. Kudryavtsev*

Social Cohesion and Reciprocation in a Tibetan Community in Nepal — 45
   by *B. N. Aziz*

SECTION TWO: CULTURES OF THE SOVIET UNION

Interaction of Cultures Among Peoples of the USSR — 79
   by *Yu. V. Arutyunyan*

Development of Traditional Aspects of National Culture in the Soviet Central Asian Republics   87
by *B. D. Djamgherchinov*

SECTION THREE: COMMUNITY AND WORLD JUDAISM

The Jews as an Ethnic Group in the Americas During the Sixteenth and Seventeenth Centuries   95
by *Seymour B. Liebman*

Ancestor Memorialism: A Comparison of Jews and Japanese   115
by *Howard Wimberley* and *Joel Savishinsky*

Some Functional and Structural Aspects of Family Life in a Communal Society: The Financial Sector of the Kibbutz Family   133
by *Frits J. M. Selier*

Jewish Communities as Cultural Units   161
by *Walter P. Zenner*

SECTION FOUR: COMMUNAL SOCIETY IN AMERICA

Eschatological Living: Religious Experience in the Shaker Community   175
by *John H. Morgan*

Religious Orientation of the Communal Counter-Culture: God, Nature, and Mysticism in Contemporary Society   187
by *David Buchdahl*

Rituals of Community in an American Religious Youth Group Meeting   209
by *E. M. Sciog*

The Country Place: An Intentional, Therapeutic Community   225
by *Geoffrey Nusbaum*

Ethnography of Religious Factors in a Politically Oriented Communal Group of New England   251
by *Raleigh E. Bailey, Jr.*

Aspects of Personality in a Communal Society by *John A. Hostetler*	281
Communitarian Experiments and the Self by *Carlos C. Drake*	293
Biographical Notes	299
Index of Names	303
Index of Subjects	307

Introduction

BHABAGRAHI MISRA and JAMES J. PRESTON

The recent emergence of various styles of "communal living" in the United States has not been adequately studied. In arranging a session for the IXth ICAES, an attempt was made to contact as many scholars who have pioneered in this new field as was possible. It was decided that older traditional communities such as the Amish and Hutterites could provide a good baseline for comparison with the recent "intentional communities" that were originally to be the primary focus of the session. As the symposium took shape, it became evident that studies of similar communities from all over the world should be incorporated and at that point, the focus became cross-cultural. This presented the difficult task of selecting representative papers that would provide a true foundation for comparative analysis. It was immediately clear that the problem of finding common characteristics on a cross-cultural basis among these divergent communities was much too complex for the present state of knowledge. Therefore, the symposium was designed as a purely exploratory dialogue that would shed some light on this hitherto neglected facet of culture and society.

The papers included here present the broad scope of this symposium. Nevertheless, each study reflects a common need to explain and interpret these heterogeneous lifestyles. This was clearly evident in the discussion that followed the presentation of papers. The participants, at that time, were looking for similar patterns of communal living on a cross-cultural scale. It was generally agreed that it was too early to arrive at any basic conclusions, despite tempting structural similarities noted in several instances.

Perhaps most interesting is the challenge presented by these studies to the evolutionary approach, which traditionally postulates a progressive model of development through various stages of increasing complexity.

The emerging "intentional communities" do not seem to fit the more traditional definitions of "tribe," "peasant society," or "nation-state." Nor do models of religious revitalization movements fully describe or explain these conscious experiments in communal life.

A particularly interesting point of contrast emerges by comparing "intentional communities" in modern technological societies with those of developing nations. There seems to be a significant qualitative difference between the two with respect to community identity. For example, communities in developing societies are caught up in the process of modernization. This results in a kind of status-oriented identity that is generally nontraditional and often based on borrowed Western models.

The "intentional communities" of the United States, by contrast, appear to be essentially transitional, experimental, and volatile by nature. Unlike traditional communities all over the world, these more recent "alternative lifestyles" do not seem to have a common set of philosophical principles. They are, by definition, nontraditional, and their objectives and goals are still nebulous, although all of them try to reject modern technology and its consequences. Despite this disenchantment with the parent society, a deeper, more significant theme may be operating. The negation of established value patterns may be only part of a larger quest to establish a utopian society. This theme is rooted in the perennial search for the nature of "self." Although it is difficult at this stage to suggest the future of these experimental communities, there can be no doubt about their influence on American lifestyles in general.

The papers included in this volume will not completely clarify the issues discussed here. It is necessary for anthropologists from different cultures to collect and codify more ethnographic data before any generalizations can be attempted. It may be that in the future more light will be shed on the durability of American "youth culture." It would be fruitful then to compare such phenomena with new styles of communal living in non-Western urban centers. Investigators would also be encouraged to better define the relations of these communities to the cultures in which they are embedded. Otherwise, the attempt to find common structural themes may result in unnecessary distortions of the unique set of cultural factors involved in the development of each community.

This volume reflects the vast range of problems presented by the study of communal living on a world scale. The arrangement of the papers under several regional headings is an attempt to bring some degree of focus to the material. It is felt that the reader will gain considerable insight from the variety of methodologies and the many different dimensions of "community" represented here. Despite the heterogeneity of these studies, there appears to be some implicit consensus that the search for "self" and "identity" is a theme of increasing significance throughout the world. In addition, though there are clear differences in the histories and levels of commitment of these communities, the interdependence of world societies today may play a major role in any structural similarities that might be perceived in the material.

We are grateful to all the participants, discussants, and coordinators of the IXth ICAES for providing us with a forum on this topic. We are especially thankful to Sol Tax for his cooperation, valued suggestions, and many vital questions as the session was being arranged around the theme, "Community, Self, and Identity."

SECTION ONE

Community in South Asian Cultures

Gods, Kings, and the Caste System in India

L. K. MAHAPATRA

That the caste system in India is not purely a secular social order, but that religious values, rites, gods, and goddesses are important in it, has been known for a long time. We need only mention the well-known fact that cults of specific deities are associated with specific castes irrespective of status in the caste hierarchy. Hocart's view (1950:59) of a new caste emerging along with a new cult is derived from this view.

Among others, Bouglé (1908:81–82; 1958:24–26) has stressed the importance of the sacrifice and the concepts of purity and pollution as distinctive characteristics of the caste order. Hocart (1950:17–18) conceives of the caste system as a ritual organization, within which the individual castes have been assigned ritual duties or services to perform; the polluting services are relegated to the vassals or serfs who do not have a share in the public or state sacrifices and thus do not have communion with the Aryan gods. This viewpoint of Hocart has certain relevance to our theme, and we shall revert to him later. Incidentally, it is important to note that Hocart has been neglected for various reasons (compare Dumont and Pocock 1958:3 ff.).

Of late, Marriott (1955:189–190) has referred to Hocart while probing the link between the caste hierarchies of little communities and the great tradition of the greater community. Marriott notes the process of filtering down from great to little communities since later Vedic times, when there were two classes of sacrifices, simpler ones of the householders with the assistance of kinsmen and elaborate ones conducted only by kings with the help of professional ritual specialists. The royal sacrifices grew more elaborate, involving greater specialization of the ritualists. Similarly, he thinks that the villagers today practice more elaborate household sacrifices and employ a larger number of specialists. He relies directly on Hocart to trace ritual relationships among castes in villages from those once prevalent in the royal palace among royal retainers. Hocart (1950:155) points out that "royal ways filter down to the common people, sometimes slowly, sometimes with astonishing rapidity, but naturally shorn of their pomp." Even a poor householder of Kishan Garhi, according to Marriott, today retains six or seven servants of different castes "mainly to serve him in ceremonial ways demonstrative of his own caste rank." Marriott adds some other facts throwing light on such royal association:

Householders and their servants formally address each other by courtly titles. Thus, the Brahman priest is called "Great King" (*Maharaj*) or "Learned Man" (*Panditji*), the Potter is called "Ruler of the People" (*Prajapat*), the Barber "Lord Barber" (*Nau Thakur*), the carpenter "Master Craftsman" (*Mistri*), the Sweeper "Headman" (*Mehtar*) or "Sergeant" (*Jamadar*), etc. About half of the twenty-four castes of Kishan Garhi also identify themselves with one or another of the three higher *varna*, thus symbolizing their claims to certain ritual statuses in relation to the sacrifice or the sacrificer of Sanskrit literary form. "Thus, the apparent degradation of the royal style becomes a step in social evolution" [Hocart 1950:155] (Marriott 1955:190).

However, the role of the Hindu kings in the evolution, functioning, and maintenance of the caste system has been very rarely considered (Datta 1968; Bose 1949; Hutton 1951; Srinivas 1952, 1955, 1966; Maynard 1972; Sinha 1972; L. K. Mahapatra 1970). Hocart has given extensive thought to it, but he goes so far when he considers the kings as gods, having priestly functions and working with the Brahman to form a sacerdotal pair, upholding the sacrificial organization for the good life on earth, that he makes the state appear as a ritual organization, and the king's palace, court, and complement of functional castes are duplicated in the god's temple, court, and ritual functionaries (Hocart 1927: 10–11; 1970:93, 105). In fact, according to Hocart, "the Church and the State are one in India. The head of this Church-State is the king" (1950:67). "The temple and the palace are indistinguishable, for the king represents the Gods" (1950:68). " . . . everyone likes to imitate his betters, the big feudal nobles the king, the small nobles the big ones, and so on . . ." (1950:155). We shall have to examine Hocart's insightful ideas carefully in the light of some empirical data from Orissa.

Although implicit in Hocart's writings, the temple organization of ritual and other services based on a caste division of labor and the relation between the state deity, the divine kings, and the vassal kings, on the one hand, and the caste system at various levels, on the other, have not been expressly analyzed in terms of the relevant empirical data. We shall attempt to do that here within the limitations of space and data. However, it is felt that in analyzing the caste system of India, it is methodologically feasible and substantially profitable to begin with a particular cultural region because there is much truth in the statement that there is hardly a single caste system, but several, each specific to a linguistic-cultural region (compare Ghurye 1961).

Orissa as a cultural region exemplifies, perhaps in an extreme fashion, the parallelism between the king's court, estates, and services, and those of the state deity. On the basis of this regional empirical study, further implications for understanding the interaction and interdependence between the gods, kings, and temples, on the one hand, and the caste system at the levels of the region as a whole, the princedoms, and the villages, on the other, can be identified and analyzed for India as a whole later on.

GOD-KING IN ORISSA

Perhaps a short introduction to Orissa as a cultural region in this context is in order. Orissa has had a checkered political history, although paradoxically its cultural continuity over a wide area in ancient Kalinga or Utkala is significant. The cornerstone of this cultural continuity in the pre-Islamic past has been the cult of Lord Jagannath, the Lord of the Universe, identified as the penultimate incarnation of Vishnu in the form of Buddha, at Puri, Shrikshetra, one of the four most sacred centers of pilgrimage (*chaturdharma*) for the Hindus. Lord Jagannath is looked upon as the protector and even the sovereign of Orissa, and the Raja of Puri (formerly of Orissa at Khurdha) officiates as his earthly deputy. The king is himself conceived as Vishnu, or Mobile Vishnu (*Chalanti Vishnu*). The institution of a state deity is perhaps as old as urban civilization itself, and we learn of it in the civilizations of Babylonia and Egypt. The Pharaohs were notably the Children of the Sun. So are many Rajput chiefs, as are also the chiefs in Orissa, who are "descended" from the gods, the sun, the moon, the ritual fire-god, Agni, and even from the serpent-god, Naga. Such a conception of divine kingship was also quite widely prevalent for a long time in Southeast Asia, where Shiva, Vishnu, Harihara, Shiva-Buddha, Bodhisatva Lokeśwara of Mount Meru, or Indra were represented in the king on earth, his palace being the sacred microcosm of the kingdom (Heine-Geldern 1942:22ff.). In ancient Cambodia, the king was an incarnation of the God-King Devaraja, who was Lord Shiva himself (Heine-Geldern 1942:22ff.). Similarly, the Raja of Puri, the descendant of the paramount sovereign of Orissa, is referred to as *Thakur-Raja* [God-King], so much so that the pilgrims used to have a *darshan* [audience] of the king before proceeding to the lord's temple. As such, he also functioned as the head ritual functionary of the Jagannath temple; "in the absence of other functionaries in cases of emergencies, [he can] ... perform all ritual services except cooking and offering food to the Images" (Patnaik 1970:88). Patnaik refers to the similarities between the rituals of the temple and those of the palace. The palace was considered as a sacred place, the abode of the God-King and Mobile Vishnu; because of this, none were allowed to enter the palace with leather footwear as in the case of a temple (Patnaik 1970). In the painted reliefs on the temple walls, the king is seen performing the twelve important festivals just as they are conducted for Lord Jagannath (Mishra 1971:114–115).

The king and the god underwent similar rituals at the time of waking up, bathing, receiving presents, eating breakfast, putting on clothes, giving audience, making offerings, and other daily rituals. In addition, the king had many special privileges, similar to those of Lord Jagannath himself, when he went to have an audience with the god. The king had vassal chiefs performing several services at the time of royal installation, coronation, and at the time of the temple visit. In the palace, the king's establishment had a vegetarian cuisine, and the queen was subject to no fewer ritual austerities (Mishra 1971:114–115). Only Lord Jagannath and the king were addressed with the reverential terms, *Manima* or *Mahaprabhu*, not only at Puri, but also in other feudal princedoms, because feudal princes are conceived as minor gods in the image of the paramount king. The paramount Raja of Orissa, at least since the days of the Ganga dynasty in about the twelfth century, has made the Jagannath cult a state cult. It may be that this was gradually superimposed on the prevailing state cults of the feudal chiefdoms, where usually some form of *shakti* [tribal goddess] was the *ishtadevata* [patron-deity] of the royal dynasty (Bhattarika in Baramba, Samaleshwari in Sambalpur, Kila Munda in Ranpur, and Hingula in Talcher, and so on.) (compare Kulke 1978).

Lord Shiva has been worshipped almost everywhere in Orissa as *Mahadeva* [Great God] from time immemorial, and the Pashupat cult was in the ascendancy from the fifth and sixth centuries. We may, therefore, visualize that Lord Lingaraj, the King of the Phallus, at Bhubaneswar, *Ekamra-Kshetra*, was the state deity of Orissa by the seventh century, when the temple is said to have been constructed by Yayati Keshari (Panigrahi 1961). But by the time of Shri Shankaracharya of the eighth century, who had visited Puri and whose monastery was established there to campaign in favor of the revival of Hinduism, the worship of Lord Jagannath and the cult center of Puri must have attained a level of all-India importance and all-Orissa supremacy in the spiritual realm.

STATE DEITY AND TEMPLE ORGANIZATION

At any rate, there is evidence that after the days of the Ganga paramount King Aniyankabhima III (who had completed construction of the present temple of Lord Jagannath), the worship of Jagannath in Orissa was more intensified than during the previous kings' times. Traditionally, thirty-six functional castes were deployed to render services in the temple. It was this king who expressly regarded Purushottama [Lord Jagannath] as the real Emperor of Orissa, he himself ruling as his representative. Thus, by the early thirteenth century Lord Jagannath might have been well established as the state deity (*rashtradevata*) although according to Mishra (1971:38), Purushottama [Jagannath] and Balabhadra were already regarded as *rashtradevatas* of Kongada and Toshali under the later Vaishnav Bhaumas by about the eighth century. Lord Jagannath was believed in so strongly as the lord and protector of Kalinga and Utkal, kingdoms of ancient Orissa (Mishra 1971:43–44), that during the reign of Purushottama Gajapati, both Lord Jagannath and Lord Balabhadra rode horses and led the Orissa soldiers to victory, according to a popular legend painted on the temple walls. This identification of the god with the king of Orissa and the king's empire as the god's realm under his protective arms must have persuaded the feudal chiefs — in addition to the fact of military or political subjugation — to become willing tributaries of a divine King-God-State polity. In fact, there is an inscription in the temple of Lord Jagannath by the paramount king Purushottama Deva that enjoins the vassal kings of Orissa to obey his orders on proper attitude and approach toward Brahmans; transgression of these orders constituted a great sacrilege and sin (*mahapataka*) against Lord Jagannath himself (S. N. Dash 1966:264). At any rate, we find perhaps no princedoms in Orissa under British occupation where we do not come across the worship of Lord Jagannath, usually with his brother, Balabhadra, and sister, Subhadra, and where a complement of functional castes does not serve in the temple as they do in the palace nearby. There is some evidence that in order to legitimize their occupation of territory and curry favor with the Gajapati kings of Orissa, the vassal kings, like the king of Bolangir-Patna, constructed temples of Jagannath, Balabhadra, and Subhadra (S. P. Dash 1962:253). Therefore, we may note that the Jagannath cult has been used for political purposes, both by the emperor and the vassal kings, at least since the thirteenth century. Again, with political purposes of espionage and public propoganda in view, the Panda system was introduced by Aniyankabhima Deva III to court pilgrims from various parts of India by learning their languages and visiting them (Mishra 1971:44). Lord Jagannath is invoked for permission to punish rebellious vassals (Mishra 1971:49). In another inscription in the temple, the paramount king threatens, presumably on the authority of Lord Jagannath, that if the people do not work for the good of the sovereign and avoid the evil path, they will be expelled from the kingdom and all their properties will be confiscated (Mishra 1971:50).

Let us now briefly consider the types of services and the number of functional castes engaged in serving in the two most important temples of Orissa, that of Lord Jagannath at Puri and of Lord Lingaraj at Bhubaneswar. The world-famous gigantic Sun Temple of Konarak, now in ruins and with no record of organized worship, need not concern us. Although it has been noted that the ritual and other services in the temple of Lord Jagannath were systematically organized in the thirteenth century, there is no justification to infer therefrom that the functional castes were not associated with the temple services much earlier, perhaps from the beginning of the temple worship in the legendary days of King Indradyumna, who, according to the Skanda Purana, constructed the first temple of Puri. Even in the days of Indradyumna, as the legend goes (Mishra 1971:82), the descendants of the Savara chief Visvavasu, known as Daita, the descendants of the Savara girl, Lalita, and the Brahman emissary, Vidyapati, known as Suara (Supakara), and the descendants of Vidyapati (by a Brahman wife?) were to serve as decorators and ministrants, as cooks, and as priests, respectively. Previous to the organization of services by Aniyankabhima Deva III, the local tradition has it that there were nine *sevaks* [servants]: (1) *Charu Hota*, (2) *Patra Hota*, (3) *Brahma*, (4) *Acharya*, (5) *Pratihari*, (6) *Puspalaka*, (7 and 8) *Dyatas* [the washerman and the barber], and (9) *Dvarapalaka* (Mishra 1971:12–121).[1] It is highly probable that every time the temple was rebuilt, it became larger and more complex, and the ritual services were further elaborated; the latter occurred also when dynasties changed. Again, just because there is a close parallel in the temple services in the Puri and Bhubaneswar temples, there is no valid reason to suspect that the services are wholly a carry-over from the temple at Puri to the Bhubaneswar temple. First, the Lord Lingaraj temple is probably 600 years older (compare Panigrahi 1961), and the associated cult center Ekamra-Kshetra is perhaps even older. King Indradyumna is said to have worshiped Lord Shiva there before Lord Jagannath in his present form appeared at Puri. Second, both Lord Jagannath and Lord Lingaraj are, as the legends run, gods of the Savara autochthones who had been recognized in some categories as temple functionaries. King Yayati Keshari, alleged to be a founder of the Lingaraj temple, is said to have brought in some Dravidian Brahmans (Bose *et al.* 1958) as temple priests because, presumably, the local Brahmans were not well versed in Shaivism at that time, and he had to elevate the temple services from tribal rites to Sanskritic ones.

The temple of Lord Jagannath engages temple servants performing

---

[1] Some of the names of these nine *sevaks* cannot be translated exactly because they are proper names. Possible meanings are (1) *Charu Hota* [the handsome head-priest], (2) *Patra Hota* [the priest in charge of vessels], (3) *Brahma* [the demiurge Brahma], (4) *Acharya* [preceptor], (5) *Pratihara* [garland-arranger], (6) *Puspalaka* [flower-arranger], (7 and 8) *Dyatas* [washerman and barber], and (9) *Dvarapalaka* [gatekeeper].

101 services or roles with their respective names, rights, duties, and perquisites (Mishra 1971). However, the actual number of castes is not ascertained from this, although castes range from Brahmans to some untouchables, and even some descendants from tribal worshippers are known to be involved. Similarly, at the temple of Lord Lingaraj, somewhat less elaborately, in 1958, 41 types of services were recorded (Bose *et al.* 1958), involving 22 separate castes, ranging over almost the same ethnic spectrum. This has also been largely confirmed by M. Mahapatra (1972), who, however, gives a tally of 30 types of services. There is no doubt that there has been wide fluctuation in the total number of ritual services (roles), at least in the temple of Lord Jagannath. Those ritual services were recorded by British officers in 1807, soon after their occupation of Orissa; at that time the number was 219. Apart from this, there were 139 types of services connected with the management of the temple. In the 1950's, the Orissa government compiled a record of rites, which gave the number of ritual services as 140. Again the number of castes involved is not given, and it is seen that many of the priestly and other castes perform several roles at the same time. The fact that specific rajas and even temple managers have been known to have introduced or discontinued specific services, offerings, fairs, and so on points to the prevalence of caste-centered core services in spite of the periodic fluctuations in the elaboration or proliferation of services. This is very clear from the stereotypical reference to *Chhatisha Nijoga* [thirty-six caste-centered ritual servants].

That almost all the caste-centered ritual services performed in the temple of Lord Jagannath were duplicated in the palace of the King of Orissa may not be far from the truth, as indicated by Patnaik (1970) or by Mishra (1971:44). Similarly, one may refer to the royal installation, attended by vassal chiefs in various roles, as bearing close similarity to the divine installation at Poushabhisheka in the month of Pousha when Lord Jagannath assumes *rajavesha* [royal attire] in a series of king-worthy rituals (*raja niti*). There is another divine installation in the month of Jyestha, known as *Rajendra-bhiseka*, auguring the proposal of marriage with Rukmini, as in the *Mahabharat*. Lord Jagannath assumes *rajavesha* again on the day of the full moon in the month of Phalgun. Not only that, but the Lord holds his royal court on Sunian day in the month of Bhadra, when his servants and subjects (temple servants and peasants and other holders of temple lands) offer him loyalty and tribute. Those Sunian rites are celebrated also in the Lingaraj temple, and this had been introduced by a former paramount king, marking the beginning of an indigenous royal calendar of Orissa. But this should not lead us to expect absolute conformity of the royal services with temple services or *vice versa*. Each system of services has its own pattern of proliferation and development, although basically the same complement of castes renders more or less similar secular and ritual services in the temple as well as in the palace. With this limitation, we may properly appreciate the concept of *temple community* developed by M. Mahapatra (1972) under this author's guidance, wherein Lord Lingaraj is seen wielding both ritual and secular authority and performing other roles through kinship, kingship, and property institutions among gods and men in his Ekamra-Kshetra. The temple servants here, as at Puri, invite the God on the occasion of auspicious ceremonies in their families; the funeral pyre is ignited with fire from the temple, at least in the case of Brahman *sevaks*; and the *Daitapati* [descendants of Savara, worshippers of Lord Jagannath] perform "funeral rites" of the Lord when a new set of images is made every twelve years. Besides the *Daitapati sevaks* take charge of the Lord's decoration, worship, and offering of fruits, and so on from the day the Lord falls ill until the end of the *Car* festival. As the *Daitapati* are considered to be family members of Lord Jagannath, they share the familial (*gyantisara*) dishes (Mishra 1971:93–96). All of this corroborates Hocart's view (1950:67) that in India, the Church and the State are one.

STRUCTURAL CONSEQUENCES OF THE GOD-KING AND TEMPLE-STATE INDENTITIES

If we accept the implications of the observations made so far, we may agree with Hocart on the essential identity of the caste organization as mediated through temple organization and the organization of services to the king's establishment. Our assertion is that such identity is all the more pronounced in the case of state deities of a kingdom, like Orissa, in which the deity is not monopolistically owned (as, for example, the Brahman priestly families monopolize Lord Pandurang of Maharashtra) and in which tribesmen abound, among whom the caste system has yet to take strong roots. That the two acclaimed tribal deities came to be elevated as state deities, one after the other, opens up a new field of promising research into the building of the Hindu state, empire, and society in Orissa, much of which was part of the Dandakaranya forests of the Ramayana era or of Jharkhand jungles of medieval times; but this is not within the scope of our discussion.

At any rate, we may still consider the major structural consequences of God-King and temple-state (or palace) identities. First, the caste system became well differentiated; rights and duties as well as hierarchical relative positions became established with reference ultimately to their ritual relevance and importance; caste regulations were not only backed by state authority, but they also acquired the character of divine dispensation. This last development can be well documented from the temple inscriptions or *Sanad* grants by various paramount kings, wherein the caste and other regulations were enjoined upon all, including the vassal chiefs and Brahmans, and which could be transgressed only at the cost of committing a sin against Lord Jagannath. In this connection, we may bring in the supreme council of Brahman scholars at Lord Jagannath's temple (*Mukti Mandap Pandit Sabha*), which sat in judgement on caste matters and rituals, among other things. The present building for this *Pandit Sabha* was constructed in 1578, but the institution appears to be much older than the buildings.

Second, the caste system, in its supposedly ideal differentiation and elaboration at the temple of the state deity and the palace of the paramount king, became the model for emulation at the temples and palaces of the vassal princes, with a *Pandit Sabha* of some sort to adjudicate on caste matters. Everything was not necessarily an exact replica of the model at the state capital and state temple. Actually, the roots go deep into the Hindu society and polity, where the king is looked upon as the authority in caste matters and is advised by Brahman scholars, who together constitute the supreme authority on caste matters in a princedom. Appeals from the level of the vassal chiefs lay before the *Mukti Mandap Pandit Sabha*, which had derived royal authority and divine ordination from the paramount king and the paramount god, respectively.

Third, the superposition of the state deity, the paramount king, and the paramount council of *pandits* on caste matters signified the spiritual, political, and social leadership of the Mobile Vishnu or God-King combination at the heart of the state and society in Orissa. That the paramount kings derived political sustenance from this trinity is without question, but this is outside the scope of the present paper. However, we have seen how the state deity cult was used for political purposes to achieve the subjugation and integration of vassal princedoms in an empire.

CASTE IN PRINCEDOMS

Although the above structural consequences have been cast in a static, timeless frame, this is not at all the case objectively. Let us take the second situation for a closer view, the one in which the caste order, political setup, and the ritual organization at the level of the princedom is shown as more or less modeled after the system evolved at the political and religious centers of the state in Orissa. This author has tried to throw some light in one of his national lectures (L. K. Mahapatra 1970) on the dual role of the Hindu king as the preserver of, and also as the catalytic agent for change in, the caste order within his domain. It can be argued, as Maynard (1972) has done, that in his original role of maintaining the traditional order, the raja gradually also, driven by logic and pragmatism, became the authority to accord recognition to the relative interactional status attained, in addition to keeping the relative ascribed status of the castes (apparently) fixed. This transition from fixity to flux gave the essential leverage to the caste system insofar as individual castes or their sections could be recognized or not recognized as having this or that ritual or caste status in a specific politically autonomous domain. It has also been this author's thesis that in India, as in Orissa, such politically autonomous entities also tended to behave as economically and socially automonous units. This, at any rate, has been the situation in most of the former princely states and zamindaries of Orissa, where the political, economic, and social (caste interactions, status equivalence, and hierarchy) boundaries tended to coincide in the recent past. If a caste or its subgroup attains a higher relative status in one princedom, perhaps because of its political or economic power or ritual purity or because of its value to the state or the king himself, this becomes the signal for the same caste or subcaste in other princedoms to claim such higher status. That the *Pandit Sabha* was not always obliging to the king or the castes in their claims is not very important. The fact that this avenue was open to the castes, by going to the local king and *Pandit Sabha*, or by going over their heads to the *Mukti Mandap Sabha* for final judgement in matters of caste rituals and status determination, added an element of dynamism to the caste order. This is not so clearly evident from the traditional model of the caste system, whether in the Hindu scriptures or in early Western "scriptures" on Hindu society. This author has even come across cases of flouting of the decision of the *Mukti Mandap Pandit Sabha* in one or two princedoms. This happened during the late British regime, when the political hold of the descendant of the paramount king of Orissa was nonexistent and the local princes did not need to fear either social or divine retribution from their people because of the prevalence of overwhelming secular trends towards social and economic freedoms in a countrywide democratic and capitalistic order.

CASTE DUTIES AS RITUAL SERVICES

It is necessary now to point out two important things. First, in the temples and palaces of princedoms, the caste organization did not exhibit as much differentiation and specialization as evidenced in the state deity's temple organization, where services were highly elaborate and sophisticated. In the variety and elaboration of caste-based services, the paramount king's palace and establishment appear to parallel closely the local Jagannath temple.

Second, the tasks allotted to particular families of particular castes in the temple, as well as in the palace, on a hereditary basis came to be invested with sanctity and privilege. It was one's religious duty, as well as a privilege, to perform the hereditary job, much as the "calling" was a religious duty in Christian medieval Europe. Hence the well-known Sanskrit saying *Swadharme nidhanam shreyah, parodharmah bhayavahah* [One's own duty is the best to perform, others' duties are bound to give fear]. This notion of religious duty elevated caste duties to what one might call ritual services. Therefore, transgression of caste duties in general came to be looked upon as sacrilege, not merely an act of criminality to be punished by the king, who was the preserver of the social order. According to Hocart, these caste services were born of the sacrifices, especially the public or state sacrifices, whose elaborate, ritual requirements were functionally differentiated, coordinated, and mediated through the caste system. He says:

... the caste system is a sacrificial organization, ... the aristocracy are feudal lords constantly involved in rites which require vassals or serfs, because some of these services involve pollution from which the lord must remain free (Hocart 1950:17).

Again, ". . . the worthy or excellent castes are those which alone are admitted to share in the sacrifice, with whom alone the gods hold converse" (Hocart 1950:18).

It is very difficult to pronounce on Hocart's theory of the origin of caste. The only positive comment one may offer is on its plausibility. The state sacrifice to which he explicitly refers is a king's consecration or priests' installation ceremony. From what is known of such rituals in the palace of the present descendants of the paramount kings of Orissa, it appears that these services are not so elaborate or differentiated as in the temple of Lord Jagannath, although there is close resemblance. Apart from that, there are many vassal rajas of the former princedoms who had been assigned services in the royal procession and other state ceremonies (Patnaik 1970:62). One vassal chief was to hold a betel leaf container, another to hold a spittoon, and still others to hold swords, golden canes, or daggers as insignia of royal authority. Such services did not always conform to the royal roles, which the godlike Kshatriya rajas were supposed to perform. On the other hand, in the daily and periodic ritual services at the state deity's temple, all the castes from the very low untouchable castes to the Veda-knowing Brahmans had their assigned tasks and statuses inside or outside the temple. Hocart might not have attached importance to the temple organization, as at the most important Temple of the Tooth in Ceylon (which he cites as an empirical source of his theory). He notes how all who officiated inside the sanctuary were Buddhist farmers. But inside the temples at Puri and Bhubaneswar several castes have ritual duties. Therefore, even if we do not accept his theory of origin of the caste from public sacrifices, because there is a lack of adequate empirical evidence to support it, at least the continuing organization of temple services in Orissa and elsewhere may supply an important basis for his assertion that caste is born of ritual, or caste is a ritual organization. Further, we may, on the basis of the facets of equivalence of the palace and the temple, agree largely with him that:

> ... the temple and the palace are indistinguishable, for the king represents the gods. Therefore, there is only one word in Sinhalese and in Tamil for both (S. *maligava*; T. *maligai*). The god in his temple has his court, like the king in his palace: smiths, carpenters, potters all work for him (Hocart 1950:68).

Again, we may also go along with him when he asserts:

> ... just as each clan has a chieftain, and the whole tribe a chief, so each clan has a temple and the whole tribe a state temple of the chief god. Thus as usual, the human organization reflects the divine, and vice versa, since the two are one. ... (Hocart 1927:105).

Hocart (1950:16), however, goes too far when he says that in India: "every occupation is a priesthood" because all craftsmen including the dancing girls, worship the objects with which they earn their livelihood. While priesthood is meaningful in the context of a community, and family rituals are far from public ceremonies, we may concede that a degree of sanctity is ascribed thereby to the caste duties, to be performed with reference to their respective religio-ethical norms. But this is true of each caste taken *individually*; there is no clue to how *a system of castes* can be viably organized, put into execution, and maintained over a long period in a particular region.

CASTE IN VILLAGES

Hocart, however, becomes very effective when it comes to the functioning of caste at the village or intervillage level:

> The king's state is reproduced in miniature by his vassals; a farmer has his court, consisting of the personages most essential to the ritual, and so present even in the smallest community, the barber, the washerman, the drummers and so forth (Hocart 1950:68).

Hocart (1950:8) logically identifies the farmers, with "feudal lords to whom the others owe certain services, each according to his caste." If we find fault with him over his ill-chosen epithet, "feudal," what he actually means is clear from the following:

The gods of the farmers, the Maruts, act as Indra's bodyguard. Since divine society is a replica of human society, we must conclude that the farmers are the king's mainstay in battle. They are just as military then as the nobles (Hocart 1950:39).

But Hocart uses a back door to induct the farmers into the sacrificial organization thus: "The farmers . . . are the support on which the monarch and the priesthood rest, and their duty is to feed the sacrifice from their lands and cattle" (Hocart 1950:39). In the state, which is a ritual organization, the others have different duties and if they cultivate, they do so only to feed themselves (Hocart 1950:41). We may not agree with him wholeheartedly on the place of the sacrificial organization at the base of the caste system and especially on the role of the farmers *vis-à-vis* the sacrificial organization. For, this role of the farmer also agrees well with the view of the society as a military organization, which he himself pointed out.

However, there is substantive truth in what he says:

This ritual organization has spread downward to such an extent that the poor cultivators in the jungle have their retainers to play the part which they alone are qualified by heredity to play at births, weddings, and funerals, but these are retainers of the community, the village, not of one lord (Hocart 1950:68).

We must again warn against absolute identities or replicas. The model is set by the court of the paramount king and the temple of the state deity, and the vassal chiefs and the temples, especially the Jagannath temple, in the princedoms largely follow suit. When we come to the village and intervillage level, this model is still valid and is looked upon as ideal, although the circumstances at the operational, interactional level do not allow for a 100 percent compliance. But let us recall how at the princedom level, representing the subregional organization of castes, the element of dynamism and flux has been as clearly evident in the variations of circumstances of each caste as in the variations between princedoms. The caste organization at the state deity's temple and the king's palace seems immutable and sets the standard by which the caste status, activities, and norms are to be tested when in doubt or dispute. Thus, this apparent immutability and stability is an important structural aspect of the regional caste system of Orissa.

Let us examine briefly the social structure of villages in Orissa, in the first instance. A large multicaste village usually has a complement of functional castes: blacksmiths, carpenters, barbers, washermen, and Brahmans, with or without potters and astrologers, who have remained, in most cases until recently, in *jajmani* relationships with the clean castes. In most villages of Orissa the cultivating caste (*Chasa*) or the militia-*cum*-cultivator caste *Khandayat* [the wielders of swords] were the landowning and economically powerful castes, which were served by all the functional castes. They conform to the significant features of *dominant castes*. The *Khandayats* especially behaved like lords and held in many cases military service *jagirs* [land grants], although there are some villages whose owners and/or dominant castes were Brahman, braziers (*Kansari*), oilmen (*Teli*), or even fishermen, and so on. The dominant castes or at least their representative, the headman of the village, who was appointed by and represented the king, exercised authority over the organization of caste-based services within the microcosm of the village. In many princely states or zamindaries in Orissa, the headman had the power to appoint or evict the village servants of functional castes, and he often took the initiative to bring a washerman or a barber to be settled on some *jagir* land under his control. He, or vicariously his (dominant) caste members, saw to it that the ritual services and other services, performed by the various resident and peripatetic members of other castes serving the village, were attended to properly, without conflict and disruption, and without intruding upon the privileges of other castes. He thus secured what is called by Srinivas *vertical solidarity* in the village. We need not go into all the facets beyond pointing out the phenomenon. The headman also saw to it that all the important agricultural and related rituals and crisis rites for village welfare were performed and that each section played its assigned role. In this sense, the headman and the dominant caste ensured the functioning of the village as a ritual, economic, and social organization. Hocart would give pre-eminence to ritual organization and derive the other facets from it. We may not grant him that; but this is not very important.

Although there may be a temple of the village goddess or other minor gods, the rituals are not elaborate and one or two castes (usually a non-Brahman, sometimes even a tribal priest) may be involved in the temple services. Thus, the services of the castes in the area cannot be readily invested with sanctity from their ritual relevance in the temple organization, and no public sacrifices are normally held on a large scale in the villages. But the chief deity is drawn into the caste disputes and into the village organization and well-being because the village assembly and the caste councils usually sit near the abode of the deity. Thus, the deity's blessings are easily invoked to seal the decisions that are made, or the deity acts as divine witness to the oaths and contracts. There is a belief that the deity will punish a transgressor if caste norms are violated. Therefore, although caste services have their ritual character derived primarily from the temple-palace ritual network, this is also locally reinforced by the involvement of the main deity of the village. The close parallel between this situation at the village level and that at the state level with the state deity and king may easily be perceived.

The question as to why the functional castes are looked upon as village servants and not as servants attached to temporal or spiritual lords can be resolved simply. In the villages there are no such powerful or affluent lords as are available at the capitals of the state or of the princedoms. Basically the peasants have a subsistence economy and do not grow much beyond their needs; hence, they have to pool their common resources, village land, or their individual resources to support the members of the functional castes (compare Hocart 1950:155).

We may also briefly note that the caste headmen in a princedom in Orissa were invested with royal authority by the kings, who formally appointed them. Thus, we find how even at the village and intervillage levels, the gods and the kings have lent their authority and sanctity to the caste organization. It is not meant that there is only a filtering down of the great tradition from upper layers of the society or from their acknowledged centers. The very fact that minor gods, caste gods, various local cults and fairs, village headmen are of crucial importance in village India indicates that the vitality and importance of local traditions are not to be belittled.

KINGSHIP AND THE HINDUIZATION OF TRIBES

In fact, there is some evidence to show how the king was instrumental in integrating minor tribal traditions with higher traditions through a process identified by Marriott (1955) as *universalization*. Thereby the king has often taken some steps to make it easier for a hill tribe to become gradually accepted as a clean Hindu caste. We may consider one case from Orissa as an illustration.

A Hill Bhuiyan priest was worshiping Kanta-Kuanri, a goddess allegedly represented by a *tantrik yantra* found by chance in the area. The Raja of Benai came to learn of its importance in the Hill Bhuiyan lore and belief. He then arranged for the annual circuit of the goddess to go up to the palace temple of the state deity and back to the hill sanctuary. On the way, the goddess was worshiped by all castes and tribes inhabiting the villages, where the ritual procession came to scheduled halts. Gradually, the tribal goddess became allied to, and even identified with, a form of Durga, a Sanskritic goddess of the great tradition, and the Bhuiyan and other low priests of the goddess thus gained higher ritual and social status from the viewpoint of Hindu society (compare Roy 1935:104–117).

In Hindu Orissa, there is a hierarchy of gods and goddesses, with the state deity, Lord Jagannath at the top, and the minor tribal gods and spirits at the bottom. The recognition of this hierarchy, as well as the several grades of purity and pollution attached to different occupations and ethnic communities, belongs to an initial phase of the process of Hinduization. To this, we may add the other concessions granted by this particular king in his anxiety to woo the politically dominant tribal group in the region, the Hill Bhuiyan. Prominent among the concessions given were that water from the tribals was acceptable to Brahman and all other castes, as if they were a clean Hindu caste and not *Mlechha*, and that the washermen caste might serve them at their life cycle rituals, as in the case of clean Hindu castes. With this background and anchorage on the fringe of Hindu society, it did not take long for the landholding, dominant, and long-settled cultivators among the Hill Bhuiyan, inhabiting the open plateaus in Bonai and other parts of Sundargarh, who sometimes owned zamindaries as vassals of the rajas of princely states, to become accepted as a clean Hindu caste of cultivators. They sometimes even claimed status equivalent with the militia-cultivator caste of *Khandayats* (compare Khandayit Bhuiyan, Paik Bhuiyan, Praja Bhuiyan; Roy 1935: Appendix B, xi–xxiv). It is also not without significance that some Bhuiyan families continue to worship the local gods and goddesses as the only appropriate agents for the welfare of all castes. A similar process might have been at work in elevating the goddess Danteswary of Bastar beyond the tribal pale (compare Sinha 1962).

Therefore, the interaction between minor traditions and great traditions is a two-way process and is very complicated. This hierarchy of gods in the Hindu pantheon, the hierarchy of "feudal" lords in princely states in Orissa, and the locally dominant political power of tribal groups and their popular and — in the folk imagination — also powerful cults of minor gods and goddesses have conjoined to open the avenues to integration with Hindu castes and Hindu religion. (The Raja of Sambalpur adopted the tribal goddess, Samalai, who was worshiped by the local Sahara [Savara], as the state deity, who came to the aid of the state during crisis [S. P. Dash 1962:301, 303–304, 307–308, 342].) As we have seen above, the rajas have played a significant role in the creation of new castes not only from among Hindus themselves, but also out of the tribal communities.

Sinha in his brilliant analysis of the state formation and Rajput myth in tribal areas of central India (1962) has thrown light on the role of the tribal chiefs and feudal overlords in the spread and intensification of Brahmanical tradition in tribal areas. The induction of ritual specialists and service castes was necessitated by the urge to follow the model of Rajput or Kshatriya rulers. This, in turn, resulted in the introduction of Hindu gods, rituals, festivals, ideas, beliefs, and values (Sinha 1958), besides effecting internal stratification based on grades of assimilation into higher Hindu caste culture and of interaction with higher Hindu castes (Sinha 1962). These processes must have gone on not only in Chhatisgarh and the former Gond states of Madhya Pradesh and in Manbhum areas among the Gond, Bhumij, and allied tribes, but must also have taken place in the Orissan princedoms, where most of the princes were either themselves of tribal origin, adopted by the dominant tribal groups, or heavily dependent on their tribal supporters.

To sum up, the state deity and the paramount divine king were served by a complement of castes, who attended to various ritual and secular tasks. But, because these tasks were performed for divinities, whether in temples or palaces, caste duties acquired the characteristics of ritual obligations. In this sense, the caste system may be conceived as a ritual organization. As the vassal kings also assumed divinity in the image of the paramount king and as the cult of the state deity spread to the princedoms, caste duties at the level of princedoms were similarly invested with ritual values. At the village levels, we find the end point in the progressive decrease in elaboration of caste services, which nevertheless retained ritual character after the model of the paramount king and the vassal princes. The vassal chiefs often played a vital role in integrating the tribal peoples in the caste system by helping to "universalize" some local traditions centering around local gods and cults. These developments in Orissa have parallels elsewhere in India; Hocart's theoretical insights probably have been largely borne out by our empirical study in one cultural region of India.

Let me finish with an attempt to answer the question as to why it is that in the Orissa region, as perhaps nowhere else, the state deity has developed such an elaborate, sophisticated, and differentiated organization of caste-based services. Orissa, known in ancient times as Kalinga, was famous as a center of Jainism and Buddhism, and some merchants of Orissa were among the first disciples of Lord Gautama. It is well known how these two puritanical religions strove to usher in a caste-free society (without *varna* and four *ashramas*). There must have been widespread, long-standing confusion of castes, anarchy in the performance of traditional duties, and economic disruptions, as pointed out by Maynard (1972), which brought, as a reaction, stiff, standardized norms and regulations to be enforced by the king. The *Kautilya Arthashastra* recites the conventional form of duties of the four *varna* and then goes on to assert: "The observance of duty leads a man to bliss. When it is violated the world will come to an end owing to the confusion of castes and duties. Hence the king shall never allow people to swerve from their duties" (Maynard 1972:90). This enhancement of royal responsibility to bring back the caste order to its normal efficacy is a plausible guess on the part of Maynard.

In Orissa, well known all over India at least since Ashoka's days, it must have been felt that the tribal component of the population would become overpowering if allowed to remain too long outside the Hindu fold. And this could not be tolerated because Orissa forms a continuous link with northern, eastern, southern, and central India. In this context, it is not surprising suddenly to find Indradyumna, the legendary king of north

India, with whom all the gods are pleased and who can go to *Brahmaloka* in his mortal body, coming to Orissa to elevate an unknown god of the local tribal Savaras to the status of a supreme deity of the Hindus of India. Similar might have been the attempt by some other king to elevate the local Shiva Linga, worshiped by the Savaras, to the status of a deity (Lord Lingaraj) of all-India importance. It is also significant that the great anti-Buddhist saint Shankaracharya is said to have visited Purushottama-Kshetra (Puri), one of the foremost sacred pilgrimage centers in the eighth century, and to have composed the famous *Jagannathashtakam*. A monastery (*math*) established by him was shifted to Puri in the ninth century where it assumed tremendous importance in the management of temple ritual (Mishra 1971:151–152). The Shaiva King Yayati Keshari, perhaps the same as Mahashivagupta Yayati II of south Koshala, the doyen of the Somavamshi emperors of Orissa, is reputed to have built the Lord Jagannath temple at Puri and the Lord Lingaraj temple at Bhubaneswar, brought Veda-knowing Brahmans from north India, held a famous public horse sacrifice, and to have reestablished Brahmanism in Orissa in the tenth century. As a result, he is popularly designated Indradyumna II (Mishra 1971:30–32).

The resurrection of Brahmanism was aided by the process of "universalization" which, it appears, must have been a very ancient and recurrent process in the orthogenetic growth of Indian civilization. But this was especially imperative and expedient in the region known as Dandakaranya or Jharkhand, which was the hinterland of the Orissa coast, where the spread of the Jagannath cult in the interior came in handy for holding up the caste services as ritual obligations — sacred and inviolable. To aid in this process, the rajas, many of whom were tribal in origin, founded numerous Brahman villages in their princedoms. No wonder, therefore, that "in the Protected States of India few chiefs have retained their position as the paramount caste authority to such an extent as the chief of the Feudatory States of Orissa, a tract long isolated and untouched by modernizing influences" (O'Malley 1932:64–65). Whether this speculation is valid or not, the fact remains that most of the numerous and powerful tribes inhabiting the northern, western, and southern hills and plateaus, such as the Bhuiyan, the Bathudi, the Gond, the Binjhal or Binjhwar, large sections of the Kond and Savara, and Bhumia, and the Amanatya, have come to be more or less assimilated to the Hindu peasantry and are often considered equivalent in status to clean castes. For once Elwin (1943) has been proved wrong, because Hinduization has not left the tribesmen in the dungeons of low menial status in Hindu society.

REFERENCES

BOSE, N. K.
1949 *Hindu Samajer Gadan.* Calcutta: Viswa-Bharati.

BOSE, N. K. et al.
1958 "Organization of services in Lingaraj Temple," Bhubaneswar: *Journal of the Royal Asiatic Society* 24:2.

BOUGLÉ, C.
1908 *Travaux sur le régime des castes.* Paris.
1958 "The essence and reality of the caste system." *Contributions to Indian sociology* II. Translated and edited by Louis Dumont and D. F. Pocock, 7–30. The Hague: Mouton.

DASH, S. N.
1966 *Jagannatha Mandira O Jagannatha Tattwa.* Cuttack: Friends.

DASH, S. P.
1962 *Sambalapura Itihasa.* Sambalpur: S. P. Dash.

DATTA, N. K.
1968 *Origin and growth of caste in India,* volume one (second edition). Calcutta: K. L. Mukhopadhyay.

DUMONT, L., D. F. POCOCK, *editors*
1958 "A. M. Hocart on caste," in *Contributions to Indian sociology,* volume 2, 45–63. The Hague: Mouton.

ELWIN, VERRIER
1943 *The aboriginals.* Oxford: Oxford University Press.

GHURYE, G. S.
1961 *Caste, class and occupation.* Bombay: Popular Prakashan.

HEINE-GELDERN, R.
1942 Conceptions of state and kingship in South East Asia. *Far Eastern Quarterly* 2:1, 15–30.

HOCART, A. M.
1927 *Kingship.* Oxford: Oxford University Press.
1950 *Caste: a comparative study.* London: Methuen.
1970 *Kings and councillors.* Chicago: University of Chicago Press.

HUTTON, J. H.
1951 *Caste in India.* Oxford: Oxford University Press.

KULKE, HERMANN
1978 "*Some remarks about the Jagannath trinity."* in *Indologentagung.* Edited by H. Hartel, V. Moeler, Weisbader, Steiner. Heidelberg: South Asian Institute.

MAHAPATRA, L. K.
1970 "The role of the Hindu princes in the caste system in India." National lecture delivered at Ravishankar University, Raipur.

MAHAPATRA, M.
1972 "Lingaraj temple: its structure and change, circa 1900–1962." Unpublished doctoral dissertation, Utkal University, Orissa, India.

MARRIOTT, McKIM
1955 "Little communities in an indigenous civilization," in *Village India.* Edited by McKim Marriott, 171–222. Chicago: University of Chicago Press.

MAYNARD, H. J.
1972 Influence of the Indian king upon the growth of caste. *Journal of the Punjab Historical Society* 6:88–100.

MISHRA, K. C.
  1971   *The cult of Jagannatha.* Calcutta: K. L. Mukhopadhyay.
O'MALLEY, L. S. S.
  1932   *Indian caste customs.* Cambridge: Cambridge University Press.
PANIGRAHI, K. C.
  1961   *Archaeological remains at Bhubaneswar.* Bombay: Orient Longmans.
PATNAIK, N.
  1970   The recent Rajas of Puri: a study in secularization. *Journal of the Indian Anthropological Society* 5:1–2, 87–114.
ROY, S. C.
  1935   *The Hill Bhuiyan of Orissa.* Ranchi: Man in India Office.
SINHA, S. C.
  1958   Changes in the cycle of festivals in the Bhumij village. *Journal of Social Research* 1:1, 24–49.
  1962   State formation and Rajput myth in tribal central India. *Man in India* 42:1, 35–80.
  1972   *A survey of research in caste.* New Delhi: Indian Council of Social Science Research.
SRINIVAS, M. N.
  1952   *Religion and society among the Coorgs of south India.* Oxford: Oxford University Press.
  1955   "The social system of a Mysore village," in *Village India.* Edited by McKim Marriott, 1–35. Chicago: University of Chicago Press.
  1966   *Social change in modern India.* New Delhi: Allied.

Commercial Economy of an Urban Temple in India: A Shift from Inheritance to Consignment Rights

JAMES J. PRESTON

The analysis of temple communities in India reveals a great structural variety. Researchers (Vidyarthi 1961; Mahapatra 1971) have paid particular attention to the large old complexes that once formed temple cities. Other studies (Gough 1970; Dumont 1970; Srinivas 1969) have been concerned with village temples and shrines. Singer (1972) focused on cultural performances in the city of Madras, but he did not conduct an extensive investigation of any one religious institution.

An urban temple in coastal Orissa appears to illustrate a new pattern of community based on *rights by consignment*, rather than the more traditional theme of *rights by inheritance*. Materials were collected during an intensive field investigation conducted in Orissa from 1972 to 1973.

RIGHTS BY INHERITANCE

Most of the larger temples of Orissa have complex networks of inherited caste duties and responsibilities. Prescribed rules govern the percentage of offerings in cash and kind to be shared among the different castes of temple functionaries. Except under unusual conditions, these traditions are strictly observed. In recent years, with the introduction of modern education and the oversupply of temple priests, there is a tendency among some functionaries to employ proxies, who act as substitutes to fulfill traditional religious duties.

The rapid increase in population has not only produced serious land fragmentation, but it also has resulted in splintering and fission among castes who share in temple profits. Thus, for example, where once two brothers might have shared a percentage of the rice offered by devotees at a particular temple, today the same portion must be divided equally among their six sons. In many cases, priests must survive solely on these diminished inheritance rights. Often the younger generation is forced to abandon their traditional priestly duties to seek other sources of income. And in many cases, these young priests leave the village of their birth to find employment in cities or to supplement their incomes by starting small businesses in the local region.

Most of the rural temples of Orissa depend heavily on incomes from the paddy produced on their lands by tenant farmers. Many priests have traditionally gathered large portions of the crops grown on inherited patrimonial lands which they have collected as partial payment for their duties in local temples. In recent years, tenant farmers are reluctant to turn over full payment in cash or kind to the priests and other temple authorities, who find it increasingly difficult to enforce their traditional rights to paddy produced on temple lands.

As long as Indian temples remain dependent on the land for the main source of their income, land reforms that threaten to restrict the percentage of profit from the crops produced on temple lands will continue to endanger the survival of this institution. After studying this problem carefully in 1960, the Aiyar Commission, investigating the state of temple endowments throughout India, expressly warned local and state legislative bodies about the danger of land reform for the survival of temples (Aiyar *et al.* 1960–62:132). Somehow these religious institutions must be given equitable remuneration whenever they are subject to large economic losses due to new legislation that limits their income from agricultural lands.

Many great temples in southern India have seriously suffered from diminished resources and are on the brink of extinction. In some states such as Mysore, Punjab, and Rajasthan, religious institutions have *not* been exempted from land ceiling laws. In such cases, only perpetual guaranteed government annuities can rectify their losses. Moreover, this kind of compensation has all the problems of bureaucracy associated with it. Indeed, in some places where state annuities have been instituted, temples have had to close down anyway, because such a long time was needed to receive payments through the bureaucratic tangle of red tape.[1]

The spreading crisis in temple economics and the fragmented patrimonial rights of priests create great stress on many land-based temples. A few urban temples, however, have managed to develop an alternative economy. Though Indian temples have long received economic support from local merchants and rich patrons in the form of cash offerings, these resources were usually invested in temple lands or buildings, which often became part of the inherited property of priests.

[1] It has been calculated that any substantial reduction in the income of the religious institutions of Andhra Pradesh would result in the closure of 95 percent of them. This would amount to 12,000 institutions (Aiyar *et al.* 1960–62:139–141).

Chandi temple in the city of Cuttack (population, approximately 200,000) has deviated from this pattern in recent years. This small but prosperous temple has no landed property. Its financial support is mostly based on a large income from the yearly temple auction, at which local merchants compete for consignment rights to several commercial shops located within the temple walls. The temple has been governed since 1970 by a local board of trustees appointed by the Hindu Religious Endowment Commission of Orissa. The effect of this government control has been to diminish the strength of the six Brahmin brothers and virtually replace the authority of the local raja who once had complete control over the temple's management.

Today the board of trustees at Chandi temple has managed to encourage commercial investment in the temple's economy. Regular wages for temple servants have been established, along with fixed rules of exchange between priests and their clients. The priests continue to enjoy their inherited rights over a percentage of the daily offerings, but these offerings have become a minor part of the temple's economy. Local merchants, who enjoy rights by consignment through the purchase of licenses to temple shops in the yearly auction, wield more economic influence over the temple than do the priests who struggle to hold onto their rights by inheritance of cash offerings at the altar.

THE DISPERSAL OF TEMPLE OFFERINGS

There are two kinds of food offerings at Chandi temple: (1) the deity's daily meals, known as *prasad* and especially prepared by the priests, and (2) offerings by devotees of sweetmeats and plantains known as *bhog*. The worshipper purchases *bhog* from temple concessions and gives these offerings to an assistant priest, who places them before the goddess Chandi. These food offerings are then blessed by the officiating priest and returned to the devotee, who either eats them in the temple or takes them home to be shared with friends and relatives.

In many temples, the *prasad*, or sacred meal of a deity, plays an important part in the economy of rice and curry distribution among the priests, who usually have prescribed rights to specific portions of this meal each day. In other words, the division of *prasad* forms part of the priests' income and is often a source of conflict between castes, who may argue over their rightful shares. For a number of reasons, the amount and distribution of *prasad* at Chandi temple is not so important as in other temples. *Prasad* offered to Chandi feeds the six Brahmin priests and five temple servants every day. Still, by comparison to many temples, where extra portions of *prasad* are sold to the public by the priests, at Chandi temple, there is no such custom, mainly because it would not be as lucrative to the priests to spend their time selling *prasad* as it is to gather cash offerings at the altar. The priests spend most of their time, therefore, supervising the collection of cash offerings to be sure that they receive their full share.

Presently a point of contention at Chandi temple is the dispersal of these direct cash offerings given by devotees at the altar on a brass plate. According to the temple's scheme (a government document outlining the rules of temple management), the temple's endowment fund technically is supposed to receive 65 percent of these cash offerings, leaving the priests with only 35 percent. This is impossible to realize, however, because the "priest of the day" has direct supervision over this money, which is usually collected by his assistants. The executive officer representing the board of trustees would like to intervene in this process, but he dares not try to do so for it would cause considerable trouble. Instead, the priests continue to take most of this cash for themselves, leaving none for the endowment fund, despite contrary rules set forth in the scheme for the management of Chandi temple.[2]

It is difficult to estimate the amount of cash offered at the altar each year because the board of trustees has not managed to intervene in this aspect of the priests' rights by inheritance. Other sources, however, bring the temple's bank account to well above 200,000 rupees each year. Seventy-five percent of this budget comes from the sale of licenses for temple concessions. There is heavy competition among local merchants for these consignment rights at the yearly auction, because the concessions at Chandi temple yield large profits, and it is considered auspicious to manage a shop inside the temple walls.

RIGHTS BY CONSIGNMENT

Each concession at Chandi temple specializes in the sale of one of the following: sweetmeats, ghee lamps, incense, flowers or haircuts. Two sweetmeat shops compete for customers among the more than 1,000 devotees who attend the temple daily. Both of these shops sell hundreds of sweetmeats. The flower concession is also lucrative, especially since flowers and garlands are easy to come by and need little preparation before they are sold.

The quality of these products is maintained at a high standard because of the keen competition among merchants who bid in the annual auction. Thus, a kind of closed-market economy has entered directly into the

---

[2] Cash offerings may also be given to the executive officer, who then turns them over to the endowment fund. Also cash may be put in one of several donation boxes located in different parts of the temple. This money is counted periodically by the executive officer and is not controlled by the priests.

temple sphere. Nash defines the relatively closed market as follows:

Markets may be less than fully open if cultural rules prevent certain kinds of persons from buying and selling there, or if political authorities through licensing or other regulatory devices control access to markets (Nash 1966:107).

The commercial competition in Chandi temple's auction is regulated with rules established by the Hindu Religious Endowment Commission of Orissa. It is theoretically open to anybody who has the money to pay the fees required as downpayment once the bid is won. But, of course, it takes people with access to cash to afford competition. Though the ownership of a particular kind of shop is not necessarily caste-bound, there is a tendency for the gardener, sweetmeat, and barber castes to purchase consignment rights to the concessions most closely related to their traditional caste occupations. Still, one can find members of the gardener caste operating sweetmeat concessions. Capital for investment appears to be more important than caste.

Though temple auctions are not confined to urban centers in Orissa, they usually play a relatively minor role in rural religious institutions. Many temples in urban and rural settings have concessions that are managed by specific castes, who pass down their inherited rights to sell goods in the temple from generation to generation. In these instances rights by inheritance are stressed, while consignment rights through public auctions are rare.

The case of Chandi of Cuttack illustrates a gradual shift in recent years from a relatively poor, landless neighborhood temple, controlled by a local raja, to a rich urban commercial temple, infused with the wealth of the mercantile classes. The Marwari, Gujarati, and Bengali merchants of Cuttack recognize Chandi as their patroness. Each year, they offer the goddess large quantities of cash, gold jewelry, and other ornamentation.[3]

In 1973, the licenses for concessions at Chandi temple brought unusually high prices. It was difficult to be sure exactly who was bidding on these occasions, because in many cases the bidders were front men for others who wanted to remain anonymous. It was also difficult to single out individual owners of concession licenses, because different families often pool their resources in order to secure a consignment.

The commercial economy of a temple like Chandi of Cuttack is linked into the larger network of its urban environment. As attendance increases due to the widening popularity of the goddess, more shopkeepers compete for space to sell their goods on the street outside the temple. Thirty

[3] There are many Oriya patrons of Chandi temple as well, despite the fact that Jagannath is the most frequently worshiped deity in Orissa.

years ago, the street in front of Chandi temple had only one shop. Today there are nearly one hundred concessions clustered around the temple entrance. These include grocery stores, tea stalls, and repair shops, which are mostly frequented by devotees and the numerous riksa pullers who spend hours waiting for customers outside the temple.

At this time, Chandi temple is not adversely affected by population pressures, though it is small in size. Indeed, it appears to be always full at peak hours. This has a psychological effect on worshippers who, when interviewed expressed their attraction to the temple because it always appears to them to be popular. Furthermore, since the temple has only six Brahmin priests, the pressures of the population explosion have not seriously cut into their shares of the profit, so as to impoverish them, as in other larger and older temples. Nor do the six Brahmin brothers rely on profits from the sale of paddy harvested on temple lands. There is also no intercaste competition among priests at Chandi temple. The single family of six Brahmin priests has managed to share equally the cash offerings at the altar with few family quarrels. Indeed, though these Brahmin priests resent the intrusion of the public board of trustees in temple affairs, they welcome the commercialization of the temple, because it attracts more devotees and thus brings them larger cash offerings each year.

CONCLUSION

Several important questions are raised by these findings. First, is the apparent shift from rights by inheritance to rights by consignment an expected direction of change for the temples of Orissa as they face financial crises? Second, does this change that incorporates the commercialism of modern India into the temple structure represent a secularization of the sacred sphere? Third, can there be a compromise between inherited and consigned sources of power and authority in the religious institutions of India? These questions are difficult to answer without further research, both in Orissa and in other states. I shall only offer here some speculations that at most will raise still further questions.

It is difficult to conceive of a solution to the financial difficulties of temples that rely on the produce from their agricultural lands for income. If land reforms are to be equitable in India, no meaningful exemptions for religious institutions will be accepted by tenant farmers. Why should a farmer pay more of his profits from produce raised on temple lands than he would pay if he were farming government lands? As the commercial economy of India extends farther into the remote villages, local institutions must face the shift from a land-based economy to a cash-centered market where competition depends more on consignment than on inherited rights. This is a gradual process and temples that are not facing financial difficulties due to overpopulation of priests or lack of income from their landed properties should have few problems. The local endowment commissions should be able to clarify disputes among different castes. If temples face more serious crisis conditions, and there are no more rich landed aristocrats to intercede on their behalf, then it would seem that there is no alternative but to commercialize these institutions.

This brings to mind the second question about the secularization of religious institutions by the incorporation of commercialism. Does this represent a corruption of Hinduism? This question is raised because it was foremost in the thoughts of many of my informants. It is important to remember here that the participation of the mercantile classes in the affairs of Hindu temples is an old phenomenon. Vidyarthi (1961) illustrates this point in his research on Gaya. It seems that the case of Chandi temple represents a far more advanced commercialization than has been previously noted. If one defines secularization as a collapse of sacred authority in the face of pressures from nonreligious institutions, such as merchants, government officials, or youth groups, then Chandi of Cuttack has not been secularized. It is quite clear that the religious authority of the priests at Chandi temple has not been altered in any significant way by its commercialization. Instead, the priests have been able to expand the ritual cycle of the temple because of increased temple income. If, on the other hand, secularization is defined more narrowly, as a corruption of the total control of religious institutions by priests and rajas, then Chandi temple has been significantly secularized. This author prefers to use the first definition of secularization here, because in India the separation of secular and sacred spheres has always been difficult to establish. There is something in Hindu philosophy itself that refuses to be reduced to a simple pair of opposites. If one assumes that sacred and secular are already hopelessly intertwined in the Indian context, then the whole issue of corruption due to the commercialization of Hindu temples is a superficial problem imposed by Western binary thinking.

The question of compromise between inherited and consigned authorities in the religious institutions of India is the most important of these issues. It would appear that as long as India remains a predominantly agricultural society, inheritance rights will remain important. There is no reason to believe that commercialism will necessarily destroy the temple as a viable community for the perpetuation of the Hindu ethical life. The old symbiotic relationship between the raja and the priest is capable of withstanding new structural interpretations with the evolution of modern Indian lifestyles. The case of Chandi temple illustrates the survival capacity of a Hindu religious institution faced with the possibility of extinction. The state governments of India are well aware of the danger of intruding too much into the affairs of local temples. Still, their task is to strike an equitable balance between land-based economies and the competitive market of modern commercial India. This is not an easy balance to maintain, but it is essential for all parties concerned to recognize the fact that rights by inheritance must live side by side with rights by consignment if India is to hold itself together in the modern world at the same time that it supports and respects its older institutions. A compromise between the old and the new is difficult to sustain, but it is essential if Hinduism is to become a vital force for future generations.

The case of Chandi of Cuttack offers an opportunity to reflect on key issues relevant to the evolution of Hinduism as manifest in its social institutions. Chandi of Cuttack exemplifies the potential versatility of the Hindu temple as a structure. The shift in emphasis here noted from rights by inheritance to rights by consignment signifies important changes in the nature of the temple community. Where once the stress was on personal, obligatory relationships through castes and kinship structures, now the temple community may be regulated by fixed rules of exchange with less personal relations between priests, patrons, and clients.

No longer can a few rich patrons control temple politics. The fall of the raja from his previous position of control over temple affairs, combined with an increase in the power and prestige of the board of trustees, has brought this temple into the mainstream of the growing commercialism in Cuttack. Though many people see this economic growth of Chandi temple as the sign of the corruption of the old pristine tradition, others support this shift, because it means that more people can participate in the temple community reaping economic, social, and ritual benefits.

The view that economic and social change are inimical to Hinduism does not hold true. The shift outlined here, from an emphasis on rights by inheritance to rights by consignment seems a viable pattern of adjustment for religious communities in India. Particularly encouraging is the fact that ritual activity has been stimulated, rather than depressed, in Chandi temple in recent years. Unlike other temples that are suffering from economic depression due to drastic reductions in profits from endowed lands, an urban commercial temple like Chandi of Cuttack is developing a viable alternative.

Nash (1966:100) says that money and economic opportunity are nearly universal solvents of static, hierarchical, and religiously defined economic systems. This assumes that religious economic systems are static. The point illustrated in the case of Chandi temple is that the high mobility of men and resources may be phrased in religious terms within a cash-profit economy, as long as the change from the old system is gradual enough to allow for the traditional elements to adjust to the idiom of the newly emerging structures. There is no validity in the idea that Hindu religion, culture, and social structure inhibit growth. Mandelbaum

(1970:641) makes this same point when he observes the following: "Particularly misguided is the notion that there must be inherent contradictions between established customs and modern innovations."

REFERENCES

AIYAR, C. P. RAMASWAMI et al.
 1960–1962 *Report of the Hindu religious endowments commission.* New Delhi: Government of India Press.
DERRET, J. DUNCAN
 1966 The reform of Hindu religious endowments, in *South Asian politics and religion.* Edited by Donald E. Smith, 311–336. Princeton: Princeton University Press.
DUMONT, LOUIS
 1970 *Religion, politics, and history in India.* The Hague: Mouton.
EPSTEIN, SCARLETT
 1971 "Economic development and social change in South India," in *Economic development and social change: The Modernization of village communities.* Edited by George Dalton, 460–491. Garden City, N.Y.: Natural History Press.
GOUGH, KATHLEEN
 1970 "Palakkara: Social and religious change in central Kerala," in *Change and Continuity in India's villages.* Edited by K. Ishwaran, 129–164. New York: Columbia University Press.
MAHAPATRA, MANAMOHAN
 1971 "Lingaraj temple: its structure and change." Unpublished doctoral dissertation, Utkal University, Orissa, India.
MANDELBAUM, DAVID G.
 1970 *Society in India: change and continuity,* volume two: Berkeley: University of California Press.
NASH, MANNING
 1966 *Primitive and peasant economic systems.* Scranton, Pa.: Chandler.
 Orissa Hindu Religious Endowment Act.
 1969 Cuttack: Cuttack Law Times.
POCOCK, DAVID F.
 1960 "Sociologies urban and rural," volume four: *Contributions to Indian sociology.* The Hague: Mouton.
RUDOLPH, LLOYD I., SUZANNE RUDOLPH
 1967 *The modernity of tradition.* Chicago: University of Chicago Press.
SINGER, MILTON
 1972 *When a great tradition modernizes.* New York: Praeger.
SOUTHALL, AIDAN, editor
 1973 *Urban anthropology.* New York: Oxford University Press.
SRINIVAS, M. N.
 1969 *Social change in modern India.* Berkeley: University of California Press.
VIDYARTHI, L. P.
 1960 "Thinking about a sacred city." *The Eastern Anthropologist* 13:4, 203–215.
 1961 *The sacred complex in Hindu gaya.* New York: Asia.

The Indian Caste Community as a Social System

M. K. KUDRYAVTSEV

The majority of the most highly developed groups in India have always had a corporate social structure based on the two pillars of the caste and the community. Each of these two systems had its own organizational principles, internal structure, and centuries-old traditions. This is why they have long been studied as independent subjects, with considerable literature devoted to each system. In Indian society, the caste and the community never existed apart from, or independently of, each other. On the other hand, under the specific conditions found in India, one presupposed and provided for the existence of the other. Regrettably, the social importance of this dualism has not yet been appreciated sufficiently. Even Mandelbaum (1970), in his fundamental work on the caste system, fails to single out the caste community as a special entity. And yet, the true nature of social relations in India at present and in the past can only be fully revealed if each system is considered as it interacts with the other.

It is often said that history is studied to gain a better understanding of the present. Depending on the character of historical sources and on the extent to which they have been analyzed, another retrospective approach may be used: the present state of the community and caste system may be studied, for instance, to determine objective criteria and to find clues to understanding of the laws that governed the development of Indian society in the past. This paper is an attempt to characterize the community and caste system on the basis of twentieth-century studies of the Indian community.

The caste organization is a definite system in itself. It was only able to evolve as a hierarchic system of social inequality under the conditions of a far-reaching property and social differentiation, or, in other words, one that is beyond the bounds of the primitive communal system characterized by social equality and lack of exploitation. It is a fact that even today many Indian tribes with rudimentary property and social differentiation have no castes. This is clearly because social equality and collective forms of ownership run counter to the very essence of the caste system.

The core of the caste system, in the form of the *varnas*, took shape over 2,000 years ago — almost in the Vedic period. The caste system became increasingly sophisticated with the development of technology, the growing division of labor, and the emergence of new occupations. It thus survived through the colonial period, the expansion of capitalism, and the establishment of the Republic.

Socially, this system is profoundly and rigorously stratified. The caste organization generally falls into several social groupings: the higher and middle ("pure") castes and the lower and lowest ("impure") castes. Specific social distinctions exist within each of these. The social status of each caste is strictly fixed and solidified by age-old traditions within the framework of the system. A sophisticated complex of social, familial, marital, and ritual relations, sanctified by centuries of tradition function within the system, with special caste self-government bodies watching over their observance.

Tradition prescribes a certain range of occupations to each caste and imposes more or less strict bans on others. The course of life has amended these prescriptions and bans over the years, generally emphasizing some and minimizing others. Thus, the number of castes linked exclusively with traditional occupations is steadily decreasing, though most castes are still classified in the hierarchy according to these occupations from which their names are derived.

Indian society is comprised of hundreds and thousands of castes. Some of these had millions of members and were spread throughout the entire country; others numbered only a few hundred or thousand and were localized in small territories amongst other castes. In principle, the castes were endogamous units; many had endogamous subcastes. An endogamous caste or subcaste generally broke down into exogamous units (*got, gotra*, and so on). These were in turn fragmented into smaller groups, which in northern India, for instance, were called *thok*, *biradari*, *kunba*, *kutumba*, *kula*, *khandan*, and so on; in English literature, these groups are known as lineages. The primary subdivision of a caste was the individual family, (which was generally large). The family was the primary exogamous cell of the caste system. Having joined her husband's family, the wife acquired membership in his caste and its multiple exogamous subdivisions; she became a member of her husband's family, usually severing all kinship ties with her father's family.

Ties of consanguinity or kinship constituted an essential element of the caste structure. The exogamous *gotras* were regarded as associations of relatives often descended from a common ancestor; the members of the exogamous subdivisions were considered to be relatives of varying degrees. In this respect, the caste organization resembled the clan-and-tribal system.

No single caste alone could exist as an independent economic unit. Coexistence with other castes was indispensable for the existence of any single caste, and castes could coexist parallel and independent of one another. Extensive ties and interactions of different castes in all spheres of social life occurred, including the production of the means of subsistence. Unfortunately, as many scholars have noted, the subject of caste interdependence has not yet been properly studied.

The village was the principal territorial unit, the arena where the castes interacted and where their local subdivisions began to figure in social relationships. It served as an organizing agent for the interaction of different castes, which numbered anywhere from ten to twenty.

Numerous case studies of Indian villages (Wiser 1958; Dube 1955, 1958; Lewis, 1958; Majumdar 1958; Orenstein 1965; Srinivas 1955; Marriott 1955a, 1955b; Pradhan 1966 and others) reveal that even today village communities still exist in various parts of the country, and in some localities, the village community acts as an important element of the social structure and a regulating mechanism in social relations. This was so even after 200 years of devastating colonial rule and capitalism, during which the villages were swept by private property relations, with elements of commodity production and capitalist forms of exploitation gaining a foothold. Under such difficult conditions, the village community structure has survived in parts of the country in varying degrees. It is best preserved in some regions of northern India, which is the reason that the material used in this paper has been drawn from the northern Indian context.

An Indian village community as a rule is comprised of several castes. Its structural elements include caste groups that differ in their property statuses, traditional occupations, and functional roles in their places in the caste hierarchy. Single-caste communities are extremely rare in India. The village seems to be the scene of an interplay between two types of social ties — intra- and intercaste. Scholarly opinion now accepts Srinivas' formal classification (1955) of horizontal and vertical social relations. According to Srinivas, the caste is the horizontal entity, whereas the village acts as the vertical element in the formula. The horizontal caste ties transcend the village boundaries, and the vertical ties are confined to the village itself. Many adherents of this classification, however, observed that the vertical or intercaste ties were not simply confined to the village, but rather, extended far beyond its borders, cementing entities that comprised many different villages.

It is important to examine these horizontal and vertical entities as a means of disclosing the social substance of intra- and intercaste ties.

The horizontal intracaste ties are primarily those of consanguinity and kinship. If these relationships are arranged in an order of increasing magnitude, that is, from the smallest unit to the largest, the resultant series would roughly resemble the following: (1) individual family, (2) a small group of related families of the *kula* or *khandan* type, (3) larger associations of relatives (for example, *thok* or *biradari*), (4) higher exogamous units (for example, *gotra* or *got*), (5) an amalgamation of several such units into an endogamous "marriage network," (6) endogamous subcaste, and (7) the caste proper.

The chain is long and intricate. Furthermore, certain elements of the chain such as the family and most small related family groupings usually reside in the same village, whereas large exogamous groups of relatives and the *gotras* may live in several neighboring villages. The network of marriage relations usually covers scores of villages situated at quite some distance from each other.

The caste structure is thus horizontal and is held together by a strictly observed tradition of family and marriage relations that form exogamous, endogamous, and hypergamous units within one horizontal entity. This appraisal of the structure of the caste organization is almost universal among scholars.

The concept of the village community as the vertical entity needs further explanation. Srinivas (1955) conceived of the village community as an organized aggregate of various castes within a single village. It is important to note that such an aggregate is essentially different from intercaste relations because it is based on relations of neighbors.

Relations of neighbors as a social phenomenon and a principle of social organization merits special attention. This principle prevailed in a socially stratified society and proved especially effective under conditions of caste organization. Indeed, the different castes in a village cannot be related by blood because of the very nature of the caste organization. Accordingly, they carry on mutual relations as fellow villagers or neighbors. The vertical ties and entities are, therefore, predominantly those of neighbors, both within a particular village and among different villages.

The village community is the nodal point of intercaste ties. It has always been the chief structural element of the community and caste system. Within the village, intercaste groupings of neighbors such as *patti*, *taraf*, *pana*, *tola*, and so on have emerged. Even within large caste groups, that is in the horizontal entity, there were similar groupings of neighbors who were not relatives, for example, people belonging to different *gotras*.

The faction known in northern India as *dhar* or *ghut*, is probably the smallest group of neighbors in the typical village. The *dhar* is a small group of families that is in conflict with some similar groups and yet forms an alliance with others. This is a recent event and was hardly known in the precolonial period. At present, the *dhars* are extremely active in the social life of the villages and are notorious for their conflicts with one another.

Groups of neighbors are organizationally interconnected at different levels. For example, the *dhars* form part of a *tola*, which constitutes a *pana*. The *panas* make up a village community. While the *dhars* are ruled by elders, the *pana*, the *taraf*, and the *patti* are governed by permanent or provisional councils of elders known as *panchayats*. Village affairs are handled by the *panchayat*.

In other parts of the country, such as the Deccan or in southern India, the villages are usually subdivided into sections, streets, and blocks, on the same principle as the neighborhood. Here, too, most villages had factions similar to the *dhars* of northern India. Though some of these groupings of neighbors did not have *panchayats* of their own, all of them were headed by elected or hereditary elders.

The transcending vertical boundaries of the village has been noted by Miller (1955) in Kerala and Smith (1955) in the Punjab among others. Indeed, along the same vertical lines, intervillage associations of neighbors comprising from two to several scores of villages were formed. Examples are the *dugama*, the *chaugama*, and the *bisagama* (Lewis 1958), or the *ganvand*, the *thamba*, and the *chaurasi* (Pradhan 1966). Each of these associations was an organizational unit of the community-and-caste system of a higher order than in the individual village. Each supervillage entity was run by its own organ of community self-rule — the *panchayat*, which had a more or less broad range of authority. The *panchayats* formed different levels of hierarchy. As was aptly shown by Pradhan (1966) this entire system was a viable and actively functioning organism even into the recent past. Thus, an association of hundreds of Jat communities in the Upper Doab took part both in the struggle against the invasion of Ahmed Shah Durrani in the eighteenth century and in the popular uprising against the British in 1857–1858.

There is no uniform pattern for either the individual community or the community system as a whole. Even the caste organization had numerous local versions. The pattern of community organization also varied substantially as in the cases of the tribes, in purely Muslim or Christian settlements where there were no castes and in villages with ethnically and religiously mixed populations. The bulk of the Indian population is organized in community patterns that exhibit some common features.

The following features are characteristic of a typical Indian community:

1. The community is a territorial unit.
2. The community has a caste pattern, that is, it is comprised of many castes.

3. A combination of kinship ties and the neighborhood principle forms an organizing element of community relations.

4. There is an inordinately large proportion of nonfarming population (engaged in trades) within the farming community.

5. There is a characteristic interdependence in the sphere of production and social relations among the different caste groups in the village.

6. Collective ownership of nonarable lands is clearly pronounced.

7. A high degree of economic, social, and organizational autonomy is enjoyed by the village community.

Still other features that are common to village communities in different parts of the country could probably be found.

Different levels of community structure emerged at various points of intersection among ties that linked relatives and neighbors; they were all organizations of neighbors, but were also permeated with family ties. Yet, these two types of social ties did not merely intersect at right angles like horizontal and vertical lines; both principles of community organization intertwined and interacted, forming a network at the nodal points where communities emerged at different levels. Apart from its structure, the caste community in some areas of northern India, such as the Doab, the Punjab, and some parts of Delhi, has retained some of its economic and social functions even into the present century. The village community played the central role in this. Though the arable land had long been privately owned by individual households, that is, families of community members, usually these lands were still controlled by the community. They were not inherited, partitioned, or confiscated arbitrarily, but in keeping with tradition. Any such operation called for the community's endorsement. In areas dominated by the private landownership *ryotvari* principle of central India, community control over land operations survived until recently, although in attenuated forms. The only exception to this rule were cases in which all the land of a village, or most of it, in such cases was privately owned by the *zamindar* landlord. In such cases the community's control became nominal or disappeared altogether. The very existence of the community became nominal, for the community members became the landlord's tenants. Still, the nonarable land was invariably owned by the community as a whole; the community set and watched over the rules for the use of such land by its members.

Production relations in the Indian community were characterized by a traditional system of placing various nonfarming groups in the production process and the division of labor among castes. This was done by rules of mutual obligations and services. Ultimately, this resulted in an extremely peculiar form of intracommunity exploitation of some caste groups by others. This system is known in northern India as *jajmani* and has been described by Wiser (1958), Lewis (1958), Gould (1959, 1964), and other researchers. Similar systems had different names in other parts of India.

Until recently, 90 percent of the population in India lived in the countryside, and the main forces of production were concentrated in villages. Therefore, the traditional production relations in the countryside by and large determined the character of the production relations of the entire society.

Moreover, these production functions constituted only one line of community activity. The primary task of the village community was to control its membership, particularly the traditional size relationship of the various caste groups. It is well known that it was not easy to escape from the village community. It was even more difficult for a stranger to be admitted to the community or allowed to settle in an Indian village. Among other things, the community, together with the self-governing caste organizations, saw that tradition was adhered to in the family and marriage relations. The community also watched the conduct of its members in day-to-day life. It controlled the observance of the routine rites and holidays. It arbitrated property and other conflicts, punished offenders of law and tradition, and organized and conducted all sorts of collective and public works in the village.

Returning to the statement that in India the corporate principle prevailed over personal relations, one is led to conclude that the social life of India's rural population is above all an incessant and pervasive interaction of the local caste subdivisions, that is, groupings of neighbors within the community.

The definition of the Indian community as a special caste variety of the village community of neighbors is of great methodological importance; such a definition permits a consideration of the socioeconomic structure that engenders the caste community as a specific, but logical, phenomenon in the world process of historical development. The general developmental trend has been for the consanguinity of kinship, the clan and tribal organization, and the collective forms of ownership and property to be superseded by territorial ties and economic relations, by class and state patterns of societal organization, and by the ultimate domination of private property. All these phenomena are in evidence in India, the sole local differences being the slow progress of this process and the peculiar forms it took in some instances. This accounts for the emergence of the caste organization in India. Caste distinctions appeared as early as, possibly earlier than, class distinctions, and both developed along parallel lines. Owing to the caste organization, the kinship ties proved to be more tenacious and adaptive. Through the centuries, they cemented the caste system. The social division of labor also took peculiar forms whereby the crafts were separated from agriculture, and became an essential element in the community's production relations. Private landownership, the chief means of production in a farming society, were not the dominant form of ownership until after the establishment of colonial rule.

This socioeconomic phenomenon profoundly affected the destiny of most of India's peoples. This also explains the extraordinary viability of the Indian caste community.

REFERENCES

DUBE, S. C.
  1955 *Indian village*. Ithaca, N.Y.: Cornell University Press.
  1958 *India's changing villages*. Ithaca, N.Y.: Cornell University Press.
GOULD, H. A.
  1959 The peasant village: centrifugal or centripetal? *The Eastern Anthropologist* 13:1.
  1964 A Jajmani system of North India, its structure, magnitude and meaning. *Ethnology* 3 (1):12–41.
LEWIS, O.
  1958 *Village life in northern India*. Urbana: University of Illinois Press.
MAJUMDAR, D. N.
  1958 *Caste and communication in an Indian village*. Bombay: Asia.
MANDELBAUM, D. G.
  1970 *Society in India*, volumes one and two. Berkeley: University of California Press.
MARRIOTT, McKIM
  1955a "Little communities in an indigenous civilization," in *Village India*. Edited by M. Mariott, 171–222. Chicago: University of Chicago Press.
  1955b "Social structure and change in an Uttar Pradesh village," in *India's Villages*. Edited by M. Srinivas, 106–121. Calcutta: Asia Publishing House.
MILLER, E. J.
  1955 "Village structure in North Kerala," in *India's Villages*. Edited by M. Srinivas, 42–55. Calcutta: Asia Publishing House.
ORENSTEIN, H.
  1965 *Goan: Conflict and cohesion in an Indian village*. Princeton: Princeton University Press.
PRADHAN, M. C.
  1966 *The political system of the Jats of northern India*. Bombay: Indian Branch, Oxford University Press.
SMITH, M. W.
  1955 "Social structure in the Punjab," in *India's Villages*. Edited by M. Srinivas, 161–179. Calcutta: Asia Publishing House.
SRINIVAS, M. N.
  1955 "The social structure of a Mysore village," in *India's Villages*. Edited by M. Srinivas, 21–35. Calcutta: Asia Publishing House.
WISER, W. H.
  1958 *The Hindu Jajmani system*. Lucknow: U. P. Lucknow.

Social Cohesion and Reciprocation in a Tibetan Community in Nepal

B. N. AZIZ

The *ga-nye* system is a mechanism of social control and mutual aid found in Tibet and in varying forms along the Himalayas in communities exhibiting Tibetan-like culture. The *ga-nye*, in its traditional Tibetan form, was carried into Nepal by new Tibetan migrants who settled there as recently as 1960. It is an action and belief system in itself, but in addition, the *ga-nye* seems to play a central part in several aspects of community interrelations. While most of this presentation will be ethnographic, it also will be an attempt to approach Tibetan society from a more synthetic and sociological viewpoint than is usually taken by specialists in Tibetan history and religion.

The way was opened for a more sociological approach to Tibetan culture by Miller's revealing paper (1956) on mutual-aid associations manifest in Tibet and some Tibetan communities in India. She documented the socioeconomic features of two types of associations, the *ga-nye* and *ki-du*.[1] During the last decade and a half, the leads Miller provided were neglected while researchers busied themselves trying to capture a pure and lost Tibet (one that probably never existed) and

---

In 1970 and 1971, I undertook intensive field research into the social organization of Tibetans settled in Nepal. The data presented in this paper were collected from one of the communities I studied. The research was funded by a generous grant from the Social Science Research Council of Great Britain. I take this opportunity to thank the Council for that support and to express my indebtedness to Professor C. von Fürer-Haimendorf for his assistance and encouragement. This research was undertaken while I was a student at the University of London School of Oriental and African Studies.

[1] These are two types of Tibetan associations. Miller notes some of the features of the *ga-nye*, but she devotes most of her paper to *ki-du*, the more corporate and economically oriented of the two. While I also observed the *ki-du* type, I make only cursory reference to it in this paper.

fighting a futile political battle for the pitiful yet promising refugees who moved into their world.[2]

Ironically today, although Tibet itself is more inaccessible to us than ever before, new and promising fields are becoming available for the researcher interested in Buddhist and Himalayan societies. The communities in the Himalaya that border Tibet show strong cultural similarities with the Tibetan, and the new communities of the recently arrived refugees from Tibet are proving to be rich in Tibetan beliefs and practices. Those communities not only maintain many traditional customs but also adjust them in interesting ways to the new socioeconomic environment and historical conditions in which they find themselves. Goldstein (1971a, 1971b, 1971c), in a number of articles, has shown what detailed ethnography can be reaped from the new fields.

It was only in 1970, during field research in a Tibetan community in Nepal, that I was able to consider Miller's suggestions and to examine for myself various forms of social organization among the Tibetans. Certainly no study of family or of local, economic, and informal political systems of the Tibetans and related groups can be undertaken without involving a study and understanding of the *ga-nye* system.[3] As Miller herself notes, *ga-nye* is like a magic word when introduced into a conversation with Tibetan informants. For the Tibetan, this word has a set of social, moral, and jural connotations. They invoke a conscious and identifiable set of thought and behavioral rules. They lead the ethnographer, just as they lead the Tibetan participant, into the heart of the society.

Data are taken from Deling, a rural community of newly settled Tibetans in northeastern Nepal, where I carried out my research. It is a village of some 1,000 people; all have moved from Gya-tri in south Tibet into Nepal over the last decade after the severe changes in Tibet.[4] The community has a certain homogeneity and distinctiveness; it is set apart socially, economically, and politically from the Nepalese host society. Most of its members know one another from Tibet. Some are kinsmen;

---

[2] The most useful anthropological accounts of Tibetan society have been carried out in the border areas of India and Nepal adjacent to Tibet. These include works by von Fürer-Haimendorf (1964), Gorer (1938), Kihara (1957), Oppitz (1968), and Prince Peter (1963). In addition to these, there have been some attempts to piece together the social structure of the Tibetans by using a variety of sources. These, all of limited use, have been not altogether successful. They include Carrasco (1959), Ekvall (1964), Bell (1928), Cassinelli and Ekvall (1969), and Stein (1962).

[3] Throughout the paper, I usually refer to the *ga-nye* as a system. While *ga-nye* means simply "close friends," and describes a personal bond, it is a system of social bonds and action. Its form and operation will be elucidated as the discussion proceeds.

[4] Deling and Gya-tri are both pseudonyms. The former applies to the new village in Nepal, and Gya-tri applies to that area in Tibet from which these villagers emigrated as refugees between 1959 and 1965. Throughout the paper, pseudonyms have been supplied for all persons whose cases are discussed.

some were covillagers, others know one another vaguely through transient meetings in the Gya-tri area. Thus, there is a firm social base in Deling for the continuation of some traditional patterns of culture and relationships. At the same time, the inevitable change caused by economic reorganization, fragmentation of families, and their incorporation into the Nepalese society create more than a mere replica of what was before.

While Deling in 1970, can be considered reasonably stable and homogeneous, it was not always like this. The new stability and intricate weave of the social matrix has developed only after some years of strain and great social flux. Earlier in its history (the community was established officially in 1963), there were serious disputes and constant changes in the population. That period of flux was followed by the emergence of a stable core of villagers. Trust developed out of familiarity; economic cooperation grew with the unified and beneficial economic innovations; and effective leadership was provided by political and spiritual leaders.

The Tibetan migrants have established ties with members of their host community, the Sherpas, Rai, and Tamang, as well as with the Newar in other parts of Nepal. There is economic and religious cooperation and a mutual respect is enjoyed among them, but the villagers of Deling rely more on each other and interact more intensively with members of their own community than they do with those outsiders.

These Tibetans are left to themselves to deal with their own affairs as much as possible. Tibetan law, as long as it does not conflict with that of the national Nepalese legal code, is respected by the Nepalese authorities. Deling is left to settle its own internal problems according to Tibetan moral beliefs and social rules. The Tibetans themselves welcome this independence, as they wish to remain outside the direct influence of others. Deling remains a jural and moral entity, as well as a socioeconomic one.

The social structure and that ongoing process of social relations that make Deling the community that it could be presented in many ways and through any one of a number of its institutions. In this paper, I have selected the *ga-nye*. There is something singularly Tibetan about the *ga-nye*, yet it displays some universal qualities in its social function and its attributes. My aim is to show both of these characteristics, as well as the personal element, the human agent, through which everything is manifested. I also endeavor to illustrate the action system as it works in regard to the community morality.

The discussion is divided into five parts: (1) the *ga-nye* as an action and as a moral system, (2) the rules and process of recruitment, (3) the reciprocal nature of the bond, (4) the role of the *ga-nye* in dispute settlement, and (5) the *ga-nye* compared cross-culturally.

THE *GA-NYE* AS AN ACTION AND A MORAL SYSTEM

The *ga-nye*[5] is a social bond; it is a feeling between two individuals as well as the name by which their relationship is known. Both the emotional and social links are related to a particular moral system prominent in Tibetan society (and separate from the religious system), which I call the *ga-nye* moral system.[6] This set of morals that directs *ga-nye* behavior has a particular nature, distinct from the moral systems that guide other social behavior, for example, family ties, economic choices, and piety.

The *ga-nye* bonds are established through a general social network such as Barnes (1954) describes. The general social network of a Tibetan in Deling is composed of kinsmen, neighbors, coworkers, special friends *(trok)*,[7] religious friends, fellow members in a club *(ki-du* or *tsok)*,[8] *ga-nye*, and covillagers. Out of that network, those recognized as *ga-nye* form one set.[9] One's set of *ga-nye*, then, is drawn from one's wider social network. It is ego-centered in that any set of *ga-nye* exists only in relation to one individual who recognizes all members of that set. Each man and the household to which he belongs have a set different from that of any other man and his respective household. Although some of one's *ga-nye* set may overlap with the *ga-nye* set of another household, they will be different and will act differently in regard to those two households. This is the nature of any network set.

Usually, most of a man's *ga-nye* set know one another; they are covillagers and of the same general socioeconomic status. They also know all of a man's household members, although they may not interact with them as frequently as they do with the head of the household. Most of the time, close association of all members of a set is neither necessary nor

---

[5] This system is different from, but not unrelated to, the merit and moral system that exists in Sherpa and Tibetan Buddhist societies (von Fürer-Haimendorf 1966). Fürer-Haimendorf himself points out: "there are indications that the Sherpas make a distinction between certain transgressions of a moral code which incur retribution in the world beyond ... and offenses affecting the interests of the community" (1966:191). The merit system Fürer-Haimendorf describes for the Sherpas operates in Deling, along with the *ga-nye* system. Like the Sherpas, the Tibetans distinguish the two moral spheres. Sahlins (1965) points out that morality systems are contained within any single sphere of reciprocation.
[6] There may be some analogies between this as a system and the honor-shame system according to which the Swat Pathans operate (Barth 1959).
[7] *Trok*, written *grogs*, is the root form for many types of friendships. The one I refer to here is most commonly called *trok-po* [male] and *trok-mo* [female]. It is a small and close friendship group; members usually join for life, and relations are characterized by extreme personal loyalty and intimacy.
[8] *Ki-du* or *tsok (tsogs)* is the corporate type of saving association contrasting with the *ga-nye*. *Ki-du*, quoted by Miller, is apparently the term most widely used in Tibet. *Tsok* was the term preferred and used by my informants.
[9] Here I follow the distinction between network and set provided by Mayer (1966:100), where "the component units of a set have a known boundary at any one time: it is not one of group membership ... but of their common connection to the central ego."

possible. Each member has his own network leading him in other directions, and some members of a set are dispersed in a number of localities of varying distances from the residence of their *ga-nye*. They do not all come together at once, and there are no occasions where all of a man's *ga-nye* meet as an unit and act corporately.

Thus, the *ga-nye* set is an unbounded group with no formal functions or goal, and no offices or internal differentiation. As noted earlier, it is both an ongoing relationship between people and an action system. As an ongoing relationship, the set exists at all times, but on specific occasions, the set, or part of it, is mobilized into various kinds of action. The persisting intimacy and daily exchange between members of the set at all times is a characteristic of the relationship, one that underlies its more aggressive role on special occasions.

A man's *ga-nye* set tends to be concentrated in his place of residence because that is where both he and his family most intensively interact. Sometimes a few members of this *ga-nye* are dispersed over a wider area in villages or towns where he regularly visits for business or religious purposes.[10] In Deling, for example, people who hardly ever move out of the village have most of their *ga-nye* there; others, who trade, are involved more closely in the wider Nepalese economic system and have to spend much time moving between markets; thus, they have a few *ga-nye* in villages along their route. Most of the people of Deling have *ga-nye* in one of the nearby monasteries that they regularly visit. At present, the respective *ga-nye* set of each member family of Deling is still growing.

For the most part, *ga-nye* act very much as kinsmen do; they visit and dine together, and they meet regularly and informally to talk. More important, but less frequently, they attend one another's life crisis rites and often participate in the settlement of a dispute among their members.

The word *ga-nye* is recognized all over Tibet and is used extensively throughout that country and in the Nepalese border villages where Tibetans are settled. *Ga-nye* is a contraction of the two words *ga-bo* and *nye-bo* — adjectives meaning, respectively, "fond" and "close." Some informants say *ga* is literally *dga* "to be fond of," but that it also may be derived from *tkar* "white." Various informants spelled *ga-nye*: *dkar-nye* or *dgah-nye*. And many people seemed to pronounce it with a slight "r." When confronted with the two possibilities, informants did not see any contradiction in the words. It still meant *ga-nye*, the bond of closeness. It could, they said, be a concept of fondness or whiteness and still be accurate for the relationship of *ga-nye*. It is no surprise, then, when it is

---

[10] Villagers generally leave Deling for only one of three reasons — to trade, to make an offering to a religious teacher and perhaps receive instruction, and to attend a political meeting. Only in very rare cases of serious illness or a life crisis ceremony of a *ga-nye* or kinsman does a man leave his village. Individuals never go to another village simply to visit.

further explained that whiteness can and does signify purity, trust, and equality — all of which are essential features of the *ga-nye* system.

Ga-nye, then, is the term used not only for the system, but for an individual, an associate — not a kinsman — who is near and dear. The relationship is characterized by feelings of respect and a limited degree of intimacy, which distinguish it from other friendships and action sets. People explained that the feeling of *ga-nye* is one of whiteness; *sems dkar-po che-wa* "we make our hearts clear," as one informant expressed it. It signifies a cleansing and removing of hindrances (impurities). A white relationship is free of malice and selfishness and is thus full of trust. A man knows who are his *ga-nye* and can tell you what he expects of them. Each person knows the rules of the relationship and often declares these in effecting or justifying an action he undertakes with a *ga-nye*. If, for example, a *ga-nye* has unflattering words for another, he will remind the latter that, as a *ga-nye*, he is trying to help. He has an obligation to speak and advise on certain matters, however unpleasant they may be.

The intimacy is not total between *ga-nye* (kinsmen and *trok* enjoy a far greater intimacy), but there is a regular exchange of information of a serious and personal nature. This develops into a feeling of closeness and exclusiveness. The trust is part of the exchange of personal information, but also it is related to the rules of reciprocity that typify and underlie the *ga-nye* system. (Later, I will discuss the economic exchange, but here I am referring to a kind of moral reciprocation.)

One trusts a *ga-nye* and establishes a degree of intimacy with him because one must do so; that is part of the bond, and no *ga-nye* bond will be established until the moral trust is reciprocated. People say, "I am your *ga-nye*, you must tell me," or "I tell you this because you are my *ga-nye*." It is unlike the intense loyalty of the *trok,* and it does not have the element of jealousy often shown between kinsmen.

The bonds between family members living under the same roof are obviously more intense; there are stronger feelings of intimacy and obligation. But in the family unit there are stronger feelings of jealousy and competition as a result of sexual relations, psychological factors, and the added complication of economic cooperation. The intimacy and trust of the *ga-nye* seems more carefully calculated and related to a different moral system. These values are more equivocal; they are guided by moral and wider community situations. It would not be inaccurate to describe them as a kind of jural relation, for the intimacy and trust is guided by the rules of reciprocation and in relation to the views of the wider society.

The *ga-nye* bond complements that of kinship and is often recruited through a kinship tie. Furthermore, it comes into action along with kinship ties on certain occasions. But it is recognized as being of a different order. That order, the moral-jural one, operates between a man and his community. It is a bond that is specifically concerned with a man's position in the wider community. The *ga-nye* set acts at times of crisis and where a man's position in the community is important.

The community recognizes some matters more than others as being of concern to it as a whole. These are the times of life crisis when a person takes a new status in the community. Life crisis events to some extent are public gatherings; the people concerned have the attention of the village focused upon them. Besides birth, marriage, and death, I include among these crises serious disputes that threaten to alter the public status or prestige of those involved and merit-making rites of an unusual scale where a man's esteem in the community usually increases.

A man's set of *ga-nye* is involved with him at the life crisis more than at any other time. The gathering of *ga-nye* at such a time is a sign of their support of a man and thus of his esteem. It is the only time when a man and the whole village can see all of his *ga-nye* set. The number of *ga-nye* at such events is noted by all concerned. And a man is pleased to count a growing number of *ga-nye* at such occasions over a period of time.

Life crisis ceremonies attended by *ga-nye* are important in the perpetuation of the bond and the public display of support at times of crisis. However, it was in the ongoing, subtle, and daily manifestations of the *ga-nye* in Deling that I observed the full significance and moral character of the *ga-nye* system. And it is in the more private sphere of operation that I shall focus.

The day-to-day events in the lives of people in Deling include those small, private crises that any and every family experiences. Most such relationships involve *ga-nye* in one way or another. *Ga-nye* are also involved in the intimate and regular exchanges that make a man and his family part of a wider community. The legal code, the political ideology, religious behavior, parental values and obligations, economic behavior — all of these are partially transmitted from a wider system through the *ga-nye* to the individual. There are, of course, other agents of communication — parents, elders, religious instructors — but even then, prescribed values are often sanctioned by the *ga-nye*.

Whatever a man's behavior, it is ultimately of concern to the community, and conversely, whatever the values and beliefs of a people (community), they must ultimately be passed down to the individual. It is the *ga-nye* who are concerned with this transfer of actions between the two spheres; the *ga-nye* are charged with making known to a man what he should do, or what impression he has given to others by his actions. In a subtle manner, they mediate between a man and the wider community.

A *ga-nye* member does not act for himself; he acts neither out of love, desire of prestige, nor power. His actions are part of his moral, social duty. For example, if a man infringes a social rule, either within the family or in the neighborhood, there will be a public reaction. Or, if a man behaves in an exceptionally positive way, it will similarly evoke a public response — approval. Whichever the case, it is the *ga-nye* who carries the response back to the man concerned. He does so as a friend and supporter, but it is often with the intention of altering the man's behavior. All that he is doing, he claims, is telling a man what "others" think or say. But in effect, the *ga-nye* puts some sociomoral pressure on a man, either by pressing him to alter his actions or by encouraging him to continue; or he may return to the community with the man's case and present it for others to consider.

As an example of one of the many minor moral infringements in Deling, I witnessed a man who was drunk and in a temper malign another who was not present. Some *ga-nye* of the absent man undertook to inform him of the incident. This served two immediate purposes: it indicated his public position to him (the maligning might have been justified and shared by others), and it gave him an opportunity to defend his honor. On this occasion, the accusation was unjust, and the *ga-nye* explicitly agreed on this and offered their support. The man neither had regard for his protagonist nor any wish to become openly involved in a dispute. So, after hearing about the matter from his *ga-nye*, he merely informed them of his position and left it to them to return to the villagers and pass on the information.

Face-saving is an important feature of Tibetan behavior, and as far as possible, public confrontations are avoided. Associated with the importance of saving one's face is the high regard accorded to etiquette, humility, and the use of intermediaries in the control of emotions. One agent of discreet behavior is the *ga-nye*. The ideal of impartiality of the *ga-nye*, and his intermediary position, make him the obvious spokesman.[11] A *ga-nye* can be counted on to reply for a man without the emotion that the latter might experience if forced to confront an opponent.

In order for a *ga-nye* to play this intermediate role, he must be aware of the disputant's thoughts and position. In expressing the trust and intimacy that are characteristic of their relationship, *ga-nye* are continually engaged in exchanging personal information with each other. They tell each other their own values, fears, plans, and encounters, but they disclose only that information they want to have discreetly publicized and that they regard as necessary for effective solutions to be arrived at in cases of trouble. Very personal information, such as that shared freely within a household or among a group of *trok,* is not generally shared with *ga-nye*.

---

[11] It has been noted throughout the anthropological literature on the subject of social control that the mediator is often a person socially outside the community. The Tibetan lama sometimes acts as a detached intermediary, applying religious sanctions to his jural role as do religious functionaries in other societies. In most intravillage matters in Deling, the religious lama is not actively involved, although he often performs divinations for disputants. It is the role of a *ga-nye* to maintain that detachment and unemotional moral position often attributed to religious men.

People know what kind of information will affect their public image, and it is usually with that in mind that they talk to *ga-nye*. For example, one of the many incidental details that will be shared with a *ga-nye* is one's merit-making expenses. If a man sponsors a rather grand ritual performance, he will tell his *ga-nye* what his expenses amounted to. The *ga-nye* will eventually inform the entire community through the network, and the man's prestige will, in this case, increase accordingly. If a man announced such facts himself, he would be considered a boaster, and his prestige would suffer. Other information about oneself that one wishes to reach the public is sent out by the same channel.

Information about oneself is received back in a similar manner. If a person under any circumstances feels that he has inadvertently and wrongly insulted another man or otherwise given a bad impression, he will find out just what has been the reaction to his behavior by consulting a *ga-nye*. His approach to a *ga-nye* is recognized as a request to find out what is going on outside. Usually before a man initiates any relationship outside his household and kinship circle, in order to act appropriately and ensure a positive response, he uses his *ga-nye* to feel out the situation for him. He may even ask the *ga-nye* to initiate a relationship. For example, if a boy or a girl fancies someone, they will ask a *ga-nye* to enquire whether or not that person is available and receptive, so he or she can proceed further with a courtship.

There are certain subjects of conversation and a manner of such exchange recognized as "*ga-nye* talk." Information reaching the members of a community through *ga-nye* has an air of respectability and authority. It is neither slander nor gossip, but it seems to have a standard and intention that people recognize and suspect. On numerous occasions, people seemed to be discussing serious questions that did not directly concern them. To my suggestions that their conversations were of no consequence and that they were interfering, they retorted: "This is our concern, we are *ga-nye* (of the person being discussed)" and "This is *ga-nye* talk."

Ga-nye talk, as contrasted with gossip or chatter, is precise and directed. When a social fact is reported to a wider group or network in a Tibetan community, the source of information is usually cited. To attribute a remark to a *ga-nye* gives it immediate credibility. There is no vagueness about statements coming from *ga-nye*, and people give these statements more weight in assessing a situation. Often, after an incident in Deling came to the public's attention, I observed villagers waiting for the *ga-nye* to talk before making their own opinion known.

Sometimes, of course, matters never reach the wider *ga-nye* network or the public. They remain in the household and involve only one or two *ga-nye*. If people have heard only rumors of troubles, and nothing from *ga-nye*, they recognize those limits and sigh, sometimes disappointed because they have been denied the opportunity to get involved even in speculation in another family's life: "Only the family and a few *ga-nye* know what really happened." Here are two cases of very limited *ga-nye* relations:

CASE 1. A widow, Tey-la, living in Deling was implicated in another family's quarrel. The wife in that family, Rinchen, had unjustifiably accused Tey-la of adulterous relations with one of Rinchen's two husbands. The two husbands, brothers sharing the common wife, were fighting with each other over a private matter, but Rinchen in an effort to hide that, claimed the fight arose over suspicion of adultery with Tey-la. Tey-la denied the accusation and eventually, when the real reason for the intrafamily quarrel became clear, Tey-la was no longer involved. But the slander caused Tey-la some embarrassment and could have defamed her reputation and threatened her other relationships. Two of Tey-la's *ga-nye*, indignant at the wrong and embarrassment inflicted on the woman, pressed Tey-la to bring libelous action against Rinchen and to demand a public apology in order to clarify her position publicly. The *ga-nye* saw themselves as the defendents of Tey-la's honor. They urged Tey-la to defend her honor and assured her that the community supported her in this matter. They were about to go on her behalf to Rinchen and demand the apology when Tey-la, a timid woman, anxious not to attract any more attention to herself, declined to assert her rights and asked the *ga-nye* to forget the matter. She said: "Already too much has been said ... people know that Rinchen was wrong ... she [Rinchen] is my neighbor and I do not wish to strain our relation further ... let the matter rest." In this case, only the few people who had urged Tey-la knew about this proposal. The matter never reached the wider *ga-nye* set or the public, as it would have had she taken action.

Sometimes, if an appropriate *ga-nye* is carefully selected in the early stages of a problem, then he or she can solve the matter. This manner is preferred by the Tibetans in Deling because it keeps quiet some private matters that could otherwise be embarrassing. Even if only one *ga-nye* is involved, he will still be seen by those concerned as representing the outside moral authority.

CASE 2. This happened in the case of Wang-bo, a young man of twenty-six, in Deling. He is a member of a family that considered itself superior, and indeed, in Tibet, they were richer and better educated than most. Wang-bo was still unmarried and living patrilocally in Deling. An attractive man, he had many girlfriends. When in 1970, he started to visit one girl rather regularly and more seriously, his family became concerned. The girl was of much lower status, with none of the prestigious qualities of Wang-bo, and his family was worried lest he would want or have to marry the girl. Wang-bo's father approached an older respected *ga-nye* of the family and asked him to speak to the boy. The *ga-nye* spoke to Wang-bo privately, pointing out not that his parents disapproved (the boy was already aware of this), but that there was some gossip in the community about the affair, and that people were surprised he had not been able to do better. The *ga-nye* only lightly chastized the boy himself (his own personal disapproval was hardly apparent) and suggested two other more acceptable girls, of whom the parents approved, for his consideration. Not long afterward, the young man stopped seeing the first girl and took a new interest in one of those suggested to him. Villagers noted this change, but were unaware of exactly how it had been effected.

THE RULES AND PROCESS OF RECRUITMENT

The method by which *ga-nye* are recruited tells us a great deal about the nature of the system and throws some light on the operation of the Tibetan family unit and its relation to *ga-nye*.

Ga-nye are recruited by two methods — either by ascription through membership in a household (birth, marriage) or by individual contact. Either way, it is ultimately a bond between members of one household and those of another. When a person joins a household by birth, marriage, or adoption, he automatically acquires as his *ga-nye* all those people already *ga-nye* to his household. As an adult, his relation to any *ga-nye* is equal to that held by another member of the household. *Ga-nye* bonds cross sexual and age differences. Thus any member of a house has *ga-nye* relations with any and each member of another household. A boy is equally a *ga-nye* of both males and females in his parents' set; some of those will be agemates of his parents; some will be his own age; and others will be very much younger than he is. Whatever their age and sex differences, the *ga-nye* tie between them is equal in value. Also if a member of a household moves into a monastery, he will retain *ga-nye* ties with all those people, lay or monastic, that he acquired through his original household. Because a man or woman enters a monastic community does not prevent that person from continuing these social relationships in the lay community. Thus, *ga-nye* bonds extend between people in monastic and in lay centers.

Recruitment through membership in a household is just that, and it is clearly defined. Since members of a household are tied together by bonds of consanguinity and marriage, becoming a *ga-nye* of that household is to a large extent the same as becoming a *ga-nye* of a kinship unit or a family. But the Tibetan household and the Tibetan family or descent group are not conterminous. Membership is held with the people in a house and not with members of an extended family. A *ga-nye* does not become one, for example, with the brother of a man, if that brother is not resident in the man's house, or, of the son of a man, if he is not a resident. If a man remains resident patrilocally, he shares all of the *ga-nye* of his father and father's father, but if he moves and thus establishes a new residence, he loses his father's *ga-nye* set and has to establish another of his own, or he may join his wife's, if he marries matrilocally. The *ga-nye* set is shared only by those members of a family occupying the same residence.

While children belong to the *ga-nye* set of their parents, they do not become seriously involved in the exchange system of the *ga-nye* until they are adults. At about age twenty, the average age at which people marry and take a full share in the household economy, children take on full rights and obligations of adulthood, including *ga-nye* relations. Before this age, Tibetan children establish a number of individual friendships within their own age category, often referring to such friends as *ga-nye*, but many such relationships are tenuous and end after only a few months, or they are marked by frequent childish squabbles. I observed a serious quarrel between two nineteen-year-old girls. (It was only one of several I noted among boys and girls of their age.) When these two girls quarreled, they severed their relations and proceeded to malign one another. Such behavior and the constant occurrence of such breaks in the *ga-nye* set of young people in Deling puzzled me, because it did not conform to what others claimed were *ga-nye* ideals. Ideally, *ga-nye* never fight, and they certainly do not change or break relations. When I asked the mother of one of the girls mentioned earlier about this, she replied: "These girls are always making and breaking such friendships. They are short-sighted and fickle at this age. The girls say that they are *ga-nye*, but really they are not. When we become friends with our daughter's *ga-nye* and her family, and they with us, then that is true *ga-nye*." She assured me: "We cannot fight with our *ga-nye*, and we cannot change the way these girls do."

Upon close examination of *ga-nye* relations between young people over the period of one year, I noticed that the friends a child claimed as his closest were, in fact, drawn from the *ga-nye* set of his own household. Out of a possible set of, say, twenty-five *ga-nye* families, a girl would likely become very close with three or four girls out of all those families and, at least before marriage, she would form a closer intimate tie with them than with any others.

For any given individual, in the normal course of his life, most of his *ga-nye* will be acquired through the household bond described earlier. Still, it is possible for him to make a new contract himself. In Deling, where many traditional *ga-nye* ties have been fragmented by the severe social changes incurred by the move from Tibet, it is common to find a number of new *ga-nye* relations established between adults. I had the opportunity to observe the initiation of a number of *ga-nye* sets. Although new and in operation for only a few months or years in Deling, as compared to those passed through generations in Tibet, these newer bonds have the same strength as older ones and exhibit the same operational features.[12]

People occasionally pointed out that they had been *ga-nye* with others for a very long time, however, that did not make the tie qualitatively different. The evidence suggests that the *ga-nye* relationship is an abso-

---

[12] For obvious reasons, it is not possible to test these differences. I inquired at length about the form of *ga-nye* relations in Gya-tri before 1959 and compared a number of disputes settled there to the procedures employed in Deling. Informants assured me that, in form and function, the *ga-nye* relations had not changed, but there is a likelihood that they have altered slightly. Still, in comparing relations in Deling between a man and a *ga-nye* contracted in Tibet (and continued in Nepal) and a new *ga-nye* made only in the last few years, they appeared to be of equal strength and intimacy. The *trok* (see Note 7), on the other hand, are quite different now when compared with their form in Gya-tri, Tibet.

lute one. A relationship between *ga-nye* does not weaken, although it may lapse into a latent period if members cease to live in the same locality. Informants never qualified a *ga-nye* relationship in the way they did other bonds with the diminutive *chung-chung* "little," or *ma-nye* "not near."

There is no such thing as good *ga-nye* or bad *ga-nye*. Often I asked a person if he were *ga-nye* with another specific person. If he were not, he would reply: "We are like *ga-nye*." This, in Tibetan, is a polite way of saying no. Or, similarly, he would say: "[No] we are neighbors," or "We are from the same village in Tibet." No one claimed they were little *ga-nye* or distant *ga-nye* as they would to qualify a coresident or kinship tie. Either they are *ga-nye*, or they are not.

The number of *ga-nye* in a man's set is precise, although not fixed. In Deling, the *ga-nye* set of most people is steadily increasing. The distribution varies, however, as does the core of the set that is active at any one time. Residence locality is the significant variable here. Because a man interacts most frequently where he lives, it is naturally there that one finds the majority of his *ga-nye*. About 70 percent of the *ga-nye* set of most Deling villagers are also residents there, although, as we have noted, most people have a small number of their *ga-nye* set in places they visit regularly on religious and commercial excursions. Some Deling people who trade regularly with other Nepalese tribes such as the Tamang, Sherpa, and Newari usually have a few *ga-nye* in those communities.

Ga-nye bonds wane if people stop interacting, usually due to a change of residence, but the bonds are never broken intentionally. They may remain latent until such time as the parties reunite. Presumably, however, they would lapse and be forgotten if, over a number of generations, parties had no contact.

In Deling, there were two household heads with large numbers of kinsmen in the village. Each of those households also enjoyed extensive *ga-nye* sets. They each had about the same number of *ga-nye* as they did kinsmen. Sometimes a family with very few kinsmen in the area also had very few *ga-nye*, but that was considered undesirable. Informants were emphatic that either kinsmen or *ga-nye* were essential, and it was preferable to have both. People like to have a large *ga-nye* set; it is a social ideal and a measure of one's popularity in the community. And, indeed, the heads of each of these two households were the most popular individuals in Deling.

Out of more than one hundred households in the village, there are only four with no kinsmen outside that residential unit currently residing in Nepal. Informants from these houses admit that they feel isolated and more vulnerable because of the absence of kinship ties. It is a handicap, and one recognized way of overcoming this handicap and securing their position in Deling is to develop a good *ga-nye* set. Each of these four families, having decided to remain in Deling, has set about consciously and purposely to develop their *ga-nye*.

One of these is the household of Dorji. Dorji had left all the members of his own family in Tibet, remarried, and come to Nepal in 1963. Neither he nor his wife has any kinsmen in Deling. They had no choice, he said, if they were to remain in Deling, but to develop a *ga-nye* set. Dorji noted that, in 1964, when his second child was born, there were no *ga-nye* well-wishers. Two years later, when his third child was born, six *ga-nye* came to his house to celebrate the event. Finally, in 1970, after the birth of his last son, there were twenty-two *ga-nye* at the birth feast. Over the last six years, Dorji and his wife had acquired an even larger number of *ga-nye* in their network.

The only people without *ga-nye* in Deling are strangers, madmen, and wild or unpredictable people. Three people were considered mad, and everyone kept away from them; as a result, they had no *ga-nye*. One unusual family had a few kinsmen in Deling but no *ga-nye* at all. Although this family is normal in most respects, it was very unpopular and suspect in the village. The position of this family is a little difficult to understand at first, because it is wealthy, and usually rich families and individuals are popular. But this family's wealth is new, acquired after the economic turmoil in Tibet and the move into Nepal. People say of this family: "They are rich, but they are also greedy; they never help other people; they do not need us ... they are too independent." Villagers strongly resent this family and one other, that of a stranger who stopped by the village for some months. Neither family participates in the life of the community; neither pays the obligatory communal fees or attends the local political and religious meetings. I attribute the unpopularity of both these families to the feeling held by others in the community that they are beyond the control of the village. Each exists, as others cannot, without the moral or economic support of other villagers.

The ideals of generosity, mutual cooperation, intimacy, and community membership cannot be imposed on them. If problems were to arise with them, there are no channels through which pressures could be brought to bear on such families. Like madmen and wild people, they cannot be dealt with. They cannot be coerced, intimidated, or appealed to morally by public opinion, because they themselves do not recognize the moral system of the village.

RECIPROCATION

Reciprocation is the second fundamental feature of the *ga-nye* bond; it is what makes the *ga-nye* ties work between two individuals within the set.

These rules, applied in a moral sphere, provide a balance of intimacy and trust essential for the operation of the *ga-nye* system.

Here I want to explore the Tibetan concepts of reciprocation as they are indicated in the language and used by the people of Deling. Root words signifying "return payment" show that they are conceived in spiritual relations as well as in economic ones. As a supernatural phenomenon, "return" is expressed by the words *las* and *lan*[13]. As a socioeconomic relationship, "return" is expressed as *nga-lak*.[14]

The karmic law of Buddhism is itself a principle of reciprocation. Essentially, it is a belief that what accrues to a person materially, physically, and mentally is a return for what he has achieved. Tibetans believe, as most other Buddhists do, that a man's retribution is a response to what he himself has expended in this or a previous life. The term Deling people commonly use to signify this kind of retribution is *las*, which may be translated as "fate" (Buck 1969:667) or simply "return." As I observed its use in various situations in Deling, *las* is conceived of by Tibetans as a kind of return payment. It is understood and employed by Tibetans to indicate a direct or indirect response to another earlier action by the recipient. *Las* is something that is received rather than given, and it can be either favorable or unfavorable.

Both *nga-lak* and *las,* then, apply to the receipt of something as a response to an earlier action. Informants explained that *nga-lak* is an economic and social fact controlled by man, while *las* is controlled in the supernatural spheres and can only be approached through a ritual medium. Another difference is that *nga-lak* can be given as well as received, whereas *las* is only received.

Nga-lak, that is, reciprocation, is a common feature of many Tibetan relationships. It is found in many social contexts and is not confined to *ga-nye* relations. Its place in *ga-nye* relations is central, however, and it is the *ga-nye nga-lak* with which I am concerned. *Nga-lak* in *ga-nye* relations refers to a specific set of rights and obligations between two members. The *nga-lak* is expressed through mutual trust, exchange of information, and specific economic return, or prestation. In some social relations, such as those of kinship among the Tibetans, some exchange is undertaken in a general manner; but in ties of kinship and neighborhood, the set of rights and obligations that guides behavior is often less specific than those guiding *ga-nye* relations.

The *nga-lak* of *ga-nye* is carefully measured with rules specifying when and how it must be made. A *nga-lak* prestation, for example, can neither cumulate into a debt to be paid when the other party can manage it nor

---

[13] *Las* and *lan* are transliterations of the Tibetan following Jäschke (1881). Phonetically, they would be *leh* and *len* respectively.
[14] *Nga-lak* is a phonetic interpretation of the Tibetan *snga-lag; sngon,* a derivative of *snga,* prefixes a number of words to denote a previous action. See Buck (1969:149–150).

can it be made in a form other than that in which it was received. To "make *nga-lak*" is to return a specific favor or item. If you do something for me, then I must "make *nga-lak*" to equalize the situation. For example, if you assist me through *nga-lak* in harvest, then my *nga-lak* is to provide precisely the same kind of assistance to you at a later date. It cannot be converted into another commodity. This acts to hold the relationship equal, and it makes the *nga-lak* a true reply rather than just a payment. Significant, too, is the permanent character of the *nga-lak*. Even though assistance is equalized by a return favor, it cannot be cancelled.[15] When a man dies, his reciprocal obligations to *ga-nye* must be taken over by his widow or son. As we have seen, this binds *ga-nye* households over a long period of time, sometimes several generations. It also serves to strengthen the corporate nature of a household. The *nga-lak* relations are part of that whole set of rights and obligations and property that is attached to a house. If there is no succeeding generation to continue payments, or if a household splits, one can imagine the difficulties that arise. The intricate ties in which a Tibetan household is bound through these types of relations may explain why Tibetans stress the ideal of unity and perpetuity of a household and not of a family or lineage.

The rules of reciprocation also define the relative size of payments, the times and occasions of transfer, and their inheritance.

The life crises — birth, death, marriage — in any household are the major occasions for reciprocal exchange. It is obligatory for a man's *ga-nye*, as well as for his kinsmen, to make their prestations at each of these occasions. In addition, the donor household must send a representative from among them to hand over the gift personally and to join in the ceremony that accompanies such an event. Payments are made in both cash and kind. Some cash is obligatory, but the additional prestations of beer, tea, or grain of some kind are customary.[16]

The amount given initially between two new *ga-nye* today is about five to ten rupees.[17] To give less than five is frowned upon as being too little, and an extraordinarily large gift is equally inappropriate, since it might embarrass the recipient. The point of these gifts is not to show off or display one's own wealth,[18] but only to maintain the bond. It is, however,

---

[15] This is the universal feature of reciprocation, first elucidated by Mauss (1966).

[16] Appropriate gifts are made according to the particular event, for example, to celebrate a birth, articles of infant's clothing as well as butter and beer are presented; grain, preferably wheat, beer, and articles of clothing are presented at weddings; only tea or beer is presented along with the cash donation in a funerary exchange. This last prestation is called in Tibetan *sems-gso*, pronounced *sem-so*, meaning condolence.

[17] In 1970, the rate of exchange was approximately twenty-five Nepalese rupees to one British pound, or ten rupees to one dollar.

[18] Cf. Alavi (1972). He contrasts reciprocation of this kind with potlatch.

customary to give a little more (perhaps 10 percent) each time there is an exchange in either direction.

Whatever the amount, it is calculated according to the size of the donation made by the other person on an earlier occasion when the roles were reversed. A man will receive differing amounts from various *ga-nye*, each gift having been calculated to reciprocate the one he gave earlier. *Ga-nye A*, attending the wedding of *B*, will determine his gift to the latter in accordance with the amount he received from *B* when there was a marriage in *A*'s household. The customary token increase will be added to indicate goodwill. Furthermore, the marriage gift is calculated according to an earlier marriage, not a birth or death. Each of the rites is kept separate, and the reciprocation for one is quite different from that for another type.

At each life crisis rite, when such prestations are made, the host *ga-nye* makes a precise list[19] of each gift and notes the name of the donor. This list is then carefully put aside for the future, when it will serve as an accurate guide for calculation of reciprocal payments. At one marriage ceremony, I observed every *ga-nye* (and kinsman) make his cash prestation in an envelope. On each was written the name of the donor, the date, and the amount of cash inside. These envelopes were collected by the groom and his assistant (they also note the other gifts in kind) during the ceremony of offering.[20] People know that the host will refer to these when making a list for himself later on. There is hardly a possibility that he will make a mistake, however, for the prestations of each guest *ga-nye* are carefully noted by all present, and there is much discussion about gifts afterwards, by villagers who did not attend the ceremonies as well as by those who did. Great importance is attached to these prestations and it is of concern to everyone.

There were several births, marriages, and deaths with appropriate ceremonies and reciprocations during my stay in Deling. After each, I had occasion to hear the accounts by some of the guests reporting the events to other villagers. The size and quality of the various *nga-lak* were meticulously recalled. They always gave precise quotations, which, according to my own observations, were amazingly accurate. One's prestation is nothing to hide, for these are matters of public concern, and people used these figures to understand relationships of the donors and

---

[19] This is called simply *ming-tho*. More generally it means household list or census (see Buck 1969:236, 467). As far as I know, there are no more specific names to denote and distinguish the various *nga-lak*. Each household possesses one, and it is inherited along with the other property attached to a household. I did not see such a list myself, but informants said most families in Deling maintained them.

[20] The term commonly applied to this part of a ceremony is *rten-'brel* (pronounced ten-del); *rten* means "stay" or "hold," and *brel* refers to a "connection" or "bond." It is a general term applied to a number of social offerings.

recipients. I often heard people ask each other how much they had given, if it was not already apparent.

The rights and obligations guiding *ga-nye* reciprocation apply to households, not to individuals. The obligation to reciprocate is held by a *ga-nye* house to every other *ga-nye* house in its set. Any member of a donor house may make the prestation; at birth and funeral rites, it is often an adult woman, but at weddings, it is more usually a senior male. If no adult is available, then an older child performs the function. If no one from a *ga-nye* household can be present to make the reciprocation, some gesture still must be made. A man may send a letter of apology and reciprocate later. Failure both to attend and to keep up the payments is a serious matter. It is taken as a sign of personal hostility between the hosting *ga-nye* and the other or as a statement of opposing political positions. If there has been a fracture in a *ga-nye* relationship, it will be at one of their life crisis rites that it will become apparent, not only to those concerned, but, just as importantly, to members of the wider community.

Attendance at a life crisis is part of the reciprocation; the rules define who attends, but it is left to the *ga-nye* to decide whether or not to attend. On several occasions, when I asked Tibetan informants who had attended their own life crisis rituals, they replied in a general way that it had been *ga-nye* and kinsmen. When I inquired further as to why these two groups came, informants replied "because of the reciprocation." In Deling, as in Tibet, it is not the custom to issue invitations to wedding, funeral, and birth feasts. It was explained to me: "When people hear [through the kinship or neighborhood network] they will know whether or not to come." "Kinsmen will come and *ga-nye* will come; they are all *nga-lak*," said one informant.

Since birth reciprocation must be made only on the occasion of a *ga-nye*'s birth celebration, and death and marriage prestations on analogous occasions, often a long time elapses before a reciprocal prestation can be made. By that time, the head of a *ga-nye* house may have died. If this happens, none of his debits and credits with *ga-nye* will be canceled; all will be carried over to his succeeding generation, usually to his brother or son. The rights and obligations remain with the household and are simply carried on by successors. Thus, the *ga-nye* rights extend through generations, as well as across age groups and sexual roles within one household.

People must then calculate over a long period of time when making or receiving a *ga-nye* gift; their own personal return can be of no significance. If a household head is making prestations near old age, there is no hope of his ever seeing the reciprocation himself. The Sherpas practice a type of reciprocation at life crisis ceremonies similar to the Tibetan. At a wedding, I observed the following: a Sherpa man, a guest about sixty, was making his offering to the bride and groom. (This is done publicly before all the assembled guests.) As he presented the gift, the man asked all present to note that since his own son was married there would not be another wedding in his own home for many years. He pointed out that by the time his grandson married, he would not be alive to receive the reciprocation of the gift he was now offering. He asked the recorders to note that the gift should be reciprocated to his son. It is neither usual nor proper for the rules to be made as explicit as they were on this occasion. Several guests criticized the man's behavior. They said it was an embarrassment and an insult to the hosts. All the people (Tibetans and Sherpas) know these rules, they said, and they understand they may have to wait a very long time for the reciprocation. To make a prestation without comment is an expression of faith in the relationship, in this case, the *ga-nye* bond.

Still, people do calculate, and those families with normal life expectations will be encouraged to enter into *ga-nye* relations with other people in relatively similar situations. The extension of the exchange between households, rather than between individuals, gives the system a corporateness and a permanence greater than that of any individual bond. It is probably this that perpetuates the system. The case of Dorji illustrates the extensive ties that can develop just over a few years and the long-term implications they can have for a family:

CASE 3. Dorji is one of the few householders who arrived in Deling without any prior *ga-nye* or kinship ties in the village. At the birth of his last child, he collected 235 rupees in cash, as well as gifts in kind from all his *ga-nye* in Deling. This sum was equal to the total of the gifts he had made to fellow *ga-nye* in the village in the process of establishing a network there. But this amount represented only the credit he had on birth feasts. More than this was still out in funeral payments to various *ga-nye*, and that much again on wedding *nga-lak* with *ga-nye*. Since his eldest child was only ten at that time, it would clearly be another decade before he would receive any of the wedding *nga-lak*. And before that, he would undoubtedly have to expend even more on gifts to some of his *ga-nye* set who might have weddings, and so on in their own households in the intervening years.

Reciprocation through *ga-nye* extends to the exchange of information as well as through ritual attendance and the prestation of cash and goods. Perhaps more than gift exchange, it is the reciprocation of information that underlies the *ga-nye* relationship. Information exchange works within a system of trust between *ga-nye* and with a *ga-nye* set. It is more difficult to measure than the specific and quantifiable items offered on the ritual occasions. Furthermore, the reciprocation of information is effected in the everyday and ongoing expression of the relationship rather than at more public gatherings. The rules are less specific, and information is usually reciprocated at the same time as it is received.

People are constantly feeling each other out and probing for information, but nothing is disclosed for free; to encourage confidence, one must first release a bit of information. Over several meetings then, even though no action is taken, and no request is made of a confidant, a basic knowledge of each other is shared by *ga-nye*. Eventually, when a crisis arises, this earlier information will help them offer the appropriate assistance.

When *ga-nye* converse, they know through the long-established bonds of intimacy and the rights and obligations what are the limits of the exchange. They distinguish between confidence among *ga-nye* and that among other groups, such as the kinship and *trok*. A man will not yield information (1) on a matter in which he does not want the advice of the community or (2) on a matter that he does not want to reach the *ga-nye* set. It is on the basis of all the information gathered over time that *ga-nye* are able to intimidate, coerce, assist, and advise one another. People recognize this and have certain expectations of a *ga-nye* when any difficulty arises. A *ga-nye* is a feedback system, and that feedback is partially a response to all the information that one has received from one's ego as well as from the wider *ga-nye* set.

THE ROLE OF *GA-NYE* IN DISPUTE SETTLEMENT

It has been some time now since anthropologists (Hoebel 1954; Gluckman 1955, 1965; Colson 1962) first illustrated how, in any social system, extensive cross-cutting ties bind people not directly related. They pointed out that the resulting social matrix operates to minimize conflict and gives cohesion to the community. The *ga-nye* set operating within a wider social network is not substantially different from those other cross-cutting systems in the way it binds people within the Deling community.

Those villagers who are not connected by such ties as kinship, membership in a *ki-du* "locality," and so on usually meet through an intermediary (mutual) *ga-nye*. If, for example, A and C are not *ga-nye*, but A and B are and B and C are, then B becomes an intermediary tie between A and C. A and C will meet when they attend the obligatory life crisis ceremonies of B. Or, in the event of friction developing between A and C, B will intervene with both his *ga-nye* (they are both members of his own set) to make them cooperate. The extensive operation of this simple principle in Deling contributes to the cohesion of the community.

Besides this, there is an explicit role of *ga-nye* in dispute settlement. Most disputes arising in Deling occur between members of the community and their settlement invariably involved the participation of *ga-nye*. Intravillage disputes most often are between members of the same household — a husband and wife, a parent and child, or siblings. Almost all the disputes I observed were between a husband and wife, but fights between siblings are also common. In each case recorded, *ga-nye* combined with kinsmen to settle the matter.

Before any positive action for a settlement can be undertaken, people must be informed, and among Tibetans, there is a long and elaborate process by which information about the disputants is gathered. Word of a break eventually reaches the *ga-nye*. It may be a kinsman or one of the involved parties himself who sends out the signals. Sometimes a man in trouble will discreetly tell a *ga-nye* the problem and ask his assistance in mediating between himself and his adversary. If one influential *ga-nye* is brought in at an early stage and is able quietly to bring about some reconciliation, then the matter is settled and goes no further. This was the case when a Deling man, Tar-gye, and his wife had a fight.

CASE 4. Tar-gye versus his wife: The wife learned that Tar-gye had spent the night with a local girl and was furious. She threatened to leave him and wouldn't let him back in his house. He regretted the incident and at first denied it, pleading with his wife that her actions were unjustified. Finally he went to a *ga-nye* and asked the latter to speak with her. The *ga-nye* approached the wife (who was obviously willing to listen) and tried to reason with her. He spoke for his *ga-nye*, Tar-gye, admitting he had indeed been with another woman. He reminded her that Tar-gye did not do this often, that he was on the whole a good husband and father, and that he promised he would not behave that way again. He also added, perhaps to relieve Tar-gye of some blame for his behavior, that Tar-gye had been with a number of other young men who had encouraged him, and that he was drunk and not fully aware of his actions. Finally, the wife agreed and the *ga-nye* returned to his home to tell Tar-gye the way was clear.

In more serious cases, information about the matter is usually first sent out to kinsmen of the disputants and through them to the set of *ga-nye*. Visits ensue, and people involved as kin and *ga-nye* rush about gathering information from the two disputants. (By this time, they will no longer be living in the same house, for one will have moved to the house of another kinsman.) The *ga-nye* and kinsmen are one group with the same aim (to reconcile the parties), and since *ga-nye* is a household bond, in such a situation, the same *ga-nye* belong to both the disputants. This group splits temporarily into two, with one side representing each of the disputants. Each gathers details of the case from its side, and then they rejoin to compare notes and discuss the matter, while the disputants themselves remain apart.

The mediating parties eventually arrive at a plan and take this to their respective sides. It may be accepted immediately; if not, the group meets again and reconsiders. The ideal solution is a complete reunion, and often serious breaches of norms are waived in order to effect a peaceful settlement.[21] *Ga-nye* try to coerce the parties by appealing to the ideals of the

---

[21] In Tibetan culture, as far as I have observed, to fight is considered worse than to break a rule. A breach of norms is more serious if it results in a fight. The concern in settling a matter

society as opposed to their own individual rights. Their advice is always for a complete reconciliation, and it is only with regret that the *ga-nye* accept less than a complete reunion. Usually the ideal — a return to normal relations — is achieved.

Only about 15 percent of serious family fights are not successfully mended through *ga-nye* participation.[22] If the *ga-nye* and kinsmen together cannot reconcile the disputants, then the division of property according to the laws of the society proceeds. Here also, it is the *ga-nye* and kin who apply the rules about division of property. Written records are made of the agreement, and *ga-nye* supervise this. Often, a reunion is effected only after one party (who, it has been agreed, is the offender) makes a public apology and pays a fine to the injured party. Indemnity will be decided by the *ga-nye* and kinsmen; they supervise its payment and accompany the disputants to the gathering arranged for the presentation.

A public apology, which is an admission of guilt, is in itself a punitive act, and usually an aggrieved person will be satisfied with this. The offender often needs support throughout this humiliating experience. It is his *ga-nye* who provide this. When he presents the white scarf[23] and beer to the offended party, he is sometimes so overcome with shame and emotion that a *ga-nye* will speak for him. When the beer and scarf are finally accepted, the matter is considered closed, and all enjoy an evening together drinking and singing. By the end of such an evening, no sign of tension remains. People insist that these reconciliations are complete once they have been accepted publicly. It is a matter of honor for a man to uphold the agreement made through *ga-nye*, and the *ga-nye* remind him of this. Furthermore, in case there is any difficulty, the *ga-nye* can use a number of tricks to ensure a lasting peace.

If neither a reconciliation nor a partial settlement can be agreed upon then the *ga-nye* are obliged to refer the matter to a higher authority in the village or in the wider political structure. People say that if *ga-nye* cannot bring about a settlement, then no one can. This indeed was borne out in the cases I observed. Still, there are a number of formal jural mechanisms in the area to which the Deling villagers can appeal.

First, there is the Nepalese court in the nearby district headquarters.

---

seems to be not to deal with the crime but to prevent parties from fighting, which is far more embarrassing and upsetting behavior (Cf. von Fürer-Haimendorf [1966: 121]).

[22] Sometimes early consultation with a spiritual leader and the employment of divination provide a solution. At the other extreme, self-help may be employed. In the event of self-help, *ga-nye* are not involved. Against their advice, the injured party attacks his wrongdoer and usually beats and abuses him publicly. As long as no personal physical harm is incurred, the matter is usually closed by such an action. But Tibetans frown upon this method of settlement. Only two cases of self-help occurred in Deling between 1967 and 1970.

[23] This is the well-known *dkar-thak,* displayed on any auspicious occasion.

This, however, is employed only in very serious matters, such as gross theft and murder. The Nepalese discourage the Tibetans from bringing minor cases to them. When approached, they usually consult a Tibetan leader from Deling and ask him to deal with the matter.

The second court of appeal, then, is the leader of Deling; he has the authority to mediate and adjudicate on local matters brought to him. In 1970, three cases were referred to the leader of Deling. On each occasion he made a proposal for settlement, but because this particular leader was so unpopular and unfamiliar with the moral system of the community, his decisions were all ineffectual.

The third formal court of appeal is the Deling council of headmen, who are elected representatives from each of the local wards of the village. They are senior men with experience and a reputation for exemplary behavior. On two occasions I learned of (there must have been many others), headmen were approached and asked to assist in a settlement. In each case, they referred the matter to *ga-nye* of the involved parties.

CASE 5. Nu-lung versus wife: One man, Nu-lung, was often locked out of his house by his wife. She kept throwing things at him and threatening to leave him. Nu-lung was a rather timid fellow who simply could not seem to manage his own affairs. He often got drunk and gambled his wages away, and this made his wife angry. It was probably because his kinsmen were tired of dealing with the constant problems arising in his household that Nu-lung finally approached his local headman and asked him to speak to the wife on his behalf. The headman declined. He said he did not want to bother with such trivial matters, and that such problems were better handled by *ga-nye*.

On another occasion, when the whole council of headmen was approached by a stranger (a Tibetan from India) who was trying to collect a long-standing debt of considerable magnitude from a Deling villager, the council referred it to higher authorities. This was in order to remove it to a jural authority completely outside the village. In this case, the council saw it as a potentially dangerous situation (their own safety was threatened) beyond their control because one of the disputants was not a regular member of the village.

Headmen in Deling are respected and have authority in a number of political and economic matters. However, they usually decline to judge cases brought either formally or privately to them. Because they usually know the social network of a litigant, headmen will approach *ga-nye* and encourage them to deal with the matter. In some cases, because a headman himself has extensive *ga-nye* ties in the village, he is drawn into a dispute, but it is as a *ga-nye* that he is involved and he does not use his power as headman under such circumstances.

The two following cases, both of which occurred in Deling in 1970, reveal the nature of disputes that arise in a Tibetan household and illustrate the dynamics of the *ga-nye* system in social control. Although neither was ideally settled, the procedures described are typical of those followed in any dispute settlement.

CASE 6. Kong-sang versus his wife, Cho-sang: In 1968, Cho-sang left her husband to live in a local nunnery. By this time, her children were almost adults and her attachment to them and her husband was declining. She no longer wanted to live with her husband, and she claimed her interests were more with religious matters. She moved into the nunnery to escape worldly matters, and a divination she had performed supported this decision. Kong-sang, the abandoned husband, did not dispute his wife's move; such a pious action as his wife's could only be condoned. However, Kong-sang did object to his wife's retaining possession of the valuable necklace that every bride brings with her to her husband's home at the time of her marriage. Usually when a wife leaves the house on her own initiative, she cannot take this or other parts of her dowry back with her. But Cho-sang did, claiming that she intended only to keep it for her son and give it to him when he married. The husband took this matter to their *ga-nye* and appealed to them. They met and consulted with both the man and his wife. They agreed that, under the circumstances, Cho-sang should retain the necklace (in Tibet, probably the rights of the husband would have prevailed) and tried to persuade Kong-sang to drop the matter. He was already quite wealthy; his wife had possession of the necklace, and she was a determined and stubborn woman. The *ga-nye* knew that Cho-sang was a difficult person to deal with, and they thought the husband would be more flexible. But Kong-sang was equally determined to press for his rights, and he refused to accept the advice of *ga-nye*. No settlement was possible then. Kong-sang took the matter to the village leader and asked him to present the case on his behalf to an outside Tibetan authority. This was done, and the decision returned was again in support of the wife. Still, that judicial body had no power to enforce the decision. Kong-sang once again refused to accept and fought with the leader who, he claimed, had not supported him. All this in addition to Kong-sang's continued ill will towards his wife earned him little sympathy in the village. The villagers knew in theory that Kong-sang was right, but all agreed that, under the circumstances, he should accept and close the matter. The *ga-nye* informed him of his growing unpopularity, due to his unreasonable and hostile behavior. Generally, such public condemnation forces a man to desist. At the time of my departure from the village, the matter still was unsettled. The *ga-nye* had asked that the matter be held in abeyance until the return to Deling of one of the couple's most experienced and senior *ga-nye*, who, it was hoped, could find a solution.

CASE 7. Nam-gya versus Norbe: In 1970, these two brothers, sharing a wife in polyandry, fought bitterly over an internal household matter. The elder brother, who had been senior in status, accused the younger man of taking too much responsibility in the household and acting without his consent. He threatened to leave and take the youngest of their children with him. The family was highly respected in Deling; they had been wealthy in Tibet and enjoyed the highest status in their former village there.

From a large group of their kinsmen in Deling, a core of those considered closest to the brothers and their wife formed an action group, which together with a core of local *ga-nye*, was mobilized to deal with the matter. First, kinsmen were called to the house and heard each disputant's case. The wife added information about the situation. Then the *ga-nye* joined. By this time, the elder brother had moved out of the house; *ga-nye* and kin therefore had to move between the residences of the two men, gathering information. Then *ga-nye* met privately with concerned kinsmen to discuss the matter. They then discussed the problem among themselves, spreading news of the case further and further through the community. Everyone agreed that it was shameful for a family such as this one to be involved in a dispute. Villagers kept reiterating that people of the status and class of these two brothers should not fight. My cook, a niece of the two men, kept saying she was very embarrassed: "My family are big people, and they are rich, I am ashamed ..." The *ga-nye* and kin approached the brothers, and reminding them of their community status and their family's honor, urged them to forget their difference and reunite in a cooperative effort as before. The brothers could not agree, and the wife, whose position it often is to keep two brothers happy and working harmoniously, was ineffective also. The *ga-nye* finally felt that there was nothing to do but proceed with drawing up rules for a division of the house and property. They met with kinsmen of the two brothers and decided on a proposal. The children, since they were all over eighteen, were allowed to decide for themselves with which brother they would go. This solution was regretted by all concerned.

THE *GA-NYE* COMPARED CROSS-CULTURALLY

The data on *ga-nye* and *ki-du* provided in Miller's paper (1956) and the reports of reciprocation systems operating in areas adjacent to Tibet (Swat, West Panjab, China) similar to that which I have noted for the Deling *ga-nye* invite some cross-cultural comparison. This should be practicable now that the Tibetan *ga-nye* is abstracted and presented as a set of sociological phenomena: a reciprocation system, a social set, a mechanism of social control with its own moral system, and a set of behavioral rules.

Extensive comparison with the *ga-nye* described by Miller is limited by the lack of corresponding data. Still, it can hardly be doubted that the *ga-nye* system she outlines is essentially the same institution I observed in Deling. The features Miller describes as characteristic of *ga-nye* — intimacy, exchange of gifts at life crisis events, reciprocation, and the absence of overt material interests or goals — all are manifest in the Deling *ga-nye* system.

The establishment of *ga-nye* relations across class and the occupational and status divisions, Miller points out, apply in Deling also, although I have not provided material about these relations in this study. The contrast Miller observes between the *ga-nye* and the more corporate formal association she calls *ki-du* is important, and investigation along this line may lead to valid generalizations about the coexistence of different types of associations.

In Deling, the *ga-nye* contrast with *tsok* associations. Again, I have not been able here to present the details of the *tsok* type of associations in

Deling. They do exist, however, and in a form not unlike that described as *ki-du* associations (Miller 1956:160–168). They are more specifically corporate economic and occupational groups.

From the presentation of her data, it appears that Miller did not have the opportunity to observe *ga-nye* in action; that may account for the absence of data on the moral and information exchange features. Miller's reliance on informants may also have hindered observation of the *ga-nye* in dispute settlement. It was only when I actually saw the *ga-nye* go into action on the occasion of a dispute that their central role in such situations became apparent.

Although I have not included material on the corporate *tsok (ki-du)* associations, this does not preclude some comment on the relation between the two different types. In Deling, both types of associations existed and had been proliferating since the founding of the village in 1963. The *tsok* grew as the economy of the village diversified and as influence from other parts of Nepal and from India was incorporated into the life of the village. The *ga-nye* sets of each household in the village were also increasing, as I have already noted in the section on recruitment, but there is no basis on which to conclude that they were interdependent. They both grew as the village itself was developing into a more integrated and rich community. Tibetan informants' comments about the interdependence or sequential relation of the two associations verified my own observations. According to these informants, the *ga-nye* and *tsok* are conceptually and functionally different. They do not rely on each other, and one does not change into the other. My suggestions that they might be associated confused informants. They were indignant at the suggestion that *ga-nye* relations could be conceived in the almost totally economic and business terms that characterize the *tsok*. They stressed the social and emotional need for *ga-nye* that could never be provided by *tsok* relations. If one simply looks at the functions of the two institutions, there is no overall correspondence of the role of one being taken over by the other. Of course, if one looks only at the economic functions and attributes of the associations, then one might be led to think of the more corporate association as a development of the less formalized *ga-nye* reciprocation.

The *ga-nye* and *tsok* exist both in urban commercial centers and in the rural villages. Deling is a rural community, and the growth of both *tsok* and *ga-nye* systems here prevents constructing an hypothesis about a rural-urban dichotomy being represented in the two. It is a tautology that, when villagers move into a town, they will reorganize themselves according to values and institutions they used back in the village, modifying these slightly to accommodate the urban economy, and so on. It would be convenient if the difference between *tsok* and *ga-nye* illustrated this, but it does not. From the reports of Deling informants, it seems that when they move into the cities of India and Nepal, they reestablish *ga-nye* links there, as well as new *tsok* membership. All that happens in an urban association is that it tends to recruit members from the same general rural area.

In one study, the rural-urban dichotomy is used as a base for understanding the development of savings associations in southwest Cameroon (de Comarmond, Soen 1972). These authors conclude that no fundamental breakdown of the Bamilèkès traditional savings association occurs when people move from their rural environment into urban centers. They attribute the form of the new modern associations of the Bamilèkè to the principles laid down in the traditional savings systems, but they point out that one does not preclude the other.

No doubt when such detailed ethnographic accounts are available on the changes in the form and membership of the Tibetan associations, some hypothesis about their development may be attempted. Until further material is available, I would like to suggest, after the observations made in Deling, that the proliferation of *tsok* is, not a response to urbanization but, more simply, a concomitant development with the diversification of economy in the village.

I have indicated throughout that *ga-nye* relations and sets cannot and should not be explained by any weakness or absence of kinship ties. Lineage is not an organizing principle in Tibetan social organization, but it must not be concluded that ties between kinsmen are weak or loosely knit. I found that people who have few kin ties in the village are often the same people who have small *ga-nye* sets; similarly, people with extensive kinship ties were found to have equally extensive *ga-nye* sets. People with no kinship ties in the village recognized that they had to work at the development of their *ga-nye* ties to substitute for absent kin ties, but they did not do this out of preference. One can see how, in dispute settlement, *ga-nye* operate to strengthen the bonds between kinsmen. And at life crisis events, *ga-nye* join kinsmen in offering support to a family.

It is important to take this opportunity to bring Tibetan society into a more realistic position with others. In the last decade, information on reciprocation systems in societies adjacent to Tibet has become available, and the time is opportune to begin some cross-cultural analysis. Although the material presented below is from societies adjacent to Tibet, it is not meant to suggest that any historical relation exists between their social systems and the *ga-nye* system of Tibet. They are selected merely to show how, in a relatively narrow geographic area, a number of variations of reciprocation systems can exist, and how each displays some of those more universal attributes manifest in the Tibetan *ga-nye*.

Ortner (1970) reports that there is a mutual aid association common among the Sherpas of Solu in Nepal. It is called *tsenga-tsali*. Ortner suggests (personal communication) that it might have similar functions to the *ga-nye* but that further data are not available.

The role of a set of close associates in settling family and local disputes is a common feature in many societies. Hu (1948:16–17) describes the mediating role of the "mourning circle" in Chinese society. The mourning circle is a group of relatives — a larger unit than the household but smaller than the clan. Like the *ga-nye* it is an ego-centered set lacking formal organization. Its members come into action occasionally to act as arbitrators and negotiators in disputes arising within and between individual *chia* [family or household].

Hu does not indicate how members of the circle are selected from a wider descent group. One important difference between it and the *ga-nye* is its kinship base; all members of the circle are tied to one another through descent. But the mourning circle functions similarly to the *ga-nye* in its participation at life crisis ceremonies of its members. As the name implies, this group is obliged to attend the life crisis of any member — birth and marriage as well as death.

In many societies, attendance at an associate's life crisis ceremonies is obligatory. The people belonging to the group to whom such obligations apply varies from one society to another. Among the Swat Pathans, Barth (1959:31–35) points out the importance of locality as the principle on which members to the Pathans' *taltole*[24] association are recruited. The *taltole* is essentially a neighborhood unit; in some ways, it is like the *ga-nye*, but it is substantially different from the latter in its corporate nature. Barth stresses the political significance of the reciprocal relations enjoined by members of a *taltole*. According to Pathan values, this political significance derives from the display of support or disapproval associated with one's presence or absence of *taltole* members. There is no mention of *taltole* members functioning as arbitrators or representatives in the settlement of disputes in Swat.

Another southern Asian association of comparable nature is the *beraderi*, found in parts of India and Pakistan. Hamza Alavi (1972) has recently provided details of the system of reciprocation in the *beraderi* associations of Punjabis in West Pakistan. Due to the excellent detail provided by Alavi, a more substantial comparison with the *ga-nye* system of the Tibetans can be undertaken. The two systems have a number of contrasting features, but there is similarity in their form of reciprocation. The *beraderi* is a patrilineal descent group, and like the Chinese mourning circle, there is a restricted set of lineage members[25] having a special set of rights and obligations. Like the *ga-nye*, the members of a *beraderi* set

---

[24] Barth (1959:31) notes that the name of the rite on which Pathan *taltole* members meet is *gham-khadi* meaning "sorrow-happiness" (cf. *ki-du* translated as "happiness-sorrow").
[25] Alavi (1972) terms this the "group of participation."

participate in each other's life crisis ceremonies and exchange goods according to a set of rules.

The system of ritual prestations and counterprestations in the *beraderi* is called *vartan bhanji* and seems to be very similar indeed to the *nga-lak* of the *ga-nye*. Alavi provides valuable details of the operation of *vartan bhanji* and elucidates the system by which a relationship in the *beraderi* is established and then maintained in equilibrium. He describes the exchange as a process of unbalanced reciprocity operating in a perpetual cycle set in motion by the constant reversal of ritual indebtedness. Additions made to a basic sum exchanged in the *nga-lak* seem almost identical to the *vartan bhanji* system. Furthermore, like the *vartan bhanji*, the *nga-lak* is essentially symbolic in nature and is perpetuated through this alternating unbalanced indebtedness. Another minor point is the existence in both systems of an account book listing the names and prestations of each donor.[26]

The two mechanisms, however, contrast strongly in their degree of corporateness. The more corporate *beraderi* is not just a set of dyadic relations, acting together with others in relation to ego on ritual occasions. It is itself a social entity; it has a specific locality and a fixed membership within that area. The *beraderi*, like the *taltole* of the Pathans, links people of disparate economic categories. Where the *ga-nye* set tends to join together people of more or less the same economic status without any corporate identity, the resulting functions and attributes of the group are bound to be significantly different. Alavi identifies the obligation established in the *beraderi* exchange as one between the *beraderi* group and the individual household, as well as that between two households. He points out that while there is some exchange expressing mutual dyadic relationships (dyadic ties are central in the *ga-nye*), payment by a Punjabi household is given or received by virtue of its membership in the *beraderi*. Another contrasting feature of the *beraderi* is its relation to the kinship structure. It is the part of the patrilineal descent group that is defined by locality. Arising from this is its role in arranging marriages between its members and those of other *beraderi*.

This comparative exercise could continue indefinitely. Without substantive data of the same features and functions, the significant variables operating in each society cannot be identified, and comparison can be of no analytical use. The comparative data provided earlier only serve to illustrate that the Tibetan *ga-nye* system is not unique as a socioeconomic system, and its central feature — reciprocation — is a widespread social phenomenon with certain implications for each community in which it occurs. Even in those aspects on which comparative data were not considered, that is, the role of *ga-nye* in dispute settlement and its operation

---

[26] The *beraderi* account book is termed *behi*.

within a restricted moral system, it is doubtful that these are confined to Tibetan society.

I have not attempted here to deal with the possible historical connections between the Tibetan *ga-nye* and similar associations found in neighboring societies. An historical explanation for the *ga-nye* could never be more than speculative, and as with any such explanation, it could tell us only about its origin. Whatever its origin, it is probably different now from what it was in the past. Now the *ga-nye* is a part of its own cultural system and can best be understood in that context.

REFERENCES

ALAVI, HAMZA
1972 Kinship in west Punjab (Pakistan) villages. *Contributions to Indian Sociology* 6:1–27.
BARNES, J. A.
1954 Class and communities in a Norwegian island parish. *Human Relations* 7:39–58.
BARTH, F.
1959 *Political leadership among the Swat Pathans.* London School of Economics Monographs in Social Anthropology 19. London: University of London Athlone Press.
1960 "The system of social stratification in Swat, North Pakistan," in *Aspects of caste.* Edited by E. R. Leach, 113–146. Cambridge: Cambridge University Press.
BELL, SIR CHARLES
1928 *The people of Tibet.* Oxford: Clarendon Press.
BUCK, H. A.
1969 *Tibetan-English dictionary.* Washington D.C.: Catholic University of America Press.
CARRASCO, P.
1959 *Land and polity in Tibet.* Seattle: University of Washington Press.
CASSINELLI, C. W., R. B. EKVALL
1969 *A Tibetan principality.* Ithaca, N.Y.: Cornell University Press.
COLSON, E.
1962 *The plateau Tonga of northern Rhodesia.* Manchester: Manchester University Press.
DE COMARMOND, P., D. SOEN.
1972 Savings associations among the Bamilèkè: traditional and modern cooperation in southwest Cameroon. *American Anthropologist* 74:1170–1179.
EKVALL, R. B.
1964 *Religious observances in Tibet.* Chicago: University of Chicago Press.
1968 *Fields on the hoof.* Case studies in cultural anthropology. New York: Holt, Rinehart & Winston.
FÜRER-HAIMENDORF, C. VON
1964 *The Sherpas of Nepal.* London: John Murray.
1966 *Morals and merit.* London: Weidenfield and Nicolson.

GLUCKMAN, M.
  1955 *Custom and conflict in Africa.* Oxford: Basil Blackwell.
  1965 *Politics, law and ritual in tribal society.* Oxford: Basil Blackwell.
GOLDSTEIN, M.
  1971a Serfdom and mobility: an examination of the institution of human lease in Tibetan society. *Journal of Asian Studies* 30:521–534.
  1971b Stratification, polyandry, and family structure in central Tibet. *Southwestern Journal of Anthropology* 27:64–74.
  1971c Taxation and the structure of a Tibetan village. *Central Asiatic Journal* 15:1–27.
GORER, G.
  1938 *Himalayan village.* London: Nelson.
HOEBEL, A.
  1954 *The law of primitive man.* Cambridge, Mass.: Harvard University Press.
HU, HSIEN CHIN
  1948 *The common descent group in China and its functions.* New York: Viking Fund Publications in Anthropology 10.
JÄSCHKE, H. A.
  1881 *A Tibetan-English dictionary.* London: The Secretary of State for India.
KIHARA, H.
  1957 *Peoples of the Nepal Himalaya.* Kyoto, Japan: Kyoto University Press.
MAUSS, M.
  1966 *The gift* (English edition). London: Cohen and West.
MAYER, A. C.
  1966 "Quasi groups in the study of complex societies," in *The social anthropology of complex societies.* Edited by M. Banton, 91–122. Association for Social Anthropology Monograph 4. London: Tavistock.
MILLER, B.
  1956 Ganye and kidu: two formalized systems of mutual aid among the Tibetans. *Southwestern Journal of Anthropology* 12:157–170.
OPPITZ, M.
  1968 *Geschiechte und socialordnung der Sherpa 8 of Khumbu Himal.* Munich: University Verlag Wagner.
ORTNER, SHERRY PAUL
  1970 "Food for thought: symbols in Sherpa society." Unpublished Ph.D. thesis, University of Chicago.
PETER, PRINCE OF GREECE AND DENMARK
  1963 *A study of polyandry.* The Hague: Mouton.
SAHLINS, M. D.
  1965 "On the sociology of primitive exchange," in *The relevance of models for social anthropology.* Edited by M. Banton, 139–236. Association for Social Anthropology Monograph 1. London: Tavistock.
STEIN, R. A.
  1962 *La civilisation Tibétaine.* Paris: Dunod.
  1972 *Tibetan civilization* (English translation). London: Faber and Faber.

SECTION TWO

Cultures of the Soviet Union

Interaction of Cultures Among Peoples of the USSR

YU. V. ARUTYUNYAN

Integration is the dominant theme in mankind's present cultural development. The growth of ethnic communities, the formation of large nations, the development of communication among nations, the fall of religious and other barriers — all these promote a steady, if difficult, process of integration of the peoples of the world. What are the real prospects for the development of a common culture for all mankind?

This is a most important question asked today of ethnographers and sociologists. It can be answered not only by pure theorizing, but also on the basis of either concrete historical materials through a retrospective analysis of the history of mankind or through studying the contemporary processes of the interaction of different cultures. This second method is particularly effective, since a comparison of historical phenomena is difficult, and since the cultural interaction of peoples in this era of scientific and technical revolution is unprecedented. The rapid proliferation of the new, common elements of culture and mass media have made this interaction extremely effective, widespread, and all-embracing.

It is natural that the present-day cultural interactions between peoples of the world attract the attention of researchers in the USSR and abroad. Yet hardly any country has so wide a cultural variation as does the USSR. Soviet science has a particular responsibility to intercultural research.

History itself seems to have staged in the Soviet Union a large-scale experiment on the interaction of different cultures, based on varying social, economic, and ideological themes. The historical heritage of the Soviet peoples varies greatly and ranges from patriarchal society to developed capitalism, from the Muslim East to the Christian West. The cultural contacts between these peoples have been of different durations; they have different experiences in historical communication. The interaction of genetically different cultures increases as the peoples come under one state, have a joint economy, and share the same ideology. It is not an overstatement to say that no country in the world, regardless of size, has such a great variety of cultures and, at the same time, such close cultural interaction as does the Soviet Union. Because of this, a summary of the cultural development of the USSR is important for the understanding of problems of cultural contact that are common to all groups.

One way to study cultural interaction is by examining the cultural fund of peoples — their songs, dances, rites, and customs. The simplest elements are then compared, and the similarities or differences of the interacting cultures and the degree of their mutual penetration are established. This method is effective when the traditional folk culture is studied and the researchers have the task of reconstructing ethnogenesis, but it is less useful for the study of contemporary societies in which professional culture plays an important role.

When comparing societies where a professional culture is dominant, similarities at one level may not be evident at another. The important variable is the degree to which a people has acquired certain features of professional culture. Therefore, it is expedient to use a special method: the analysis of cultural consumption i.e., how widespread certain features of the culture are, rather than the cultural fund.

The Institute of Ethnography of the USSR Academy of Sciences has undertaken this kind of research into the cultural interaction of the nations of the Soviet Union. These studies make it possible to solve four fundamental problems, which are described as:

1. Establishment of ways that the development and the growing closeness of the nations are influenced by the specific features of their culture histories, by the degree of development of their national cultures, and by the nature of the historical experience of relationships among the peoples.
2. Establishment of the way that the cultural development of a nation is influenced by the degree of industrialization and urbanization and by the development of mass media and international contacts.
3. Establishment of the variables governing the changes of the inner structure of national cultures (infrastructure through the correlations between material culture, language, art, and local values).
4. Establishment of the common and specific features in the cultural makeup of different peoples.

The scope and nature of the comparative research conducted on a countrywide scale in the Soviet Union determines the methods used and the organization of the research. In order to reflect the multiplicity of the Soviet nations, the selection of cultures should be significantly large; this sample includes approximately 40,000 people. By the method of taxonomic analysis, on the basis of thirty-five specific features, republics were chosen that would offer examples of economic development and urbanization, historical experience, and cultural history. Moldavia, Georgia, Latvia, Uzbekistan, and the Russian Federation were surveyed between 1971 and 1975. The author hopes the summary of data on the social and cultural development of the native populations of these republics will considerably enrich the theory of culture.

Several research methods that have rarely, if ever, been employed in either ethnography or sociology are used here. These methods involve the combination of descriptive materials concerning individuals, obtained through polling, along with objective data describing the environment. All the information is processed by a computer, making it possible to obtain a clear-cut picture of environmental influences on the cultural development of the individual.

A primary research instrument is a questionnaire, used to formalize the biography of each person polled. The interviewer obtains information about the factors and channels of the social and cultural development of an individual. This enables researchers to judge the relative importance of certain factors in a person's development. The selection also enables the researchers to create a combined portrait of a nation and its several subcultures. The specific social and cultural features are judged not only on the basis of formal measures, such as the level of education, but also on the basis of the overall nature of that particular cultural and national orientation. The actual behavior of individuals and their cultural values are established.

Research has already been completed in some republics. The material obtained thus far suggests that a single cultural structure exists throughout the USSR. This superstructure is based on the uniformity of the USSR populations, where every nation is comprised of similar groups. The objective basis for this singular culture common to the entire Soviet society has been created by industrialization and urbanization. These are historical processes that take place all over the world, but their effect has been qualitatively heightened in the Soviet Union by a number of specific factors that accelerate cultural integration.

The most important of these factors is a unified economy that has served to change the cultural configurations of the Soviet republics. It is known that the specifically national features in material life lose their importance and play a secondary role in all industrially developed countries. This process has been rapid in the Soviet Union, with its unified economic system and countrywide division of labor. Large-scale industrial production of consumer goods provides a wide choice of products, with which locally produced handicrafts cannot compete. Mass production may reflect national traditions — in architecture and construction, for instance — but these national preferences in material culture have a limited distribution. In every case, practical considerations are always outstanding. It is more important that goods be comfortable, cheap, and durable than that they reflect national tastes. Tastes are relatively stable only in the choice of food, the sphere in which the competition from mass production has thus far been less keen. With reference to other elements of material culture — housing, interior decoration, clothes — the advantages of industrial production are obvious to all, and the higher the degree of urbanization of the people, the weaker are preferences for the national culture. For example, 18 percent of Moldavians and only 5 percent of Russians in the city of Kishinev would like to have Moldavian national features in interior decoration. National foods make up 36 percent of the favorite dishes of the Moldavians and 13 percent of those of the Russians.

The development of industrial forms of material life under the conditions of a uniform economy increases the similarity of the material culture in the developed republics and promotes the formation of a culture that is common to the entire Soviet Union.

Another important factor in the development of cultural uniformity in the country is in connection with the unified Soviet political system. The Soviet cultural policy is essentially the same with regard to every nation and nationality. A single educational system operates all over the Soviet Union with the same cultural standards applying to every people; secondary education is equally obligatory for every nationality. This single cultural policy brings the standards of cultural consumption of different peoples closer together. The differences in cultural consumption between urban and rural populations and various social and professional groups are not directly connected with specific national features.

Unity of ideology is also an equally important condition for the creation of a common culture. All the religious and other ideological barriers, which in the past separated one people from another, have been removed. Even among the peoples, who in the past professed Islam, the influence of religion has been largely minimized. Thus, in the rural areas of the Tatar Autonomous Soviet Socialist Republic, only one-third of the population think of themselves as believers. Most of these are older, illiterate, and unskilled professionally.

This uniform system of social and moral standards and values is typical for every nationality of the USSR. Distinctions here are also between urban and rural populations, as well as between different classes and professional groups. The same system of overarching values is accepted in identical social and ecological spheres and in similar social groups throughout the different nations of the USSR.

Thus, the intensive international communication within the Soviet Union and the unified ideology of the Soviet people create a basis for the integration of spiritual culture. A uniform system of values and common moral standards has developed.

This unity manifests itself with particular clarity in the social and moral values of the peoples living under similar conditions, such as the Moldavians and the Russians living in Kishinev. We have detected between these peoples no differences in social and moral values. However, certain differences in values still exist in family life and daily living. For instance, 67 percent of the Russians believe that it is better for a woman to work than to run a house, while this view is held by only 57 percent of the Moldavians. Correspondingly, the Russians value a woman's professional abilities more than her being a good home maker.

The present day professional forms of culture play an important role in creating a common culture for the entire Soviet Union. The development of a national professional culture takes place in the Soviet Union through a unified ideology of social and moral values.

Evidence shows that it is a professional culture, and not folk culture, that plays a special role in the interaction and mutual penetration of the multiple cultures of the USSR. The republics that have a developed fund of professional culture have more opportunities to exert a cultural influence on other peoples. On the other hand, in nations where local cultures are less developed, cultural assimilation takes place more readily. The historical logic of cultural evolution is such that the nations that formerly had a less developed culture now have more rapid cultural development. The leveling-off process among various national cultures promotes the development of a common culture.

The development of cultural uniformity among the Soviet nations does not mean that they are culturally homogeneous. Certain national distinctions remain, including social, class, socioecological, and professional distinctions. The nations that were more highly developed in the past have a relatively higher percentage of intelligentsia and workers, while the nations that were more backward have a higher percentage of peasants. The Soviet nations also differ in the ratio of urban to rural populations. These social distinctions determine the different levels of actual consumption by the peoples and are reflected in professional culture, the standards of consumption, and the system of values. Today, these republics are complex historical formations that differ ethnically (although ethnic distinctions increasingly are being erased) and also in their respective sociocultural features, which are determined by different economic and social factors.

It stands to reason that these distinctions will gradually disappear, since the main trend of Soviet society is aimed at the liquidation of major differences between urban and rural populations and between classes and social and professional groups. This trend will gradually lead to a complete social and cultural leveling-off of the nations. How will this affect the ethnic peculiarities of the people?

This question can be answered with the data from a homogeneous social and ecological environment where different nationalities already have essentially the same social structures as in the Moldavian capital of Kishinev. Both the Russians and the Moldavians living in Kishinev have similar social and professional structures, common levels of education (the Moldavians, on the average, have nine years of schooling, and the Russians ten), the same standards of consumption, and similar patterns of leisure time. In their leisure time, they read books (88 percent of the Russians and 78 percent of the Moldavians) and go to the theater (70 percent of the Russians and 60 percent of the Moldavians).

At the same time, local levels of culture continue to differ greatly. The Moldavians prefer national Moldavian styles of art; 74 percent have national preferences in music, and 81 percent, in dance. The majority of Moldavians (58 percent) prefer their national wedding ceremony with its archaic features. The Russians, by contrast are much less oriented to folk rites and folk art; only 40 percent prefer the national style in dance, and 24 percent prefer the national style of wedding. The Russians have a strong orientation toward professional types of Russian art.

The leveling-off of cultural consumption, therefore, does not lead to a restriction of local cultures; those local cultures with a progressive character are being preserved, and thus, the cultural range of the peoples widens. This can be illustrated linguistically. The Moldavians study Russian intensively. In Kishinev, with its mixed ethnic environment where contacts between the nationalities are frequent, 70 percent of the Moldavians speak fluent Russian. Every new generation contains a larger proportion of people with a good command of Russian, demonstrating the intensity of the linguistic assimilation. While only 32 percent of the Moldavians over sixty years of age speak Russian well, 82 percent of the Moldavian young people in Kishinev speak fluent Russian.

Moreover, just as contacts with Russian culture as a whole have not destroyed Moldavian national (mainly folk) culture; the Moldavian language has not been forced out of use by the Russian language. Eighty-nine percent of the Moldavians in Kishinev have a good command of the Moldavian language. Professionals of all ages of the Moldavian population have a high percentage of people with a good command of the Moldavian language. The percentage of people speaking Moldavian did not drop below 80 percent in any of the groups investigated. Thus, under conditions of active international contact, the Moldavians, while acquiring the culture of another people, continue to enjoy the wealth of their own cultural fund. This is a sign of the optimum cultural development of the Moldavian people.

National psychology, based on an awareness of national interests and a national self-awareness, helps to preserve the ethnic elements in the culture of a nation.

The growing cultural similarity in the Soviet Union does not weaken the solidarity within a single nation or the intensity of national feelings. Depending on the stage of cultural development, different mechanisms come into play to preserve and strengthen national solidarity. The scientific and technical revolution exerts a twofold influence on national, social, and cultural development of the Soviet nations. On the one hand, it increases national similarity, equalizes, and promotes mutual understanding. On the other hand, due to the development of mass media and other cultural channels of communication for the purpose of national consolidation, there is a growth of national self-awareness among the people of the USSR.

Thus, even in the Soviet Union, where there exists strong incentives for cultural integration, it is a common culture, rather than a homogeneous ethnic culture that is being formed; cultures are growing closer, but they have not blended. Cultural integration is a long and complex process that dialectically combines international and national features. In the long run, the rates of ethnic integration depend on the intensity of social processes, the liquidation of social distinctions, and the creation of economic abundance.

Development of Traditional Aspects of National Culture in the Soviet Central Asian Republics

B. D. DJAMGHERCHINOV

National traditions and customs are often related to specific historical periods and socioeconomic conditions. Traditions and customs in the present-day Soviet Central Asian Republics differ from those that existed in prerevolutionary times. Many old traditions have changed considerably and, to a great extent, have lost their initial meanings.

Traditional aspects of national culture die off or change, following changes in economic relations, in sociopolitical conditions, and in the spiritual life of the people. As a result of the triumphant socialist revolution, revolutionary transformations have been brought about throughout the Soviet Union, but these have been particularly profound and dramatic in the Soviet Central Asian Republics. These changes have preserved and developed the finest features of traditional culture in this part of the Soviet Union.

In the course of the socialist construction of the USSR, formerly backward peoples have been consolidated into new socialist nations. The territories of Kazakhstan, Kirghizia, Tajikistan, Uzbekistan, and Turkmenia offer examples. Industrialization, cooperation in agriculture, and cultural revolution have promoted economic and cultural ties among the republics and nations.

The implementation of Leninist principles in national policy has preserved and promoted the basic positive features of traditional culture, as exemplified by the preservation of the national languages of the Central Asian peoples and their transformation into developed literary languages; the preservation and further development of technological knowledge in the traditional branches of the national economy (cattle-breeding in Kirghizia and Kazakhstan, cotton growing in Uzbekistan, Tajikistan, and Turkmenia, Astrakhan sheep breeding and carpet making in Turkmenia, and so on); preservation of the finest customs such as communal aid (the *asar* of the Kazakhs, the *khashar* of the Uzbeks); hospitality;[1] reverence toward older people;[2] national forms of entertainment; and traditional contests (such as the *aityah*, which is a contest among improvisational folksingers).

Love for the mountains and woods of the Kirghizes, the boundless steppes of the Kazakhs, and the cotton fields of the Uzbeks are still glorified by the poets and writers of these nations. The love of the Soviet Central Asian peoples for their land and their patriotism have become particularly deepened in Soviet times. Only Soviet power has made them masters of their own land and destiny.

The Soviet cultures and traditions in the different nations have been drawing closer together with every passing year, becoming more unified. In the course of common work, studies, entertainment, and active cooperation in sociopolitical and cultural activities, people of different nationalities adopt their neighbors' finest traditions, customs, working experiences, and know-how. At present, all major work collectives in the Soviet Union are multinational. This is also the case with the Central Asian Republics; for example, the builders of the Toktogul hydropower project in Kirghizia include men and women of some forty nationalities.

The expansion of international ties among the peoples of the Soviet Union brings new elements to the local national cultures. National languages are enriched through extensive mutual borrowings of expressive words; nations adopt traditions and customs of their neighbors; and marriages of people of different nationalities result in new blood ties that play a major role in bringing different nationalities closer together.

The many Soviet cultures can be compared to a rainbow, the beauty of which lies in the harmony of the different colors. Although the structural forms of these cultures are diverse, the content remains the same. This is not to say that centuries of tradition have been lost in the cultural life of the Soviet Central Asian nations. To the contrary, the preservation and development of local cultural traditions are expressed through work experiences and aesthetic principles, which are passed from generation to generation.

The condition of applied arts in these nations serves to illustrate this point. Applied arts have developed in different ways in Central Asia, although the cultural contacts maintained over many centuries have brought a certain affinity of cultures to the region, which is characterized by a uniformity of styles that sets these arts apart from those of other regions and countries.

The traditional applied and decorative arts of Central Asia and Kazakhstan include ceramics, carpet making, the making of weaving and

---

[1] Every nation in Central Asia has its specific customs of hospitality and, quite logically, considers hospitality to be a traditional feature.
[2] The lack of respect for the elderly is strongly condemned by public opinion.

fabric decoration, wood and bone carvings, jewelry making, metal chasing, embroidery, and gantch-work, (gantch being a local variety of stucco or plaster). These folk arts have rich, long-standing traditions, and all are being practiced at present. Yet these arts do not show any traces of conservatism, and, they are even in a state of continuous transformation.

Today, craftworkers continue to produce exquisite samples of applied art that both adopt and develop historical traditions. These traditional artistic principles have found their way into consumer industries. Traditional folk designs and color schemes, for example, can be observed in contemporary fabrics, clothing, jewelry, and other designs. In this way, local artistic traditions have given birth to new works of art and new consumer goods that are in keeping with the tastes and requirements of the Soviet peoples.

For instance, Turkmenia continues to be known for its magnificent long-nap carpets, which have been treasured in many countries. Today, traditional handmade and machine-made carpets are being produced in Turkmenia. The art is also being practiced in Kazakhstan, Kirghizia, and Karakalpakia. This specific national style of carpet making continues to progress. The collective experience of individual carpet making in Central Asia has given rise to carpet factories and workshops in Tajikistan, Kirghizia, and Kazakhstan. Traditional Uzbek fabrics, with their specified designs and color schemes, are now being produced not only in Central Asia, but also in the Russian Federation.

Centuries-old traditions of Central Asian art have now been recognized in many countries of the world. Especially famous are the ceramic wares of Uzbekistan and Tajikistan. This art has preserved historically evolved local traditions. A marked progress is evident especially in the quality and design of ladies' jewelry.

Traditional folk decorative designs also find their way into modern architecture. In the Soviet Central Asian Republics, this is especially manifest in the interior decoration of public buildings, which incorporate works of art based on folk tradition. Most impressive is, for instance, an architectural design incorporating gantch-work.

Folk elements continue to form the basis of the Soviet Central Asian Republics' applied arts and largely determine their development. Many works of art that originated in the Soviet Central Asian Republics are appreciated outside the USSR and in other nations within the USSR. Thus, this art manages to become international without losing its national features.

A forced division of Central Asia and Kazakhstan before the revolution, along with weak economic and cultural ties among the nations of that region, left its imprint on the spiritual life of the people. Education was sporadic, and the local spoken languages of the masses were unrelated to the norms of the literary language. In many cases, such literary forms simply did not truly exist. Of great importance in the formation of the present-day norms of the literary languages of the Soviet Central Asian nations are traditions extending back to such outstanding enlighteners as Chokan Valikhanov, Ibrai Altynsarin, and Abai Kunanbayev of Kazakhstan and to famous *akyns* (folk poets and singers) such as Toktogul Satylganov, Togolok Moldo, and other poets of Kirghizia, who were democratically oriented. Yet, genres such as short stories, essays, novels, comedies, and dramas only became part of the spiritual life of the Soviet Central Asian nations in the postrevolutionary period.

It is significant that folklore plots have not disappeared in Soviet times. Their literary value has withstood the test of time, and they have proven to be a fertile soil for the development of other related art forms such as opera, ballet, and musical drama. In music, there has been a transition from the one-voiced melodic line and unison to polyphony. Mutual cultural enrichment of the Soviet Central Asian nations is manifest in such fields as painting, graphic arts, and, especially, in cinema.

Tremendous changes have taken place in the outlook of the people. The development of a new scientific perspective, based on the general laws of the evolution of nature, society, and ideology, has been in keeping with the vital interests of the toiling masses. At the same time, scientific attitudes have helped to transform the local cultural heritages. The Marxist-Leninist outlook has exerted an all-round influence on the spiritual culture of the Soviet Central Asian nations by eradicating conservative customs and traditions rooted in religion. Of course, this was not only a result of the dissemination of progressive scientific ideas. In the long run, the customs and traditions of a people reflect their psychology and the existing material conditions of life and social relations.

Radical socioeconomic transformations were accompanied by gradual profound changes in customs and traditions. For instance, in prerevolutionary Kirghizia and Kazakhstan, the *saan* [a lease of milch cows to poor peasants in exchange for work] and the *kuch* [a lease of draught animals to be paid off by work] were traditional forms of exploitation of poor relatives or villagers by the landed aristocrats. The *barymta* [plunder of an offender's cattle] was also a scourge for the toiling masses. The establishment of the dictatorship of the proletariat and the abolition of private ownership of the basic means of production has eliminated the economic and social foundations of the *kuch*, *saan*, *barymta*, as well as other feudal or patriarchal customs and traditions.

The change from private to public ownership of the basic means of production was also a major reason for the preservation and further development of the finest democratic features of traditional national cultures among the Central Asian Republics. These old but progressive traditions include the *ashar* [which is mutual aid among peasants joining together for some particular work demanding many hands], reverential attitudes toward seniors, and the care of old people, among others.

New patterns of everyday life in family and social traditions have emerged in recent years; these include wedding festivities that are in sharp contrast with the Muslim tradition, birthday parties, and jubilee celebrations. It should be noted that, in the past, the Kirghizes celebrated the *balanyn tuulgan kunu* [a child's birthday]. They also used to invite friends and neighbors to the *zhentek toi* [a party during which a child is put to bed] and the *tuahoo nesuu* [a party to celebrate a child's first step]. Until recently, the clergy imparted a religious content to these celebrations, but at present, these celebrations are assuming a new form. Funerals are often arranged today as civil burial rites, although religious and ancient pre-Muslim magic rituals still persist.

At present, the Kirghizes are beginning to observe a still newer ritual tradition of "silver" and "gold" wedding anniversaries. These customs have been borrowed from other fraternal Soviet nations.

The disappearance of conservative traditions and the spiritual revitalization of progressive traditions, which acquire a new socialist content, have been a result of profound changes that are still underway in the economy, political life, and class structure of Soviet society. This process is accelerated by the systematic political and educational work of the Communist party and the Soviet state.

SECTION THREE

Community and World Judaism

The Jews as an Ethnic Group in the Americas During the Sixteenth and Seventeenth Centuries

SEYMOUR B. LIEBMAN

The identification of the Jews as an ethnic group or race has been discussed by anthropologists and ethnologists for over a century (Herskovits 1966). Their peoplehood is undeniable. Their status as an ethnic group is clear, since they possess a religion that outlines the daily routines of life history, nationalistic beliefs, culture, indigenous customs, international language (Hebrew), and a pattern of learned behavior that has been socially transmitted from generation to generation.

There are subgroups within the general ethnicity that evidence traits other than those associated with the religious beliefs of the major group and that are held in common with non-Jewish ethnic groups. Iberian or Sephardic Jews could scarcely be singled out from their Iberian-Christian neighbors. Only the activities involved in the practice of religion identified them as Jews.

Jews as an ethnic group are subdivided into religious denominations and distinctions that result from differences in places of national origin, family traditions, folklore, and subgroup history. The religion, Judaism, is comparable to the axle on a wheel. The axle is the basic religion held in common by all subgroups. The spokes are the various groups, each of which have identifiable differences. The Jewish anthropologist, Raphael Patai (1971) has ably described the schisms and differences among Jews. This paper deals with one of the major groups, Sephardic Jews. True Sephardim are those who inhabited the Iberian peninsula and their lineal descendants. I have briefly discussed elsewhere the psyche of the Iberian Jews in the New World (Liebman 1970:52–55). In addition to discussing their religion, I will also touch upon the association of the Sephardim with their Catholic and Indian neighbors in the New World between 1550 and 1700.

It is my view, based on over twelve years of research on the history of the Jews in the Americas during the colonial period, that the social contacts between Jews and their non-Jewish secular neighbors were not marred by the religious intolerance of the Spanish church symbolized by the Holy Office of the Inquisition and its tribunals. Many Catholics throughout the Americas knew that their neighbors and friends were Jews, but they neither reported this to the Inquisition officials nor mentioned it to their confessors.

The Holy Office had three tribunals in the New World: (1) Mexico, the vice-regal seat of the vice-royalty of New Spain, which included all of the present southwest United States, Mexico, Central America except Panama, and the Philippines; (2) Lima, the vice-regal seat of Peru, which covered all of South America except Brazil, until 1610; and (3) Cartagena, the seat for New Granada, which was carved out of Peru and included Panama, Colombia, Venezuela, and the Spanish islands in the Caribbean.

Jews have lived as a dispersed people ever since their biblical beginnings. At no time did they all reside in the Holy Land, although their residence in the Diaspora was not always obligatory. Until A.D. 70 Judaism was also a proselytizing faith. The dispersion and proselytizing were two of several factors that produced many variations in the religious ceremonies and in their secular lives. Many of these variations were due to acculturation. This acculturation extended to Jewish liturgy; to the secular language, which, at times, also was incorporated into their liturgy; to food and clothing traits; and to almost every aspect of their group mores. The absence of dogma and doctrine in Judaism, except for the belief in a unitary God, facilitated acculturation.

The differences among the Jewish people are almost as many as among the ethnic groups with whom they lived (Patai 1971). Some of the differences are minor and appear principally in superstitions and attire. When an ethnic group is a small minority surrounded by a single, homogenous group possessed of a religious culture that is antipathetic to that of the minority group, the process of acculturation may take place at a more rapid rate than under other circumstances. The hostility of the Spanish Catholic church and the Spanish throne to Judaism drove the Jews to the secret practice of their faith. The factors of hostility and secrecy played vital roles in their group life. If they had elected not to live as Jews, they would have suffered no impediments, since they were not only integrated into the Spanish colonial society but were easily assimilated.

The historiography of the New World contains little mention of the presence and activities of the Jews during the colonial period. Passing mention is found in some Spanish works concerned with the Church *vis-à-vis* the Jews as a religious group. The sources quoted in these works are the proceedings and documents of the Inquisition and the letters sent to Spain by secular and church officials. C. R. Boxer and a few others have made brief comments on the economic aspects of the lives of the Jews, but they say nothing of the normal or usual facets about the lives of members of this ethnic group. I have attempted to supply these insights in my own writings (Liebman 1970). Manuel Tejado Fernandez (1954) and Lucía García de Proodian (1966) also have assayed this task, but the clearest overtones of anti-Semitism pervade their works, and most of their sources are secondary or tertiary (Liebman 1971).

It is difficult to ascertain, even from original Inquisition files, the social and political life of the expellees from Spain in 1492 and from Portugal in 1497 who wended their way surreptitiously to the New World under false or forged licenses and through other subterfuges. The uprooting of heresy, the suppression of dogmatizing[1] by some of the Hebrew New Christians or Marranos or Judaizars or crypto-Jews,[2] and the attainment of spiritual homogeneity among the Crown's subjects were the avowed goals for the papal establishment of the Holy Office in Castile and Aragon in 1478 and elsewhere a few years later. It was this goal that also motivated the later decree of expulsion.

CAUSES FOR ETHNIC SURVIVAL

There are four main reasons for the survival of the Jewish ethnic group from 1550–1700 in the Americas despite powerful opposition by the dominant authorities. The motivating and supportive factors were:
1. Messianism and strong religious beliefs and practices,
2. Endogamy and the role of the Jewish female,
3. *Farda* and its contribution to the revival of indigenous culture,
4. Spiritual oppression with its effect upon Judeo-Spanish stubborness.

Messianism and Religious Beliefs and Practices

According to Kohn (1948:356): "Messianism is primarily the religious belief in the coming of a redeemer who will end the present order of things, either universally or for a single group, and will institute a new order of justice and happiness."

Barber (1941) wrote: "The Messianic doctrine is essentially a statement of hope. . . . The general sociocultural situation that precipitates a messianic movement has been loosely described as one of 'harsh times.'"

If it were not for the belief in the coming of the Messiah, who would

---

[1] See Appendix 1.
[2] See Appendix 1.

release Jews from oppression throughout the world and inaugurate a reign of peace for all mankind, Jews would have long ago abandoned Judaism. As a concommitant of this hope for surcease from persecution, Jews denied the "messiahship" of Jesus. They saw throughout the civilized world some seventeen centuries after his demise that peace had not come, that his disciples were warring against each other, and that man's inhumanity to man was still prevalent. Catholicism did not appear to be aware that Jews viewed this situation as an anachronism in the Christian position.

Although Catholicism preached that the Mosaic laws were fulfilled and completed by the crucifixion and the resurrection, Jewry continued the practice of the "old laws," because they were convinced that the Messiah, as foretold in the prophetic writings, had not yet come. Both faiths believed in the prophetic writings, but Catholic theologians chose to show by selected passages from the prophets and by exegeses and mistranslations[3] that Jesus was the one foretold. The Jews refuted this by insisting that the person foretold could not be separated from the conditions that would prevail if and when he came.

There are basic differences between the Jewish and Christian concepts of the messianic era. Jewish messianism had "a wider, more universal aspect, as well as a more spiritual meaning . . . and the Messiah would bring to all mankind justice, deliverance from misery and pain, a blossoming of the life of the spirit and a reign of brotherhood and peace. Messianism was thus a philosophy of history and a theodicy that explained the ways of God" (Kohn 1948:357). The Jewish philosophies of history, people's history-mindedness, and the belief that they are a people chosen to convey the laws of God to all mankind stem from the Bible and rabbinical exegesis. The rabbis interpreted the Bible to differ between Jews and non-Jews, indicating that the non-Jews have a responsibility to observe the seven Noachian laws (Hertz 1940:1:81, Genesis 9:4–7), whereas the Jews are to observe as many as possible of the 613 laws codified later by Maimonides. In the Ethics of the Fathers (a part of the Talmud), there is the statement that everyone, regardless of faith, who lives a moral life has a place in the world hereafter: "The kingdom of God is then understood as a universal kingdom of peace and justice, still a kingdom of the earth but metapolitical" (Kohn 1948:359).

Messianism was, and still is, an intrinsic part of the daily prayers of all Jews. During the period from 1605 to 1644, the Jews in New Spain believed that not only was the Messiah coming in the not-too-distant future (A.D. 1666), but that he was to be born of one of the women in New

---

[3] Catholics have translated the Hebrew word *"almah" in Isaiah 7:14* as "virgin," so the verse read: "Therefore the Lord Himself shall give you a sign: a virgin is with child, and she will bear a son, and will call him Immanuel." In the New English Bible (1970), the translation of "young woman" has been adopted as the Jewish philologists have contended.

Spain (Liebman 1970:255). (Jews in other pa­
lieved that the year of the coming of the Messiah
pressed no knowledge from where he would come.,
los Angeles named her daughter Geronyma Espe
believed that Esperanza (Hope) would bear the Mess
1649). When Geronyma failed to produce a son, the hop
to Juana Enriquez, a granddaughter of Juan Rodriguez
son, Gaspar, did not show evidence that he was the anti
then Ines Pereira was considered as the mother whose son
the reign of peace.

From 1550 to 1580, the Spanish Jews were predominant among the Jews in the New World. They were mainly males and of the conquistador type. When Spain assumed dominion over Portugal in 1580, many Portuguese Jews fled to the Americas. A greater religious fervor was aroused by their incursion into the Spanish vice-royalties. Their incursion rose to a crescendo in 1605 with the issuance of the Papal Bull of Pardon, which was adopted by King Phillip II. Those Portuguese Jews who inhabited the vice-royalty of Peru called it the promised land (Medina 1956:65; Liebman 1971:176). The Portuguese Jews included many of the descendants of the Spanish Jews, some 100,000, who had left Spain in 1492 and had paid a head tax for permission to enter Portugal. Consequently, the term "Portuguese Jews" is generic and includes all Iberian Jews who brought with them strong beliefs in the efficacy of prayer and the acknowledgment that most Jews were sinners because they did not abide by full compliance with the Mosaic laws. They were thus considered to be living a fraud because they posed as Catholics, followed some Catholic rites, and even received the sacraments.

As expiation for their sins, they resorted to an unusual degree of fasting. This custom of fasting almost became an end in itself, a virtue, rather than a *via mecum* for atonement. They fasted on *El Día del Perdon* or *El Gran Día*, known elsewhere as Yom Kippur, the Day of Atonement, and also from sunrise to sunset on Mondays and Thursdays. Three other fasts observed by Jews throughout the world were also observed in the Americas, and Jews also recognized those days referred to in non-canonized books of the Jews as fast days. Two such books were the Book of Tobit and the Book of Judith, which are part of the Apocrypha. Since normative Judaism does not recognize these as religious books, while Catholicism does, the fasts derived from them must be considered a result of acculturation. Very few copies of the Hebrew version of the Bible are known to have been in the Americas, so the Jews were relegated to the use of the Vulgate version.

References can be found in numerous *procesos* [the Inquisition trial proceedings] to Jewish prayers, and especially to the *Amidah*, a Hebrew word meaning "standing." The weekly version of this prayer is known as *oneh Esreh* [the eighteen benedictions], and it is longer than the ...ath and Holy Day Amidah. The prayer is recited in silence while standing with the feet held together. Pedro Arias de Maldonado stood on bricks so that he could not move his feet while praying (de Bocanegra 1649).

For the recital of prayers on the Sabbath and other holidays, at least a quorum of ten men are required. No house of worship was necessary for Judaism, since it is a home-oriented religion. The prayers and the books (the Torah) are the prerequisites. Written copies of prayers were available at times, but copies of the Jewish Testament (the Five Books of Moses, which was called the Old Testament by Christians) in Hebrew were rare. Since Judaism exhorts its disciples to learn as early as possible, a great transmission of oral learning has always existed, especially in the Americas. In numerous *procesos*, one reads of prayers that the people had learned in their youth that were recited from memory. Henry C. Lea (1922:208) and Cecil Roth (1958:276) erroneously carried this oral transmission to absurdity when they wrote that the youngest Carvajal daughter, at the age of seventeen (two additional errors since she was neither the youngest nor seventeen), could recite backwards the Psalms of David (there are 150 Psalms) plus the Prayer of Esther (there is a Book of Esther) plus hymns.

The Sabbath observance includes abstinence from work. For a male not to open his store entailed some risk. Some did open their shops, but they refused for one reason or another to conduct business. Illness served as a subterfuge. Women did no sewing or cooking on the Sabbath. *El ani*, also known as *adafina* [Jewish stew], was prepared on Fridays and left in the oven until Saturday. Juana Enriquez was so orthodox that she cut the meat into bite-sized pieces and cut the bread prior to the onset of the Sabbath. One woman berated another for brushing her teeth on Saturday, since this was work. It is not, however, the author's contention that all the Jews in the Americas were orthodox or that there were no backsliders among them. Jews ran the gamut from orthodoxy to almost nonobservance.

Although male circumcision was not universal, the proportion of those who had been circumcised was considerable. The number may have been greater than thought since the ordering of a physical examination by the Inquisition was rare. It was usually ordered when the prisoner continued to deny his Judaism or Jewish practices, or would not make a full confession, including the names of all those Jews whom he knew.

Endogamy and the Jewish Female

Judaism is opposed to marriage of a Jew with a non-Jew (Hertz

1940:11:34). Judaism has also been opposed to proselytizing for the past 1,900 years, and frowns on the conversions of non-Jews for the sake of marrying a Jew. In the Americas, endogamy was almost sacrosanct, not only for the survival of the group but also for the individuals who practiced the ceremonies of their faith. The danger was that a Christian spouse might report Jewish observances to a confessor.

Pious women, some of whom were notable dogmatizers, served as teachers of the faith to their offspring. Julio Jiménez Rueda (1948:120) referred to Beatriz Enriquez, burned at the stake at the December 8, 1596, auto-de-fé, as "the greatest dogmatizer among the women, with the exception of the Carvajal women." One of the outstanding female dogmatizers was Blanca Enriquez (no relation to Beatriz). The inquisitors called her a "rabbi," and she did serve in that capacity from 1638 to 1639. (The Hebrew word "rabbi" means teacher.) When Juan Pacheco de Leon, alias Salomon Machorro, came from Italy and was considered for the post of rabbi in 1639, Blanca examined him to determine whether he was qualified (Liebman 1970:268). Many Jewish women in the Americas have been added to the long roll of martyrs in Jewish history (Liebman 1970:186).

There are several cases of uncles who married nieces, and of marriages among other relatives. Family intermarriage was practiced not only to insure the "purity of blood," as noted by Americo Castro, but also to permit an observant Jew to perform the rituals without fear of hostile detection. It also insured that only those foods permitted to Jews would be served in the home (no pork or fish without scales, and so on) and that fowl and meat would be prepared in accordance with Jewish law.

Women decapitated the fowl with a special knife that was inspected prior to each use to insure that there were no nicks on the blade. They faced East (toward Jerusalem) and recited special prayers of thanks. Cattle and lambs were ritually slaughtered by men. The thigh vein and the suet around it were removed by the women in accordance with Jewish law. (Coincidentally, North American Indians cut and threw away the hamstrings of the deer that they killed [Frazer 1923:357].) The women would hang the fowl by the legs after decapitation, allowing the blood to drain into a pan of water, which was then poured onto the earth. These things were usually done after the servants had retired and prior to their arising early in the morning. Women also performed the religious ceremonies of washing and shrouding the dead.

It is beyond the scope of this paper to list all the household practices and religious responsibilities of women, and those who seek them can turn to the primary sources.[4] Such research will reveal that the religious observances of the Jews in the New World ran the gamut of Jewish ritual,

---

[4] See Appendix 2.

and that, until 1700, except for the necessity of concealing Judaism, the Jewish communities in the Americas resembled the communities of their co-religionists in other lands. A stranger from "free lands" might have noted the absence of some customs, but would not have felt at a loss. Not only the daily and religious life of the Jews within their own ethnic group can be reconstructed from the research, but also their relationships with the dominant group.

Endogamy produced some interesting developments until 1649. Many parents sought spouses for their children from distant places. The closeness of the relationships within each faction of the ethnic group (the Jews were not united, but they were subdivided into factions, especially in New Spain) caused the members of each faction to entertain a somewhat familial relationship to other group members that was not conducive to marriage. Studies of the Kibbutzim in Israel have disclosed that marriages are rarely contracted between group members. The reason advanced is that when boys and girls grow up together in close social contact, the resulting relationships are similar to those of siblings. Consequently, men seek their brides in other kibbutzim or elsewhere.

In New Spain, brides for the men were often sought in Peru, because it was believed they were better educated in the Jewish traditions. Young men from heavily populated Jewish centers in Italy were sought as grooms. Some were from Pisa, Florence, and Bologna, and a few came from Provence, France.

Farda

Farda is defined in the old Spanish dictionaries as a form of tax or contribution paid by Jews and Moslems for the support of their respective communities in the Holy Land. In the *procesos* [trials] of three men in New Spain (Ruy Diaz Nieto, Diego Diez Nieto, and Thomas Treviño de Sobremonte), reference is made to *farda*, and the story is told of these practices among the Jews.[5]

Emissaries came to New Spain from the Holy Land. They were learned men who remained in one area for periods varying from three to six months to study with the people. These emissaries provided a refresher in Jewish learning. After the completion of their stay, they made a collection for the support of the Jewish communities in the Holy Land. This custom helped to strengthen Judaism by fresh infusions of learning and the maintenance of identity with the Promised Land.

---

[5] In Peru, the custom was somewhat different and is discussed elsewhere (Liebman 1971:184–189).

Spiritual Oppression and the Judeo-Spanish Psyche

The Bible refers to the Jews as "a stiff-necked people" almost twenty times. Henry C. Lea (1922) wrote many years ago that their Catholic majesties and the Spanish Church erred in establishing the Holy Office of the Inquisition in order to achieve religious homogeneity. This institution succeeded only in driving many converts back to Judaism. Lea believed that, if Spain had decreed complete religious equality and freedom for all Jews within their realm, within fifty years, the Jews would have assimilated and abandoned Judaism. The French sociologist, Georges Friedman (1967:241), wrote: "Assimilation can become total only when anti-Semitism ends." He and other sociologists concerned with the survival of Judaism assert that more liberal church attitudes, the abandonment of all racism, and the end of all anti-Semitism will foretell the demise of Judaism.

Instead of migrating to the Ottoman Empire, Holland, or parts of Italy where they could openly observe their faith, the Jews came to the Americas in the sixteenth and seventeenth centuries, bringing with them all the traits of the Spaniard. They elected to live under the inquisitorial sword of Damocles because they preferred to be among Spanish-speaking people and those who shared a secular ethnicity with them. "The Jews expelled from their fatherland, that is, Spain, in 1492, felt themselves . . . as Spanish as the Christians" (Castro 1954:466). Approximately 100,000 Jews had moved to Portugal in 1492, and when many of their descendants returned to Spain in 1580 as false Christians, they also spoke Spanish and felt an identification with Spain even though they detested the Church. Fernando Diaz-Plaja (1968:13) lists pride as the first of the seven deadly sins of the Spaniards and writes: "It is quite possible that this pride is, as Castro thinks, an inherited Jewish or Arabic characteristic."

ACCULTURATION AND MODIFICATION OF JEWISH RITES

Jews have believed in magic and superstition since their establishment as an identifiable ethnic group. Their superstitions were often borrowed from the dominant groups and others among whom they lived (Trachtenberg 1961:120). Some of the most common superstitions in the Americas were of Spanish origin (Liebman 1970:85). The belief in demons was rampant. Even the orthodox family of Justa Mendez threw freshly slaughtered meat under her bed when she died to sate any demons who might prevent her ascension to heaven. An almost universal custom among Jews was to empty any jars of water when a resident of the house died, and another was to cover all mirrors or turn them to face the wall for a week after the burial.

The secret Jew in the New World elevated fasting as a religious rite. Coincidentally, this is also a Catholic rite observed on certain days of the Catholic religious calendar in Spain (Longhurst 1950:91). Those fasts of the Jews that could not be related to Catholicism required other pretexts to disguise their Jewish significance. Some couples would commence a dispute as they sat down for their midday meal and then feign a state of anger that caused them to stalk away from the table. Others would leave the house in the morning and say that they were to be luncheon guests at another's house. Some went horse-back riding, and others alleged upset stomachs or gave other excuses. Except for the sunrise to sunset fasts on Mondays and Thursdays and on the three days preceding Purim (which usually falls in March), all other fasts commence at sunset and end when the evening stars appear on the following day. Fasting was a non-conspicuous method of expiating one's sins. Fasting was also used as an expression of thanks for divine blessings. It was also resorted to as a means of averting evil events. Here the line between religion and superstition becomes very thin.

Individuals could pray in the privacy of their homes three times a day, as some did. Silent praying alone on weekdays is consonant with Judaism. On the Sabbath and Holy days, however, congregational praying is required. The problem of meeting in large groups and praying aloud on the Sabbath was solved by Juana Tinoco and others. She set many Jewish prayers to the melodies of Catholic hymns so that passerbys would hear the music and regard the sounds as choir practice (Liebman 1970:70). To heighten the deception, the names of Jesus and Mary were interpolated; these names were said in raised tones in case there were eavesdroppers.

The Inquisitors did not order a physical examination of male prisoners in the majority of cases in the New World. The examinations, when held, were to determine whether the prisoner had been circumcized; they occurred only in those cases where the prisoners continued to deny Jewish practices or failed to give full confessions of his own acts as well as the names of those who observed with him. One case with a humorous touch involved a man who explained that the Mark of Covenant had been made on him by a barber in Puerto Rico who advocated surgery on his sex organ to cure his unnamed disease. This man vehemently denied that it had religious significance. Some circumcisions were performed in an untraditional manner. Instead of a circular cut of the prepuce, a longitudinal cut was made. In one case, that of Duarte de Leon Laramillo, the father cut out a small piece of flesh from the shoulders of three of his children.

Pork, usually prepared in an *olla* as a stew, was one of the food staples of the general populace in the Americas. Some Jews would not eat pork under any circumstances; others felt that they could not refuse to eat it when at the home of others. Some put their fingers in their throats when they returned home, causing regurgitation. As a precaution, the consumption of meat was kept at a minimum and fish, vegetables, eggs and olives were a staple diet, especially prior to and at the end of the fast. Meat was eaten on Fridays and during Lent as a token of rebellion against the church.

An absence of images of Jesus, Mary, and other saints would cause suspicion among Gentile guests. Thus, while they were present, many Jews would flog crucifixes accompanied by imprecations directed toward the figure impaled on it. Burning and other acts of vandalism, such as breaking an arm of an image, were also perpetrated.

Perpetual absence from mass and other church functions would also arouse suspicion so Jews occasionally attended, but they averted their eyes or placed a handkerchief to their faces during the holding aloft of the Host. And if they took a wafer, they did not swallow it, but surreptitiously expectorated it.

During Passover, Jews are obliged not to eat bread made with yeast or any leavening, they are supposed to eat matzot or *pan cenceno*. The Jews observed Passover during Holy Week, when they baked their matzot in a round, small shape so that they had the appearance of tortillas. One doctor in Peru prescribed matzot for some patients with stomach disorders, and then during Passover week, alleged that he had a stomachache so he could also prescribe it for himself.

One of the practices taken from Catholicism was that of praying on the knees. Jews have not prayed in that position since the year A.D. 70 when the temple in Jerusalem was destroyed by the Romans. Jews in the Americas, however, would prostrate themselves and would also kneel when praying alone or with the congregation. Some clasped their hands or held their palms together during prayers, customs that are unknown to normative Judaism.

Judaism has no saints, and there is no particular reverence paid to any mortal, including Moses, who is known as "our teacher" or "the lawgiver." Yet, in the Americas, several people refer to "Saint" Moses and applied "Saint" to some of the prophets and patriarchs. Juana Enriquez acknowledged that she had made the "seven stations of Saint Moses."

Speaking to the dead or having visions are foreign to Judaism's beliefs. Yet, one finds a practice in the New World of Jews standing in silence at the grave of one newly interred until one of the mourners exclaims that he or she has seen the soul of the departed ascend into heaven. Dreams are interpreted by specialists, and contacts with the dead are used in divination (Trachtenberg 1961:241).

The Sabbath candles are lighted by women who recite appropriate blessings and prayers. This act, prior to sunset on Friday, inaugurates the

Sabbath. According to Jewish law, these candles are not to be extinguished. In order to avert suspicion, many Jews did not snuff out the candles in their homes on the other nights of the week so that the continuous burning of the Sabbath candles appeared to be the usual household practice.

A custom borrowed from the Indians was that of placing in the mouth of the deceased a piece of grain or a piece of a coin. It appears that this practice may also have been observed by the Catholics, since I have not found any questions put to Jewish prisoners by the Inquisitors about the reason for this custom. The broken coin could not have been intended for Charon as passage across the River Styx although the Indians have a similar belief in the crossing of a river. The grain would not have been sufficient as food for the trip to some other nonworldly paradise.

Death rites were drawn from Jewish customs, as well as from superstitions. Finger and toenail parings of both the living and the dead were never carelessly cast away, but they were always gathered together and burned. This superstition is still followed by some European Jews. It is part of the religious ritual for cadavers to be washed externally and douched internally. In the Americas, the hair under the arms and around the genital area were also shaved.

The *proceso* of Francisco de Leon reveals that his aunt, a pious and learned woman, prayed three times a day, each time for about an hour, always facing east and with a kerchief over her hands. This last act is unknown to any modern rabbi. One day, while visiting the home of a Mexican journalist, I was shown a four-foot statue that was an enlarged replica of a statue in the Mexican Museum of Anthropology and History. The original came from the island of Jaina, which had a Mayan cemetery. The figure is "a standing woman with loose tunic, holding a tubular bag." The statue has a cloth or kerchief over her clasped hands. If this is not the origin of the custom practiced by the aunt of Francisco de Leon, it may be that some Catholic women followed this practice, which then spread.

One of the superstitions practiced by the women involved running into the street immediately after the death of a family member and standing at a nearby corner screaming. This screaming and wailing was to scare away demons that might be lurking in the vicinity and to hasten heavenward the soul of the departed. This custom is still followed by the Jews in the Maghreb, where Spanish Jews settled in great numbers in 1391.

There were many ceremonies of the Jews that had their counterparts in Indian rites. American Indians with whom some of the Mesoamerinds are distantly related also had the concept of messianism (Barber 1941:663, fn. 3). I believe the reason that I have not found any Indian slave or servant being an informant or witness against a Jew is that the Indians felt a bond of kinship, however close and amorphous, with the Jews. This bond may have resulted from the fact that Indians were regarded as "no gente de razon" by the church and were enslaved. These Indians witnessed the Jews in the autos-de-fé being persecuted for their god and had also had their own gods taken away from them by the Spaniards. Thus, both groups were the victims of Catholic oppression, and this may have been instrumental in creating a feeling of empathy.

DECLINE AND DECADENCE

Franz Boas wrote: "Not every culture is characterized by a dominant character" (Benedict 1961:xvii). The Jewish ethnic group is one of those possessed of a dominant character, which is its religion. There would be no ethnic group without the religion. Should the knowledge and practice of the religion decline, the members of this group would cease to be an identifiable outgroup, and the distinctions between them and the ingroup would become blurred and ultimately disappear (Benedict 1961:8).

By the end of the seventeenth century, a serious decline in numbers in the Jewish ethnic group in the Americas had set in, and a decadence in the practices of Judaism had reached catastrophic proportions. The principle factors contributing to these developments were the following:

1. The arrests of a great number of Jews and their leaders, commencing in Peru (1634), New Granada (1636), and New Spain (1642). The arrests in Peru and New Spain culminated in the "great" autos-de-fé of 1639 and 1649, respectively.
2. The establishment of open Jewish life in Holland and Denmark, a return of the Jews to England starting in 1656, and the concomitant cessation of immigration of Jews to Spanish America.
3. The reduction of religious oppression in the Americas toward the close of the seventeenth century.
4. The disillusionment in the pseudo-Messiahs between 1630 and 1666.

The Arrests of the Jews

There were several reasons for the massive arrests in the vice-royalty of Peru, New Granada, and New Spain, but they are not germane to this paper. The greatest number apprehended was in New Spain. Over 400 Jews were arrested, among whom were the leaders of the three principal factions. Many were prominent in society, the royal court, and especially in the economic life of the colonies. Most were incarcerated and languished in the Inquisition cells for almost seven years. Many more escaped and were never caught. The greatest blow to the Jews was the arrest of their religious leaders. There is no record of the entry of any Jews into New Spain during the seven-year interval. In Peru, where the interval between incarceration and the auto-de-fé lasted about five years, the entire vice-royalty suffered an economic debacle. Again, one finds no trace of Jews coming to any part of South America during this period.

The decline of Peru was due in no small part to the bankruptcies that resulted from the sequestration and confiscation of the Jews' property, the nonpayment of debts, the drying up of capital, the idling of the silver mines of Potosi, and the absence of the Jews as merchants and renters of mule trains. The decline in Peru had an adverse effect on New Granada and its own "round-up" of Jews, causing many of them to flee and reestablish themselves in the Caribbean Islands, which were shortly thereafter taken over by the English, French, and Dutch. They also settled in Dutch Surinam or the Wilde Kust, which was on the mainland adjacent to New Granada. These Jews achieved a certain amount of revenge by turning to the smuggling business and establishing their bases in Barbados, Jamaica, Martinique, Trinidad, and Surinam. They traded with the Spanish colonists in New Granada and later established new Jewish colonies in Coro and Barcelona that are now cities in Venezuela.

Holland, Denmark, and England

The names of these nations spell a new era of Jewish life in Europe, beginning with the seventeenth century. With the achievement of Holland's independence from Spain and the gradual granting of religious privileges to the Sephardim, Jews could live in Amsterdam, continue to speak Spanish or Portuguese, practice their faith openly, and engage in economic enterprises the size of which exceeded anything that had been possible in the Americas.

Cromwell's accession to the request of Rabbi Menasseh ben Israel of Holland to permit the Jews to return to England, from which they had been expelled in 1290, opened new avenues to the Iberian Jews. King Christian IV of Denmark invited the Jews of the "Portuguese nation" to participate in the economic life of his realm, and Hamburg, Altona, and Gluckstadt became pivotal economic centers between western and eastern Europe, as well as between Scandinavia and southern Germany.

The Netherlands also opened its New World possessions to the Jews. Thus, by 1660, Jews were engaged in industry, commerce, and agriculture in Surinam and as plantation owners in neighboring Cayenne. The sugar trade, which was lost to them in 1654 by the recapture of Brazil from the Dutch, was recouped in the Caribbean Islands. The Jews asked themselves: "Why go where one's life is at stake when one can have all the advantages and none of the disadvantages by going next door?"

The Abatement of Religious Oppression

Of course, the Spanish church and the Holy Office of the Inquisition did not eliminate all the Jews from the Spanish Americas. They did succeed, for an extended period, in forcing the Jews completely underground, out of the capitals and large urban areas, and curtailing their immigration. In New Spain, the Jews moved their diminished numbers to Monterrey and its environs in northern Mexico. In New Granada, they moved to Medellin and the surrounding areas, and in Peru, they went to the area around Tucúman and Cordoba. Moreover, they went without religious or secular leaders. The attrition of competent religious leaders led to the decline of religiosity.

Numerous trials were held before all the tribunals after the middle of the seventeenth century, but comparatively speaking, these were insignificant. The Inquisition became more concerned with the inroads of Protestantism in the New World, the importation of its literature, and the rise of Freemasonry. The Inquisition began slowly to be more a political arm of the state than the religious protector of the purity of the church.

After 1665, the *procesos* dealt with wealthy Jews, some of whom were foreigners, and the punishments administered were usually monetary; they never involved complete confiscation; and there were few burnings at the stake. It is possible that the 2,000 charges filed ca. 1662 against the three venal inquisitors in New Spain by Dr. Pedro de Medina Rico had a mollifying effect on their successors.

The Jews who remained in the Americas found that they were mostly alone. The mainstream of world Jewry either forgot them or ignored them. Although they were unmolested, there was no infusion of new blood through immigration and no religious inspiration. The emissaries for *farda* found it of little profit to seek a few Jews in the hinterlands. There were larger and more prosperous communities in Europe, and efforts there achieved greater rewards. A study of any Jewish community in the Diaspora during the past 2,000 years reveals that isolated Jewry cannot survive, nor can it remain vital without new immigrants, most of whom are dedicated to learning opposed to assimilation. Assimilation tolls the death knell for any ethnic group whose dominant character is religion. The greatest number of Jews migrating to Israel from North and South America within the past decade are orthodox Jews who see no future for traditional Judaism on these continents.

The Jewish world found itself with a shortage of spiritual leaders and qualified teachers by the middle of the seventeenth century. These shortages deprived the remnants of the Jewish ethnic group in the New World of the opportunity for learning and enlightenment in basic Judaism. As each decade passed, one finds a decline and atrophying of religious practices in the Americas. Superstition frequently supplanted valid religious concepts.

The Pseudo-Messiahs

New World Jewry suffered three disappointments in the hope for the birth of a Messiah from among their own numbers. World Jewry suffered an even keener disappointment in the disillusionment with Sabbatai Zevi, who had proclaimed himself the Messiah in Europe in 1648. He had charisma, was a learned Jew, and seemed to fulfill the conditions described in the Kabbalah and Talmudic sources in support of his claim. Literally thousands of Jews in Europe abandoned their businesses and homes to follow him to Constantinople, where he proposed to confront the sultan and receive legal possession of the Holy Land for all Jewry. To the consternation of most of his followers, the sultan had him jailed in 1665. After two years in jail, the sultan presented him with the alternative of death or conversion to Islam. Zevi converted.

The cliché that hope springs eternal in the human breast finds more than adequate confirmation among the Jews. Although disillusioned, most Jews did not despair or abandon hope for the coming Messiah. The handful of rabbis who had not accepted Sabbatai exhorted the people to trust in God and to rehabilitate themselves spiritually. Only then, they said, could the arrival of the authentic Messiah be expected.

The disillusionment was strongest among the remaining Jews in the Americas. They were the ones who lost all hope. In their new areas, there was little interference from the local representatives of the Holy Office. The Jews lost the incentive to affirm or reaffirm their faith. Their practices fell into desuetude. There was an erosion of the ethnic group members, especially through exogamy, and those who remained lost interest in the maintenance of the group. The *coup de grace* came shortly after 1700, when the Hapsburg dynasty came to an end in Spain and the Holy Roman Empire and the Bourbon dynasty took over the Hispanic throne. Interest in the Jew faded, and assimilation was accelerated.

APPENDIX 1: TERMS

Some confusion exists in the use of certain words. The following will serve either to define or clarify their meaning.

JUDAIZAR AND THE SPANISH WORD JUDAIZANTE. While dictionaries confine the meaning of these words to one who observes Jewish rites, a study of literally hundreds of *procesos* reveals that these words were used by the Inquisitors and their subordinates as synonyms for Jews and Jewish. In my translation of the Relacion of the 1649 auto-de-fé (Liebman 1973a), the interchange of *judio* and *judaizante* appears on almost every page.

MARRANOS AND CRYPTO-JEWS. Those interested in the philology of "Marrano" and its history are referred to the leading article on the word (Malkiel 1948: 175–184). As used herein, the word describes people who publicly professed Catholicism in the Spanish colonies, but who secretly practiced Judaism, who regarded themselves as Jews and were of Jewish ancestry. If all of the foregoing existed, it is of no importance whether they were baptized or received other sacraments. Gerson D. Cohen, former professor of history at Columbia University and presently president of the Jewish Theological Seminary and a graduate of the seminary, wrote: "... no matter how Christianized a Marrano way of life may have become ... they need not — and — apparently did not — cease to be a Jewish group historically, sociologically, and even religiously" (Cohen 1966:181).

CRYPTO-JEWS. Crypto-Jews were Jews who practiced their faith secretly. The few who would deny full Jewish status to these secret observers erroneously use "Marrano," "crypto-Jew," or "Judaizer" to indicate either lack of credence in the sincerity of the observances or in the validity of Inquisition *procesos*, or they imply that the words that they use mean some breed of hybrid or half-Jew, statuses that are nonexistent in Judaism.

CONVERSOS AND NEW CHRISTIANS. Not all converts to Catholicism were insincere. Many Jews opted for Catholicism even prior to 1492. In fact, some of the more virulent anti-Semites were former Jews. However, there were many converts and New Christians who were crypto-Jews and Marranos. Many of these were called "Hebrews New Christians" by the Inquisition. The failure to prefix "Hebrews" did not mean that New Christians without the appellation were not of the "*caste y generación de los judios.*"

DOGMATIZER. The crypto-Jews, or Marranos who were learned, often were people who attempted to bring back into the fold of Jewry those who had converted or who were the descendants of Jews who had converted. Being a dogmatizer was a heinous crime in the eyes of the Inquisition. During the period covered in this paper, most dogmatizers were Portuguese Jews who were considered more observant than were the Spanish Jews who had never been in Portugal.

APPENDIX 2: SOURCES

The principal source of data on the history of the Jews in the New World are the Inquisition files in Mexico and Peru, the Archivo Historico Nacional de Madrid, the Bibliotecas Nacional in Madrid and Santiago de Chile, and the Archivo de las Indias in Seville. There are forty-seven volumes of original Inquisition documents and *procesos* in the Henry E. Huntington Library, Pasadena, California, many in the Thomas E. Gilcrease Institute, Tulsa, Oklahoma, and in several other places around the world. Many have been lost by fire, pilferage, the ravages of time and so on. The *lacunae* are partially filled by secondary sources. José Toribio Medina is the most fecund author with seven volumes on the Inquisition in the New World to his credit, but none of his volumes is devoted exclusively to Jews. His references to them are in the form of statistical information, punishments, and the itemization of names and evidences of esoteric random facts and some errors.

The time to accept his works uncritically and to place undue reliance upon them is long past. The distinguished Amero-Hispanist, Charles Gibson, put it succinctly: "Students have tended to rely excessively on the writings of Jose Toribio Medina and Henry C. Lea" (Gibson 1970:1553). While Medina is invaluable for copies of correspondence much of the balance of his writings are derived from *relaciones de las causas*, reports sent to the Suprema in Madrid by each tribunal of pending and adjudicated cases for a preceding year or longer.

Medina did no work in Mexico. He relied upon Luis González Obregón who may have consulted several original papers, but most of Obregon's reports to Medina were predicated upon the *relaciones*. Henry C. Lea relied upon Medina and, to a limited extent, upon Gonzalez Obregon. Genaro Garcia's books are also based upon the *relaciones* and some of his working papers (almost all included in his printed works) are at the University of Texas Library. Since the *relaciones* are secondary sources, at best, then those who wrote on the basis of these, are tertiary sources. Investigation and study of original *procesos* reveal countless errors in Medina and Lea, and in Cecil Roth who synthesized Medina and Genaro Garcia. Roth is even a worse offender because he never distinguished between Portuguese and Spanish Jews and the vast difference in the quantity and quality of religious observances. At best, his works are a most general synthesis.

We have not supplied the archival references for many of those individuals named in the paper. These references can be found in Liebman (1964). Where we have utilized a *relacion*, we have so designated it and it is usually Bocanegra whose virulence against Judaism symbolizes the nadir of religious bigotry.

REFERENCES

BARBER, BERNARD
   1941   Acculturation and messianic movements. *American Sociological Review* 6:663–669.
BENEDICT, RUTH
   1961   *Patterns of culture*. Boston: Houghton Mifflin.
BOXER, C. R.
   1952   *Salvador da Sá*. London: Athlone.
CASTRO, AMÉRICO
   1954   *The structure of Spanish history*. Princeton: Princeton University Press.
COHEN, GERSON D.
   1966   Book review on the *Marranos of Spain*. *Jewish Social Studies* 29:178–184.
DE BOCANEGRA, MATHIAS
   1649   *Relacion del auto de fe de 1649*. Mexico: Antonio Calderon.
DIAZ-PLAJA, FERNANDO
   1968   *The seven deadly sins*. Translated from the Spanish. London: Pan Books.
FRAZER, JAMES GEORGE
   1923   *Folk-lore in the old testament*. New York: Tudor.
FRIEDMAN, GEORGES
   1967   *The end of the Jewish people?* Translated from the French. New York: Doubleday.

GARCÍA DE PROODIAN, LUCIA
- 1966 *Los Judios en America*. Madrid: Consejo Superior de Investigaciones Cientificas. (See also essay review of this book by Liebman, Seymour B. *Jewish Social Studies* 33:63, Jan. 1971, No. 1.)

GARCÍA, GENARO
- 1906–1910 *Documentos ineditos o muy raros para la historia de Mexico*, volumes five and twenty-eight. Mexico: Libreria de la Vda. de Ch. Bouret.

GIBSON, CHARLES
- 1970 Essay review in *American Historical Review*. 75:1553.

HERSKOVITS, MELVILLE J.
- 1966 "Who are the Jews?" in *The Jews: their history, culture and religion*, two volumes. Edited by Louis Finkelstein, 1489–1509. Philadelphia: Jewish Publication Society.

HERTZ, J. H., *editor*
- 1940 *The pentateuch and haftorahs*, five volumes. London: Oxford University Press.

JIMÉNEZ RUEDA, JULIO
- 1948 *Herejías y supersticiones en la Neuva España*. Mexico: UNAM.

KOHN, HANS
- 1948 "Messianism", in *Encyclopedia of social sciences*, volume ten, 356–363. New York: Macmillan.

LEA, HENRY C.
- 1922 *The inquisition in the Spanish dependencies*. New York: Macmillan.

LIEBMAN, SEYMOUR B.
- 1964 *Guide to Jewish references in the Mexican colonial era; 1521–1821*. Philadelphia: University of Pennsylvania Press.
- 1970 *The Jews in New Spain*. Coral Gables, Fla.: University of Miami Press.
- 1971 The great conspiracy in Peru. *The Americas* 28:176–190.
- 1973a *The great auto-de-fé of 1649*. Coronado Press.
- 1973b *The inquisitors and the Jews in the New World*. Coral Gables, Fla.: University of Miami Press.

LONGHURST, JOHN E.
- 1950 *Erasmus and the Spanish inquisition*. Albuquerque: University of New Mexico Press.

MALKIEL, YAKOV
- 1948 "Hispano-Arabic *Marrano* and its Hispano-Latin homophone." *Journal of American Oriental Society* 68:175–184.

MEDINA, JOSÉ TORIBIO
- 1899 *Historia del tribunal del santo oficio de la inquisición de Cartagena de las indias*. Santiago de Chile: Imprenta de Elzeviriana.
- n.d. *La inquisicion en el Rio de la Plata*. Buenos Aires: Editorial Huarpes S.A.
- 1952a *Historia del tribunal del santo oficio de la inquisición en Chile*. Santiago de Chile: Fondo Historico y Bibliografia J. T. Medina.
- 1952b *Historia del tribunal del santo oficio de la inquisición en Mexico* ampliada por Julio Jimenez Rueda. Mexico: Editorial Navarro.
- 1956 *Historia del tribunal del santo oficio de la inquisición de Lima*. Santiago de Chile: Fondo Histórico y Bibliografia J. T. Medina.

PATAI, RAPHAEL
- 1971 *Tents of Jacob*. Englewood Cliffs, N.J.: Prentice-Hall.

ROTH, CECIL
  1958 *History of the Marranos.* New York: Meridian Books.
TEJADO FERNANDEZ, MANUEL
  1954 *Aspects de la vida social en Cartagena.* Chapter 11.
TRACHTENBERG, JOSHUA
  1961 *Jewish magic and superstition.* Cleveland and Philadelphia: Jewish Publication Society and World Publishing.

Ancestor Memorialism: A Comparison of Jews and Japanese

HOWARD WIMBERLEY and JOEL SAVISHINSKY

Any discussion of Jewish and Japanese life between individuals who are familiar with only one of the two patterns is likely to give rise to the exclamation, "You don't mean to say they're like that, too!" Plath (1964), in his inquiry into how the Japanese treatment of the dead reflects the institutional molding of affect, noted that these particular effects might be comparable to those of other peoples, such as Americans. Zenner (1965) briefly elaborated on this point by noting a number of interesting similarities between Japanese and Jewish memorial practices. Since Zenner's initial comparisons, however, little systematic ethnological work along these lines seems to have been undertaken. Finding Zenner's observations rather remarkable, in the winter of 1972–1973, we undertook a preliminary study of middle-class, Jewish New Yorkers of Ashkenazic descent, in which we attempted to integrate library research materials with field observations in order to develop a balanced account of this American subculture for further comparisons. In this report of our findings, we have analytically divided the data into historical, structural, and psychological categories for comparison with the well-documented Japanese case.

JEWISH MEMORIALISM[1]

The Historical Dimension

The Jewish religion is suffused with metaphors of kinship, and it derives its charters of authority from genealogy. The dominant figures of the Old

---

[1] Maurice Freedman (1958) distinguishes between ancestor worship and memorialism, using the latter term to refer specifically to domestic household rites. In this essay, we are

Testament are patriarchs in a literal and corporate sense: the Jewish people are "the seed of Abraham"; they are his "household" and the "house of Aaron"; their God is the "God of our Fathers," that is, of Abraham, Jacob, Isaac, and their descendants. And the people are, by virtue of their heritage and the covenants made by their "Fathers" with Yahweh, the "Children of God." In the Old Testament, and in subsequent commentaries on it, religious, priestly, and political authority are usually validated on a genealogical basis, and there is throughout a strong consciousness of patrimony, family ties, and kinship obligations. In more recent centuries, the inhabitants of the rural communities (*shtetls*) of Eastern Europe maintained this kinship imagery at both the communal and the national levels: they saw themselves as members of *Klal Isroel*, "the entire Jewish people the world over" and, as Landes and Zborowski indicate:

The *shtetl* Jews consider all members of the Jewish community to be related to each other through kinship ties, a belief expressed formally in the collective terms *B'nai Israel*, Children of Israel, and in the acceptance of the three Biblical patriarchs as the ancestors of all Jews (1950:462).

Despite the pervasiveness of kinship in early Jewish history and its writings, there is no biblical sanction or authority for actual ancestor worship or memorialism, nor do these appear as a formal part of early orthodox Jewish ceremonialism. Some biblical scholars suggest that early Hebraic religion actually contained many remnants of ancestor worship from pre- and non-Israelite sources in the Middle East, but that the early patriarchs and prophets attempted to suppress these practices from the faith. In the case of the two liturgical prayers most directly related to memorialism and commemorating the dead, *Kaddish* and *Yizkor*, the former, an ancient Aramaic text, is literally a "sanctification" of God that only later became associated with ceremonies of mourning. The prayer itself lacks any mention of the dead, although after its incorporation into the liturgy, its recitation was believed to help "redeem the dead parent from the sufferings of Hell (*Gehinnom*)" (Zenner 1965:481).

It is probable that the Kaddish was formulated after the destruction of the first Temple and was recited primarily after a lecture or discourse on a Torah theme. It then slipped easily into the worship service, into which its themes and responses fitted admirably (Lamm 1969:52).

---

dealing with both household and communal modes of memorializing deceased persons and have not followed a strict dichotomy in our use of these terms. We suggest in the text that neither Jewish nor Japanese people literally "worship" their ancestors, and hence, we employ the term "*memorialism*" in a broad sense to cover activities and observances that have elsewhere been designated as "worship."

The memorial service of *Yizkor* [Recalling the Dead] was introduced into Jewish services during the period of medieval pogroms, and it was "instituted so that the Jew may pay homage to his forbears and recall the good life and traditional goals" (Lamm 1969:196). In both cases, then, memorial prayers have become part of the liturgy, either through the reinterpretation of a prayer from another context or through the introduction of a service during a specific historical period.

In contrast to the relative silence of early biblical and liturgical sources on the theme of ancestors, and as the history of the memorial prayers illustrates, there has developed an unmistakable complex of beliefs and services directed toward helping, placating, memorializing, and maintaining ties with the deceased. The specific content of the *Yizkor* and *Kaddish* prayers also reflects the fact that orthodox Judaism rejects the notion of direct *worship* of ancestors, and instead, conceives of memorial prayers and observances, in the words of one of our rabbinic informants, as "*reverence and respect* for the dead," a reverence that this rabbi derived from the biblical injunction to "honor thy father and mother."

While some Jewish memorial observances incorporate biblical and liturgical elements, others exist outside the formal framework of Judaism, and they have evolved as an adjunct set of participations, some of which are clearly folkloristic in nature. Rabbinic authorities, for example, repeatedly emphasize the biblical, Talmudic, and orthodox rejection of ancestor worship as a "monstrous blasphemy" (see, for example, Lamm 1969:211). Yet, cultural and historical studies of European Jewry consistently reveal a belief in the efficacy of prayers directed to ancestral spirits as a mode for obtaining help and guidance. Trachtenberg (1970) provides extensive documentation of these and similar practices among Ashkenzic Jewry in the medieval period, noting their similarity to non-Jewish beliefs of this era and their persistence among Ashkenazic Jews into more recent times (Pollack 1971). The practice of paying annual visits to the grave of the deceased, the pattern of naming their children after ancestors, the making of charitable donations on behalf of the deceased, and the belief that the dead and the living can intercede on one another's behalf are widespread Ashkenazic patterns which have no specific biblical sanction.

On a number of these memorial practices, Ashkenazic and Sephardic Jews show some basic divergences. Sephardic Jews, for example, name their children after living, rather than deceased, ascendants. These differences are indicative of the fact that observances and beliefs pertaining to the dead show a great deal of regional and historical variation among the many Jewish groups that have developed during the last 2,000 years.

Structural Features

To understand the structure of Jewish memorialism, it is necessary to look at the structure of both the Jewish family and the Jewish "people" as a religious and historical community. Ancestral practices among East European Jews are bilateral in breadth but shallow in genealogical depth. Observances, memories, and involvements concerning the deceased usually include a person's own and his parents', children's, and grandparents' generations, but they rarely extend deeper into genealogical time. That is, they center on people of whom there is still a living memory among family members. There is no specific kinship principle that designates which persons, beyond parents, spouses, siblings, and children, should be memorialized. In the case of parental siblings, for example, initial research indicates that decisions in the matter of memorialization may be made in an *ad hoc* and personal manner, that is, the decisions on kinsmen such as aunts and uncles may more often be situational rather than strictly ideological in nature: those kinsmen with whom an individual had close, warm ties are most likely to be memorialized, regardless of their specific degree or line of relatedness. In some cases, this may result in mostly patrikin being memorialized; in other cases, matrikin; and in still other instances, there is a combination of deceased persons from both lines.

From a personal point of view, then, significant kinsmen among Jews constitute a bilateral, consanguineal kindred rather than a unilineal, corporate descent group. This noncorporate tendency is reinforced by the lack of any consistent unilocal, postmarital residence pattern among Jews. It is from among this bilateral network of people that memorialized kin — those for whom *Kaddish*, *Yizkor*, and *Yahrzeit* are observed — are most likely to be found. Also, unlike systems that emphasize unilineal descent, men and women do not become responsible for the memorialization of members of their spouses' families of orientation or identified with them. It should be noted, however, that the literature on *shtetl* cultures of Eastern Europe indicates that people were often likely to have warmer and more extensive ties with matrikin than patrikin, due to the fact that mothers provided the expressive focus of familial relationships and often turned to their own kin for assistance in rearing their children. This fact could conceivably lead to a matrilineal emphasis in memorial practices, a possibility worth further statistical investigation (Landes and Zborowski 1950:452–453, 459).[2] *Shtetl* Jews also occasionally practiced an initial

---

[2] The authors' comment: "It often happens that the mother's relatives are the ones best known to her children, even, in [some] cases, to the entire ignorance of the father's kin. Informants born and reared in the *shtetl* area have told us of never having met paternal grandparents, especially the paternal grandfather, until the age of thirteen or fourteen" (1950:452).

uxorilocal residence pattern called *kest*, in which a young couple lived with, and were supported by, the bride's parents for a period stipulated in the marriage contract; this pattern, too, could have conceivably contributed to a matrilineal emphasis. If confirmed, such a matrilineal trend in memorial practice would contradict the patrilineal ideology of Jewish family life.

Another important structural feature of Jewish life is the pervasive sense of community that Jews have fostered among themselves before and since the Diaspora. Jews have lived their complementary lives, as family and as community members, with equal intensity, and there are several ways in which the individual involvement at both these social levels is revealed in memorial practices. For example, death notices are displayed in public places in many New York Jewish communities, and funeral services, especially for particularly righteous persons, become as much communal as family affairs. In the culture of the *shtetl*, all the members of a community would memorialize a well-loved scholar or rabbi, for the deceased's spirit was believed to watch over and guard the village as it had in life. Such a communal orientation in mourning observances, in which death is seen as affecting "the entire group and not only the surviving relatives...", has applied, generally speaking, from biblical times to the present day, in relatively self-contained Jewish communities. To the members of a *shtetl* community, the *shtetl* itself was an extended family, and in death, as in all life crises, both the family and the community took an active part.

These communal overtones are further emphasized by the fact that the recitation of major memorial prayers, such as *Kaddish* and *Yizkor*, can only occur in the presence of a *minyan*, a group of ten adult Jewish males. Hence, these are often said in a communal context at a synagogue. One rabbinical commentator on Jewish mourning has observed:

The Jewish experience has taught that such values as peace and life, and the struggle to bring heaven down to earth, of which the *Kaddish* speaks, can be achieved only in concert with society, and proclaimed amidst friends and neighbors of the same faith (Lamm 1969:163–164).

There are other ways in which the community has become both a participant in and repository for the memorialization of the dead. Prominent public places have often been used by a dead person's survivors to commemorate his or her memory. Since at least Roman times, a prime means of doing this has been by making contributions to synagogues in the name of the deceased; traditionally, such acts are publicly advertised by the display of permanent plaques or mosaics in the temple bearing the names of the donors and the person being commemorated. This practice is still followed extensively among Ashkenazim in the United States. In a similar vein, it is customary for a person reciting *Yizkor* in a synagogue to make a donation to the temple on behalf of the deceased. Zenner notes:

> In both Israel and the United States, Jewish religious and secular institutions are full of plaques which are in honor of a contributor and in memory of that person's deceased relations. In one synagogue, even the fluorescent lights contained the name of a contributor. Synagogue ornaments, Israeli forests, and institutional buildings commonly are named in memory of deceased relations of the contributors. The relations remembered are generally parents, spouses, siblings, and children of the donors (1965:482–483).

Four things are accomplished simultaneously by means of these charitable acts. First, the deceased is memorialized, and he or she is honored by means of an act of generosity and charity — actions that are among the most righteous and praiseworthy that a Jew can perform. Second, as one Yiddish saying goes: "Charity saves from death" (from Proverbs 10:2), and so generous individuals are both honoring a kinsman and thereby assuring their own good fate in the afterlife. "Thus, he who performs a good deed is taking out 'afterlife insurance in *Olam Habo*,' the world to come."[3] Third, and most visible in the case of memorial plaques, the deceased's memory is enshrined and displayed in such a way and in such a place that the whole community of worshippers has its attention drawn to the deceased and his or her name, and the memory is thus guaranteed of perpetuation, honor, and homage as long as the synagogue or institution itself shall survive. Fourth, and perhaps less consciously, the deceased's surviving kin have drawn attention and honor to themselves as well, for each thought of the dead that the plaque invokes carries with it a reminder of the concern, love, and respect that the dead person's family bore the deceased both before and after the demise. As was customary in the *shtetl* concerning all such benevolent acts, people thus publicly displayed their generosity and their care for family, and thereby demonstrated the increase in their personal *zkhus* [merit] (Zborowski and Herzog 1962:196–197). Memorials at the communal level thus become a commemoration for the dead and self-advertisements for the living.

Memorial plaques and *Yahrzeit* candles provide a physical clue to the structure and function of memorial practices, and there are a number of other visible symbols that also reflect in part the content of Jewish ancestral behavior. These other symbols include annual grave visits, the recitation of *Yizkor* and *Kaddish* by the deceased's survivors, the display of memorabilia in family homes, and the names borne by a person's descendants. Particular given names, for example, may be passed on

---

[3] Zborowski and Herzog (1962:195). Cf. the latter's comments (1962:191–213) for an extended discussion of the place that charity occupies in traditional Jewish culture and psychology. Trachtenberg (1970:157) provides some specific examples from the medieval period of Ashkenazic Jewry.

indefinitely within family lines; and since the bearer of a name is believed to honor and incorporate the nobler qualities of his or her namesake, there is created a conscious sense of continuity and identity, which, at a given point in a family's history, may often include the living memory of individuals whose lifetimes cover a span of four or five generations. Furthermore, the structure of the naming pattern offers a good reflection of the bilaterality of the Jewish family kindred: individuals may be named in memory of either male or female ancestors on both their father's and their mother's side.

Psychodynamics

Psychodynamically, Jews experience a strong sense of obligation toward parents and ancestors, including the obligation to honor their wishes and ideals and prove oneself worthy of their heritage. This behavioral pattern is reinforced and given poignancy by parental adherence to an ethic of suffering and sacrifice for one's progeny. *Alles for die kindere* [everything for the children] is a saying that embodies the parental ideal that life is lived for the sake of one's offspring, and that all necessary sacrifices are to be made on their behalf. While the content of the maxim carries with it an air of altruism, Jewish family life also possesses a strong undercurrent of obligation and indebtedness. The children are repeatedly — sometimes directly, sometimes indirectly — reminded of the parental sacrifices that have been made for them, and so they grow up with a strong consciousness of their parents' expectations and hopes. In the United States, as Zborowski and Herzog note for the *shtetl*: "Children are reminded constantly of all their parents have done and suffered in their behalf" (1962:294).

Balancing this sense of obligation is an awareness of the advantages which individuals acquire as part of their ancestral heritage, that is, a person benefits reciprocally from the reputation and accomplishments of one's forbears through *yikhus ovos*, which is high status based upon one's ancestry and genealogy. In the *shtetl*, the number of learned and wealthy individuals that a person could count among the family ancestors was a prime determinant of one's social position. This form of ancestral status and self-consciousness still persists among Jews of Ashkenazic descent in the United States. People are quick to point out that their ancestors in Eastern Europe were *sheyneh layt* [literally "beautiful people," that is, high class, learned, and/or wealthy] rather than *prosteh vidn* [low class, working, or common Jews].

Individuals are thus proud and fortunate to have learned persons or rich individuals in their genealogies, for such people can thus invoke *zkhus ovos* [the merits of their ancestors] when appealing to God for help.

The ancestral merit of this kin can benefit not only individuals, but families and communities as well. The influence of a righteous man is indeed great, as Zenner (1965:482) notes, for he "may protect or atone for his ancestors, his contemporaries and his posterity, through his righteous deeds." People who enjoy high status and spiritual help based on *yikhus ovos* and *zkhus ovos* thus live their lives against a backdrop of family and community history, and they are consequently likely to feel a strong sense of indebtedness to their ancestors, coupled with the obligation to honor and to prove themselves worthy of this ancestral inheritance and merit.

Within this psychological context of sacrifice, expectation, and honor, homage to significant ancestors may be shown in a number of ways; these include not only such aspects of formal worship as *Yahrzeit* lights and the recitation of *Kaddish* and *Yizkor*, but also the fulfillment of the deceased's wishes by those still living. Parents and elderly Jews give frequent expression to their concern for what they want their descendants to achieve in life. The Jewish concept of *naches*, denoting the joy and gratification enjoyed by a person because the worthy actions of someone else both please and favorably reflect upon him or her, is most salient within the realm of kinsmen. Parents and grandparents look to their descendants, rather than to their own accomplishments, as the prime source of their *naches*: for a person to give a parent or grandparent *naches* is to perform a great secular *mitzvah* [good deed]. The establishment of a family, the pursuit of righteousness, the love of learning, and the rewards of a profession — these and other goals may be urged upon a child or adult, either directly by an elderly grandparent or, indirectly, through the invocation of a deceased parent's or grandparent's memory by a concerned and psychologically subtle parent. Childhood and later life are thus experienced against a backdrop of ancestry and with a sense of continuity that links the hopes of one generation with the accomplishments of another.

The psychological efficacy of these family patterns rests upon a mutual dependency between elders and youngsters and between the living and the dead. The young depend upon their elders, not only for physical necessities and emotional support, but for approval and validation as well. Parents honored in life may be further honored in death, and the neglect of parents' wishes during their lifetimes may be compensated after their demise.

Conversely, the living look upon their eventual death with a comparable sense of dependency directed toward their survivors and descendants. The living are very concerned about how their survivors will remember and honor them after their death. Religious Jews are especially anxious for an heir — particularly a male heir — so that there will be someone to say *Kaddish* for them upon their demise; their happiness and security in the afterlife and their chance to avoid the dismalness of *Gehinnom* are believed to rest upon the efficacy of this prayer and the regularity and sincerity of its recitation.

The problem of family psychodynamics warrants some special consideration of the role of women and mothers within the theoretically patriarchal Jewish households. Mothers often have a predominant position of power and moral authority, and their sway over husbands and children is notable as their induction of feelings of guilt and obligation in their children is pervasive and characteristic. In seeking to understand some of the structural and psychological dynamics of these situations, it is relevant to consider the jural and legal position of women in Jewish culture. First, Jewish women are in possession of fewer rights and privileges than are men; and if women are to express themselves and realize their capacities, they have to do it outside of the economic, political, scholastic, and religious spheres permitted to men. The household and its family members, on the other hand, provide an arena where women are not nearly as restricted as they are outside the home, and the concentration of their expressive and instrumental activities into these channels thus becomes comprehensible. If husbands and children are one of the main creative and expressive outlets available to women in Jewish culture, then the emotional investment by women in their spouses and offspring is an understandable consequence; and the development of certain psychodynamic bonds between them, such as guilt, resentment, and obligation, is an expected outcome.

Given these family and ancestral pressures upon Jews, there are a number of ways in which resentment and guilt may arise within families. The dynamics of guilt within the family may have several sources; for one, persons may be oppressed by the sense that they mistreated the deceased during his or her life, perhaps through stinginess, a lack of care, or a failure of understanding. In the case of the death of an elderly parent, if the later years were characterized by declining health and were spent in a nursing home, hospital, or similar setting, where people other than one's own children cared for the parent, then the children may be particularly susceptible to guilt feelings over their lack of commitment and personal attention to the stricken parent. Grown children who have lived their adult lives with an intense awareness of what their parents wanted them to become and to accomplish, but who feel that their lives have been an inadequate realization of their parents' dreams, may experience self-recrimination and shame along with the guilt occasioned by a parents' death. A married person who has lost a spouse may suffer a comparable sense of personal failure and inadequacy if the spouse's death engenders feelings that one never provided for or treated the deceased with the care, consideration, and consistency that was deserved and that one had promised. Guilt may also arise from the unresolved resentments, quarrels, and jealousies of the relationship, the psychological residue of which becomes especially oppressive when death seems to prevent any possible reconciliation. The death itself even may be a cause of anger and resentment, stemming from the sense of loss, abandonment, and rejection experienced by the survivors.

In each of these circumstances, Jewish memorial practices provide a number of ways for dealing with the emotions involved. People may try to achieve forgiveness from the dead through certain customary procedures. In one such observance, when a dead person lies on his deathbed, it is customary for relatives, neighbors, friends, and acquaintances to "ask pardon" of the deceased "for all possible insults or offenses they may have inflicted on him during his life." One Israeli custom "has the mourners place a stone on the covered grave and ask forgiveness for any injustice they may have committed against the deceased" (Lamm 1969:67).

Of deeper psychological import are those memorial observances whose purpose is to display respect and reverence for the deceased. *Kaddish*, *Yizkor*, and *Yahrzeit* are prayers said at periodic intervals over a long span of time, and they thus serve to maintain a tie with the deceased and exhibit the sincerity of the mourner's love. The necessary recitation of the first two prayers in a congregational setting, among a group of fellow-mourners, provides the bereaved with a continual reintegration into the community and its supporting sentiments and is thus productive of a sense of comfort and consolation.

Mourners may derive satisfaction not only through directing their prayers and thoughts to the deceased, but they may also reinforce their own convictions regarding the sincerity of their feelings and sense of bereavement. Guilt and grief may thus be simultaneously assuaged.

Naming one's child after a deceased parent or grandparent also provides a highly visible embodiment of respect and continuity. Traditional Jews are especially concerned about having their spirit and memory perpetuated by means of their name. As one Hebrew text says, "A man's name is his person" and "His name is his soul" (cf. Trachtenberg 1970:78). It is considered to be a personal and family tragedy if individuals lack descendants who could honor and perpetuate their memory in this way: "for a namesake is another link with the continuing community" (Zborowski and Herzog 1962:321). In traditional families, where such a naming pattern is followed, a young child will be reminded of the ancestor after whom he or she has been named, and special emphasis is often put on the personal qualities of the deceased, which the child is expected to emulate. Here again, then, a memorial observance weaves the threads of history and morality into the fabric of a young person's life and takes a life from the past — a memory, an ancestor, and a name — as a model for the present.

While not an orthodox practice, many Jews do direct certain memorial prayers to the deceased themselves, often asking for forgiveness, aid, or advice, or inviting the departed to share in some *naches* that the family or community is enjoying. It is customary to visit gravesites during times of individual or family crises, and the anxiety-ridden person may seek to communicate by prayer with a deceased parent, grandparent, or spouse, asking them for guidance or for help in a dilemma. Trachtenberg (1970:64) notes that, in the medieval and subsequent periods, there has always been a belief that the deceased could help the living, especially the righteous and the related among the departed. Thus, "the ancient practice of visiting the cemetery to entreat the good offices of deceased relatives or scholars persisted. . . . In addition to such individual visits, there grew up the custom of the entire congregation repairing to the cemetery annually on several occasions . . . 'that the dead may beseech mercy on our behalf.' " Another type of communication between the living and the departed is reflected in the dream folklore of the *shtetl*, which "abounds in anecdotes of fathers, mothers, grandparents, rabbis, who appeared in dreams to save someone [or a community] from disaster or point the way to success. . . . [In sum, then], the deceased continues to live within the community" (Zborowski and Herzog 1962:310–311, 380).

Charity, as we have seen, may also provide an avenue for memorializing the deceased and maintaining ancestral ties. As an illustration of this, we cite the case of one female informant in New York who keeps a *pishke* [charity box] in her desk drawer — a *pishke* to which her recently deceased mother had regularly made contributions. Whenever this woman's own children face a crisis, such as an important job interview or a school exam, she places some coins in the *pishke* and calls on her mother to intercede on the children's behalf. This woman also keeps her deceased mother informed of family *naches*, such as good school report cards, weddings, and births and places money in the *pishke* on each of these occasions as a charitable thanks-offering.

This case is neither unique nor isolated, because Jewish folk practice, both in New York and Eastern Europe, seems to have consistently held to such beliefs, even in the face of orthodox disclaimers. Relationships between the living and the dead were thus viewed in terms of a reciprocity of interest and influence. For the believing but somewhat less-than-orthodox Jew, one can thus reestablish, through memorialism, the kind of dependencies that one had with the dead during their lifetime. From this mutual interdependence between the living and the dead, one thereby achieves the kind of comfort that can be derived from continuing intergenerational ties beyond the individual's lifetime. Dependency, comfort, and continuity, so intrinsic to the ethics and psychodynamics of the Jewish family and community, acquire a degree of permanence and pervasiveness through their embodiment in the mechanics of memorialism.

Death can also be an intensely moral experience among Jews. It is in regard to this ethical dimension that memorial observances may involve the individual and the family in a wider sense of communal and ethnic responsibility. Through the experience of guilt, remorse, and bereavement, a sense of moral obligation can be reawakened or created in individuals to better fulfill their parents' hopes and dreams — a moral sense often involving the consequent need to reform their lives. The dual intimations of mortality and responsibility, which are reinforced by repetitive memorial practices over time, may thus impel family members to treat kin and community members more humanely and adhere more closely to the moral tenets of the religion and the community. Since such a consciousness is usually phrased and experienced in terms of one's proper behavior "as a Jew," there is also a reaffirmation of one's collective responsibility and conscience in the community of *Klal Isroel*, the Jewish people.

The intensified sense of mortality may not only lead to a personal reformation, but it may also alter an individual's perception of specific family ties. A surviving spouse or child may turn to his or her own child as a means for fulfilling the dreams and wishes of the deceased spouse or parent, just as the mourner may now see that same child as his or her own vehicle for personal immortality. The obligatory period of joint family mourning, *shiva*, and the somewhat less intense period of *shloshim*, fully bringing together by force the spouse, children, and siblings of the deceased into a therapeutic community of brief duration, provides a setting in which a range of contradictory emotions may be resolved, just as it simultaneously allows the family to draw lessons from the life of the deceased by remembering and recreating his or her personality and life history. The reunion of the mourning group at the time of the unveiling of the deceased's gravemarker again illustrates the repetitive nature of memorialism, a feature that enhances its moral and psychological efficacy. While Jewish memorial beliefs do not attribute to the dead the kind of jural authority that anthropologists have identified in some other cultural systems of ancestor worship, Jewish patterns do enable the deceased to exercise a degree of moral authority and to convey a sense of comfort and dependency that may even exceed that which they exercised in life.

The moral experience of death, like other aspects of Jewish memorialism, also has a dimension of reciprocity to it, that is, as a complement to the notion of ancestor *zkhus*, it is possible for the living to have a moral impact upon the dead, a feature that finds its embodiment in the concept of "the merit of the children." Adults whose lives were marked by faults and vices may be redeemed after their death through the exemplary behavior of their progeny. Both their memory in the community and their fate in *Olam Habo* may be blessed and preserved by virtue of their children's merit. While parents cannot redeem an erring child by virtue of their own good deeds: "The reverse is possible! The deeds of the child *can* redeem the life of the parent, even after the parent's death. It is a neat reversal, a 'merit of the children' " (Lamm 1969:159–160).

Finally, the moral experience of death can occur not only at the individual and family levels, engendering in these persons a communal consciousness, but also, structurally and psychodynamically, whereupon the moral impact of death can be seen to operate at the actual level of the community itself. The community not only participates in the funeral, but it traditionally takes over the responsibility for funeral and burial arrangements for the bereaved family, just as the community bears a corporate responsibility to support scholars, widows, orphans, and the indigent. The death of a great scholar, rabbi, or leader may prompt a community, by means of various memorial practices, to restate and reaffirm his ideals; to renew a sense of moral commitment and purpose; and often to institutionalize the continuity of the deceased's work and memory through a memorial fund, the creation of scholarships, or the formation of an association, school, or other institution dedicated to his ideals. While certain medieval Ashkenazic beliefs emphasized the punitive, retributive, and threatening nature of deceased spirits and couched the language of death and mourning with many euphemisms, more recently, contemporary Jews appear to have played down these aspects of belief in comparison to the supportive and moral role of the deceased.

The members of a community may observe *Kaddish*, *Yizkor*, and *Yahrzeit* for an honored person, just as they would for a member of their own family; they thereby reflect the familial nature of the Jewish community and the congregational nature of the Jewish family. One can suggest that perhaps compensating for the relatively shallow genealogical depth of Jewish familial memorialism is the great breadth of its communal dimension. While these community practices may fall short of the actual worship of the deceased or the bureaucratization of his or her charisma, they may, in fact, constitute the communalization of his or her memory and morality.

At this larger structural level, the community thus does for itself what the congregation does for the individual mourner. Mourners, through necessarily communal participation in the more formalized aspects of memorial observance, renew their sense of affiliation with Jewish history and custom and the Jewish people, and they benefit from the comfort of tradition and a sense of dependency on the community, God, and their ancestors. Just as individual mourners recite *Kaddish* in a community of mourners and thereby call to the attention of others their grief, loss, and piety, now the community itself calls the individuals' attention to this greater loss and involves them in a community that is itself bereaved.

These multilevel psychodynamic effects illustrate the relationship of ancestral practices to social solidarity and continuity. In the Jewish case, the dimensions of solidarity and the depth of continuity are broader and deeper than are those of some other cultural systems; solidarity and continuity are simultaneously familial, communal, and "national," but since jural authority rests more with Talmudic tradition and rabbinical precedent than with the ancestors, the focus is more on moral authority, which finds its sources in the existential, historical, and ancestral forces that animate the individual's life.

DISCUSSION

Historically, ancestor memorialism has been an important component of both Jewish and Japanese folk religion since the earliest of recorded times. Its significance, however, in the prevalent religious orthodoxies of the two peoples is quite different. In Japan, ancestor memorialism plays an important role in Buddhist and Shintō rites. In orthodox Judaism, on the other hand, ancestor worship, as well as many of the aspects of ancestor memorialism described here, are specifically condemned by Jewish religious authorities. A number of functional models can be erected that could conceivably account for this difference, but a historical inquiry into its origins is well beyond the scope of this study.

At the structural level of analysis one finds that, while both cultures employ kinship terminologies that reflect bilaterality, the lineal parent-child relationship is expanded into a descent ideology that employs ancestor reverence as a major theme. Among Japanese, the focus of this ideology is the household, although it may be extended to the national level via the concept of the family-state. In the Jewish case, the focus has been the local community, with historical extensions to the broader concept of the "People of Israel." The rural *shtetls* of Eastern Europe provided a prime social context within which deceased persons were memorialized, and this has been continued, to some extent, among Ashkenazic Jews in the United States. Our pilot study (in New York City and its suburbs) of the saying of *Kaddish*, the lighting of *Yahrzeit* candles, and the naming of children after ancestors shows that spouses separately memorialize the dead of their natal families — there is no Jewish equivalent for the Japanese *ie* [a vertical lineage consisting of member families, living and dead, which are all related by blood lineally and collaterally].

At the psychological level of analysis are many similarities in the emotional content of the memorial practices of the two peoples that arise from similar childrearing experiences. Japanese and Jewish children are highly prone to feelings of guilt when they fail to meet expectations as communicated to them by their parents. And parents in both societies, especially the mother, are able to produce this response by their expressions of pain and self-sacrifice when a child fails to achieve objectively stated goals. Furthermore, rejection of family and community dependence is both difficult and laden with anxiety, so that memorial practices find suitable psychological support.

If the supposition that similarities in childrearing experiences, together with their consequences with regard to personality formation and family dynamics, account for the observed similarities in Jewish and Japanese memorial customs, then this conclusion may be of help in the resolution of certain questions regarding Japanese memorial practices. Smith (1966), Plath (1964), and Ooms (1976) have presented data that answer the questions: "Who are the ancestors?" "What emotions do they engender?" and "How are they symbolized?" They show how the identification of the ancestors is related to household structure, how their assumed emotional attributes are related to the institutional molding of affect, and how the symbolic conceptualization of the ancestors is structurally similar to the life cycle of the living. Yet, when one considers the question of why there are ancestral practices in Japanese society, one is not quite satisfied with the answers provided. Smith alludes to the force of tradition, though it was not his objective to answer why, but rather, who. Ooms (1976) points out that most Japanese no longer believe in the reality of ancestral spirits or in their ability to affect the living, an observation that we suspect is equally true of American Jews. At one point, he attributes the continuation of Japanese memorial practices to the emotions they induce, without indicating why these emotions should provide sufficient motivation. Later, he suggests that contemporary Japanese memorial rites have been weakened by semantic depletion and that they now exist as survivals perpetuated by a kind of historical momentum. To illustrate their terminal state, he reports the view of an informant who felt that "ancestor worship was meaningless and rather a burden," though this informant also reported that she would eventually undertake these activities at the proper time. Plath suggested that Japanese ancestor worship provides its adherents with comfort and emotional security due to the importance of maintaining family ties — ties that include those between the living and the dead. With regard to the emotional content of these ties, he noted that hostility directed toward the ancestors is suppressed and that they are thought to be benevolent and concerned with the welfare of their descendants.

In our view, Japanese ancestor memorialism is not perpetuated by tradition, nor by the feeling of security it provides in Plath's sense. In light of our comparison with Jewish data, we conclude that ancestor memorialism among Jews and Japanese exists as an expressive model of idealized social relations through which participants overcome feelings of hostility and personal deprivation.[4] Human institutions, such as the family, are often less than perfect and seldom wholly satisfying to individual members. Cooperation within any cultural enterprise is likely to involve certain psychic costs — costs that somehow must be accounted for and justified. Within the memorial practices of Jews and Japanese, the attitudes of gratitude and dependence that are stressed would, when sincerely felt, promote cooperation, but the rites also stress an identification of oneself with one's ancestors who are the forbears of one's living group to the extent that any sacrifice for it is equally a sacrifice for oneself. Lebra (1976) notes that members of one Japanese religious sect specifically equate ancestor worship with self-worship. Wimberley (1969, 1972) also noted that members of the Japanese religion Seichō-no-Ie hold a similar view.

We do not suggest that ancestor memorialism among Jews and Japanese exists solely to contain hostility, expiate guilt, and promote selfless devotion to one's group. Other ends may equally be served. In the Japanese case, however, it is notable that, where ancestors are held responsible for the suffering of their descendants, the social affairs of the descendants are seldom in order. Lebra notes that this disorder need not arise from the simultaneous application of different principles of social organization, in which case a structural explanation would be called for, but rather, that it typically arises from various individual circumstances. What is particularly impressive about her findings is that again and again, the reason given for ancestors having harmed a descendant is not that they were acting in the capacity of moral arbiters, but rather, because they desired assistance. In short, they needed a descendant on whom they could depend, as do the living with regard to each other. In the Seichō-no-Ie case, the prevailing view is that, if one gets right with one's ancestors, one will get right with one another.

In this paper, a synoptic view of memorialism among American Jews is presented and discussed with regard to its form and significance as it relates to a further understanding of Japanese memorial practices. At this juncture, we suggest that detailed case studies of instances of Jewish memorial activities be undertaken either to establish or to disprove our expectation that the intensity with which they are undertaken is related to the degree of self-deprivation and hostility engendered within the individual by the group with which he or she is identified. Furthermore, we suspect that, as a result of memorial practices, the participant becomes less individuated and comes to see self-sacrifice for the group as an objective good.

[4] For a bibliography and discussion of expressive models as cultural units related to the resolution of psychological conflict, see Roberts and Ridgeway (1969:223–245).

REFERENCES

FREEDMAN, MAURICE
1958 *Lineage organization in southeastern China.* London School of Economics Monographs in Social Anthropology 18. London: Athlone.

LAMM, MAURICE
1969 *The Jewish way in death and mourning.* New York: Jonathan David.

LANDES, RUTH, MARK ZBOROWSKI
1950 Hypotheses concerning the eastern Jewish family. *Psychiatry* 13:447–464.

LEBRA, TAKIE SUGIYAMA
1976 "Ancestral influence on the suffering of descendants in a Japanese cult," in *Ancestors.* Edited by William H. Newell, 219–230. The Hague: Mouton.

OOMS, HERMAN
1976 "A structural analysis of Japanese ancestral rites and beliefs," in *Ancestors.* Edited by William H. Newell, 61–90. The Hague: Mouton.

PLATH, DAVID W.
1964 Where the family of God is the family. *American Anthropologist* 66:300–317.

POLLACK, HERMAN
1971 *Jewish folkways in Germanic lands (1648–1806).* Cambridge, Mass.: M.I.T. Press.

ROBERTS, JOHN M., CECILIA RIDGEWAY
1969 Musical involvement and talking. *Anthropological Linguistics* 11:223–245.

SMITH, ROBERT J.
1966 *Ihai:* mortuary tablets, the household and kin in Japan. *Transactions of the Asiatic Society in Japan*, third series (9):1–20.

TRACHTENBERG, JOSHUA
1970 *Jewish magic and superstition — a study in folk religion.* New York: Atheneum.

WIMBERLEY, HOWARD
1969 Self-realization and the ancestors: an analysis of two Japanese ritual procedures for achieving domestic harmony. *Anthropological Quarterly* 42:37–51.
1972 The knights of the golden lotus. *Ethnology* 11:173–186.

ZBOROWSKI, MARK, ELIZABETH HERZOG
1962 *Life is with people.* New York: Schocken.

ZENNER, WALTER P.
1965 Memorialism — some Jewish examples. *American Anthropologist* 67:481–483.

Some Functional and Structural Aspects of Family Life in a Communal Society: The Financial Sector of the Kibbutz Family

FRITS J. M. SELIER

The form of family life that developed in the Israeli kibbutz during the first decades of the twentieth century was entirely different from that prevailing in the countries of origin of the kibbutz founders, who were mainly East European immigrants, and showed no similarities to the Western family pattern.[1] In the kibbutz, important family tasks were taken over by communal institutions, and family life met with remarkable reserve, sometimes with opposition. Since the establishment of the first kibbutz in 1909, however, various internal sociocultural changes have brought important modifications in the kibbutz movement, so that the kibbutz of today differs in many respects from the settlement of 1909. The kibbutzim have evolved from *community-centered* to *family-centered* communities, though not all at the same rate: some kibbutzim have remained more community-centered than others.[2] The kibbutz family has come to resemble increasingly an average Western urban family in which the wife works outside the home. The family has been, as it were, "emancipated," and has regained a great deal of its traditional functions and importance. Still, to the Western observer it does not look familiar; the communal kitchen and dining hall, and the collective educational system that most kibbutzim practice, are in themselves enough to show that the difference with the Western family is considerable.[3]

My investigations were made in 1968 and again in 1971. The first time was in the framework for an M.A. in cultural anthropology at Amsterdam University. The second time was with a grant from the Netherlands Organization for Pure Research.

[1] See Appendix 1.
[2] This is also pointed out by Ellemers (1962:343). Talmon-Garber (1965a) uses it for her typology of different collective settlements.
[3] In a slowly increasing number of kibbutzim of the ideologically most moderate federation "Ichud Kahvutzot Vehakibbutzim," children now again sleep in their parents' house. Some of the oldest settlements never introduced the collective system of education.

This article describes the financial function of the kibbutz family in various sociocultural circumstances. A developmental background, discussion of the distribution of family tasks between marital partners (the conjugal organization), and other aspects of kibbutz life are used to show the modifications in the financial sector of family life, which are the main focus of this paper.

FAMILY AND COMMUNAL LIFE: A DILEMMA

A *communal group* may be described as a social group in which the interpersonal relationships are especially of a spontaneous, informal, and primary nature. By definition, such a group cannot be large. Implicit in the concept is the express endeavor of the members of the group to act conjointly in as many respects as possible (collective organization).[4] All group members identify intensely with this objective. The commune differs in this respect from other social groups, such as the army, where a certain amount of joint action is among the paramount values.

The communal group is, moreover, characterized by some form of collective ownership of property and often by the principle of sexual equality. This last feature does not, in the author's opinion, belong in a general definition, for in some communal groups, such as the Hutterites in North America, there is considerable differentiation of rights and duties between the sexes.

The strong identification with group aims may be due to the fact that the group is a *Wahlverwandtschaft* ["based on a spontaneous communion of kindred souls ..." (Talmon-Garber 1965b:261)]. The commune is then an *intentional* group; it is explicitly intended for its common way of life. The group members are above all united by their desire to realize a communal life. In such a group, ascriptive ties play no role; group membership is based on equality of aim only. Schmalenbach's concept (1961:331–347) of *bund* applies here as well. The *bund* results from a voluntary choice made by persons who know they are bound by the same ideals. Identification with group values and group aims, often revolutionary in character, may be so intense precisely because group membership rests on idealism and free choice. Schmalenbach remarks further that a social group that is primarily based on a common ideal demanding great devotion and sacrifice from the individual will often constitute a precarious and unstable social system. For such an exacting ideal can usually only

---

[4] A collective organization is characteristic also of consanguineous groups such as the *extended family*. Its members are an economic and sometimes also a domestic unit. However, members of this group were born in it, whereas members of the communal group joined voluntarily.

be kept up in a "state of emotional ecstasy," which is often "a fleeting thing."

Communal groups, however, frequently have *functional* aspects as well. Often they are born from necessity or viewed as a means to a specific end outside the ideal of communal life. Apart from the common ideology, an antagonistic external situation (*frontier situation*) may make some form of collective organization desirable. The communal way of life is then seen as the one suitable way to survive hostile opposition or economic hardship.

Another term demanding our attention is *familism* which has been defined as a "form of social organization in which the interests of the individual are subordinated to those of the family group (Heller 1970:73). This definition can be accepted, but with the addition that not only the interests of the individual, but also the interests of the community are subordinated to those of the family (see also Banfield 1958). *Antifamilism* may then take the form of individualism or collectivism.

The communal society is characterized by collectivism, not only on account of its collective organization, but also because of its antifamilistic viewpoint. The family and the encompassing communal group are, in a sense, contradictory social institutions: "There is a certain incompatibility between commitment to a radical revolutionary ideology and intense collective identification on the one hand and family solidarity on the other" (Talmon-Garber 1965b:260–261). Or, formulated in Parsonian terms: "Family ties are based on an exclusive and particularistic loyalty which sets the members of the family more or less apart from the rest of their comrades.... Families may easily become ... foci of intense emotional involvement and infringe on the loyalties to the collective" (Talmon-Garber 1965b:261).[5]

For this reason, groups for which community life is a supreme value are often antifamilistic.[6] The communal way of life itself makes for limitation of place and meaning of the family, because its collective institutions fulfill the tasks that are elsewhere carried out by the family. The communal ideology, moreover, put social mechanisms into operation to eliminate, or at least reduce to a minimum, any phenomena that threaten community life.

---

[5] The divisive power of family life in a larger community is also found in the modern west European communal movement (Koinonia 1970:24). Campbell (1964) described this function of the family in his study of a Greek shepherd's community. Gluckman (1950:76–77) and Lutfiyya (1966:180) did the same for an African and Arabic situation respectively. See also Bott (1964) and Talmon-Garber (1962).

[6] Antifamilism is found in the Japanese "kibbutz" (a collective settlement after Israeli example), see Yamare (n.d.), and in several American communal groups, both religious and socialist, in history as well as contemporary, see Hinds (1878); Bestor (1959); Holloway (1966); Bennett (1967) and Hostetler (1967). Coser (1951) reported on the antifamilistic politics of early Russian communism. Collective groups organized from necessity or as a means to achieve a military end often have an antifamilistic trait, see Gluckman (1950).

Although it is true that the family and the collective are competing foci of emotional involvement and identification, they are not incompatible social facts. A controlled coexistence is possible, though at the expense of both family and communal life.

The Israeli kibbutz is one example of communal life. It has the features of both an intentional and a functional communal group.[7] In the kibbutz, the antifamilistic attitude is reinforced by an emphasis on sex equality.[8] Initially, such traditional family tasks as housekeeping and childrearing are felt to hamper the wife in finding full scope for her abilities. Collective organization is looked upon as providing one of the solutions for this problem.

COLLECTIVE CONSUMPTION: FROM "COMMUNE OF POVERTY" TO "COMMUNE OF PLENTY"

In the kibbutz, both production and consumption are collectively organized. Up to about 1935, the collective settlements were characterized by an exceedingly close-knit communal life and a pronounced antifamilistic position. Marriage and family life received scant attention. Marriage was regarded as a purely private matter that should not manifest itself in community life. The wedding was not ritually underlined; the man and wife simply asked for a room, and when this was allocated to them, their union was socially accepted. Such symbols as wedding rings were not used. In public, man and wife were expected to emphasize their role of *chaver* or *chavera* (comrade, fellow kibbutz member) rather than that of spouse. And even within the family "... relations ... were patterned to a large extent on relations between comembers and emphasized equality and companionship" (Talmon-Garber 1965b:266).

Publicly demonstrated mutual affection was ridiculed. Kinship terms were avoided: children called their parents by their given names; spouses talked about each other as "comrade ...," often followed by the given name. Married couples tending to withdraw too often to their rooms were strongly condemned (see for this and other antifamilist symptoms, for instance, Spiro 1954; Talmon-Garber 1965b). Family life hardly existed.

---

[7] Talmon-Garber (1965b), explaining the rise of the Israeli kibbutz, distinguishes between ideological and situational factors. For the ideological factor (in European youth movements), see Meier-Cronemeyer (1969) and Becker (1946). Also see (in Marxist Zionism), Spiro (1956). For the kibbutz as a reaction to the traditional East European way of life, see Schwartz (1950) and Diamond (1957). Viteles (1967:1–69) gives interesting details on the situational factors.

[8] Aspiration for equality between man and wife is no prerequisite for a communal society. The Hutterites of North America, a community in many respects comparable to the kibbutz, know a very traditional and authoritarian man-wife relationship (Bennet 1967; Barkin and Bennett n.d.; Hostetler 1967).

In most kibbutzim, children did not sleep with their parents; instead they were housed and educated collectively. Domestic and nursing family tasks were practically nonexistent in this phase. Even the function of the family in the sphere of reproduction was limited and the birthrate was kept low for a long time.

While antifamilism was imposed by ideological factors and the communal way of life, it was also due to economic circumstances. In this period, the kibbutz was a "commune of poverty" (Leon 1969:82). Everything the members possessed had to be given up for the purpose of economic construction. The fulfillment of either familial or individual needs was out of the question.

The distribution system in this phase, known as *communa alef* [first commune] was determined by the ideal that each gave according to his or her capacity and received according to his or her needs, irrespective of personal abilities, work capacities, or personal tastes and preferences. The family played no part as a single unit. Goods were distributed to individual kibbutz members and children, with the married couple only counting as one unit in the distribution of living space.

The room, as the apartment for man and wife was called, was scantily furnished for a long time. Most kibbutzim started as tent-camps. Later, it became possible to build simple wooden barracks, which could be imaginatively furnished by the occupants themselves ("We lived on orange crates"). Not much furniture was required because the room was minute and served for resting and sleeping only. For recreation, the members went to the common hall, the only space that could be lighted and heated and the only place where they could find more or less comfortable chairs, a newspaper, and a radio. The image of the kibbutz inhabitants spending their evenings folk dancing and community singing dates from this earlier period. They also took all meals in the communal hall as there was nothing to make "eating at home" possible in the rooms.

Clothing was regarded as collective property. Members took their washing to the common laundry and received other garments in return, often from the top of the pile, regardless of size or preference (see also Spiro 1956:21, Stern 1965:52). All attention was directed to work. Neglecting one's personal appearance and wearing obviously used work-clothing were regarded as signs of industry.[9] What was not covered with the dust of labor, was soon looked upon as a luxury, superfluous and often called bourgeois. The women desired to participate in kibbutz life in as great equality with men as possible. All this is evident in the concept of *chalutziut* [a complex of values and attitudes that ideally should characterize the true pioneer who was expected to be concerned with nothing but

---

[9] Abraham Slonsky's song about the members of the third aliya (immigration wave) glorifying poverty and shabby clothes has become well known.

labor]. If possible, this ethic consisted of working the soil with bare hands.[10]

Gradually, in the *communa beet* [second commune], the distribution of goods was to some extent regulated and standardized. In many respects, it still depended on the direct needs of the members, but for some articles, distribution became subject to general rules. At the same time, however, attempts were made to allow some scope to personal preference.

In this phase, the older settlements began to show the first signs of prosperity, and the ascetic and consistently task-oriented pioneer mentality began to bear fruit. As the kibbutzim consolidated their economic positions, ideological reformulation allowed for the partial restoration of some of the functions of family life.

After the children's houses and the other communal buildings had been improved, the living quarters for married couples were renewed. The wooden barracks were replaced by one-and-a-half room stone-constructed apartments with a modest cooking corner. A single room lavatory and shower took the place of the common sanitary facilities. A system of points was evolved for the allocation of apartments. Age and years of membership determined whether a couple was entitled to a new apartment. After a number of married years, they were allowed to furnish the rooms once and for all. Gradually more domestic appliances were allowed. After heated ideological discussions, the electric kettle was generally permitted, which opened the way to making coffee or tea "at home." A refrigerator and radio for each family soon followed. Pocket money, formerly a negligible amount, was raised considerably. Some kibbutzim proceeded to allow yearly holidays for its members.

The system of clothing distribution was changed as well. Mainly at the insistence of the women, clothing had already been marked for size, so that the members could at least find clothes that fitted. Then it became customary to distribute the clothes according to a quota system based on norms dictated by the federations of kibbutzim which had, in the meantime, been established. Each kibbutz member could now receive a fixed number of clothes per year. The norm system was also applied to household linen and other goods. Carelessness about centrally allotted garments seems to have been a reason for changing the original *communa alef* system (Spiro 1956:21). Although the clothes were still communal property, the kibbutz members became responsible for their care. They

---

[10] One of the highest ideals of the first kibbutz pioneers was to cultivate their own land. It should be remembered that in Europe, Jews as a rule were forced to follow nonproductive occupations, since agriculture and trade were closed to them. The result was a reversed pyramid of professions: many intellectuals, shopkeepers, and artists, but few workmen or farmers. The desire again to cultivate "the land of their fathers" has been an incentive to Zionism in general and to kibbutz movements in particular. This was the origin of the mysticism around labor and especially manual work, which is part of the complex of values called *chalutziut*.

could inform the kibbutz store when they felt entitled to new goods. Buying was established centrally. In most kibbutzim, members are expected to accept what they get. Still, this leaves a little room for personal taste.

THE TAKTZIVIM

A complex system of budgets (*taktzivim*) was evolved for various purposes in the kibbutz in 1950. After the establishment of the state of Israel in 1948, the living standard rose rapidly, both nationally and within the collectives. For most kibbutzim, there began a time of relative security in which semimilitary functions fell into the background. The implementation of these functions was, moreover, largely relegated to the regular army, just as other tasks that the kibbutzim used to fulfill were taken up by national institutions. For many kibbutzim, this meant a termination of the *frontier situation,* one of the factors that made collective organization imperative.

Increasing prosperity made it possible to attend to individual and familial needs.

The kibbutz is no longer a place where everybody is *equal in poverty* . . . Today's kibbutz member eats much better and is better housed and clothed than ever before. The kibbutz has succeeded in attaining a cultural and economic level which is not lower, and in many respects higher than that of Israel's urban workers (Darin-Drabkin 1962:82).

In many cases, the apartments were enlarged by the addition of an extra room, which could be used for meals, since most families prepared their afternoon tea and other small meals "at home." Where the children no longer slept in special children's houses at night, another room was added. The larger houses were often furnished better, too; a sofa and chairs to match and a bedroom suite belong to the normal equipment of a kibbutz house today. The family has a bookcase, often well stocked, a record player, and sometimes (especially in the older settlements of the Ichud) a television set. All this makes domestic life more attractive, but it has also considerably enlarged the complex of family tasks.

The distribution of goods and services in kibbutzim can no longer be spoken of, in general, but the various types of settlement must be considered separately.

In the kibbutzim affiliated to the federation "Kibbutz Artzi Hashomer Hatzair" ("Kibbutz Artzi"), formal distribution still takes place directly according to need. That is to say that although regulation of distribution and consumption has gained ground, need is still the decisive factor in determining whether the members receive what they are entitled to according to the general rules. These rules may be summarized as a system of points (distribution of houses) and norms (distribution of clothes). Whereas, the members in former days simply got what they requested, they are now usually free to choose within the limits of their allowance. They no longer have to depend on what the kibbutz warehouse happens to have in store. If desired, clothes can be bought in town, usually from shops also affiliated to the kibbutz movement.

In the settlements of the federation "Ichud Hakvutzot Vehakibbutzim" ("Ichud"), regulation has proceeded further. Here, goods are increasingly distributed according to general standards irrespective of direct need: the members can obtain goods they are entitled to, whether they need them or not. After 1950 this federation, which is the one least oriented to communal life, evolved a system of "personal budgets." Instead of establishing a quota according to norms or points, these kibbutzim fixed different amounts of money for various articles. The amounts are put at the disposal of those entitled to them and can be spent as the receiver thinks fit. In this way, a maximum of scope is given to personal preference.

The Kibbutz Artzi does not formally accept this system, although in some of its settlements, it is practiced with caution. Indeed, members increasingly urge the legalization of this system. The point of that federation is that the personal budget system may facilitate an unequal distribution of goods. According to the points and norms system, those who do not need anything, get nothing, but with the personal budget system, everyone can demand to receive the amount to which he is formally entitled. As a consequence, nonsmokers may use their "smoking budget" to supplement their "clothing budget," or members who have received garments from relatives may use their "clothing budgets" to improve their furnishings. Moreover, the Kibbutz Artzi people say:

> ... if through saving soap, more chocolate can be bought for the children, commodities become valuable not in themselves but according to their worth in terms of money, *which takes us back to the capitalist method of evaluation* (Leon 1969:87, italics added)

In the Ichud, on the other hand, it is thought unjust when the accidental fact that members do not smoke or have already obtained articles in one way or another means that they are not given what all the others get.[11]

The size of the personal budget and the nature of the articles for which it is allotted vary in each kibbutz, though the federation has laid down some lines of policy. Each member gets around (Israeli) £200.– for pocket

---

[11] For discussions on a federative level, see Viteles (1967:344 ff) and Leon (1969:79–98).

money, to which all kinds of extra allowances may be added. The yearly per capita clothing budget varies from Isr. £150.– to £300 and is generally more for women and less for men. As in the Kibbutz Artzi, furniture in the Ichud is usually distributed according to norms. There may be a furniture allowance for each family of a few dozen pounds a year for occasional renewal. In the kibbutz I studied in 1968, members were urged to establish a regular furniture budget as well. For purchases in the kibbutz shop (an institution to be found in most kibbutzim today), a monthly amount is often allotted. Some commodities are free, others, especially luxury goods, have to be "bought." The members usually do not get this allowance in cash, but in coupons that function as a kind of "kibbutz money." Members who are short of coupons have to pay for their purchases out of their own pockets with money saved from other budgets, a procedure that is not formally allowed but often followed.

Budgets may be allotted for various other goods. Fixed amounts are often laid down for the purchase of books, garden plants, theater visits, and visiting parents or grandchildren. Also, those kibbutzim that use the personal budget allot a yearly holiday allowance per member. The most recent development is that of a holiday allowance for children, so that they may share their parents' holidays.

Initially the personal budget was individually administered and distributed, that is, to man and wife separately. As it turned out, however, spouses tended to combine their allowances. Sometimes the amounts were pooled among relatives living in the same kibbutz, since needs may vary. An investigation carried out by the Ichud (1967:103) showed that among 410 respondents from nine different Ichud kibbutzim, 36 percent did not object to family members sharing their personal budgets. In those kibbutzim where children slept at home and were not housed collectively, this percentage was even higher (44 percent).

Today the personal character of the budget does not receive so much stress. Man and wife are generally allowed to use each other's allowances, while the amounts are often recorded administratively as family budgets. These new freedoms have enlarged the possibility of planning and, with it, the need for some form of financial control.

The most recent development in the Ichud is the *taktziv kollel* [total budget]. An amount is yearly fixed per member or family without specified allocations. The members are expected to manage on this amount and pay for their various kinds of needs. It will be clear that this system requires more of a financial policy and planning on the part of the members. As an intermediate solution, some budgets (pocket money, clothes, and recreation) are sometimes combined in one total budget, while for other kinds of expenditures, the personal budget or allocation according to norms remains. In general, members can only draw part of the total budget in cash, receiving the remainder in coupons. Often the supplier sends the bills directly to the kibbutz administration where the amount owed is recorded on the card of the member concerned, so that absolutely no money or other securities change hands.

EQUALITY ASPIRATIONS

In the kibbutz movement, there existed initially a marked tendency to realize sex equality. The equality ideal was one of the factors that led to collective organization.[12] Such communal services as a central kitchen, dining hall and collective education system would, it was hoped, release women from traditional tasks of housekeeping and childrearing, so that they could participate in the economic process and in community life on a basis of complete equality with their spouses. The well-known kibbutz stereotype of women driving tractors, handling guns, or building houses dates from this earlier period. Moreover, the striving after equality rested on a predominantly masculine ideal. Whereas women aspired to tasks that were traditionally performed by men, the men rarely took up traditionally feminine activities such as education, childrearing, or work in the clothes stores or sewing rooms. The situation was reversed within the family (Talmon-Garber 1965a:148). Most of the emphasis there was put on the husband's participation in traditionally feminine activities. He kept the room tidy, and the young father minding his child became a familiar kibbutz picture. But, in the initial phase of the kibbutz there were few tasks to divide within the family. As time went by, the equality ideal and the corresponding reality underwent drastic changes. In the kibbutz of today, women rarely perform any traditionally masculine work, nor do they aspire to it. Their wish to retain a "feminine" appearance often underlies this. They do not like field labor, it is said, because the sun has a harmful effect on the skin. Nor are women, in many cases, welcome in the productive economic sector. Male labor has turned out to be more effective, as a man can continue doing heavy work for longer periods and need not interrupt his work from time to time.[13] In the kibbutz that I investigated in 1968, only 6 percent of the women worked in one of the productive branches of the kibbutz. The average percentage for the five kibbutzim I studied in 1971 was 10 percent.

Work in the nonproductive service sector (such as the kitchen or children's houses), which is nowadays mostly done by women, enjoys less prestige than tasks that directly support the kibbutz economy. This presents the kibbutz woman of today with a great problem, which I will only briefly discuss here (see especially Rosner 1967, 1969).

[12] See note 7.
[13] Members in the kibbutz speak of *"ha tragedia habiologit shel ha isha,"* [the woman's biological tragedy].

While on the one hand, women often are no longer admitted in the productive sector and usually do not aspire to work there, they are not always quite satisfied by their tasks in the service sector. New possibilities for employment are scarce, although attempts in that direction are being made within the kibbutz movement.[14] Being isolated in the service sector, moreover, the women have partially lost their involvement in the economic system of the kibbutz, which has become exceedingly complex. In consequence, they feel less capable in matters of administration than do the men. Although attendance at the *assiva* [general assembly] has fallen off everywhere, women take part even less than men.

It is partly in reaction to this situation that women wish to stress once more their traditional role. Now that family life has regained several of its functions, it has become possible for them to find fulfillment within it. Their work in the service sector has prepared them better than the men for the execution of family tasks. There may be more factors that could explain this development. The socialization of the *vattikim* [old-timers or kibbutz founders], for instance, who grew up in Europe, has not been wholly eliminated. The kibbutz has become more open as well, so that the "outside world" increasingly makes its influence felt.

The kibbutz woman now accentuates her femininity by using makeup and dressing fashionably. And although within the family, there is no question of a rigid separation of sex roles: "A fairly specialized albeit flexible and fluctuating division of labor has emerged in most families" (Talmon-Garber 1965a:146). In contrast to the situation outside the family, where labor division on the basis of sex is generally accepted, there is a striking gap between ideology and social reality within the family. Verbally, speaking in the abstract, kibbutz members often emphatically profess their belief in an ideal of sex equality, but, in practice, obligations and responsibilities are distributed between marital partners as a matter of course. Sharp role differentiation in many respects is prevented only by the fact that women still work outside the home (they work fewer hours nowadays), and family tasks remain relatively slight.

THE CONJUGAL ORGANIZATION: CONCEPT AND MEASUREMENT

Conjugal organization is defined to mean the division of family labor between man and wife. The tasks to be carried out by each of them at

---

[14] Several kibbutzim decided to set up a factory, partly because of the new possibilities of employment for women. Such monotonous work, however, does not satisfy everyone. Nowadays women have more opportunities to work outside the kibbutz, as a physiotherapist, for instance. Some members also want to maintain the collective housing system for children as a provision of employment for women in the children's homes.

home form an important part of their conjugal roles. Conjugal organization has been regularly researched for some decades. The studies of Herbst (1954), Blood and Wolfe (1960), and Bott (1964) have become classics in the field.[15] The numerous studies that appeared later are either based on these older investigations or are merely replications.

In spite of this long-standing interest in conjugal organization, such research is still faced with considerable problems of theory and methodology. Recent studies often simply replicate older ones and do not aim at augmenting the apparatus of measurement or lead to theoretical reflection. Aside from this, these studies tend to limit the conjugal organization to the structure of "family power" or "decision making." Recently a discussion has arisen with reference to this type of research (Safilios-Rothschild 1970; Turk, Bell 1972; Olson, Rabunsky 1972; Sprey 1972).

For many years it has been assumed that we knew what "power" or "decision making" really was and that all we needed to do was find a good measure of it. It now appears that it is a very complex set of not very closely related phenomena. The same thing has happened over and over again in the social sciences. There is scarcely an interactional variable that has not floundered in the same morass (Broderick 1972:213).

It has become clear that a distinction should be made between authority, influence, and the movement of deciding. "Family power," which is measured by means of questionnaires, is usually conjugal authority, the formal power coupled normatively to the conjugal role. It is more difficult to establish which of the spouses, in fact, exerts more influence. Participant observation is the technique most suitable here. The use of questionnaires may establish who has responsibility for final decisions, but this often yields merely a normative relation of power and not a picture of the process itself.

This investigation focuses, not on "family power," but on the conjugal division of tasks, or in other words, a behavioristic approach. This division has been measured by the method usually applied in this type of investigation: a questionnaire that offers the respondent a choice from five possibilities: (1) the man always carries out the task, (2) he usually carries out the task, (3) man and wife carry out the task equally, (4) the wife usually carries it out, (5) the wife always carries out the task.

When the answers are widely distributed over the five-point scale, the extent of *role-stereotyping* may be considered to be slight. When practically all the answers are at one extreme end of the scale, there is great *role-differentiation*: the task is then coupled to one of the conjugal roles.

---

[15] Bott's study is slightly out of place here, since she was particularly interested in the relationship between the conjugal organization on the one hand and the social network of contacts between spouses on the other. Most other studies do not focus on this special relationship.

This method of inquiry has some imperfections. One question that arises again and again is that of the relation between the value of findings and the social reality itself:

... researchers have often assumed that in using self-reports of wives to obtain measures of the family power structure they are obtaining valid measures of "objective reality." What they are really dealing with are invalid measures which only describe "subjective reality" (Olson, Rabunsky 1972:231).[16]

Objections have also been voiced against inquiries made exclusively among respondents who all occupy identical positions. Often they are women, who are usually more easily accessible than men, or children (Herbst 1954). For this investigation both male and female informants were approached.

As the aim was to measure actual behavior, the usual procedure of asking a limited number of questions (eight or ten) concerning tasks that are regarded as representative of the main sectors of family life was not followed; instead, a series of concrete questions on each task was designed, both in order to measure actual behavior and to avoid normatively colored answers as much as possible. The questionnaires contained eighty-five questions on task division alone. After examining the gathered data for consistency, it was assembled into one score. The questions touched on daily recurring situations so that the respondents were encouraged to relate what actually happened. Although in this way, the normative factor was to some extent suppressed, the subjective element of individual perception was still not wholly eliminated. Through observation and informal conversation, other data was collected to establish the extent of divergence between "objective" and "subjective" facts. The questions frequently gave rise to candid talks, which lead to opportunities to observe various family situations.[17]

Another problem in this type of investigation is that the data relating to one family sector or to the total of family functions are expressed in one general total score. It is true that such a general score may facilitate comparison within the material, but it is also of limited significance. The

---

[16] Cultural anthropologists may find these observations rather surprising. Used to the technique of participant observation, they take it for granted that the "reality" they observe differs from that reflected by the informants. Most likely, such statements come from investigators who predominantly use questionnaires.

[17] The investigation of a family gives rise to particular technical problems. Most families are small, closed social groups and their internal functioning is not perceptible from outside. The investigator must live with the family in order to observe several families. Even if the family agrees to take him in, it still remains to be seen whether this serves any useful purpose because he has a considerable influence (thermometer effect). These problems particularly crop up at the investigation of modern Western urban families, hidden as these are behind the walls of their apartments. In such cases, the questionnaire is often the only useful means of investigation.

selection of tasks about which the questions are to be asked is fairly arbitrary. The investigator may, for instance, have included too many questions on activities associated with the feminine role, thus distorting the overall picture. Moreover, in such a general score, no account has been taken of the importance of various tasks. These should be weighed separately.

For these several reasons, no general total score is given here. The activities that were on the whole found to be "feminine," "masculine," or "neutral" are averaged and mentioned separately (values over 3.5; less than 2.5; between 3.5 and 2.5, respectively).

TAKTZIV ISHI, TAKTZIV ISTI

Huguet (1963:159), Komarovsky (1961:270), and Leplae (1968:26) found in France, the United States, and Belgium, respectively, that routine activities in the financial sphere of the family are often carried out by one of the spouses, while decisive action and important decisions are taken jointly and after mutual consultation. Male or female role dominance depends on the nature of the routine tasks involved. Huguet found that incidental expenses, especially if they are clearly concerned with the world outside the family, are met by the man, while current expenses appear to be taken care of by the wife. Indeed, routine expenses are usually related to matters commonly regarded as belonging to the feminine sphere, such as the care of food and clothing. The man seems, further, to take charge of any tasks requiring more complex financial techniques.

In short, as these investigators and others have shown, in the conjugal organization of the financial affairs of Western urban families, both man and wife participate. It should be added that, in many cases, the wife's share is the largest because she is the one who takes care of the short-term expenses that are especially characteristic of family finance. The study carried out by Blood and Wolfe (1960:Table 2, no 1) confirms this general picture (see Table 1 on facing page).

At first sight, the conjugal organization of this sphere in the Israeli kibbutz corresponds reasonably well with what was found elsewhere (Blood, Wolfe 1960:Table 2). Here, as in Belgium and the U.S., the regularly recurring expenses of food and clothing fall into the woman's terrain (Blood, Wolfe 1960:Table 2, no. 2 and 3) with one difference: man and wife, in the kibbutz, often take joint charge of food budgets. Both in the United States and in Belgium, the man usually deals with complex financial matters (Blood, Wolfe 1960:Table 2, no. 4 and 5), but such decisions are often taken after mutual consultation. In the kibbutz, however, individual members are not called upon to make important

Table 1. Financial task division: a comparative perspective (in percent)

Country item (see Key)	USA 1	Belgium 2	Kibbutz 2	USA 3	Belgium 3	Kibbutz 3	USA 4	Belgium 5	Kibbutz 6
Number of respondents	731	472	255	709	472	231	716	466	283
Female activity	41	62	69	53	71	45	14	5	3
Man and wife together	34	37	24	33	25	40	42	28	23
Male activity	25	1	7	13	4	15	43	67	74
Total	100	100	100	99	100	100	99	100	100

Source: Blood and Wolfe 1960; Leplae 1968.
Key: 1. Takes care of the money and the bills.
2. Clothing budget.
3. Food budget.
4. Decides about taking out life insurance.
5. Decides about insurance firm.
6. Takes care of money and bills outside the kibbutz during holidays.

financial decisions, so that, in general, the kibbutz family is not concerned with financial activities of long-term importance. The kibbutz family has a series of modest budgets that require small-scale planning to cover clothing and food. There was only one task in the kibbutz that is particularly performed by the men: the care of money and bills when the family leaves the settlement. This obligation does not frequently occur and hence the expression of *taktsiv ishi, taktsiv isti* [the personal budget is the woman's budget]. "They [the men] are usually not much interested in this small-scale budgeting and leave the planning and management of the family 'finances' to their wives entirely" (Talmon-Garber 1965a: 275–276).

It has already been demonstrated that in the kibbutz nowadays, there is a tendency towards sex-role differentiation. This is particularly noticeable outside the family situation, but to some extent also within. Although much has changed in the kibbutz movement, I want to emphasize that compared with the Western urban world, the kibbutz is still characterized by a marked role interchangeability. This is certainly true in the domain of family finances. In the kibbutz, husband and wife usually take decisive action together on matters requiring long-range planning or the withdrawal of money. Minor financial activities are left to the woman. In the Western urban family, man and wife manage some of their financial affairs together, while each controls their own domains. Their roles are more varied than in the kibbutz, where only the woman has her own special task apart from communal activities. The absence of a special role for the man can be explained not only by the lack of importance of the financial sector, but also by the kibbutz ideology, which formally stresses role equality and the fact that this is considered not *chalutzi* [according to the way of life of the true pioneer] when the man pays much attention to consumptive activities. The man regards it as bourgeois to concern himself with money and expenses. He would rather leave these matters to his wife. It may be expected that the kibbutz man will take a more active role in the management of family finances when aspiration for equality has diminished and members of the kibbutz are less influenced by traditional kibbutz values.

MASCULINE AND FEMININE PERCEPTION

Management of the clothing budget was found to be a woman's activity on the average. Behavior related to food and furniture budgets scored neutral, and these were often handled by both husband and wife. The question of who took out money from the secretariat also scored neutral. It has already been mentioned how the care of bills and money during holidays is commonly a sole "masculine activity" in the financial sector.

Generally men and women had the same perception of task division. The slight majority of women has no particular influence on the total score. The two categories differ only significantly in their answers to the question of who takes care of the money and bills during holidays (see Table 2.). To this question, the women score more masculine than the men

Table 2. Financial task division: perception of man and woman (by standard deviation scores)

	Women (N = 170)	Men (N = 113)	Total (N = 283)
Female activity	3.63–0.97	3.67–1.00	3.69–0.94
Neutral	2.99–0.76	2.97–0.76	2.98–0.76
Male activity	1.81–0.84	2.07–0.89	1.92–0.87

themselves. Possibly it embarrasses a man to admit that he concerns himself with money outside the kibbutz. Interest in such bourgeois matters is regarded as not *chalutzi*. Women seem to feel a lesser need to stress this kibbutz value.

Granbois and Willett (1970) and Scanzoni (1965) have pointed out that in an investigation of married couples, it is unnecessary to concentrate "on methods to overcome systematic bias inherent in responses to role questions. At this point, there simply is no evidence of such bias." The author's investigations also show that, although husband and wife may have slightly different pictures of reality, the difference is not systematic so that, owing to the great number of respondents, the eventual scores show no striking deviations. It should, however, not be ruled out that a systematic difference could occur for specific questions or under other sociocultural circumstances. Consequently, it is undesirable to rely on information obtained exclusively from women.

IDEOLOGICAL AND STRUCTURAL VARIABLES

It has already been argued that the communal way of life, and consequently, antifamilistic tendencies are, in most cases, not completely, but at least largely, dependent on the measure in which the value and norm pattern stipulates such a group.

Kibbutzim that are less focused on communal life than others may be expected to have a less comprehensive collection organization. Therefore, a greater role differentiation might be expected between man and wife in the kibbutzim less directed towards communal life, at least if no special circumstances necessitate equal roles for spouses.

Table 4 shows that there is a greater role differentiation in the Ichud kibbutzim than in the settlements of the federation Kibbutz Artzi. This role differentiation finds expression not so much in a more pronounced role of the woman as in a more generally assigned task for men to handle the money during holidays ("the male activity"). In all types of settlements, the woman already has her role established in the financial sector. The difference in score between the Artzi and Ichud about the "male task" is significant (5 percent; $t=2.103$). Yet ideological attitude (together with the importance of family life) is not the only influence on task division.

Table 3 shows that, although the two Artzi settlements have the same distribution system, the man participates more in the domain of family

Table 3. Task division in five kibbutzim

Kibbutz	Alef (N = 68)	Beet (N = 46)	Gimmel (N = 75)	Dalet (N = 43)	Yod (N = 51)
Female activity	3.81	3.63	3.81	3.58	3.49
Neutral	2.99	2.89	3.13	2.84	2.96
Male activity	2.15	1.98	2.01	1.58	1.69

finances in Beet than in Alef. The same is true of the two Ichud kibbutzim Dalet and Gimmel. Apart from the general ideological factor, the age of the settlement is found to influence the nature of the task division. The difference in score of the "male task" between older and younger kibbutzim (2.08 and 1.78 respectively; see also Table 4) is markedly significant (1 percent; $t=2.627$). The conclusion that must be drawn here is that the less ideological and the younger the kibbutz, the more pronounced will be the man's financial role in the family (Dalet, 1.58). The reverse is also true: the more ideological and the older the kibbutz, the smaller his part will be (Alef, 2.18). The quality of "age of the kibbutz" is attended with several other characteristics (see Appendix 2). First, a young kibbutz is in most cases, not as rich as the settlements founded before 1930. Second, they are seldom large, and third, most young kibbutzim have a young population. Economically difficult situations such as occurred in the

Table 4. Task division: ideological and structural variables

	Alef and Beet Artzi (N = 114)	Gimmel and Dalet Ichud (N = 118)	Alef and Gimmel Old (N = 143)	Beet and Dalet Young (N = 89)
Female activity	3.72	3.70	3.81	3.61
Neutral	2.94	2.99	3.06	2.87
Male activity	2.07	1.80	2.08	1.78

beginning of the kibbutz movement no longer exist. The national standard of living and the many forms of assistance guarantee even the newly founded settlements sufficient subsistence. The collective organization and the nature of the man-wife relationship then becomes a deliberate choice, rather than a necessity. The young kibbutzim of the frontier may be exceptions, but they are not included in this study. Explanatory variables should be found, particularly in other characteristics. The size of the group certainly affects the form of social life. Other things being equal, it would seem easier to bring about communal living for a group of 200 than for a group of 600 people. The smallness of the group is no guarantee, however, of successful communal life. Also essential is the generally accepted aspiration to live as a commune.

The third factor is the age of the settlement and the structure of the kibbutz population. In the younger kibbutz, young people can be found who were seldom brought up in a kibbutz (only 4 percent of the members of the kibbutzim Beet and Dalet were born in a kibbutz), but often they were recruited from the kibbutz movement and sometimes from outside.[18] Ideologically, they take a different stand from the *vattikim* and their children who constitute the members of the veteran kibbutzim. Rosner (1967:50) writes on this subject that: "The egalitarian attitude will be most strongly entrenched in the younger kibbutzim, least in the veteran settlements. . . ." By egalitarian, Rosner also means an undifferentiated role relationship. He explains this as follows: "These women [i.e., in the younger settlements], in their more recent past, took the positive step of joining a kibbutz, and this rational decision was partly based on the expectation of gaining equality." Rosner found his hypothesis confirmed in a number of cases.[19] It seems likely to this author that young people, on joining the kibbutz, know very well that the kibbutz ideal of equality between man and woman has not proved to be wholly realizable. Besides, these young people are motivated not so much by a pioneer's idea as by the values and norms of their own time, which they have adopted from the intruding Western urban pattern of life. In this pattern, the conjugal organization, compared with that of the kibbutz family is characterized by a greater measure of sex-role differentiation.

When young people join the kibbutz, they realize a conjugal relationship that, when influenced by their free choice of kibbutz life, may be less differentiated than if they had remained in town, but certainly is more

---

[18] Members of the younger kibbutzim are predominantly recruited from various youth movements connected with the kibbutz federations. The federations have also established offices in many cities all over the world to recruit new kibbutz members. This method has not been very successful, and many kibbutzim contend with a shortage of manpower because their natural increase of members is insufficient.

[19] The author does not agree with Rosner's hypothesis as his own data contradict this hypothesis.

differentiated than the relationship known by the *vattikim* that often cling to traditional kibbutz values. This line of argument explains one of the best results of his investigation, that in the younger kibbutzim, the man has more explicitly his own task in the management of the family finances than in veteran settlements. Structurally, the family in a young kibbutz approaches the Western urban family, where family tasks are even more evenly distributed between husband and wife than in the veteran kibbutzim.

Rosner also supposed that the younger members of the veteran kibbutzim who were born and raised in the kibbutz (members of the second generation) would show the least egalitarian attitude:

They received educational training in the kibbutz and youth movement, which stressed equality between the sexes. But the reality of kibbutz life, which they accept as being the realization of these educational values, has produced differentiation in roles, and this, too, is accepted as being natural and as fitting these values (Rosner 1967:50).

In the author's study, the *vattikim* from the two older settlements scored 2.19 on the question about the husband's role in managing the family finances, whereas the members of the second generation scored an average of 2.01. In general, the men of the second generation have more their own financial task than the *vattikim,* but less than the members of the younger kibbutzim. Born from *vattikim* and raised in the kibbutz, they still seem closer to the kibbutz ideal than members of the younger settlements who often come from outside the kibbutz.

VARIABLE FAMILY FUNCTIONS

Komarovsky (1962:48–81) defines the conjugal division of family tasks as a structure characterized by a *balanced exchange.* Given a specific task division, it could be said that: "If the advantages of differentiation are to be realized, there must be some balance in the tasks assigned to different positions." And "If the tasks assigned to one actor become overwhelming, the distribution may be questioned on the basis of legitimacy and fair exchange" (Campbell 1970:52). It is clear to this author that factors such as power and traditional views can play an important role in this respect. The burdening of a woman with more special tasks will neither necessarily lead to a redivision if these tasks are normatively connected with her role nor will she be able to pass on part of her extra burden if this is not within her power. The potential of carrying a specific task load is limited. In the kibbutz, such factors as values, norms, and power hardly play a role in this respect. There are no signs that one of the partners can control the task division, and kibbutz ideology still prescribes role interchangeability.

The man was first inclined to leave all the housework to his wife. Working fewer hours than her husband, she had more opportunity. It was found, however, that one hour was not sufficient. Now there is a general aim to free the women even more from community work. In practice, the man usually helps his wife or even takes on special tasks himself. This leads to the assumption that an increase of the domestic burden will necessitate a redivision of the tasks in which the man takes charge of some of the work alone or together with his wife.

In the Kibbutz Yod, the children do not live collectively, but they sleep "at home." For the women, this has increased their household tasks and for men, their roles in the financial sphere (see Table 3). Also in this kibbutz, fathers of families with many children (that is, more than two children under fifteen years of age) undertake the male tasks in this sector almost single-handedly (see Table 5). Both in the younger and older settlements, the participation of the man is greater among respondents

Table 5. Task division and family size

	Kibbutz Yod		Young Kibbutz		Old Kibbutz	
	few children	many children	few children	many children	few children	many children
Female activity	3.39	3.55	3.84	3.60	3.86	3.81
Male activity	1.89	1.40	1.87	1.74	2.13	1.80

with many children than among those with fewer than two, or no children, under age fifteen. The man has a more defined role when there are more young children in the family and consequently more tasks to do in the way of housework, education, and finances.[20] The man will also participate more in the "female" task of the financial sector. The Kibbutz Yod is, however, an exception: a larger family here does not lead to a greater participation of the man in all the tasks, but to a more marked role differentiation in which each partner specializes in his "own" tasks.[21]

In most cases, the length of kibbutz membership is an indication of

---

[20] Even when the children are collectively housed, the parents retain a share of their care and training, a task that will increase with the number of dependent children. In the Ichud kibbutzim, the children join their parents after school and stay until they go to bed. In the settlements of the Kibbutz Artzi federation, this is done during weekends and usually once a week. The affectionate relationship between parents and children is an important contribution to the children's upbringing. In the Ichud kibbutzim, parents tend more and more to take over the tasks of the children's house, such as the care for the child's clothes. Parents also prepare meals when their children are "at home" (four o'clock tea).

[21] Campbell (1970:52) made a close examination of the relationship between family size and conjugal organization. "The newlywed stage is characterized by a more equalitarian pattern of task performance. After the birth of their first child, the wife's total workload increases. This is likely due to the added amount of work that she can comfortably perform as a result of a more complete specialization in family affairs. The increased workload of the

the country of origin. Groups from certain countries often arrived in a body. Many of the *vattikim* came from East European countries. Members of the younger settlements are most often born in Israel, though not in a kibbutz.

APPENDIX 1: BACKGROUND ON THE KIBBUTZ

The kibbutz is a communal settlement in Israel, usually situated in the country (with the exception of a few urban kibbutzim), and varying in size from a few dozen to 2,000 members. Most kibbutzim are somewhat isolated, thereby forming separate municipalities. Kibbutzim are sometimes called collective settlements. The kibbutz has more of an appearance of a holiday resort or bungalow camp than of an average European village. Most kibbutzim are agricultural farms; some also have important industrial undertakings. Characteristic of the kibbutz is its collective organization of production and consumption. The community is administered by an assembly of members, which appoints an executive secretary.

In principle, the members of a kibbutz earn no money; they work for the community, which, in return, provides for them in most respects. Everything is common property with the exception of a few personal articles.

Characteristic of most kibbutzim is the collective training system. The children are housed in separate children's homes, where they are brought up by kibbutz members who receive special training for this work.

In 1971, Israel had some 230 collective settlements, mostly organized within one of the kibbutz federations. Each federation is connected with a political party. About 3 percent of the Jewish population of Israel, ca. 80,000 people, live in kibbutzim. Their important role in the construction of the state of Israel gives them more importance than these figures suggest.

The kibbutzim are united in three larger and some smaller federations. The federation "Ichud Hakvutsot Vehakibbutzim" is connected with the moderate, socialist Mapai party. The federation "Kibbutz Artzi Hashomer Hatzair" is connected with the Mapam, a party based on Marxist, socialist principles. Both federations comprise about 75 settlements. The federation Kibbutz Artzi has more ideological principles about communal life than the Ichud federation. An ideological middle course is adopted by the federation "Hakibbutz Hameuchad," which numbers some 60 settlements and is connected with the Achud Haavoda party. Together, these three federations comprise about 90 percent of the total kibbutz population. The federations offer their members technical, financial, and educative facilities. The federations also give directives for communal life and collective organization.

APPENDIX 2: POPULATION SAMPLE

Stratified population samples were selected so that the main categories of kibbutz members were represented as much as possible.

---

wife is no respecter of tradition, as more time is spent handling money and bills and making household repairs. The wife's time is not inexhaustible, however, for among fourth parity families, husbands again assume a greater share of the task load."

Kibbutz	Alef	Beet	Gimmel	Dalet	Yod	Totals
Population						
Ideology	A	A	I	I	I	
Age	x	y	x	y	x	
Size*	580	200	600	210	400	1990
Number families	150	45	140	36	90	461
Economy	1 and 2	1	1 and 2	1	1 and 2	
Sample						
Number families	46	35	51	28	34	194
Men	27	15	33	18	20	113
Women	41	31	42	25	31	170
Total number of respondents	68	46	75	43	51	283

Key: Ideology: A = Belonging to the most ideological federation (Kibbutz Artzi).
   I = Belonging to the least ideological federation (Ichud).
Age: x = Founded before 1930; y = after 1950; z = between 1930–1950.
Economy: 1 = Agriculture; 2 = Industry.
* relates to the number of kibbutz members as well as the kibbutz children and the other categories of inhabitants (temporaries, for instance).

In Kibbutz Yod, included in the sample because of its deviating educational system, the children sleep "at home." Women turned out to be slightly better represented than men. In the total sample the settlements affiliated to the Ichud predominate, which has been taken into account in the total score.

APPENDIX 3: CASES

The number of observations of activities in the sector of family finances is restricted. Financial actions do not occur every day and they are often difficult to perceive.

Kibbutz "Gan Siva" (1968)

Shmuel, *vattik*, born in Germany, says: "I wanted a sliding door with nontransparent glass between the living room and the bedroom. This was very expensive. Of course in such cases, I do consult my wife about our finances, and we thoroughly discuss the matter."

Chaver Moshe, *vattik*, born in Poland says: "When my son expressed his wish to have a camera, we considered our different budgets, together with his older brothers."

Channa went to Tel Aviv today to do some shopping. She told how she first went to the secretariat to take out fifty Isr. pounds. "In former times I would have had to announce this long beforehand," she added.

Kibbutz Alef (1971)

The Rachman family receives me kindly, but with some reservations. He is from Russia and is willing to explain the system of *taktsivim*, but he continually consults his wife, who is busy cleaning the room.

Kibbutz Beet

I had an animated discussion about the budget system with the Avi family, who were *sabras* [born in Israel]. They came from outside the kibbutz and are about thirty-three years old. They regarded the questionnaire as unsatisfactory. The woman explained that clothes are distributed according to norms and that there are "prosperous" years in which they get much and "lean" years in which they get less money. Other aspects are elaborately elucidated. She complains that some budgets are not sufficient. Her husband, dressed in officer's uniform, takes a lively part in the conversation, correcting and adding to her statements. He explains: "The various budgets are not sufficient, but most members seem to manage quite well. It is obvious that money must be coming from outside. You should have asked where the money comes from, that is much more interesting!"

Kibbutz Gimmel

Naomi, from Poland and one of the founders, explains the quarrel over the smoking budget that raged some years before: "It was proposed to distribute smoker's requisites no longer according to need but to give everyone a fixed sum. Those who did not smoke would then save the money. There was protest because this was considered in conflict with the essence of the kibbutz idea, and it was predicted to be the end of the kibbutz. Everything has turned out all right, however, and we are still here, but some members took the matter so personally that they left the kibbutz."

Kibbutz Dalet

In this kibbutz, the *taktsiv kollel* has been introduced only a few years ago, and then even partially. Esther, a young woman from Haifa, who has studied sociology, says: "Many women still find it difficult to resist the temptation of spending all their money at once."

Menachum, born in Israel (not in a kibbutz) from a Dutch mother, proudly shows his wallet in which he keeps differently colored allowance coupons. He says: "I can use these all over the country preferably in shops affiliated to the kibbutz movement because of the discount. Of course, you have to consider your budget, but it does not matter if you spend too much. They deduct that from next year's balance."

Menachum further mentions how in the (kibbutz) shop many things are to be had "free." "People often take advantage of this." He, too, tells how some members complain that allowances are not sufficient, but that personally he manages quite well. He confides to me that he himself deals with everything concerning money and bills. His work is outside the kibbutz (he is responsible for the cotton crop in the kibbutzim of the region, looks after the machines, and arranges financial matters connected with the cooperation for which he has a car at his disposal). He explains his large share in this task by pointing out that he is a veteran member (thirteen years) of this kibbutz and therefore better acquainted with the customs than is his wife, who came from another kibbutz.

REFERENCES

BANFIELD, E. C.
1958 *The moral basis of a backward society.* Glencoe, Ill.: Free Press.

BARKIN, DAVID, JOHN W. BENNET
n.d. "Kibbutz and colony: collected economies and the outside world." Unpublished paper.

BECKER, HAVARD
1946 *German youth: bond or free.* New York: Oxford University Press.

BENNETT, JOHN W.
1967 *Hutterian brethren: the agricultural economy and social organization of a communal people.* Stanford, Calif.: Stanford University Press.

BESTOR, A. E.
1959 *Blackwood utopias.* Philadelphia: University of Pennsylvania Press.

BLOOD, ROBERT O., DONALD M. WOLFE
1960 *Husbands and wives: the dynamics of married living.* Glencoe, Ill.: Free Press.

BOTT, ELIZABETH
1964 *Family and social network* (second edition). London: Tavistock.

BRODERICK, CARLFRED B.
1972 Editorial. *Journal of Marriage and the Family* 34 (2):213.

CAMPBELL, FREDERICK L.
1970 Family growth and variation in family role-structure. *Journal of Marriage and the Family* 32:45–53.

CAMPBELL, J.
1964 *Honour, family and patronage.* London: Clarendon.

COSER, L. A.
1951 Some aspects of family policy. *American Journal of Sociology* 52:111–129.

DARIN-DRABKIN, H.
1962 *The other society.* London: Victor Gollancz.

DIAMOND, S.
1957 Kibbutz and Shetl. *Social Problems* 5:68–99.

ELLEMERS, J. E.
1962 Familie en nederzettingin Israel: over enige niet-voorziene ontwikkelingen bij sociale planning [Family and settlement in Israel: some contingencies in social planning]. *Tijdschrift van het Koninklijk Nederlands Ardrijkskundig Genootschap* 79:340–350.

GLUCKMAN, MAX
1950 "The kingdom of the Zulu," in *African political systems.* Edited by M. Fortes and E. E. Evans-Pritchard. New York: Oxford University Press.

GRANBOIS, DONALD H., RONALD P. WILLETT
1970 Equivalence of family role measures based on husband and wife data. *Journal of Marriage and Family* 32:68–72.

HELLER, PETER L.
1970 Familism scale, a measure of family solidarity. *Journal of Marriage and Family* 32:73–80.

HERBST, P. G.
1954 "Conceptual framework for studying the family," in *Social structure and personality in a city.* Edited by O. A. Oeser and S. B. Hammond. New York: Macmillan.

HINDS, W. A.
  1878 *American communal and cooperative colonies.* Oneida, N.Y.: Office of the American Sociologist.
HOLLOWAY, MARK
  1966 *Heavens on earth, utopian communities in America 1680—1880* (second edition). New York: Dover.
HOSTETLER, JOHN A., G. E. HUNTINGTON
  1967 *The Hutterites in North America.* New York: Holt, Rinehart & Winston.
HUGUET, M.
  1963 *Conceptions différentes des rôles de l'homme et de la femme à l'interieure de la famille.* Edited by M. J. and P. H. Chombart de Lauwe, M. Huguet, E. Perroy, and N. Bisseret. Paris: C.N.R.S.
ICHUD
  1967 "Report of an investigation made under the instruction of the federation *Ichud Hakvutsot Yehakibbutzim.*" Unofficial publication in Hebrew.
JANOWSKY, O. I.
  1959 *Foundations of Israel.* New York: D. van Nostrand.
KOINONIA-GROUP
  1970 *Het kommune boek* [The commune book]. Utrecht: A. W. Bruna.
KOMAROVSKY, M.
  1961 "Class differences in family decision making on expenditures," in *Household decision making, consumer behavior.* Edited by N. N. Foote. New York: University Press.
  1962 *Blue collar marriage.* New York: Random House.
LEON, DAN
  1969 *The kibbutz, a new way of life.* Oxford: Pergamon.
LEPLAE, CLAIRE
  1968 "Structuur van de taakverdeling en de machtsverdeling bij het echtpaar" [Structure of the task-division and power-division among spouses] in *Het Echtpaar.* Edited by Pierre de Bie. Rotterdam: University Press.
LUTFIYYA, ABDULLA M.
  1966 *Baytin, a Jordanian village.* The Hague: Mouton.
MEIER-CRONEMEYER, HERMANN
  1969 Judische jugendbewegung. *Germania Judaica* 8:1–9.
OLSON, DAVID H., CAROLYN RABUNSKY
  1972 Validity of four measures of family power. *Journal of Marriage and the Family* 34:224–235.
ROSNER, MENAHEM
  1967 Women in the kibbutz: changing status and concepts. *Asian and African Studies, Annual of the Israel Oriental Society* 3:35–68.
  1969 "The change in the perception of the equality of the woman in the kibbutz." Unpublished paper in Hebrew.
SAFILIOS-ROTHSCHILD, CONSTANTIA
  1970 The study of family power structure: a review, 1960–1969. *Journal of Marriage and the Family* 32:539–553.
SCANZONI, JOHN
  1965 A note on the sufficiency of wife responses in family research. *Pacific Sociological Review* 8:109–115.

SCHMALENBACH, HERMAN
1961 "The sociological category of communion," in *Theories of society*. Edited by Talcott Parsons et al., 331–347. Glencoe, Ill.: Free Press.
SCHWARTZ, ELI
1950 Communal settlements in Palestine. *American Journal of Economics and Sociology* 9:191–203.
SHEPHER, JOSEPH
1969 Families and social structure: the case of the kibbutz. *Journal of Marriage and the Family* 31:567–573.
SPIRO, MELFORD E.
1954 Is the family universal. *American Anthropologist* 56:838–846.
1956 *Kibbutz: venture in utopia*. Cambridge, Mass.: Schocken.
SPREY, JESTE
1972 Family power structure: a critical comment. *Journal of Marriage and the Family* 34:235–239.
STERN, BORIS
1965 *The kibbutz that was*. Washington, D.C.: Public Affairs Press.
TALMON-GARBER, YONINA
1956 The family in the collective settlements. *Transactions Third World Congress Sociology* 4:116–126.
1962 Social change and family structure. *International Social Science Journal* 14:468–487.
1965a "Sex-role differentiation in an equalitarian society," in *Life in society*. Edited by Thomas E. Lasswell et al., 144–155. Chicago: Scott, Foresman.
1965b "The family in a revolutionary movement," in *Comparative family systems*. Edited by M. Nimkoff, 259–287. Boston: Houghton Mifflin.
TURK, JAMES L., NORMAN W. BELL
1972 Measuring power in families. *Journal of Marriage and the Family* 34:215–224.
VITELES, HARRY
1967 *A history of the co-operation movement in Israel*, volume two. London: Valentine Mitchell.
YAMARE
n.d. *Formation of a communal settlement in Japan: a case in Shinkyo*. Osaka: Osaka City University.

Jewish Communities as Cultural Units

WALTER P. ZENNER

The purpose of this article is to apply Naroll's operations for defining a cultural unit to Jewish groups in order to stimulate the use of dispersed ethnic entities in cross-cultural comparative research and to examine certain questions about the relationship of culture to speech community and political boundaries raised in the course of this exercise.

In recent years, Naroll published several papers (1964, 1968, 1970) that have stressed the necessity to define the boundaries of a cultural unit in cross-cultural correlation. Naroll's definition of such a unit is observer oriented. He is less concerned with the subjective definitions of group boundaries used by actors than with objective differences,[1] regardless of the views of the participants. Naroll's critics, especially Bessac (1968), Leach (1964:299), Hymes (1968), Moerman (1965), and Barth et al. (1969) have stressed the actor's view of the situation.

Barth's distinction between ethnicity, which is a social structural boundary, and culture is implicit in the subtitle of his book on ethnic boundaries, "the social organization of cultural variation." One of the articles in that volume (Blom 1969), in fact, deals with a case in which ecological and cultural variation did not result in a deep-rooted ethnic boundary. Barth's analysis is parallel to the distinction between structural behavior and identificational assimilation made by American sociologist Milton Gordon (1964). A group may be separate in structure and identity, yet its

This paper was prepared under a faculty research grant (020–725A) from the Research Foundation of the State University of New York. Thanks are due to Stephen Childs, Craig Henrikson, Robert Carmack, John Mason, Werner Cohn, James L. Newman, G. de Rohan-Csermak, and others who read and criticized an earlier version. The author assumes sole responsibility for the content.

[1] Saying that Narrol is concerned with objective differences does not mean that he is only concerned with observed behavior. Naroll (1964:280) clearly states that the cultunit is for analyzing "social and cultural patterns as they exist in the minds of culture bearers."

members may come to resemble closely outsiders in their behavior. It is now necessary to view not only race, language, and culture as separate aspects, but ethnicity and culture must be viewed that way as well. To the Boasian proposition that there is no necessary causal relationship among race, language, and culture, one may now add that there is no one-to-one relationship between ethnicity and culture. The connection between an ethnic group and a cultural unit is, therefore, a problem for investigation. Naroll's original article (1964) was an effort to deal with a cultural unit, even though he used the term, "ethnic unit." Since his goal is a cross-cultural comparison of behavior and norms, rather than of ethnic identification per se, he might consider characteristics such as a group's name for itself and similar aspects of group identification separately. A group's sense of sameness obviously influences behavioral norms, but there is no one-to-one relationship between this sense and the norms.

For Naroll's purposes, the Jews as a group constitute an interesting problem. Naroll himself has referred to them as an "ex-tribe" or "ex-cultunits." This is a named group whose members have a common history and a sense of common destiny, and who are quite conscious of boundaries between themselves and others. Nevertheless, modern Jews, such as those in America, are distinguished neither by their speech nor by political autonomy, which are among Naroll's more salient features. Concerning their religion, Naroll also writes:

Millions of people in the United States today call themselves Jews, but neither believe in the truth of the Jewish holy books nor attend Jewish religious services. They all, however, claim descent from people who did believe and did attend. These, in turn, claim descent from members of the ancient Jewish states of Israel or Judah. (1970:731).

Naroll sees the Jews and other "ex-cultunits" (or "hyphenated cultunits"), as aggregates "whose bonds of unity are the conditions of their forbears rather than their own condition." While admitting the possible utility of defining such groups for certain studies, Naroll decides to ignore them for his studies.

Most authorities would agree that Naroll's definition of the cultunit as "people who are domestic speakers of a common distinct language and who belong either to the same state or the same contact group" does not apply to American Jews. After all, American Jews and other groups discussed by Naroll (for example, non-Basque-speaking Basques, Maronites, or Moerman's Lue) are in an advanced stage of behavioral assimilation, even if there is some lag in their structural and identificational assimilation to their neighbors.[2] But what does one do with the middle

---

[2] The terms "structural," "behavior," and "identificational assimilation" are borrowed from Gordon (1964). It should also be pointed out that American Jews, by and large, speak the same English dialects as their neighbors of similar class, with some minor differences

category of Jews who "did believe in the Jewish holy books and did attend Jewish religious services," even though they did not live in a Jewish state? These were the communities who constituted the bulk of Jewish history. Like other minorities and like peasantries, the traditional Jewish groups represent subsocieties and part-cultures that deserve greater consideration in cross-cultural comparison than they have received. The cross-cultural samples of Murdock have either neglected this type or found it difficult to handle. Groups are either selected as if they were full-cultures representing larger populations, such as the Lebanese (Orthodox Christians) or the Palestinian Druzes (Israeli), or they are not dealt with. In the former case, I have used parentheses to indicate what is unmarked in the ethnographic atlas (Murdock 1967:194–197). These labels are misleading in that the community used as a sample is specialized. Why should Arabic-speaking peasants or post-peasants be representative of Lebanon as a whole? Can a Christian village represent all religions in Lebanon? Similarly, is an Israeli Druze community a good sample of all Druzes?

The classification of groups such as these involves consideration of complex societies (or social fields) in which one finds several cultures and subcultures, some dominating others. Naroll has proposed that culture-bearing units in such a field may be seen as belonging to either the Aztec-type or to the Aymaran-type. The Aztec-type is defined as:

People who belong to a state in which unintertelligible dialects occur and who are domestic speakers of a dialect intelligible to speakers of the *lingua franca* of the state, that is, the dialect in which state officials usually transact their business (1970:733).

The Aymaran type is defined as:

People who belong to a state in which unintertelligible dialects occur and who are domestic speakers of a dialect not intelligible to speakers of the *lingua franca* of the state (1970:733).

Most of the Jewish groups can, it will be argued, be considered either Aymaran-type groups or ex-cultunits within an Aymaran-type or Aztec-type unit.

NAROLL'S OPERATIONS FOR DEFINING CULT UNITS

In finding cultunits, Naroll proposes two strategies. One is to map all the cultunits in a given region. In the case of "primitive," stateless societies,

---

and, in some cases, occasional use of Yiddish (or other languages) for foods, jokes, and the like. For structural distinctions between premodern and modern Jewish communities, see Zenner (1967, 1968). For a description of groups that maintain communal autonomy in the U.S., see Poll (1962).

this involves the definitions of linguistic and political boundaries, followed by a mapping of contact gaps that determine the dates when particular traits are present, and finally, a mapping of actual cultural boundaries. Because of Naroll's definitions, these will tend to coincide with political and linguistic boundaries. The other strategy (used in state-societies) is to find the cultunit affiliation of a given settlement, which involves working from the individual community and mapping the linguistic and political boundaries from the small unit to the large (Naroll 1970:737–739). By showing how Naroll's operations may be applied to Jewish groups, one can illustrate the way cultunits are defined.

APPLICATION TO JEWISH GROUPS

Naroll's definition of the cultunit fits the Yiddish-speaking Jews of the pre-eighteenth-century kingdom of Poland, and later, of Tsarist Russia and other states of Eastern Europe. In the case of those living under the role of German speakers, one may question whether the Yiddish spoken was unintelligible to those speaking standard German, although there are indications that this was the case (at least as much as the Tyrolean dialect). Two problems exist from Naroll's viewpoint: the Jews did not live together in contiguous areas, a point emphasized in his 1964 paper and downplayed in the 1970 version. Rather, they were dispersed in clusters among populations belonging to various language groups. The other problem is whether one is dealing with one cultunit or several.

Yiddish-speaking Jews were dispersed throughout several eastern and central European states, especially after the partitions of Polish kingdom. In the period preceding World War 1, one could find substantial numbers in the Tsarist, Austro-Hungarian, and German empires, as well as in Rumania. Yiddish-speaking Jews who did not use standard Polish, Russian, German, or Rumanian obviously fit the definition of an Aymaran-type unit. From Naroll's view, it is problematic whether this was one cultunit or several. Naroll sees the political boundary as determining the unit. Margaret Mead (1952:13–14) answers this query by an affirmation that Yiddish-speaking Jewry was a single cultural entity, "whether they paid taxes and marketed in Polish or Ukranian or Hungarian or were ruled by Czar or Emperor."

While this is in essence the position of Max Weinrich and his successors (Weinreich 1953, U. Weinreich 1954, 1963; Herzog, Ravid and U. Weinreich 1969; Lewis 1972), the use of extensive diffusion studies, with regard to language and other culture traits, leaves them an opening. Past and present political divisions are among the features that lead to the differentiation of both dialects and local customs. In the area of language, they could conceivably lead to a great enough differentiation to cause the loss of intertelligibility. This leads one to suggest that, rather than considering Aymaran-type units (and even the Aztecan-type) as existing solely within the boundaries of one state, one should adopt concepts and procedures that Naroll has used in dealing with the stateless (Hopi-type) units.

In such societies, Naroll suggests the use of contact boundaries and contact links. As defined by Naroll (1964:286), a contact link is two nuclear families . . . if every year one of the members of each speaks directly to one of the members of the other." In the case of nonliterate Hopi-type units, Naroll (1964:286) specifies that one must assume that, where the distance is more than 200 kilometers, no contact exists unless there is evidence to the contrary. This obviously does not apply to Jewish groups in eastern Europe as well as elsewhere, where long-distance contacts such as commercial fairs, pilgrimages to Hasidic rabbis, and attendance at schools existed.

The data on the distribution of cultural and linguistic traits that accompanies the Weinreichs *et al.* dialect geography studies and the efforts to explain this distribution shows how these may be used. For instance, Herzog (1964) relates the extinction of certain lexical and cultural features in northeastern Poland to the history of restrictions on Jewish settlement in certain regions, to the movement of settlers along certain trade routes as the restrictions eased, and to a tendency of settlers on a frontier to "lighten the cultural baggage which they bear with them."

While Herzog's study does not concentrate on the political aspect, it does provide much of the data needed for defining contact boundaries. What has been written about the Yiddish-speaking Jews applies to Ladino-speaking Jews of the Balkans and Turkey. Again, there is an Aymaran-type unit in which the language spoken domestically is not intelligible to native speakers of the state's *lingua franca*. In this case, too, the speakers of Ladino (also known as Judeo-Spanish) were demarcated from local Jews who spoke languages such as Greek and Arabic and from Gentiles who spoke languages other than Ottoman Turkish. The Gentiles constituted separate Aymaran-type units. Many of the non-Ladino-speaking Jews were, in fact, assimilated into the Ladino community (Bernadette 1952).

A more difficult case occurs when the Jews speak a dialect of either the state *lingua franca* or of a language spoken by other segments of the population. It is fairly easy to dismiss modern American Jews who are often nonpractitioners of traditional Judaism as being members of an ex-cultunit, but this does not apply as easily to medieval German or Arabic Jewries. In these situations, Jews apparently adhered to the dictates of Jewish law, ideologically and practically. The degree of intertelligibility of the dialect spoken by Jews and Gentiles in such contexts must be treated in a case-by-case manner.

Using Blanc's summary of data on social dialects in the Arab world, one would conclude that the Arabic spoken by Arabophone Jews was generally not unintelligible to other speakers of Arabic (Blanc 1964:12-16). In Baghdad, one found that distinctive dialects were spoken by Jews, Christians, and Muslims. Jewish and Christian dialects belonged to one type of Mesopotamian Arabic, although differing one from the other, while the Muslim dialect belonged to another type. Blanc (1964:170-171) explains these differences on the basis of migration to the city and similar historical developments.

Except for Hebrew loan words, the Baghdadi Jewish dialect, as recorded by Blanc (1964), is apparently intelligible to other speakers of eastern Arabic. The words of Hebrew origin found exclusively in the Jewish dialect include the vocabulary of Jewish religious practice and some words that might be useful in the marketplace and other interethnic situations (including the words for danger, bribe, and thief). Since the Jewish community lacked war-making power, by Naroll's tests, the Arabophone Jews of Baghdad would be part of the same cultunit as their other Arabophone neighbors. Under the Ottoman Turks, this would be the Aymaran-type, while under an independent Arab government, this would be the Aztec-type.

If one follows Naroll's typology of culture-bearing units, one finds some traditional Jewish (and other minority) groups classed as separate Aymaran-type units, while some will be classed as segments (or ex-cultunits) of either Aymaran-type or Aztec-type units. Since all of the Jewish groups are subordinate and lack sovereignty, the main criterion for classification becomes linguistic. In fact, the approach applied here raises questions regarding the relationship of language and political relations to other aspects of social and cultural life.

LANGUAGE AND THE MINORITY CULTUNIT

Dell Hymes (1968) suggested that Naroll's assumptions about the relationship of language to social units are problematical. Hymes pointed out that communication and mutual intelligibility depend on several factors, "of which sameness or similarity is but one." Hymes suggested that different codes may be used for communication in different aspects of culture, such as with regard to "languages of religion."

This has particular relevance to Jewish units, since Hebrew constituted an important medium of communication within and between traditional Jewish communities. There are suggestions that even Jewish communities that shared mutual intelligible languages with their Gentile neighbors also made use of Hebrew for purposes of privacy, whether in the religious or other areas.

There is some suggestion that Hebrew vocabulary was used not only for areas of ritual, but for other areas as well. As was noted earlier, in Baghdad terms that might be used in the marketplace or other interethnic situations were Hebrew. As Denison (1971) points out, Jewish dialects and languages such as Jewish German (Western Yiddish or Eastern Yiddish) and Yiddish served as concealment codes.[3] In non-Germanic eastern Europe, the Germanically based Yiddish "went a long way towards meeting the need for concealment." In Germany, however, a special vocabulary was needed. Thus, among the cattle dealers and other Jewish trades people of Germany, a Hebrew vocabulary is found, including the use of Hebrew numbers for the discussion of prices and wares. Even within groups that Naroll would define as ex-cultunits, one finds regions of activity in which mutual intelligibility is lacking.

The use of the concept of domestic speakers of a language also has complications in the Jewish case. In modern times, one can find Jewish families in which two or three languages are used in a household, sometimes over more than one generation (such as Hebrew and Yiddish or Hebrew and Arabic in Israel, or Ladino or French and Arabic in some Egyptian Sephardic households). Poll (1962:273–274) suggests a similar situation among the Hungarian Hasidim of the Williamsburg neighborhood of New York City, who simultaneously use some English mixed with Hungarian as well as the Hungarian dialect of Yiddish.

POLITICAL BOUNDARIES OF THE CULTUNIT

As indicated, there are problems with Naroll's use of political criteria in defining the cultunit. With regard to the Jews, it seems advisable to use contact links, rather than the boundaries of a state in defining the limits of the unit. In fact, Naroll appears to view the state as crucial in setting the blueprint for cultural and social patterns of those societies defined as Aztec-type and Aymaran-type cultunits. This poses several problems. First, many premodern states did not have the kind of power and authority assumed by Naroll. Second, states differ widely in imposing a blueprint for behavior on those who live under their control.

One must look to Naroll's definition (1970:731) of the state as a "territorially ramified territorial team occupying at least ten thousand square kilometers of land whose leaders assert and wield the exclusive right to declare and conduct warfare" in the first instance. The term "territorially ramified" allows for this fairly large unit to be made up of

---

[3] Western Yiddish and Eastern Yiddish are defined linguistically. Roughly speaking, the centers of Western Yiddish were in Germany and related areas, while Eastern Yiddish was spoken in Poland and other parts of eastern Europe. See Herzog, Ravid, and Weinreich (1969) for further discussion.

component "territorial teams," that is, groups of "people whose membership is defined in terms of occupancy of a common territory and who have an official with the special function of announcing group decisions — a function exercised at least once a year."

While somewhat awkwardly stated, Naroll's definition fits others used in anthropology. The use of arbitrary criteria, such as the minimum of an annual announcement of group decisions (which assumes some sort of collective leadership) and of occupying at least 10,000 square kilometers is obviously a device needed for comparative purposes. The remainder of the definition is compatible with the view that states, and even primitive states, claim the right "to monopolize the use of force" (for example, Adams 1966:44).

The monopolization of force by the state, however, is much less clear with regard to such premodern governments as the Holy Roman Empire, sixteenth-century Scotland, nineteenth-century Iran or Morocco than with regard to modern states (for examples, see Vinogradov and Waterbury 1971). Keddie (1971) points out that the word "state" only attained its modern meaning in European languages in the sixteenth century, and that it is somewhat absurd to speak of a monopoly of the legitimate use of physical force for governments that lacked significant standing armies. While the combat between the nomadic tribes, urban factions, governors, and other groups may not completely fit Naroll's definition of warfare as "public lethal group combat between kin groups," obviously, if the government of a state is unable to monopolize force within its boundaries, it is likely to be permeable with regard to outside cultural influences as well. Goitein (1971:1, 403–405) has demonstrated the degree to which medieval Jewish communities maintained contact over often hostile political boundaries. They were allowed extensive autonomy, even in the realm of law enforcement, as long as they paid their taxes and did not overstep limited bounds. The state did not use its power to impose the dominant culture on them.

Naroll's model of the Aztecan-type cultunit consists of a centralized state that not only controls violence within its boundaries, but imposes a common culture on its population. Examples of such imposition are certainly found in premodern, as well as modern times. The Roman Empire is probably the most striking example. Nevertheless, even there one finds that cultural diffusion did not stop at the boundaries of the empire, which, in any case, were in flux. The Romans were influenced by alternative blueprints from Iran, as well as by their own subject peoples, of whom the Jews were one. Similarly, there were communication links between the Palestinian Jews within the Roman Empire and the Babylonian Jews within the Sassanian Empire throughout the period prior to the Arab conquest in the seventh-century. The communication link cannot be dispensed with in dealing with cultural units of this type.

An alternative to Naroll's effort to define territorially homogeneous cultunits is found in Anderson (1971). In dealing with medieval and early modern Europe, Anderson defines three culture areas (or co-traditions), those of the aristocrats, the burghers, and the peasants. The aristocrats had other aristocrats as their reference group, not burghers or peasants living in their own geographic region. Their cultural patterns were spread throughout Europe and moved independently of the others. If burghers or others sought to imitate it, then the aristocrats would modify it to differentiate it further. The diffusion of the burgher culture similarly was not limited by locality. Although Anderson does not go into the communication links of the medieval Jews and gypsies, their communication links were similarly autonomous.

Only the culture of the peasants was different. Here, there was a lack of mobility that prevented the establishment of an independent communication network. Yet, in spite of this, one finds similarities among peasants in various parts of Europe. Anderson suggests these similarities are explained by the fact that the aristocrats in different parts of Europe imposed similar patterns on their cultivators. The case of the peasants is of the type implicit in Naroll's Aztec cultunit, while the other cases would require greater stress on communication links.

The use of contact links in analyzing cultural units would not negate the use of political boundaries, but it would supplement them. Rather than assuming that the political boundary is the key, one would use it together with trade routes, language, and ecological features as explanations of why particular divisions occur. Another aspect, religion, which has up to this point been neglected, should be considered in terms of its relationship to ethnic boundaries and cultural units.

RELIGION, ETHNICITY, AND THE CULTUNIT

Religion was not previously used in defining the cultural unit because Naroll explicitly omitted it. He (1964:289; 1970:735) was obviously well aware of its role in determining group membership and cultural differences in Eurasia. His use of language and political boundaries and his exclusion of religion, in fact, reflects both arbitrariness and reliance on modern nationalist criteria for the definition of the nation. The Jews, of course, are a classic example of an ethnic group whose identity has been determined by religious ideology, both Jewish and Gentile. In addition, the Jewish religious blueprint of a society has played an important role in determining Jewish behavior.

In the Middle East, sectarian affiliation often determines the norms for cousin marriage, divorce, and inheritance patterns, as well as for openness to acculturation from the outside (Zenner 1972). At the same time, during the Greco-Roman and medieval periods, even traditional Jewish societies were faced with cultural patterns that rivaled those of their own religion. Works such as Goitein's monumental study (1971) record how the behavior of Jews during various periods resolved the possible contradictions.

CONCLUSION

Naroll's attempt to define culture-bearing units has been useful in challenging anthropologists to deal with the relationship between the culture-bearing unit and the norms and behavioral practices to which they adhere. Traditional Jewish communities, in many cases, fit his categories, albeit with some minor modification. Nevertheless, Naroll's use of linguistic and political criteria and his neglect of other criteria such as religion have problems. In some measure, this is due to the fact that he and other cross-cultural correlationists have tended to neglect groups such as the Jews, the gypsies, and other dispersed populations. There has been a tendency to think in terms of nonliterate tribes and bands, on the one hand, and modern states, on the other. With some exceptions (for example, see Ember and Ember 1972), such studies have also neglected processes of acculturation. It would be well for them to test this methodology on such problems.

REFERENCES

ADAMS, ROBERT McC.
   1966 *The evolution of urban society.* Chicago: Aldine.
ANDERSON, ROBERT T.
   1971 *Traditional Europe.* San Francisco: Wadsworth.
BARTH, F., *editor et al.*
   1969 *Ethnic groups and boundaries.* Boston: Little, Brown.
BENADETTE, M. J.
   1971 *A Mediterranean society: the community* volume two. Berkeley: University of California.
BESSAC, F.
   1968 "Cultunit and ethnic unit: processes and symbolism," in *Essays in the problem of tribe.* Proceedings of the Annual Spring Meeting of the American Ethnological Society. Edited by June Helm. Seattle: University of Washington Press.
BLANC, HAIM
   1964 *Communal dialects in Baghdad.* Cambridge, Mass.: Harvard University Center for Middle Eastern Studies.
BLOM, JAN-PETTER
   1969 "Ethnic and cultural differentiation," in *Ethnic groups and boundaries.* Edited by F. Barth. Boston: Little, Brown.

DENISON, N.
1971 Review of Die Reste des Juedisch-Deutschen. *Jewish Journal of Sociology* 13(1):118–120.

EMBER, C. R., M. EMBER
1972 Conditions favoring multilocal residence. *Southwestern Journal of Anthropology* 28(4):382–400.

GOITEIN, S. D.
1971 *A Mediterranean society: the community*, volume two. Berkeley: University of California.

GORDON, M. M.
1964 *Assimilation in American life.* New York: Oxford University Press.

HELM, JUNE, editor
1968 *Essays in the problem of tribe.* Proceedings of the Annual Spring Meeting of the American Ethnological Society. Seattle: University of Washington.

HERZOG, M. L.
1964 "Channels of systematic extinction in Yiddish dialects," in *For Max Weinreich on his 70th birthday*, 93–107. The Hague: Mouton.

HERZOG, M. L., W. RAVID, U. WEINREICH, editors
1969 *The field of Yiddish: studies in Yiddish language, folklore and literature*, (third collection). The Hague: Mouton.

HYMES, DELL
1968 "Linguistic problems in defining the concept of tribe," in *Essays in the problem of tribe.* Proceedings of the Annual Spring Meeting of the American Ethnological Society. Edited by June Helm. Seattle: University of Washington.

KEDDIE, N. R.
1971 The Iranian power structure and social change, 1800–1969. *International Journal of Middle Eastern Studies* 2:3–20.

LEACH, E. R.
1964 Comment (on R. Naroll: Ethnic unit classification.) *Current Anthropology* 5:4:299.

LEWIS, B.
1972 The emergence of modern Israel. *Middle Eastern Studies* 8:421–427.

MEAD, MARGARET
1952 Introduction to *Life is with people*, written by M. Zborowski and E. Herzog, 13–14. New York: International Universities Press.

MOERMAN, MICHAEL
1965 Ethnic identification in a complex civilization. *American Anthropologist* 67:1215–1230.

MURDOCK, GEORGE P.
1963 *Outline of world cultures* (third revised edition). New Haven, Conn.: Human Relations Area Files.
1967 Ethnographic atlas — a summary. *Ethnology* 6(2): passim.

NAROLL, RAOUL
1964 On ethnic unit classification. *Current Anthropology* 5:283–312.
1968 "Who are the Lue?" in *Essays in the problem of tribe.* Proceedings of the Annual Spring Meeting of the American Ethnological Society. Edited by June Helm, 72–82. Seattle: University of Washington Press.
1970 "The culture-bearing unit in cross-cultural surveys," in *A handbook of method in cultural anthropology.* Edited by R. Naroll and R. Cohen, 721–765. New York: Natural History Press.

PATAI, RAPHAEL
  1971 *Tents of Jacob.* Englewood Cliffs, N.J.: Prentice-Hall.
POLL, SOLOMON
  1962 *The Hasidic community of Williamsburg.* Glencoe, Ill.: Free Press.
VINOGRADOV, AMAL, JOHN WATERBURY
  1971 Situations of contested legitimacy in Morocco — an alternative framework. *Comparative Studies in Society and History* 13:22–54.
WEINREICH, MAX
  1953 *Yiddish and Yiddishkayt.* Mordecai Kaplan Jubilee Volume, 481–514. New York: Jewish Theological Seminary.
WEINREICH, URIEL
  1963 "Culture geography at a distance — some of the problems in the study of East European Jewry," in *Symposium on Language and Culture.* Proceedings of the 1962 Annual Spring Meeting of the American Ethnological Society. Edited by V. Garfield and W. Chafe. Seattle: University of Washington Press.
WEINREICH, URIEL, *editor*
  1954 *The field of Yiddish: studies in Yiddish language, folklore, and literature.* New York: Linguistic Circle of New York.
  1965 *The field of Yiddish* (second collection). The Hague: Mouton.
ZBOROWSKI, M., E. HERZOG
  1952 *Life is with people.* New York: International Universities Press.
ZENNER, W. P.
  1967 Ethnic assimilation and corporate group. *Sociological Quarterly* 8:340–348.
  1968 Syrian Jews in three social settings. *Jewish Journal of Sociology* 10:101–120.
  1972 Some aspects of ethnic stereotype content in the Galilee. *Middle Eastern Studies* 8:405–416.

SECTION FOUR

Communal Society in America

Eschatological Living: Religious Experience in the Shaker Community

JOHN H. MORGAN

The religious communism of the Shakers is built upon the foundation of an understanding of the "second coming" of Christ as a social incarnation. The Shakers themselves use the terms "communistic" and "communitarian communism" more frequently than do any others to describe the total nature of their community in which all goods are held in common. Within Shaker circles, the formal term for their communitarianism is "the united inheritance."[1] In addition, there is a rather substantial and still growing body of literature on collective settlements, past and present, in the social sciences, especially in the fields of social anthropology and social psychology.[2] There is no question of the value of these studies for increased understanding of collective settlements. The nature of this study precludes the utilization of these materials since our focus, through the Shaker's literature, is on how the Shakers themselves understood their religious experience of community. This approach may be charac-

---

[1] Just a sampling of Shaker literature is enough to determine that the often used term "communism" is a readily acceptable term descriptive of Shakerism. For example, see Evans (1871a), Allen (1897) and Andrews (n.d.).

[2] In the past two decades, there has been a surge of interest in social analysis of collective settlements and millenarian movements. Of increasing interest in sociological circles is the work of Dr. Yonina Talmon of Hebrew University. Her specialization is in collective settlements, and she has made an important contribution to the subject in "Pursuit of the millennium" (1962:125–148). A few other important works are Aberle (1962), Cohn (1957), Hobsbaum (1959), Worsley (1957; 1961), and Wilson (1961). Another book of profound impact in religious community studies is Turner (1969). This is an analysis of rites of passage in religious communities ranging from the Franciscan Order in the Middle Ages to the hippies and Hell's Angels of the 1960's. Of special interest in terms of an understanding of the place of Shaker studies in social anthropological perspectives are his chapters on "Liminality and Communitas" and "Communitas: Model and Process." Finally, Rosabeth Moss Kanter (1972) has illustrated a sociological understanding of the phenomenon of communal settlements.

terized as a "folk exegesis" suggestive of the sensitive insights of Turner (1969).[3] Through such an approach, one can hope to come to see better the way in which the Shakers themselves understood their ideological and communitarian formulations as expressive of their experience of Christ-as-community.

The Shakers had no intention of establishing an expression of Christian experience in community that was totally new in the history of the church. To the contrary, as Morgan (1972) has suggested, they were insistent upon their continuous relationship with the "primitive church" of the dispensation of Jesus and the apostles. Yet, it must be remembered that for Shakers, continuity did not mean a static continuation of the same ecclesiastical forms or any other forms, for that matter. The *Millennial praises* (Wells 1813), their earliest hymnal, contended that forms and structures "must be limited to their period of usefulness: for no gift or order of God can be binding on Believers for a longer term of time than it can be profitable to their travel in the gospel."

Central to the Shakers' understanding of the participational experience of union with Christ in the church was the communal experience of the first gathering of the church described in the Book of Acts, where they "had all things common . . . sold their possessions and goods, and parted them to all men as every man had need." "Union in church relation" is the characterization Shakers give to their experience, which for them is similar to the experience of the first Pentecostals.[4] Christ socially incarnate in community makes reasonable, and indeed logical, this communistic enterprise. Evans (1871b:97) says: "Brotherly love, community of interest, community of goods! This picture of first century Christianity . . . has ever affected the imagination of men." Morgan (1973a) has shown that it is as natural for this "community of interest" to express its union with Christ as it is for the human body to express its unitive nature through the cooperation of all its constituent parts in its life-processes. Just as the hand does not keep back service that it is uniquely designed to render to the rest of the body, so neither is it characteristic of Christian union for any part of the social body of Christ to keep back anything: services, finances, and so on, or any other means of contributing to the welfare of the body. Evans (1871b:97) notes: "Christians have sighed over communistic Christianity's lost delights, sadly supposing it an impossibility under present conditions."

For the Shakers, the fundamental explanation of their communistic community is their religious experience (Morgan, 1974a.) The centrality of their understanding of union with Christ finds expression in their

---

[3] Turner calls it "native exegesis." Professor Bhabagrahi Misra suggests using the term "folk exegesis," since the word "native" has a colonial overtone.

[4] A sample of recent studies of the Pentecostal experience in modern times includes Hollenweger (1972), Nichol (1971), Ford (1970), and Samarin (1972).

"united inheritance." They were also aware of the social and economic advantages of and attractions to the communal way of life. This is evidenced in the literature on socialism by F. W. Evans (1890a,b), who was first attracted to the Shakers by the socioeconomic dimension of the tradition.

At the beginning of the nineteenth century, Youngs (1808) suggested that, in the light of all the turmoil in society with its "extraordinary changes, revolutions and remarkable events . . . rolling on, through the physical, political, moral and religious world," there is no hope that is more promising or that has greater expectations for society than "the formation of associations in which all the members can enjoy equal rights and privileges, physical, and moral, both of a spiritual and temporal nature, in a united capacity" (Green and Wells 1827:1-3). The Shakers observe that although men everywhere seek such a society, their many attempts end in failure because something is lacking in their community.

It is well known that with their wisdom, skill, benevolent designs, unity of intention, convenience of location and confidence of success, they have soon failed in their expectations, and been scattered as before . . . Not withstanding these general failures, we (Shakers) are prepared to show that there is a sure system, founded upon the principles of a unity of interest in all things. . . . (Green and Wells 1827:1-3).

That which is missing is the recognition of the centrality of the religious experience of Christ's presence in the community of faith:

The United Society of Believers (called Shakers) was founded upon the principles of equal rights and privileges, with a united interest in all things, both spiritual and temporal and has been maintained and supported in this Society (Green and Wells 1827:1-3).

Even though collective settlements recognize the importance of socioeconomic equality, they are doomed to failure unless they also recognize as primary the spiritual nature of the communal experience. The confidence of the Shakers in the success of their communitarian experience was built upon the experiential vitality of the realization of union with Christ embodied in their communal life (Morgan, 1973b).

Shaker theologians Green and Wells make a strong case for the superiority of the Shaker variety of communal life on the basis of historical witness of other recorded communistic attempts and their inevitable failure. Writing in 1851, they invite anyone to instance "any other religious institution which has stood fifty years without a visible declension of the principles and order of the institution" (Green and Wells 1851:18). Though man seeks for this shared life in Christ, his attempts consistently seem to fail except in Shakerism, for the "central Society of this community has now stood upon the ground of a united and consecrated interest, and maintained the institution of equal rights and privileges in all things, both spiritual and temporal, for more than sixty years" (Green and Wells 1851:18). This longevity itself is alleged as a "sufficient test of the superior principles upon which this institution is founded ... and its progressive improvement can be ascribed to ... the blessing, protection, and government of Divine Power and Wisdom...." (Green and Wells 1851:18). The Shakers were aware that these were strong and serious claims, but their experience in communal life had convinced them beyond question that they existed by a divine will.

In spite of this emphasis on the sanction from the heavenly sphere, or perhaps because of it, the Shakers escaped the traps of the romantically naive "utopianism" of so many communistic attempts. Theirs was a communal effort of a spiritual nature, and with the spiritual maturation of its leaders, the society was able to establish and maintain itself in all its subsequent developments. The spiritual reality of the community was the foundation upon which the practical considerations of communal living were made. Although the Shakers were able to prosper economically through the years, "the temporal interest held by the United Society never was intended, nor can be, appropriated to the wealth or personal aggrandizement of a few" (Green and Wells 1851:18). Indeed, the "temporal interest (of the society) is held in conformity to the order of the Primitive Church of Christ," for it was social and not individual in its nature and intention:

This dedication does not end with the lives of those who thus dedicate it, but is designed to descend in perpetuity to a regular heirship, who can never apply it to any other purposes than those stipulated in our *Constitution or Covenant* (Green and Wells 1851:18).

As is suggested in this citation dealing with the practical economic issue in communistic communities, there are doctrinal overtones relative to the Shaker concepts of covenanting and its centrality in their idea of salvation in community.[5] Nonetheless, in all of these considerations of constitutional arrangements relative to economics, the Shakers would have us know that these "temporal arrangements, however economical, fall far short of unfolding the inward principle by which the concern is managed" (Green and Wells 1851:27). This "inward principle" is that which is of

---

[5] The following citation from Elder Richard McNemar (1831) will indicate the nature of the Shaker's doctrine of covenantal soteriology.

"When one makes a promise to another, and that promise is accepted, this constitutes a *covenant* or *agreement*. Thus the promise of eternal life was made to Christ before the foundation of the world, and accepted by him in behalf of all his seed. In this promise, or *covenant of life*, the *Father* and *Son* were perfectly united ... The *covenant* itself, is absolute, unconditional and inviolable...."

special concern for our purposes, for it lies at the core of the Shakers' religious understanding of their communistic community (Morgan, 1976).

A "theological" anthropology of Shakers is crucial here for us, because their understanding of man is that he is of a "divine" nature, "God in miniature," and God's "earthly representative." For Shakers, there is no more explicit exemplar of this divine nature than the communistic community itself. Fraser says: "Such a community is a manifestation of the divine in man . . . [for] every act of goodness (epitomized in classless communism) is a divine act" (Fraser 1890?:2). This manifestation of the "divine in man" is of such force in humanity that Fraser suggests "where the life and love of God is shed abroad in human spirits there is no need to manufacture a community having goods in common; *it springs up of itself*, and is the result of the internal forces of divine relationships" (Fraser 1890?:2; emphasis added).

The pervasiveness of these internal forces of divine relationships is further commented upon by Andrews: "People in all times seem to have been aware that there is not only a disposition but a necessity in man's nature, leading him to fraternize, to congregate into communities and live in as close relation as the nature of his circumstances would permit" (Andrews n.d.:1). Often, however, the very people who were most conscious of these "internal forces" failed in their communal attempts, for they refused to recognize as central the spiritual nature of the undertaking. Whereas the family relation as the seedbed for human existence was the first great necessity of the race, Andrews (n.d.:2) suggests that the communistic relation is also a great necessity, a kindred necessity of equal importance: and although not primal, it is final and completes what the other begins.[6]

Regardless of what motivating forces — moral, economic, or social — the world ascribed to the Shaker lifestyle, the Shakers themselves asserted that "the purpose of the life is not communism, but the living in practical work of a highly developed spiritual life, requiring strong, devoted natures" (White and Taylor 1905:307).[7] Communistic commun-

---

[6] Andrews establishes a binary relationship between the "family relation" and "church relation," the first epitomizing the relationship in the natural sphere, and the second, that relationship in the spiritual sphere. Thus: "That true communistic relation . . . requires that a man be governed by the liberal sentiments, an equal care for his fellowman. . . . No matter what the society, whether savage, civilized, or Christian, there must needs be a common bond of union, a universally pervading element in which all interests center, and toward which all aspirations point . . . in order to have that degree of harmony which creates and which alone sustains society. In natural generative society, this harmonial bond is the reproductive instinct culminating in the family relation. . . . In the spiritual regenerative society, this harmonial bond is love — love to God, supreme, and neighbor as self in the communistic relation"

[7] In this connection, the authors call attention to the elders and elderesses and the qualities demanded of those offices, namely, "delicacy, strength, courage, persistence, hope, energy,

ity is not the intention — it is the product — of the higher developed spiritual life. Men do not set out to build a communal way of life and become spiritual thereby; to the contrary, they ultimately build a communistic society as a manifestation of the divine nature exemplified in the higher spiritual development. In order for the doctrine of realized eschatology to be actualized on this earth, the work of bringing about those characteristics of the kingdom must begin in the religious community as the social incarnation of Christ. Evans says:

> If God is to wipe away all tears from all eyes, so that there is no more sorrow, no more sighing, no more pain, physical nor mental, then there must be abolition, not only of slavery, but of land monopoly, poverty, oppression, sickness and disease, — of army, navy, doctors, lawyers, priests, landlords, of debtors and creditors, of rich and poor; in the New Earth, each one sitting under his or her own vine with mutual National Cooperation; and in the New Heavens, all being brothers and sisters, they enjoy all things in common in a Heavenly Community (White and Taylor 1905:308).

Lest it be thought that Elder Frederick Evans is speaking of a "heavenly abode" in the traditional sense, it must be remembered that, for Shakers, the "heavenly life" is created wherever and whenever men and women come to know consciously that Christ has come in religious community, and thus, there is no waiting for union with Christ and "at-one-ment" with God in an afterlife. This "heavenly community" spoken of by Evans is the experiential reality of Shakers in their Christed community. Keeping in mind the two orders mentioned above, that is, the natural order of family relations and the heavenly order of communal life, once that communal life is entered into, the heavenly or angelic life is begun.

The natural order of family relations can be perfect for those who will strive to attain the heights of it, as it leads toward ever higher spiritual levels, for "were the conditions of this order adhered to, in obedience to God's laws written in the physiological relations of man's being, a race of worthy, capable and moral men and women might be produced, serving God in serving mankind" (White and Taylor 1905:298). But because of man's moral state, one in which he continually commits sin, that is, negating the spiritual realm by claiming the supremacy of the natural, he is not moving toward the spiritual plane where men and women "lay aside

---

endurance, patience, and a power of penetration little short of divine." These qualities are needed because of the kind of people who seek admission to the society, for example, "various classes and conditions of men and women, all degrees of culture and ignorance, all stages of mental and spiritual development come for admission. The sincere and the hypocritic, the deceiver and the self-deceived, the crank and the fool, the humbug and the fanatic, the weary, the lame, the lazy, the hungry, — the deadbeats from life's thousand paths, all come knocking at the doors of the Shaker Community."

selfishness, live harmoniously, by moderate labor gain a sufficiency of physical necessities and in unison attain a higher spiritual, a richer intellectual development, than is possible on the individual, competitive plane" (White and Taylor 1905:298).

Shakers continually insist that their quest is not for a comfortable system of socioeconomic communitarian living in which physical and mental pressures might be avoided. There are a "spiritual family." As an inevitable and natural outgrowth of their experience of union with Christ, and as a result of the recognition of man as "divine," they have produced a communal life that reflects their experience empirically, a communistic community, conceived of as the "united inheritance" (Morgan, 1974b). Dunlavy, (1847:242) in speaking of the miracles that were performed by Jesus and his apostles as undeniably true for that day, says: "it is also undeniable that the use of them gradually subsided, no doubt, as the necessity for them ceased, and their use was superseded by the more permanent, substantial and genuine fruits and evidence of the Gospel — charity, union and good works."

These are the qualities that maximize the spiritual potential of communal life as Christ Incarnate, namely, love, union, and good works, which are the higher gifts of the Second Christian Church, the Millennial Church. The past good is ever being superseded by the present good, which, in due time, will likewise be surpassed. "To constitute a true church of Christ, there must necessarily be a union of faith, of motives and of interest, in all the members who compose it" (Green and Wells 1827:58). This union of faith is a key to establishing the continuity of religious community in its practical workings. For Shakerism, this "union of faith" is a eucharistic experience that is continually repeated in the ongoing life of the community. Green and Wells continue:

[there must be] one body and one bread, [and] nothing short of this union in all things, both spiritual and temporal, can constitute a true church, which is the body of Christ ... wherever that body exists, it will bring into operation every individual talent for the general good of the whole body. And here is the prayer of Jesus answered: 'That they may be one, even as we are one' (1827:59).

In order for the community to maximize the spiritual realization of Christ's existence in union with the body of believers, there must be a primary interest in bringing to the common life every talent and every gift that might be found in the collective community. Thus, paradoxically, there is an emphasis on the individuality of each member that directly correlates with an emphasis upon the body collective. Let us note a few observations by Shakers in order to introduce this correlation between the individual and the community as experientally verified in their communal life.

"Union," as we have seen, "is the distinguishing characteristic of the true followers of Christ . . . [and] it is an essential part of the worship of God" (Green and Wells 1827:94). "Union in church relations" is the motif that runs throughout Shakerism, for it is this sense of unity on the spiritual plane that is crucial in their understanding of social incarnation. Hence, this awareness reaches its highest point in the collective consciousness of the community during common worship. As Green and Wells explain:

Where a body of Christians are united in Spirit, they cannot but feel a peculiar blessing when united in their religious devotions. Indeed the true union of the Spirit has a direct tendency to produce a harmonious order in the exercises of divine worship . . . [for] such is the harmony of the heavenly world, and such must be the harmony of the Christian church, in its completed order (1827:94).[8]

Worship for Shakers encompasses much more of life than just those times of "religious devotions" that are held in the community during the day and week. The unitive spirit itself is worship, and every activity of the believers-in-community is worship. Green and Wells summarize this sense of union as divine worship:

It will doubtless be granted, that no one can worship God for another; that each one must exercise his own faculties in the service of God, and not depend on the exercise of another's faculties. And hence the necessity of a harmonious unity in divine worship, that each individual may participate in the united devotions of the whole body, and mutually contribute to the strength, and share in the harmony of all. Union is the strength of God's people, and the glory of divine worship. Thus united in spirit, and inspired with divine love, a whole assembly can move in harmonious order, and devote the active powers of soul and body to the giver of all good . . . (1827:94).

Shakers understand union to entail a full recognition of the differences that exist in any collective body of human beings. To minimize individual uniqueness proper to each person is not to reach union, but rather social confusion and individual discontent. Union in the religious communistic community is a "harmonious order" and activity in which each in his own gift and talent contributes to the welfare of the whole. There is no substitute for the unique gift each one has, for if anyone holds back his own gift, then the body is not built up. This sense of union as worship is recognized to be unlike the usual understanding of union.

---

[8] "Where there are diversities of operations, there may appear a want of harmony to a spectator who knows not *the things of the Spirit*; but when these operations proceed from the same Divine Spirit, as they must in the true order of the Church of Christ, those exercised thereby feel a heavenly harmony, one-ness and union in the Spirit" (See 1 Corinthians. 12:4–12).

This union is of a different nature, separate and distinct from all the union which can possibly subsist among the children of the flesh, professed Christians and others... [because in this spiritual union] true believers are able to maintain and increase ... gathering together, more and more, as they increase in the work of God in Christ ... (Dunlavy 1847:267).

Growing together in the spiritual work of Christ means that each individual in the community utilizes each of his gifts and talents to its full potential for the increase of the welfare of the society. Dunlavy says:

[The] very existence of such a union proves it to be of God, and in the Spirit of Christ ... [for history records] that such a connection in a united interest cannot be supported by any cause [social, economic, and so on] separate and distinct from the Spirit of Christ ... [but the fact that a society] does exist in a united interest therefore proves the agency and indwelling of the Spirit of Christ.... (1847:271).

The multiple failure of others and their own success is indication enough for Shakers to substantiate their claim that a communistic society must be the result of and not the aim of a religious community; reliance upon the primacy of the spiritual, rather than on the natural sphere, is the cause of success.

This "union," which exists in the Shaker community, is the result of the presence of "love" in the hearts of each member. This love, like the union that it produces is different from the love known in the natural world. Dunlavy states:

[The] love of the body of Christ is peculiar to his members, separate and distinct from all love of the children of this world [otherwise, it would not distinguish them], so its operations must be such as do not pertain to any rank or class ... to prove the present agency and indwelling of the Spirit of God[9] (1847:266).

Shakers are uninterested in discussions of love as an ideological abstraction. Their interest is in love, as it is demonstrated and manifested in life. "Now the immediate production of love," says Dunlavy (1850:4), "is union — such a union as the world knows not." Union produced by this love is the characteristic mark of the Christian in the world, for "where such a union is not manifested ... the true evidence of Christianity is wanting" (Dunlavy 1850:5). Just as this love and union together are uniquely characteristic of the Christians in communion with Divinity, it consequently precludes the possibility of a counterfeit community, for it

---

[9] On the nature of love, Dunlavy makes the following comment: "But let it be granted that love is not known by intuitive knowledge; that is, gift and sensation, or internal affection of love is not visible, or in the abstract, to the natural man, it can nevertheless be discovered in its operations; for as faith without works is dead, being alone, so love without effects would be a contradiction of terms. 'But whoso keepeth his word, in him verily is the love of God perfected; hereby know we that we are in him' (1 John 2:5). Love therefore is manifested by its operations as the cause by the effect" (1847:266).

is by these characteristics that they are "known and distinguished from all other people" (Dunlavy 1850:14). It is the Shaker experience in religious community that constitutes the verification of this form of life.

The communistic community is the empirical demonstration of unitive participation in the Christ-Life. Union and love of Christians is that which establishes their relationship with God, and this relationship is explicitly manifested in the communal way of life in which all are equal and all things, spiritual and material, are held in common. According to Dunlavy (1847:249): "Christians know themselves to be of God in Christ ... by the work of God in them and the fruits which they bring forth." The being of "God in Christ," which characterizes a community of believers as Christian, is not, as it may seem to suggest, something that is hidden in the spiritual realm, for "the first description of the Church ... by which they are known, is their doing the will of God" (Dunlavy 1847:249).

The "doing" is the sign to the world. "The same rule of judgment, and the same marks by which Christians know themselves, and know one another, so as to apprehend the body of Christ collectively, serve in the main, to prove to the world and to all men, who are the true Church" (Dunlavy 1847:249). If the world cannot recognize the community as the body of Christ collectively, then it must not be the body of Christ. Shakers emphasize the importance of the world as the witness of the natural sphere to verify that they were truly the embodiment of the Christ-Spirit.

This paper attempts to understand the meaning and nature of the communal experience of the Shakers as they themselves perceive and explain it. This type of approach is advanced here not as an alternative to the sociohistorical perspectives but as a necessary complement to them, at least to the extent that the inquirer wishes to comprehend more fully the meaningfulness of the communal life as experienced by actual participants. This brief inquiry has been facilitated by the voluminous literature written by Shakers as they were striving for deeper and more exhaustive ways of expressing the "communal experience" as actually lived in day-to-day activities.

To test this phenomenological approach to the understanding of the Shakers' worldview and tradition, two different manuscripts were submitted to the presiding officer of the Shaker Society, Sister Mildred Barker. She was asked to judge the accuracy of the interpretations. On both occasions, she commended the works as significantly emphatic and sympathetic to the "experiential category" in the communal lifestyle of the Shakers.

REFERENCES

ABERLE, DAVID
1962 "A note on relative deprivation theory as applied to millenarian and other cult movements," in *Millenial dreams in action*. Comparative studies in society and history, supplement. Edited by Sylvia L. Thrupp. The Hague: Mouton.

ALLEN, M. CATHERINE
1897 *A full century of communism*. Pittsfield, Mass.: Eagle.

ANDREWS, W. WATSON
n.d. *Communism*. Mt. Lebanon, N.Y.: Shaker Community Pamphlet.

COHN, NORMAN
1957 *The pursuit of the millennium*. New York: Essential Books.

DUNLAVY, JOHN
1847 *The manifesto, or a declaration of the doctrine and practice of the church of Christ*. New York: E. O. Jenkins.
1850 *The nature and character of the true church of Christ proved by plain evidence*. New York: G. W. Wood.

EVANS, FREDERICK W.
1871a *Shaker communism: or test of divine inspiration. The second Christian or Gentile pentecostal church, as exemplified by seventy communities of Shakers in America*. London: J. Burns.
1871b *Religious communism: A Lecture by F. W. Evans. Delivered at St. George's Hall, London*. London: J. Burns.
1890a *Capital and labor: wail of a striker*. Mt. Lebanon, N.Y.
1890b *The country: A new earth and new heaven*. Mt. Lebanon, N.Y.

FORD, J. MASSINGBERD
1970 *Pentecostal experience*. New York: Paulist-Neuman.

FRASER, DANIEL
1890? *Analysis of human society: Declaring the law which creates and sustains a community having goods in common*. Mt. Lebanon, N.Y.: Shaker Community Pamphlet.

GREEN, CALVIN, SETH Y. WELLS
1872 *A summary view of the millennial church or united society of believers*. Albany, N.Y.: Packard & Benthuysen.
1851 *A brief exposition of the established principles, and regulations of the United Society of Believers called Shakers*. Albany, N.Y.: Packard and Van Benthuysen.

HOBSBAUM, E. J.
1959 *Primitive rebels*. New York: Free Press of Glencoe.

HOLLENWEGER, W. J.
1972 *The Pentecostals: the charismatic movement in the churches*. Minneapolis: Augsburg Publishing House.

KANTER, ROSABETH MOSS
1972 *Commitment and community: communes and utopias in sociological perspective*. Cambridge, Mass.: Harvard University Press.

McNEMAR, RICHARD
1831 *A review of the most important events relating to the rise and progress of the United Society of Believers*. Union Village, Ohio: Union Press.

MORGAN, JOHN H.
1972 "English Quakerism's forgotten legacy to America: the shaking Quakers." *Friends Quarterly of London* 17(g): 272–275.

1973a "Religious communism: the Shaker experiment in Christian community." *The Shaker Quarterly* 13(4): 119–131.
1973b "The Baptist-Shaker encounter in New England: a study in religious confrontation in eighteenth-century America." *The Shaker Quarterly* 13(1/2): 152–163.
1974a "Experience as knowledge: a study in Shaker theology." *The Shaker Quarterly* 14(2): 43–55.
1974b "The Shaker experience: two centuries as debtors to God." *Quaker Life* 15(12): 10–11.
1976 "The 'inward principle' of communal life in the Shaker society." *Communal Studies* 3(1): 9–14.

NICHOL, JOHN
1971 *Pentecostals: a history and contemporary survey of the Pentecostal movement.* Plainfield, N.J.: Logos Press.

SAMARIN, W. J.
1972 *Tongues of men and angels.* New York: Macmillan.

TALMON, YONINA
1962 Pursuit of the millennium: the relation between religious and social change. *Archives Europeenes de Sociologie* 3:125–148.

TURNER, VICTOR W.
1969 *The ritual process: structure and anti-structure.* Chicago: Aldine.

WELLS, S. Y., *compiler*
1813 *Millennial praises, containing a collection of gospel hymns, in four parts: adapted to the day of Christ's second appearing.* Hancock: J. Tallcott.

WHITE, ANNA, LEILA SARAH TAYLOR
1905 *Shakerism: its meaning and message. Embracing an historical account, statement of belief and spiritual experience of the church.* Columbus, Ohio: Fred J. Heer.

WILSON, B. R.
1961 *Sects and society.* Berkeley: University of California Press.

WORSLEY, PETER
1957 *The trumpet shall sound.* London: MacGibbon & Kee.
1961 Rebellion and revolution. *Science and society* 25:26–27.

YOUNGS, BENJAMIN S.
1808 *The testimony of Christ's second appearing.* Lebanon, Ohio: John McClean, Western Star.

Religious Orientation of the Communal Counter-Culture: God, Nature, and Mysticism in Contemporary Society

DAVID BUCHDAHL

Today's communes represent one of the more dramatic developments of the loosely associated counter-culture in America. It is obvious that they both reflect and contribute to the processes of historical change that confront us, but their meaning and significance are disputed by participants and observers alike. Personal estimations are likely to depend on a number of conflicting interests, as well as on one's own historical consciousness.[1] I, myself, see the communes as being essentially involved with the transformation of a religious consciousness that has contributed to the peculiar development of Western society over the last several centuries, namely inner-worldly asceticism. This type of asceticism could not easily retain its meaning as an orientation to life in the present century. Depending as it does on a particular conception of God, it has grown steadily weaker as belief has suffered from attacks by the great iconoclasts — Darwin, Nietzsche, and Freud. Several decades were required before this iconoclasm transformed itself from an outrageous attack into an acceptable posture. To be an atheist today is not shocking, it is rather boring. And while theologians (some of them anyway) looked for awhile toward the "secular city," other natives were discovering the springs of the sacred buried in the forest, spurning the American tower of Babel, and searching for a god in the garden.

The first draft of this paper was written during the first months of 1973. I would like to thank David Schneider, Talcott Parsons, Bhabagrahi Misra, Victor Turner, and Milton Singer for their helpful comments and criticism. My research on the counter-culture extended from 1969 to 1973, a year of which was spent on a commune in eastern Washington. In this revised version, I have maintained the "ethnographic present" if only to heighten the reader's sense of how quickly the present becomes the past in our contemporary world. For a more extended treatment of the rural communes, see Buchdahl (1974).

[1] For three quite different depth-historical views of the hippie counter-culture, see Thompson (1972), Nuttall (1970), and Snyder (1969).

Nietzsche's words, written nearly a century ago, have a special meaning in a contemporary context:

> Once the sin against God was the greatest sin; but God died and these sinners died with him. To sin against the earth is now the most dreadful thing, and to esteem the entrails of the unknowable higher than the meaning of the earth (1954:13).

The meaning of the earth is one of those ultimates that keeps haunting the mystic consciousness. Nietzsche was still close enough to the Enlightenment to think that man embodied this meaning, an idea shared by today's militants, who claim the moral supremacy of Nietzsche's "ubermensche." But mankind is only one of the earth's manifestations, and its significance is questionable. The firm denial of a homocentric world is an unquestioned premise of today's mystic.

A change in the conception of God is a cultural event of some magnitude, especially because the character of a culture is heavily influenced by the notion of God that predominates within it. American culture bears the imprint of a particular conception of God — the God of Abraham, Isaac, and Jacob — mediated through Protestants such as Calvin, Cotton Mather, and Billy Graham. The counter-culture represents an elaboration of reality independent from that notion and draws its character from a quite different, if not altogether new, understanding of what God is. The difference is implied in a comment that a young man made to me as we talked about our experiences with LSD. "I heard someone say that acid is the way that God decided to come to America. You know," he added without a trace of irony, "I think that's true." To understand this statement, and the whole essence of the counter-culture (and in just what way it is "counter"), it is necessary to look more closely at the concept of "god" as a cultural item. The object will be to discover first not how it is defined in other cultural traditions, but how it operates as an ordering concept within a symbolic universe.

GOD AND REALITY

Individuals inhabit various spheres of the culture that surrounds them in the form of retrievable information, and their travels throughout the symbolic universe can be more or less restricted. But however narrow particular horizons may be, man's symbolic representations of reality imply some horizon beyond which lies the unthinkable, and within which is contained all-that-which-is. Cultures have mechanisms to express or symbolize this state of affairs and to allow thought to address itself to the unity that is occasionally felt or perceived. In Western thought, the concept of God has served this purpose and continues to function in the same manner today for significantly large numbers of people. The ultimate source of all reality, God is at the same time the embodiment of the horizon and all that lies beyond — the representation of the "wholly other." It is around this concept, variously defined, that Western man has articulated his worldview, formulating his ideas of human nature, morality, society, and life and death.

One can deny the God of the Bible, but in order to think about reality completely, some sort of god-term is still required for a coherent symbol system. Kenneth Burke (1961:25) suggests that the requirement results from a purely linguistic motive, "a logic of entitlement that is completed by the rising to ever and ever higher orders of generalization" in our designations or mappings of reality. "Such a secular summarizing term would be technically a god-term in the sense that its role was analogous to the overall entitling role played by the theologian's word for the godhead." Even when the concern is directed to the realm of natural events, some concept of this sort has been necessary for those attempting a complete and coherent linguistic specification of reality. Hence, in Aristotle, one finds the concept of an unmoved-mover, and in a more recent system, Whitehead develops the notion of God as the Principle of Concretion, a principle that thought requires in order to account for any concrete actualization, as opposed to sheer potentiality.[2]

Whitehead's discussion of God is revealing in this context because of its resemblance to Burke's argument. Whitehead writes:

That which is metaphysically indeterminate has nevertheless to be categorically determinate. We have come to the limit of rationality. For there is a categorical limitation which does not spring from any metaphysical reason (1967:178).

That is, it springs, as Burke suggests, from the very logic of words and thought, from linguistic categorization. One could also say that man requires a god because he uses symbols to describe and categorize his experience. Persons have a god because they talk to one another, not because of any metaphysical necessity (except insofar as talking to one another is seen as a metaphysical necessity). Systematic philosophy, which is the attempt to convey reality accurately in linguistic form, is preoccupied with God as the mystic who contemplates the ultimate concept in silence, trying to move through the words and closer to the reality they conceal and reveal.[3]

---

[2] For Aristotle's discussion of God as the unmoved mover, see his *Metaphysics*. A concise statement of Whitehead's view of God can be found in Hartshorne and Reese (1953:273–285).

[3] It seems that Durkheim had something like this in mind in his conception of divinity. He writes: "For as the role of the categories is to envelop all the other concepts, the category *par excellence* would seem to be this very concept of totality" (1915:489). Durkheim's mistake was to think that "the concept of totality is *only* the abstract form of the concept of society: it

One can discern the linguistic aspect of the god-term in Anselm's classic definition of God as "a being than which nothing greater can be conceived." Alan Watts (1972:116), one of the chief theologians of the counter-culture, displays this aspect quite neatly when he renders the Sanskrit formula "sat chit ananda" as "the which than which there is no whicher." It is also evident in a recent statement by Paul Ricoeur (1973), in which he argues that the word "god" refers to "the total space of linguistic discourse." Perhaps certain primitive creation myths are simply the transformation of this historical process into its opposite, depicting the creation of the world and man through the spoken word of some anthropomorphic deity. The linguistic source of the deity is transformed into creation through God's speech. One finds such an idea — a suggestion of the dialectic that exists between the human condition and its reflections in culture — in Genesis, of course, as well as in other places.[4]

One can see, then, that while the systemization of reality leads to the notion of a god-term, the latter exerts a definite influence on further understandings of that reality. As a symbolic operator, the god-term serves to close and complete the categories, to mark the limits of thought, but it also determines the nature of the reality from which it was derived. Burke (1961:35ff) refers to this process as a "dialectic of attribution," in which he sees the "upward way," where the god-term takes on the characteristics of the natural order (power, personality, reason, and so on) and the "downward way," wherein the natural order is recharged with these now sacred attributes.

The impact of this process in the West has been extremely significant, for it is through the concept of God that the idea of an enduring moral and natural order has been legitimized. Whitehead, in his search for the antecedent conditions for the rise of modern science, argues:

> There can be no living science unless there is a widespread conviction in the existence of an Order of things, and in particular an Order of Nature.... We have to trace the rise of the instinctive faith that there is an Order of Nature which can be traced in every detained occurrence. It must come from the medieval insistence

---

is the whole which includes all things, the supreme class which embraces all other classes" (1915:490). Men, at some time, might confound the space of society with space in general, as he suggests, but generally, they know that the totality is greater than the social space. This is precisely why separate concepts of society and divinity continue to have meaning. It is not the case, as Durkheim believed, that "at bottom, the concept of totality, that of society and that of divinity, are very probably only different aspects of the same notion" (1915:490, fn. 18). Rather, each of these have a common aspect of universality and are therefore easily related. But divinity is the totality *par excellence,* the totality of totalities, one might say, which, because of its unique and insurpassable status, is understood and greeted as the "wholly other."

[4] For example, see also the creation myths of the Oiutu and Maori (Radin 1957:329, 354). In this connection, a statement by Levi-Strauss (1966:252) is especially interesting: "Language, an unreflecting totalization, is human reason which has its reasons, and of which man knows nothing,"

on the rationality of God, conceived as with the personal energy of Jehovah and with the rationality of a Greek philosopher. The search into nature could only result in the vindication of the faith in rationality (1967:12).

The civil order, or the order of law, has also been established on the basis of this deity. From the Mosaic code to the divine right of kings, it was the will and power of God that legitimized civil authority. When Grotius tried in the seventeenth century to argue for the idea of law merely on the basis of the Good, which had worked adequately for the Greeks, he was condemned to prison by an ecclesiastical court.[5] When Hobbes argued in the *Leviathan* (ch. 13) that it was Nature and not God that "hath made men so equal," the only order in society arose from the application of brute force. Instead of some sort of Augustinian harmony existing before the rule of law, there was only a "war of all against all." It is apparent that, in the West, any notion of order, in nature or in society, has usually depended on the belief in this rational and transendent God — Jehovah, the creator of the universe.

There also has been in the West another and quite different conception of God, one in which God is understood as a substance that permeated the entire creation, including man and the natural world — a sacred spirit, perhaps, or the "stuff" of the universe. This concept has received many and varied expression, but one of the most beautiful occurs in the following lines from Wordsworth's poem, "Tintern Abbey":

And I have felt
A presence that disturbs me with the joy
Of elevated thoughts; a sense sublime
Of something far more deeply interfused,
Whose dwelling is the light of setting suns,
And the round ocean and the living air,
And the blue sky, and in the mind of man
A motion and a spirit, that impels
All thinking things, all objects of all thought,
And rolls through all things.

It is this something abiding in the sun and sea and sky, and even in the minds of men, that represents the god-term of the counter-culture. It is not exactly Nature itself, but a more diffuse idea of Spirit, which exists as a vital force within it and unites all of nature's manifestations.

From this perspective, it can be seen that the counter-culture is only a specific manifestation of a recurring theme in Western history, a theme that is made possible by the potential diversity of interpretations that a cultural system will always yield. It is the most recent attempt to find

---

[5] Grotius is a central figure in the development of modern thought. If Locke had followed him more closely instead of relying on theological conservatism, we might today be one nation under the god, instead of under God (see also Ernest Cassirer [1955:234–241]).

meaning in an immanent God, and to worship this Being in all its varied forms. In the present time, people are following the plea made by Diderot in the midst of the Enlightenment. Men, he said, had banished divinity from the world and confined it to sacred sanctuaries. "Madmen that you are, destroy these enclosures.... Liberate God, see him everywhere where he actually is, or else say that he does not exist at all" (Cassirer 1955:166). In such a view, God as a transcendent creator has no special place. Divinity is everywhere. The earth is sacred substance.

SUBSTANCE AND CODE

In order to consider the impact that such different conceptions of God have upon cultural systems, it will be helpful to employ David Schneider's notion (1969:124) that various cultural domains are "structured in terms of the dual aspects of substance and code for conduct." In any cultural system, units must be defined; the world as experienced must be named — and substances must be identified. Moreover, the substances must have recognized states of being, ways of behaving, or as Schneider puts it, codes for conduct.

If substance and code are incorporated into the elaboration of any cultural system, it is clear that different cultural traditions have given these parameters varied emphasis, have conceived of their relationships differently, and have found various means of expression. It seems that substance and code can be relatively dominant *vis-à-vis* one another within a particular tradition or in different periods of a single tradition, as culture is transformed over time by consciousness. Cultures are historical events, and, like individual consciousness, they develop their own conflicts and oppositions. Still, their development occurs within a particular context of thought and is subject to partial determinations by concepts that are taken for granted or widely held in that context. In the West, then, the concept of God has played a major determining role. Yet, that concept has itself been subject to varied interpretations, and there is a relationship between these interpretations and the elaboration of culture in terms of substance and code.

One can discern the nature of this relationship in the original creation myth, the story of Eden. It is possible to interpret creation as the outpouring of God's own Being into definite form. Instead of standing apart and creating the world *ex nihilo,* God created it out of himself. Such an interpretation was offered, for instance, by Johnathan Edwards. "The disposition to communicate himself in his own fulness, which we must conceive as being originally in God as a perfection of his own nature, was what moved him to create the world" (in Miller 1956:198). It is possible to see man, on this account, as partly divine, sharing in God's substance.

God blew his own breath into Adam's lung and shaped him from the clay he had used to form the earth.

An immanent conception of God stresses this element of divine substance present in all of reality. When taken to its logical conclusion, it denies any differentiation between God and the world. Both are understood as different manifestations of the same reality. In Europe in the fourteenth century, for example, the Brotherhood of the Free Spirit developed an immanent conception of the deity and spoke in this manner:

> He who recognizes that God does all things in him, he shall not sin. For he must not attribute to himself but to God all that he does. One can be so united with God that whatever one may do, one cannot sin. I belong to the liberty of nature, and all that my nature desires I satisfy.... I am a natural man. The free man is quite right to do whatever gives him pleasure (in Cohn 1961:183).

Similarly, in Eden, man required no code and needed only to obey a single prohibition. All creatures lived in harmony, and life in the garden was itself a cause for worship and celebration. But once expelled from the garden, man's being becomes stained with original sin, and his separation from God becomes the defining feature of their relationship.

A transcendent conception of God emphasizes this separation between man and the divine. A thoroughly transcendent god is completely absent from the world. What man has to live by is God's word — pronounced by the prophet and turned into a code. Such a God requires a constant effort on the part of man to maintain contact. Man can do this by faithful adherence to God's law, or by constantly confessing his sin of godlessness, inherited or self-acquired. A transcendent god deprives all substance of divinity, or sacredness, and the code assumes a much greater importance within the cultural system. The worship of nature becomes heretical pantheism, for the proper relationship with a godless nature is not worship but mastery.

There is then a correspondence between the conception of God, on the one hand, and the articulation of the cultural system in terms of substance and code on the other. The more that God is immanent, the more sacred all substance becomes, and codes receive less elaboration. A sacred quality invades every item of reality, endowing each with a special significance. A transcendent God brings about a greater preoccupation with code. In the development of Western culture, this has meant both a code of nature, or laws of nature — "order of nature" — and a code for man, or laws of society — an "order of law." Man follows God's law here on earth in order to sustain or prove his relationship, and he searches for an order in nature that will reveal the mastery of design.

Certain cultural traditions seem to epitomize the possible alternatives. In Judaism, code has clearly been dominant. Law is highly elaborated and given ultimate importance. The people who defended a rigid monotheism against their neighbors became the People of the Book. The way to be united with God, to be a Jew, is to follow His code. Hence a converted Jew, one who accepts the law, is a Jew of full and equal status to a Jew by birth, that is, an individual who is related to other Jews by blood. The man of status is the prophet, the law-giver, the ruler, and the rabbi. Every man was enjoined to study the law, even if this meant postponing a family. In the act of sexual intercourse, which is where elaboration in terms of substance is most likely, individuals were directed to concern themselves with the law:

A man should accustom himself to be in a good mood of supreme holiness and to have pure thoughts when having intercourse. He should not indulge in levity with his wife.... He should not converse with her, whether at copulation or immediately before it.... When having intercourse, one should think of some subjects of the Torah, or of some other sacred subject; and although it is forbidden during this act to utter holy words, yet thinking them is permissible, even meritorious. (Ganzfried 1963:100).

Weber (1963:83) reports that, in nearly all periods of Jewish history, the Jewish peasantry suffered an inferior status. "The rustic," Weber writes, "was virtually identified with the godless, the rural dweller being politically and religiously a Jew of second class."[6]

One can contrast Judaism and its extreme emphasis on law and code with Taoism in China. In Confucian thought, virtue was associated with the notion of "Li" or heaven, a transcendent deity and the source of moral principles. The word "tao," signified the "way," an ethical code for the individual to follow. Creel (1953:81) reports that "as Confucianism developed, it came to demand that the individual dedicate himself more and more completely to a fixed code for action." The Taoists reacted against this stress on a complicated code. In contrast, they offered a minimal code, based on the concept "te," which Creel (1953:87) says refers to "natural or instinctive primitive qualities or virtues, as opposed

---

[6] There is, of course, in Judaism, the divergent strain of Chasidism, which interestingly, developed among the peasant communities of Russia and Eastern Europe, generated tales rich with natural symbolism, and was concerned with the female element of God that was immanent in the world, the *Shechinah*, as well as with the holy sparks distributed in all things in this world. Moreover, it is interesting to find that Jewish theologians are reacting today against this alienation from the natural world and demanding that the Jew pay attention to the earth and not merely the law. Rabbi Everett Gender (1971:238) has even argued: "The present institutional alienation from nature was not always the case, and that it is, in fact, a comparatively recent development." Gender (1971:24) points for instance, to the celebration of Rosh Hodesh, the holiday of the new moon, and Succoth, the celebration of the harvest: "A vital and relevant Judaism for this age must begin to reclaim seriously its nature heritage." Arthur Greene (1971:201), speaking of ways of living that might become satisfactory for today's Jew, suggests: "Others might find their fulfillment in the redemptive robustness of physical labor, particularly such as would involve them with the realms of animal and plant." And, of course, there is the Song of Solomon.

to those enjoyed by social sanction or education." Tao came to represent the primal stuff of the universe, as well as the totality of things, the "wholly other" that is also the "wholly same," as noted in the *Tao Te Ching* 1922:ch.25):

Something mysteriously formed,
born before heaven and earth,
in the silence of the void,
standing alone and unchanging
ever present and in motion,
perhaps it is the mother of ten thousand things,

I do not know its name.
Call it tao.
For lack of a better word, I call it great.

Tao Te Ching, ch. 25.

The esteemed man in Taoist thought is the man closest to nature — the peasant, the woodcutter, or the fisherman. If there is an order in nature, it is only the order found in the patterns that the eye beholds, in the bark of a tree, the arrangement of a flower's petals, or the spots on a bird's breast. Or it is found in the cycle of the seasons — in visible transformations of substance and not in abstract relationships. In Taoism, "god" is fully immanent, and the construction of reality subordinates the elaboration of the code. This does not imply any lack of ethical sensitivity, but it is simply a shift in focus. Instead of complex legal tables that specify right conduct, code is subsumed in the natural order. It is enough to say that "Man follows earth, earth follows heaven, heaven follows Tao, Tao follows what is natural" (*Tao Te Ching*, ch. 25).

These examples are not arbitrarily chosen. Judaism has been a major influence in shaping Western thought. With the inheritance of the Hebraic God, the code has always been highly elaborated. Theology, philosophy, and the natural and social sciences have always been preoccupied with discovering the order of things. In America, through the Puritan experience, the Hebraic influence has been especially strong. The New World became the American Israel, and the puritans, God's chosen people, struggling in the wilderness to realize the promise of an earthly kingdom. The biblical paradigm has been used repeatedly, especially in the interpretation of America's role in the world. "The great wars of our history have all to a considerable extent been regarded as Armageddon, which surely was near. After the war had been won and evil conquered, an era of peace and prosperity would begin" (Tuveson 1968:215). Today, it is the advocates of the counter-culture who borrow the imagery of the apocalypse, convinced that the last days are at hand, unable to believe that corruption should flourish so effortlessly in the world. There are, on the other hand, striking similarities between the religious orientation of the counter-culture and the Taoist concern for simplicity and surrender to nature. Moreover, it was through Taoism that Mahayana Buddhism became transformed into Zen, a cultural tradition that continues to exert a steady influence in American thought, especially on those persons who were instrumental in the early development of the counter-culture.

The East is important, however, not because it has something different to offer, but because it has developed so richly those ideas that often existed only on the margins of Western thought. The East has focused on areas that remained, at best, minor themes in the West; at worst, they were often denounced as heretical, rarely taken seriously, or conceived as something dangerous and alien — a counter-culture.

Early Christianity represents an emergence of this opposing theme, and, in many respects, remains a model for all latter-day counter-cultural manifestations.

If, in Judaism, there is a vision of a transcendent God with whom man maintains contact by following a prescribed code, early Christianity re-establishes divinity in the world. Jesus was the "word made flesh" — code transformed into substance. And this man, this god-person, represents not only a model of good conduct, but a superhuman being capable of assimilating and transforming all mankind. His code, moreover, especially in contrast to the complexity of Hebraic law, was absolutely minimal: "Do unto others as you would have them do unto you" — to love God with all your heart, and to love your neighbor as you do your self. But the symbolic consequence of his person was to reaffirm the divinity and unity of man. In his bodily substance, all men could be united.

Viewed abstractly, the historical development of Catholicism can be read, in part, as a gradual return to the Hebraic emphasis on code. God becomes trinitarian and resumes his transcendent position. Man, as a sign of contact, can ingest divine substance, but this does not transform his own flesh. Confession takes the place of obedience to the law. Christ's death and resurrection become the symbolic representation of salvation, while his simple ethic often seems hidden by evangelical fervor and the institutional labyrinth of the church. The world is once again shorn of God, and the church joins hands with the state to maintain order in the earthly kingdom.

Within American culture, one can locate this same opposition: the divergent conceptions of deity and the subsequent impact on one's orientation to reality. Puritanism, with its Calvinist conception of an absent, yet all powerful God, was preoccupied with right conduct. A person's behavior was understood as proof of his election into the community of saints. But Puritanism is a complex ideology, and it reveals nicely the divergent emphasis on substance and code for conduct within its own development. Perry Miller's essay, "From Edwards to Emerson," focuses on this problem. He writes:

> The point may be put thus. There was in Puritanism a piety, a religious passion, the sense of an inward communication and a divine symbolism of nature. One side of the Puritan nature hungered for these excitements... but in Puritanism there was also another side, an ideal of social conformity, of law and order, of regulation and control. At the core of the theology, there was an indestructible element that was mystical, and a feeling for the universe which was almost pantheistic. But there was also a social code demanding obedience to ethical law, a code to which good people voluntarily conformed and to which bad people should be made to conform (1956:192).

Puritans were inspired to display their mystical leanings often enough. And whenever they did, in the form of the Antinomian preaching of Anne Hutchinson, in the Quaker dissent, or in the "great revival" led by Johnathan Edwards, the authorities responded in a consistent fashion — with condemnation, repression, and expulsion. From the very start of the American experiment, those who defended the social codes in the name of law and order demanded that people "love it or leave it." When Quakers insisted on returning to the Massachusetts Bay Colony after repeated warnings, the magistrates even executed a handful, hoping to discourage the others (see also Erikson 1966:107–137). Their misconduct, however, seemed far less serious than this sort of punishment would suggest. Sometimes they did commit rather bizarre acts: men would attack the honor of the magistrates as they sat in court, and on at least two occasions, Quaker women paraded nude in public.

In *Wayward Puritans*, Erikson (1966:127) notes: "One of the most interesting aspects of the Quaker crisis was that no one seemed very concerned to describe what the Quakers were talking about in theological terms." One unfortunate convert to Quakerism was hauled into court, where he addressed the bench in the following manner:

Wharton (the Quaker): Friends, what is the cause and wherefore have I been fetched from my habitation where I was following my honest calling, and here laid up as an evil-doer?
Magistrate: Your hair is too long, and you are disobedient to that commandment which says "Honor thy mother and father."
Wharton: Wherein?
Magistrate: In that you will not put off your hat before the magistrates (in Erikson 1966:128).

Three hundred years of historical change have not altered the circumstances. Hippies are not asked very often to explain their theological positions. Indeed, today many people would be shocked to discover that they even had a theological position. It is enough that their hair is too long and they show disobedience to the respected officers of the law.

THE CIVIL RELIGION AND THE COUNTER-CULTURE

Now that the basic viewpoint has been established, one can look more closely at the present situation. The same polarity is present today in what has been called the American "civil religion," on the one hand, and the diffuse manifestations of the counter-culture, on the other.[7] Today, the civil religion constitutes the quasiofficial view of the law-and-order Establishment. It is represented at the highest levels of government by such respectable clergy as Billy Graham, D. Elton Trueblood of the Yolkfellows, and Norman Vincent Peale. In recent years, these men have emerged as the spiritual coaches for a sophisticated kind of fundamentalism. The civil religion is a faith that feels as comfortable with military bands as it does with church choirs, as was made clear at Nixon's second inauguration and at Lyndon Johnson's funeral. Indeed, the choir at the Johnson funeral performed the war song of the civil religion, "Onward Christian Soldiers." It is a faith that transforms imperial armies into God's warriors. It is certainly no accident that our worst enemy still appears as a "godless" communism. There is much less objection to the communism of the monastery or other groups who explicitly follow the model of the primitive church. The God of this civil religion is Jehovah — the transcendent creator and law-giver. At Nixon's inauguration, God was addressed by a Baptist preacher, a Jewish rabbi, and a Greek Orthodox priest.

Intellectuals either accept this God, however quietly, and go about examining the order of nature and society, or they do without it, searching for patterns in the laboratory or in history that might reveal and constitute a temporary truth. But truth, it is believed, continues to reside in the codes and structures. If there is a disenchantment with particular legal or social codes, more basic structures of matter and mind can be conjured for faith or worship, and people learn to live with a cultural and moral relativism. But for the majority of the American public, the concepts of truth and right retain a more straightforward matter-of-factness, and neither relativism nor agnosticism satisfy many. Most Americans, the not-so-silent majority, still trust in God, as is indicated on the coinage of the realm, even though they may not always trust in the leaders of His

---

[7] The notion of a "civil religion" received wide attention after the appearance of Robert Bellah's article, "Civil religion in America" (1970:168–193). Bellah was eager to make clear that civil religion was something more profound than a self-righteous national idolatry, but he realized that it could often appear in that form, especially with respect to America's role as a world power. He also recognized the more complex issue of God as a central symbol in this civil religion, and suggested the serious consequences that a reformulation of the God-symbolism might involve. "If the whole God-symbolism requires reformulation, there will be obvious consequences for the civil religion, consequences perhaps of a liberal alienation and of a fundamentalist ossification that have not so far been prominent in this realm" (Bellah 1970:183).

chosen people. America is right — the "American way" continues to be right — because it is ordained and directed by God. Divine creation is still taught, along with evolution, in the public schools, and the President asks the nation to aid him through the power of prayer.

It is the civil religion that serves to legitimize the official code of the nation. Officers are sworn in with one hand on the Bible and the other hand pointing toward God. The civil religion upholds modern society as the exemplary way of life and calls for civility in social behavior. People ought to follow the proper code in their daily lives, as well as obey the legal statutes. One of the most revealing clichés of the Establishment is "equal opportunity," a phrase that indicates the basic nature of the system. The whole game is one of action, in which certain procedures are to be followed, and all entries are to be given a fair chance to play, that is, to conform to the sanctioned code for conduct. The idea of equality, referring by itself to our natures, to our substance as individuals is not generally present in the rhetoric of the Establishment's leading speakers. One loses sight of the fact that each human life is equally a representative of the species, and all represent an equal amount of being and becoming.

The counter-culture, with its own leaders and religious gurus, represents the alternative view that has been outlined above. One finds a renewed attempt to ground code in substance, to find truth in nature, in cycles of birth and death, in the instinctual needs of the body, in our natures as creatures in a world of matter. Currently, certain drugs take on the attribute of sacredness that, at other times, was attached to the wafer and the wine. Ingesting these substances endows an individual, it is believed, with clarity of vision that reveals the world and the self, more fully allowing one to "see" the unity that exists between the organism and the environment.[8] As one person expressed it, "Peyote gets you back into the earth." Through sacred substances the self is reunited with all substance, and the mind apprehends the substantial unity of the universal organism.

The elementary substances of the planet as experienced in everyday life — earth, air, fire, and water — also become sacred substances in this context. Ramon Sender, formerly a member of the Bruderhof community and an important figure in the development of the counter-culture in northern California, composed the following four prayers for the Morning Star Faith:

Earth: O earth, be fruitful
   Thou art our own Mother's breast.
   I share you with all life.

---

[8] See also Castaneda (1971) for a particular account of this kind of "seeing."

Air: O air, scented with early mists
 Thou art our Mother's breath-aura.
 O wind in the trees,
 Only thou, only thou.

Fire: O light, high fire of being,
 O sun, Father-Mother united
 Out of thy brilliance we flew
 to a half-lit planet
 Only to find Thy Light buried in
  the dust-dance of matter.

Water: O water, sparkling from the spring,
 Thou art our life-current.
 Our brooks race into Thy rivers,
 Our efforts merely dam Thy flow,
 Ocean, Ocean, womb of life.

Sender n.d.

People achieve an earthly salvation, a purification of their own spirit, by breathing clean air and drinking clean water; by digging in the earth to raise organic foods, pure uncontaminated substances; by rejecting electricity and returning to fire for light and warmth; by standing naked in the sunlight. An abstracted vision of nature preoccupied with structure and code is replaced by a vision of the world that delights in the surface reality and textures and finds meaning in the direct communion with these great cosmic symbols. One's relationship with these substances becomes the determining factor in the conduct of everyday life, influencing the nature of work, creating new orientations towards the environment, and transforming the acquired values of an urban society.

There is a certain irony involved in the official protest against drugs and communes that highlights this divergent emphasis on substance and code. A great deal of propaganda on both sides of the LSD issue has prevented a clear apprehension of the truth, but legal authorities were quick to adopt the argument that the drug could do real damage to the genetic code. Antidrug films were fond of showing babies with birth defects and attributing these to the use of LSD and other drugs. I am certainly not competent to judge on this issue, but it is interesting that on both sides of the controversy people recognized that what is really at stake is the human being as a creature. And where the "acid-freaks" saw the emergence of a new consciousness and a new man, the "authorities" could find only the abominations of the natural order. One side looked for visible changes in the conduct of everyday life; the other sought to find changes in the invisible code of substance.

In the thought of the counter-culture, along with the veneration of natural substance, there exists a rather thorough antipathy toward formalized codes or doctrines, a feeling that finds a positive expression in the commitment to individual freedom. The possibility of freedom actually becomes a focal issue — one not simply of freedom from institutional codes, but also the freedom from social and cultural conditioning whose grip is much more pervasive.

There is today (as always) the question of whether freedom is a viable concept. If it is not viable in fact, should it be maintained as a value? B. F. Skinner (1971:26) suggests, for example, that hippies are simply people trying to escape from aversive conditions, a form of behavior that is as much conditioned by situational contingencies as any. From this viewpoint, the creation of communes is not an indication of human freedom, but it is a conditioned response brought about by rapid and unplanned change, social disintegration, or threats of an ecological crisis or nuclear holocaust. They are, like the Melanesian cargo cults, a parody of liberation rather than being the "real thing."

The real issue here is not the survival or validity of Skinner's autonomous man as a cultural concept; it is the affirmative demonstration of freedom from particular codes of conduct that are themselves human creations. From the perspective of the counter-culture, a person is certainly conceived of as a product of the social environment; indeed one blames it for most of one's woes. People are even willing to accept the fact that they are not single, autonomous agents, that they are simply a focal point of matter and energy in a much wider force field. They also stand ready, however, to demonstrate their ability to create a new environment, even if it means adopting a voluntary primitivism that they know is utterly impractical as a model for widescale reform. Like Skinner, they will create new environments, setting up new sets of contingencies and new programs for reinforcement. If they are not demonstrating their freedom, they are at least asserting their desires to engineer their own destinies. But wise hippies know something that behavioral engineers have forgotten:

There's a difference between intention driving us on,
and mystery pulling us on. Mystery will always
educate and correct. Intention can go off the end
of its own limb.   (Brand 1971)

Their methods reveal the basic creativity of the human organism, which is, indeed, the foundation for all thought about freedom.

If one wanted to find a general ideological position congruent with these ideas, anarchy would be the most suitable. Many of the communes are explicitly anarchistic, being open to anyone who wants to come and be free from formalized organizational patterns. Anarchy, however, need not be associated with ideas of chaos and disorder. Anarchy is rather a commitment to a minimal elaboration of codes. At the commune where I lived for one year, for example, there were only two stated rules: (1)

anyone could come, and no one would be asked to leave, and (2) new houses should be constructed out of sight of others already built. The aim of the anarchistic ideal is harmony without rigid structures and mutual aid without social coercion. What is desired is the freedom from sanctioned law and custom, which no longer carry conviction. Herbert Read (1971:40) writes in *Anarchy and order*:

The organic life of a group, a self-regulative life like the life of all organic entities, is stretched on the rigid frame of code. It ceases to be life in any real sense and only functions as convention, conformity and discipline.

Read's language reveals that people are still in the realm of nature, treating the community and the individual alike as organic processes that have their own natural laws. For the anarchist, however, the basic natural law is not self-preservation or the survival of the fittest, but equity, "the principle of balance and symmetry which guides the growth of forms along the lines of the greatest structural efficiency" (Read 1971:41). It is the principle of justice that is fundamental and sometimes contradictory to law. Read continues:

The tendency of modern socialisms is to establish a vast system of statutory law against which there no longer exists a plea in equity. The object of anarchism on the other hand is to extend the principle of equity until it altogether supercedes statutory law (1971:41).

The whole drift of anarchism in today's communes is radically to confront the Establishment's equation between law and order. Again the similarity with Taoist thought is striking:

The more laws and restrictions there are
The poorer people become.
The sharper men's weapons,
The more trouble in the land.
The more ingenious and clever men are,
The more strange things happen.
The more rules and regulations,
The more thieves and robbers.

Tao Te Ching, ch. 57.

MYSTICISM AND COMMUNITY

This is enough by way of an initial sketch to indicate how the contemporary situation can be understood in terms of the dichotomy present in the elaboration of any cultural system — the dual parameters of substance and code. Different cultures have evidently found quite different ways of combining these parameters — combinations that affect the entire cultural style. It is also apparent that the conception of God, or the nature of the deity in a particular tradition, seems to be an important factor in determining how the elaboration will be carried out. It is in the rural communes that one finds many of today's mystics, grounding their daily life in the substantial unity of which they are a part. In this case, the elaboration of substance takes place as a celebration of the body and a worship of nature: letting your hair down and anointing the body with oils, going naked in the forest, sitting in silent communion with others, and letting the sun warm your back as you plow the earth.

The founder of the commune in which I lived shared this orientation to reality, although his behavior might not seem consistent with a mystic withdrawal from the world. He was always at work — gardening, making saddles and other leather goods, building a stable or a dome or a wash house, or helping other people get settled in. But he once commented to me:

There is more going on in a mud puddle in terms of beauty and activity than anything man has accomplished. The only thing man has got that is special and worth saving is a special awareness that can be developed. What I hope is that everyone could develop this kind of awareness. I would want man to be able to be conscious of everything without messing it up all the time. Just be observers, to be able to know everything and to see everything (personal communication).

Here is the mystic orientation presented in the most ordinary style — the desire to contemplate all of reality.

To accomplish such aims, even to understand them, people have gathered together to practice mutual aid and to simplify their lives. Then each day can become a step toward the realization and accomplishment of one's goal. Communal life becomes a series of moments that, taken together, constitute a complex religious performance. They become not merely representations of a particular religious orientation but "enactments, materializations, realizations of it — not only models of what people believe, but also models for the believing of it" (Geertz 1966:29).

If one views the communes as a complex ritual process, it becomes obvious that the concern for community per se is not, after all, a primary value. Communes provide a liminal field in which redemptive transformations can occur (see also Turner 1969). The back-to-nature journey is undertaken with fellow companions, all of whom share a common orientation and, hence, see some value in making the journey together. Still, there is always the knowledge that one may pick up and leave, that there are like-minded people elsewhere who share the same visions and goals.

One must be careful, therefore, not to confuse the present communitarianism with the older tradition of thought, which generally maintained a belief in the redemptive qualities of the community itself. This point has to be clearly understood. Philip Rieff (1966:70) has summed up the classical position nicely:

The view elaborated most thoroughly in our historic social theories, whatever their other differences, was that men were healthy only when they were good citizens. In short, security cured; and security came through membership in an "organic" community. This was the basis of conservative and radical political theory alike: community cures through the achievement by the individual of his collective identity.

Rieff (1966:53) calls the community that works in this way a "positive community." It is positive because it "guarantees some kind of salvation to the individual by virtue of his membership and participation in that community." For many people, such communities continue to exist, either in the form of the small town, the ethnic group, the denominational sect, or even the nation. The symbolic systems that constitute the definitions of these communities still maintain their viability, but it is equally true that, for others, the symbolic systems are no longer compelling, which means that commitment becomes spurious.

Where the community fails to provide a "cure," the family can become elevated as a substitute — an island of collective life within the wider network of contractual relationships. But as Rieff (1966:53) notes: "these collections of little islands . . . are themselves infected by the negativity of the larger community and become manipulative arenas themselves, rather than oases of escape from the larger arena."[9] This is even more true, perhaps, of the many urban communes. Filled as they are with people dissatisfied with the nuclear family, they become a larger "family" that frequently serves to make the manipulative games all the more complex and potentially destructive.

The journey to the rural communes, however, results generally from a quite different sort of orientation. Here it is not membership in a community that "cures," for the commune merely provides the social framework that makes the whole complex ritual possible. When the ritual is successful, what "cures," is the discovery of a reality more fundamental and more permanent than any particular community — the reality of the natural world. There are people who would argue that such a position is no longer tenable. George Kateb (1967:11–12), for instance, suggests that modern utopianism has:

severed its connections with primitivity, ignorance, and innocence; in sum with nature.... Not because nature never was what the stories say it was... but because

---

[9] The family itself has gone through its own historical transformations. For a history of modern family life, see also Aries (1962); for a view of family as a private utopia, see also Kirk (1972); and for a study of the pathology of family life, see also Henry (1973).

even an idealized state of nature (whether "nature" is mountain, plain, forest, or sequestered island) no longer answers to our sense of reality or to our expectations of reality.

But the aim of the communes is the reappropriation of nature as the ground of reality, and the cure comes when people are satisfied with this reality and cease to look elsewhere for their salvation, when they can understand themselves as natural creatures. It comes when people move beyond idealizations — even the idealized community — so that natural reality begins to determine ones expectations. Healthy individuals are not citizens in good standing, but human creatures alive to their senses, living in "affectionate company with the sky, winds, clouds, trees, waters, animals and grasses" (Snyder 1969:116).

If there is a community to which they belong, it is the human species — the community of man: an idealization, of course, for the gap between natural species and moral community is profound. Yet, even daily, more of these persons find each other — natural creatures, earthlings, citizens of the world. What they create and experience is not then a community in the sense of some particular form of organization, but rather, a unique awareness of their unity that derives ultimately and mysteriously from their mutual recognition. This sense of unity has been given various names — "communion," the "essential *we*," and "communitas." Such a union does not diminish the individuality; on the contrary, it accentuates the individuality of those who are united by conferring upon each the status of a whole and worthy creature. If there is leveling in these unions, it is symbolic leveling that is surpassed by an actual increase in dignity and worth.

So the outlook of the rural communes is communitarian in a peculiar sense. As one observer has accurately noted: "Personal fulfillment, rather than strength or endurance of the group, are the measures of success for these communes" (Kanter 1972). Consequently, it is only rarely that one finds the faith in particular models that characterized the social experiments of the nineteenth century, nor does one generally encounter systematic efforts to interrupt ordinary conjugal relationships for the sake of community, as in the celibacy of the Shakers or the controlled promiscuity of the Oneida community. What one does find almost always is a willingness to experiment with many forms of social relationships in order to find the arrangements that will best satisfy the requirements of the immediate situation. What one witnesses in the communes is the kind of association that Kropotkin had envisioned, where:

the fullest development of individuality will combine with the highest development of voluntary association in all its aspects, in all possible degrees and for all possible purposes; *an association that is always changing, that bears in itself the element of its own duration, that takes the form which best corresponds at any given moment to the manifold strivings of all* (in Buber 1958:13).

When all the present fascination with these rural communes has elapsed, mystics will still be developing their visions of truth, seeking new forms of association in which the religious spirit can flourish. Perhaps this modern mysticism can have as much impact on the world as the inner-worldly asceticism that led to the development of the current social realities. Or, perhaps, it will remain a special path that provides joy and meaning for the few who find it.

REFERENCES

ARIES, PHILLIP
    1962 *Centuries of childhood.* Translated by Robert Beldick. New York: Vintage.

BELLAH, ROBERT
    1970 "Civil religion in America." in *Beyond belief, essay on religion in a post-traditional world.* 168–193. New York: Harper & Row.

BRAND, STEWARD, *editor*
    1971 *The last whole earth catalog.* Menlo Park, Calif.: Portola Institute.

BUBER, MARTIN
    1958 *Paths in utopia.* Translated by R. F. C. Hull. Boston: Beacon.

BUCHDAHL, DAVID
    1974 "American realities: anthropological reflections from the counter-culture." Unpublished Ph.D. dissertation, University of Chicago.

BURKE, KENNETH
    1961 *The rhetoric of religion.* Berkeley: University of California Press.

CASSIRER, ERNEST
    1955 *The philosophy of the enlightenment.* Translated by Fritz C. A. Koelln and James P. Pettegrove. Boston: Beacon.

CASTANEDA, CARLOS
    1971 *A separate reality.* New York: Simon & Schuster.

COHN, NORMAN
    1961 *The pursuit of the millenium* (second edition). New York: Harper & Row.

CREEL, H. G.
    1953 *Chinese thought.* Chicago: University of Chicago Press.

DURKHEIM, EMILE
    1915 *The elementary forms of the religious life.* Translated by J. W. Swain. New York: Free Press.

ERIKSON, K.
    1966 *Wayward puritans.* New York: Wiley.

GANZFRIED, LOUIS
    1963 Code of Jewish law. Abridged from translation of *Shulchan Aruk.* New York: Hebrew Publishing.

GEERTZ, CLIFFORD
    1966 "Religion as a cultural system, in *Anthropological approaches to the study of religion.* Edited by Michael Banton, 1–46. London: Tavistock.

GENDER, RABBI EVERRET
1971 "On the Judaism of nature," in *The new Jews.* Edited by James R. Sleeper and Alan R. Mintz. New York: Vintage Books.
GREENE, ARTHUR
1971 "After Itzik: toward a theology of Jewish spirituality," in *The new Jews.* Edited by James R. Sleeper and Alan R. Mintz. New York: Vintage Books.
HARTSHORNE, CHARLES, WILLIAM L. REESE, editors
1953 *Philosophers speak of God.* Chicago: University of Chicago Press.
HENRY, JULES
1973 *Pathways to madness.* New York: Vintage Books.
HOBBES, THOMAS
1955 *Leviathan,* in *Philosophers speak for themselves.* Chicago: University of Chicago Press.
KANTER, ROSABETH
1972 *Commitment and community.* Cambridge, Mass.: Harvard University Press.
KATEB, GEORGE
1967 "Utopia and the good life," in *Utopias and utopian thought.* Edited by Frank E. Manuel, 239–259. Boston: Beacon.
KIRK, JEFFREY
1972 "The family as utopian retreat from the city: the nineteenth century," in *The family, communes and utopian societies.* New York: Harper & Row.
LEVI-STRAUSS, CLAUDE
1966 *The savage mind.* Chicago: University of Chicago Press.
MILLER, PERRY
1956 *Errand into the wilderness.* New York: Harper & Row.
NIETZSCHE
1954 *Thus spoke Zarathustra.* Translated by Walter Kaufman. New York: Viking.
NUTTALL, JEFF
1970 *Bomb culture.* London: Paladin.
RADIN, PAUL
1957 *Primitive man as philosopher.* New York: Dover.
READ, HERBERT
1971 *Anarchy and order.* Boston: Beacon.
RICOEUR, PAUL
1973 "Religion and the philosophy of language." Unpublished lecture, University of Chicago Divinity School.
RIEFF, PHILIP
1966 *The triumph of the therapeutic.* New York: Harper & Row.
SCHNEIDER, DAVID M.
1969 "Kinship, nationality and religion in American culture: toward a definition of kinship," in *Forms of symbolic action.* Seattle: University of Washington Press.
SENDER, RAMON
n.d. "Morning star open land." Unpublished manuscript.
SKINNER, B. F.
1971 *Beyond freedom and dignity.* New York: Bantam, Vintage Books.
SNYDER, GARY
1969 *Earth house hold.* New York: New Directions.

TAO TE CHING
  1922   Translated by Gai Fu Feng and Karen English. New York: Vintage. See chapter 25; edition is unpaged.

THOMPSON, WILLIAM IRWIN
  1972   *At the edge of history.* New York: Harper & Row.

TURNER, VICTOR W.
  1969   *The ritual process.* Chicago: Aldine.

TUVESON, ERNEST L.
  1968   *The redeemer nation.* Chicago: University of Chicago Press.

WATTS, ALAN
  1972   *In my own way.* New York: Pantheon.

WEBER, MAX
  1963   *The sociology of religion.* Translated by Ephraim Fischoff. Boston: Beacon.

WHITEHEAD, ALFRED NORTH
  1967   *Science and the modern world.* New York: Free Press.

Rituals of Community in an American Religious Youth Group Meeting

E. M. SCIOG

"The Seekers" is the young adult group of the High Street Congregational Church, Old Town, East Coast, United States. Members of the group are students drawn from a number of colleges, junior colleges, and universities in the metropolitan area, as well as young professionals and academicians residing and working in the area.

As one of the older urban areas of the East, Old Town is noted as one of the more gracious and pleasant environments, although it, too, has its share of urban blights, pollution, slums, and social conflict. Its proximity to the major urban centers of the East and its high prestige as a residential location have attracted young professionals from diverse backgrounds, and the quality of the academic institutions surrounding it draws a highly mixed student body.

Within this environment, the High Street Church, like many other traditional religious bodies, has long sponsored youth groups, such as the Seekers, in an attempt to bring this population into its orbit.

The membership figure for the Seekers at present is approximately 400, and the average weekly meeting attendance is 350. In comparison with other church-sponsored youth organizations in the Protestant community, the group is extraordinarily large. The average membership of such an organization is between 15 and 30.

The members and sponsors of the Seekers are themselves aware of the great discrepancy in numbers between themselves and other comparable organizations. This discrepancy, which has developed within the past three or four years, is a phenomenon inexplicable to the group other than in terms of the power of God. This interpretation of their growth is founded in one of the basic beliefs of the group, one common in American Protestantism — millenarianism. This belief centers around what is known as the "second coming of Christ." The "second coming" is the key symbol of the process in which Christ will return to earth, rule a thousand years, and then end the world, rewarding the faithful with eternal life. This thumbnail sketch of millenarianism outlines the goal of all adherents to this belief. The Seekers are specifically postmillennialists, who believe in the active role of man in bringing about a Christian world prior to the advent of Christ, as opposed to premillennialists, who deny that man can do anything and say that Christ will set the world right after his coming.

The Seekers consider themselves to be actively involved in this process of regenerating the world, in anticipation and preparation for the predestined rule of Christ. Their interpretation of millenarianism demands that the world be made "good" before Christ will enter it. This "making good" [their own term] consists of both a theological and a social component. First, the world must be converted to Christianity or, as they put it, everyone must find Jesus. Second, the social world must be articulated with Christ's teachings on interpersonal relations, that is, love thy neighbor as thyself. This social relationship is known as the fellowship.

The Seekers are, in their own way, intensely mission oriented. Their ultimate goal is the Christianization of the world, but their immediate concern is with the community around them, particularly their friends and acquaintances. The prime method of conversion is for an individual to capitalize on crisis situations, in which family, friends, and acquaintances might find themselves at some time or another and attempt to convince the sufferer to accept a religious solution. Divine intervention is also called upon by a believer on behalf of a certain individual. This request is carried out during the meetings of the group, and petitions of this type occupy a substantial portion of the meetings.

In recent years, however, the rate of conversion and the sudden climb in membership have far exceeded the amount of effort that the Seekers have contributed to God's work. It is, therefore, obvious to them that many of their new members have been directly converted, not through any human agency, but through the power of God.

An interesting belief associated with this type of millenarianism, which the group's growth has reinforced, is that men alone are not sufficiently capable of remaking the world, and that God must take an active hand in the work to be done. Further, these conversions through the act of God have had the effect of confirming a belief in the ultimate disposition of the world, as well as spurring many members on to greater efforts at converting their friends and relatives.

Several years ago, the Seekers was no larger than any other similar organization in the city. Because membership records have been and, in fact, still are rather carelessly kept, awareness of any membership growth came very slowly. Even in retrospect, several informants, the clergyman included, could not determine the rate of growth prior to 1971. All agreed, hazily, that around 1968, the group began to get larger. Membership at that time was approximately 50 persons. Although no one had ever been concerned about keeping a record of membership, by the summer of 1972, the story of how the group had grown was beginning to evolve. Then the membership was nearly 200. That previous autumn, only ten months earlier, the group had numbered barely 150. In the autumn of 1970, it had been only 100. Between 1968 and 1970, agreement on figures for any particular months or seasons is impossible to obtain. The membership, or more properly, the attendance figures, for the autumn of 1972 literally staggered the group, being double their previous number, and the preceding chronology has become fixed in the oral history of the Seekers.

There is no way to substantiate objectively this chronology of group growth, which was obtained from four of the most senior members of the group and the clergyman. Their version has formed the basis of the group story. In reality, the growth curve of the group most likely approximates the chronology, but from the point of view of the membership, this story actually represents their historical growth.

The great crowd of newcomers in the autumn of 1972 necessitated the removal of the meetings from the basement classroom of the church to the sanctuary on the floor above, which was the only place within the church large enough to hold a meeting. At first, the incredulity of the minister and older members was expressed both privately and publicly. No one could believe that such an unprecedented jump in membership could be permanent. Most people expected attendance to drop drastically within a few weeks. To the astonishment of all concerned, membership continued to increase throughout the autumn until December, when the estimated attendance was 400.

A very interesting observation I made was the fact that the actual number of people was never counted. Informants always spoke in approximations. Authoritative pronouncements on attendance figures were never made by anyone in my presence or during the course of any meeting I attended. Neither, as far as I was able to ascertain, was such an announcement made at meetings I did not or could not attend. On three occasions, I made head counts, one each in September, November and December. From my figures attendance varied between 360 and 390.

The Seekers' membership is socially homogeneous. The age of members ranges from eighteen to late twenties. White, middle-class (or aspiring middle-class) college students and young professionals are the rule. White, blue-collar workers are rare, as are middle-class blacks. Ghetto-dwelling, lower-class blacks are never seen. The ratio of men to women is about equal, only slightly favoring men. Most members are unmarried.[1]

---

[1] The information presented here was acquired by a number of informal surveys of members. In this way, background information was accumulated on more than a third of the

In other aspects, their heterogeneity is outstanding. Members are drawn from a wide variety of regional backgrounds, coming from every major geographical area of the country and from rural and urban areas alike. Religious backgrounds are also highly varied. A high percentage is Catholic (approximately 40 percent). Methodists, Lutherans, Episcopalians, and Baptists are also represented. Some continue to practice their original religions, attending their own churches for regular Sunday service and coming to the Seekers meetings as well. As a group, the Seekers are well aware of their religious heterogeneity and appear to be proud of it. They believe that at least half of their present membership is composed of former Catholics, although, as in the case of accurate membership figures, no one has ever kept count.

As an official part of the church organization, the group is under the leadership of one of the resident clergy, Reverend Hanson, the appointed "minister of youth." He is in charge of leading major portions of the meetings and also is responsible for the administrative matters that confront the group, such as deciding on dates for religious retreats, organizing travel arrangements for such retreats, and choosing scriptural passages to be studied by the group. He considers himself, and is so regarded by the rest of the clergy at the church, as a kind of spiritual guide to the group. Group members refer to him as "a good guy," "a very nice man," and "someone you can talk to." While Reverend Hanson may indeed function as a spiritual guide in intimate encounters with individuals or small groups, his role in the specific ritual gathering with which this paper is concerned, the Sunday evening meeting, is strictly that of a Master of Ceremonies. He engages in the minimal participation necessary for maintaining order and the smooth flow of the meeting.

During this meeting, the minister is assisted by a self-selected group of subordinates known as "lay ministers." Members of the lay ministry are drawn directly from the general membership of the Seekers. Anyone fulfilling one basic criterion is eligible. This criterion is sufficient commitment to the group to engage in a large amount of voluntary labor, mostly organizational in nature. This work consists of assisting the minister in administrative affairs, such as handling paperwork. The lay ministers also host the infrequent social affairs of the group and assist in the conduct of the main meeting.

A new member of the group is confronted with a hierarchy of leadership, although the only clear demarcation is between the minister who is an ordained member of the clergy and the rest of the group.

The Sunday evening meeting of the Seekers is conducted within the

---

membership. No official records are kept. Assessment of the social characteristics of members was aided by the practice of publicly introducing newcomers. Newcomers would be obliged to stand and tell their names and occupations as well as places of origin.

framework of the High Street Church's organization of Sunday affairs. At the morning service, 10 A.M., the time schedule of the various church group meetings is available for the congregation, together with the week's order of worship. The Seekers meeting is always listed on this schedule. This meeting is the main weekly event for the group. It is the only time when all members of the group come together. During the course of an ordinary week, several small group meetings, led by one or more of the lay ministers to discuss scripture and to pray, may or may not be held. At most, one or two of these meetings will be held in any given week, and attendance averages about fifteen persons.

Outside the context of purely group activity, that is, the meetings and infrequent social gatherings noted above, members form small friendship cliques. Members who are college students may room together. Groups of friends visit and entertain each other and go to restaurants and movies. Other members of the group date, go steady, or are engaged. Belonging to the Seekers has certain social advantages for many members.

Sunday at the High Street Church is an exceedingly busy day. Besides morning and evening services, the church sponsors many special groups. Classes are held on the Bible, and lectures on topics relating to the teachings of Christ are given at least twice a month. Besides these general types of meetings, the church sponsors numerous age-graded groups. There are groups for children, high school students, young marrieds, and business people. None of them, however, approaches the size of the Seekers or can match its heterogeneity of regional backgrounds or religious faiths.

These other groups have little relevance to the Seekers. Aside from having a clergyman as the official leader of the group, most members of the group (those who are not members of the congregation) have almost no contact with the church outside of the Seekers. The existence of other church-sponsored groups is known, but this is irrelevant to participation in the Seekers. No group actions, that is, socials or lectures, are prepared in concert with other groups; nor does the recognition of any group other than their own within the church structure or even the recognition of the church itself ever become a necessity for members.

The Seekers meeting is actually split into two parts. The first part consists of a lecture on some biblical topic; this begins at 5:30 P.M. and ends at 7. Less than a third of the full membership ever show up for this lecture. The average attendance over a period of ten weeks was 125 persons. Many of the lay ministers attend this part of the meeting. Following the lecture, a supper of sandwiches and punch is served. Members stand about the lecture room, located in the basement of the church, and engage in informal conversation for half an hour.

At 7:30, the regular evening service is conducted; those group members who attend the lecture also attend this service, which lasts an hour.

This church service has a typical Congregationalist format, consisting of hymn — prayers — sermon — hymn — prayers — closing hymn; the central element is the sermon. (This pattern is meant to be schematic, and the category of prayers encompasses such elements as benedictions, and so on.) This general pattern of the service varies little from church to church in the Congregationalist services in other areas of the country. Minor variations are found particularly within the prayer category. At the conclusion of the service, the congregation is asked to clear the sanctuary quickly so that the Seekers' meeting can begin.

The part of the congregation that does not belong to the Seekers leaves and those Seekers who do not attend the regular evening service arrive for the evening meeting. Most of the group attend only this one weekly meeting and see their "brothers" and "sisters" only at this time. The group spends a good deal of time becoming settled. Greetings are exchanged and informal conversation is carried on. People inquire into events of the past week and comment on absent friends. During this time, small, more acquainted groups stand about together waiting for the meeting to start. In actuality, however, the tendency to sit with friends is counterbalanced by an explicit injunction to sit with strangers and others with whom one is only minimally acquainted. In several instances, I had been conversing with four friends prior to the start of the meeting and had expected to sit with them when we were called to order. (It is customary to stand and converse before the meeting is called to order, so most people do not choose their seats until they are required to sit down.) In all such cases, however, I never sat with more than two of the persons with whom I had been conversing. When the time comes to be seated, groups of four or five tend to break up into couples and trios that sit quite a distance from each other. With such a large number of people attending meetings, especially within the last eighteen months, many people do not know even a substantial number of the members. Individual members are, however, quite enthusiastic about meeting new brothers and sisters.

About fifteen minutes after the regular evening service has ended, one of the lay ministers steps up to the microphone, which is set up in the front of the sanctuary, and calls the meeting to order. At his word, the groups of friends disperse for the remainder of the meeting. As the crowd settles down in the pews, the lay minister welcomes members and visitors to the meeting.

All meetings are opened by one of the lay ministers. In the case of the particular meeting, which I shall describe, Jack officiated. Other lay ministers whom I observed assisting the minister in this capacity were Paul, Jim, and Mike. I never observed a woman undertake this task, although there are a number of women lay ministers. One of these persons always shares the burden of conducting the meeting with the minister.

As Jack called the meeting to order, several instrumentalists milled about in the front, tuning their guitars, and someone was fussing with the overhead projector. Tim, Don, and Peggy, on guitars and piano respectively, provided the accompaniment. After a slight period of confusion, everyone was finally ready to begin, and Jack put the verses of the first hymn on the projector, raised his hands to gather the full attention of the assembly, and shouted into the microphone: "And a one, two, three!"

In an excellent imitation of a symphonic maestro, Jack (who actually is a legitimate music major at a nearby college) conducted the several verses with great gusto. His lighthearted and joyous approach to the whole business communicated itself to the group, and they responded to his goading to sing louder for the Lord with enthusiasm. He put up the verses for the next hymn amid a scattering of applause and shouts for some special favorite tune.

In general, Jack prefaced his introduction of each hymn with comments such as: "You remember this one," and "We haven't done this in a while." Every few meetings, a new hymn or hymns are taught to the group as a whole, and they have built up quite a repertoire. Because most members of the group know the repertoire of hymns available, people hazard guesses as to the identity of the next hymn and comment in satisfaction if one of their favorites is chosen.

The hymns that are sung are joyful and rendered in a semifolk-style to the accompaniment of the guitars and piano. The verses and tunes are sometimes composed by talented members of the group or taken from hymnbooks and jazzed up a bit. The central themes of the texts are praise at the salvation of man by Christ and affirmation of a service commitment to Jesus. A sample verse of one of the most popular hymns follows:

Jesus came down to be our Savior.
Jesus came down to be our Savior.
Jesus came down to be our Savior.
He is the Way. He is the Truth. He is the Light!

Occasionally the *Pilgrim Hymnal* will be taken out, and something will be sung to a more traditional rhythm and accompaniment, such as the well-known verses of "Stand up, stand up for Jesus."

After three or four hymns have been sung, each more boisterous than the preceding one (because Jack encouraged foot stamping, hand clapping, and loud singing), Jack announced that it was time to get on to the next item on the agenda. Visitors, in the persons of interested members of the congregation and curious parents, but particularly prospective group members, abound at each Sunday meeting. It is the second order of business to effect their introduction to the group at large. Jack asked the visitors to stand and tell their names, occupations, and hometowns. It generally takes quite a bit of time before these introductions are completed, but the entire group always listens with full attention, and several people in any pew, including all the lay ministers and a large number of ordinary members, as far as I have been able to ascertain, take notes.

After all the strangers had been identified and welcomed, Jack surrendered the microphone to Reverend Hanson, who proceeded to the third part of the meeting. Following a short welcoming speech of his own, Reverend Hanson opened his New Testament to the biblical passage of the week. Each week, a certain passage of scripture is designated for meditation and discussion. Members are advised to read the passage during the week and come prepared to say something about it at the following meeting.

Although officially designated as a discussion, and referred to as such by members when they describe the elements in the Sunday evening meeting, that which ensues is not precisely a discussion in the common sense of the term.[2]

The minister began by citing the source and the page number of the scriptural passage for the benefit of those not in possession of that knowledge. He then addressed the group with the question: "Who has something to share?" A scattering of people raised their hands, and the minister selected volunteers at random; each of them, in turn, stood and addressed the group as a whole.

The nature of this sharing or, as the minister sometimes phrases it, "contribution," is couched in terms of the relationship of the passage to (preferably) recent personal experiences of the contributor:

In the passage, Paul talks about being steadfast and unyielding in faith no matter what trials you are undergoing. And I guess if he can say that and really mean it in his predicament, being in prison and all that, I can stick out the troubles, the little everyday troubles that I've been having. After all, he had a rougher time than I've ever had yet. It kind of bucked me up to have somebody give advice like that to someone like me, when he's in a really bad situation like that. So I decided to stick out the troubles I'd been having on the job, and not let them get me down the way they had been, and trust in God that everything will turn out all right in the end if I stick to my faith and pray. But since I read that passage, things have been a lot easier.

These comments, of which the above is typical, consist of the application of the passage to individually unique and often rather vaguely or generally stated experiences. Most often the passage is interpreted as a remedy to a currently stressful situation or mental state. The association

---

[2] The manner in which I am describing the organization of the Sunday evening meeting, as a division into four parts: hymns, introduction of strangers, Bible discussion, and sharing, is not my own construct, but it is the way my informants perceive the structure of the meeting.

of the passage may also refer to an individual's total life orientation, as follows:

I realized that he was saying in the passage just what I've been trying to do in my life, but he sort of put it in a clearer perspective — like a revelation.

"Revelations on reading a Bible passage" would certainly be a more appropriate description of this part of the meeting than "discussion," and, indeed, members do occasionally speak of this part of the meeting as "sharing what God has revealed to you in the scriptures."

The "discussion," then, consists of a static series of revealed statements — testimony. There is never any critical discussion of the merits of any particular interpretation. Each is accepted, solemnly and without comment, as worthy in itself as a revealed truth.

After six or seven people commented on the Bible passage to the group as a whole, the minister instructed the members to break up into small groups and discuss the passage among themselves. The members did this by including eight or so individuals seated nearest them in a circle. In ten consecutive weeks, I was never in a small group with the same people.

Ideally, each small group is led by one of the lay ministers, who initiates the discussion, prompts each member of the group who has read the passage to make a comment, and fills up the silences with relevant talk. Visitors, whose position has been marked by members of the group, are apportioned among a number of small groups. Outsiders are never allowed to remain as outside spectators, but they are incorporated into a small group.

The explicit purpose of these small groups is to give everyone a chance to say something. The minister, on occasion, makes this function absolutely clear. Upon closing the discussion and ordering the formation of small groups, he will sometimes say: "I'm sorry we haven't time to hear everybody who has something to say, but although you can't tell it to the whole group, you can share your observation within the small group." Informants say they feel obliged to say something if they have read the passage, and they feel that the only persons who have a valid excuse for not having something to contribute are visitors and those who were not able to find out what passage was assigned.

If everyone in the group has made his contribution before the minister signals for attention, the lay minister, either alone or with some talkative members, assumes the responsibility for making further interpretations of the passage. Often individuals are asked by the lay minister to elaborate on the circumstances of the situation to which they are applying the passage.

At this point, the lay minister sometimes takes the microphone and initiates a short interlude of singing. There seems to be no set rule about singing at this point in the meeting. Weeks may go by without any singing, and then for two or three weeks in a row, Jack or one of the other lay ministers will get up and say: "Let's sing a hymn." Usually only one hymn is sung, in the same folk style as the opening ones and with the same kind of text, stressing joy in salvation.

When the hymn ends, the minister rises and initiates the final segment of the meeting by asking, "Does anybody have anything he or she would like to share with the rest of the group?" This part of the meeting is called "sharing" by group members, and all consider it to be the most important event of the meeting.

The structure of this final phase of the meeting is the same as that of the Bible discussion. After Reverend Hanson asked his question, several people raised their hands; individuals were chosen at random. In general, things that are shared with the group as a whole are those that have been classified by members as having great importance. Because almost all sharing is articulated in terms of personal experience, comments made to the entire group are expected to be of great personal importance, even catastrophic to the teller.

Those things considered to be worthy of sharing with the entire membership are such events as a confession of personal acceptance of Christ, the conversion of someone not present, the discovery of other Christian groups or fellowships in Jesus in other places, and the announcement of a very great personal experience or tragedy.

After six or seven individuals spoke, the minister declared that the time had come to form small groups, but he first asked if there was anyone left with an important message to share. After the last of these most urgent "sharings" was aired to the group at large, people formed their small groups again.

An interesting feature of this part of the meeting is that, immediately after something was shared, the group as a whole offered a silent prayer for what was shared, whether it was the death of a member or a close relative of a member or the discovery of another group like themselves. During the moment of prayer, the minister invited members to say a prayer aloud. At this, several people in succession composed a spontaneous prayer about the particular sharing. If the thing shared was of great joy, a prayer of praise was composed; if tragic, one of consolation. In general, the graver the thing shared, the longer the time spent in prayer. Occasionally, the minister will be one of the contributors of a prayer.

The particular function that members perceive for these prayers varies with the nature of the thing shared. They believe that all happy things that happen to them are the result not only of their own efforts but of divine dispensation as well. They believe that one must work for personal goals, material gain or praise, or the conversion of a non-

Christian, but the ultimate attainment of these is the result of the influence of Christ. When something particularly happy or unexpected happens, this event is attributed to the intervention of Christ, and he must be thanked appropriately through prayer. Conversely, suffering is also attributed to God or Christ, either as being some sort of test of faith or the fulfillment of the unknowable will of God. In these cases, one prays for courage and a steadfast and unwavering belief in the fact that this is the will of God and ultimately good.

When the meeting again broke up into small groups, the explicit intent, as before, was to provide everyone with the opportunity, or perhaps obligation, to participate. The lay minister again took charge and initiated sharing by being the first to say something. Then each member of the small group was gently prodded in turn to contribute. Although visitors and newer members are not highly pressured to share, the group is gratified if such persons do say something. After the second meeting, I attended, several people in my small group told me how nice it had been that I, a new member, had felt moved to share something with them.

In this setting, it is very difficult to avoid sharing. Once the lay minister has said his or her piece, he or she will indicate with a nod or a glance the direction about the circle in which the comments should flow. If the person whose turn it is to share says nothing, a very long, anticipatory silence ensues. Either individuals are very firmly determined not to speak and so endure the silence, or they become increasingly uneasy and ultimately capitulate. Sometimes one member of the group will ask, with great concern: "Haven't you anything you'd like to tell us?" Having been the focus of such a silence in a later meeting, I can say without reservation that it operates as a very powerful sanction and can elicit the cooperation of all but the most determined individual.

People who do not have anything to say or cannot think of anything feel that they somehow have let the group down. This self-judgment is reinforced by the disappointment that others in the small group display when someone refuses to participate in the sharing. In addition to feeling that one has not lived up to the norms of the group and that one is considered deficient as a member of the Seekers by the group, this circle of sharing generates a very powerful emotional atmosphere. This emotional tension is not physically expressed by such phenomena as speaking in tongues or movements. It is highly internalized, but members are aware of it just the same, and the tension increases as the round of the circle is made. Members are loath to break this circle by silence and dislike it if anyone, other than recognized outsiders and newcomers, remains silent.

During the second month of attending the group meetings, I once deliberately refrained from sharing, a course that very much annoyed the group and destroyed the atmosphere. I might indeed have been regarded as a kind of spoiler of the "magic."

The things shared in the smaller groups are much more mundane and even petty compared to those shared with the membership as a whole. An illustration of sharing is presented below — an abridged sequence of small-group sharing from the meeting of August 27, 1972.

Ann [lay minister]: My husband has had the flu and is still in a bad way. I'd like you to pray that his convalescence will be quick. Also, we're trying to form a Christian discussion group in the high school where we teach, and we're hoping that it will be successful.
Dave: Lately, you know, I've been talking to my roommate Steve about Jesus, and he's beginning to seem more interested. Now he's asking questions. I want you to pray that he'll find Jesus soon because he's been leading a really unhappy, empty spiritual life and he needs him.
Paul: I've just been realizing how much my life has changed since I met Jesus, and I've been happier than ever before, I've been a Christian for almost a year now, and I just wanted to share my joy in Jesus with all of you.
Mary: I've found a new job working with really nice people, and I love it. Jesus answered my prayer with this work, and I really feel that he's showed me my proper place in the world where I'll do his work best.
Tom: Well, I've decided that I really want to go on to college, and I've applied to City College. I feel that this is what Jesus wants me to do, so the last few weeks I've been praying awfully hard that I'll be accepted and sure would appreciate your help.
Ellen: My dad's been terribly ill since last week. He had a heart attack and really needs your prayers to give him spiritual support.
Neil: In the last few days, I've been faced with the choice of what to do with my life for the next few years and I'm not sure what the right thing to do is. I've been praying, but Jesus hasn't shown me the way yet, or maybe I just can't hear him. Maybe if you put in a prayer or two for me, I'll be able to see the way Jesus wants me to take.

Only after everyone had had his or her say were the prayers concerning these sharings offered. The group was silent and, at random, individuals in the group composed a short prayer about one or several of the sharings. The prayers fell into three general groups: petition, praise, and consolation.

Dear Lord, we thank you that Ann's husband is recovering his strength and pray that he will soon recover completely in order to carry out your work.

Jesus, thank you for what Paul told us tonight. When he told us of the change in his life found through you, we see that you are surely the Truth and the Light.

Dear Jesus, may Ellen's strong faith in you sustain her and her family through this terrible time in their lives, and we pray, if it be your will, for her father's speedy recovery.

Each sharing was mentioned in prayer at least once, and often more. When the creativity of the group had become exhausted and a prolonged silence signaled a tacit agreement that enough had been said, the lay minister took over and voiced one last conclusive prayer for the group. Everyone then subsided into a grave, meditative silence to await other groups that were engaged in an identical procedure.

This exact same pattern was followed by all the other small groups. In a membership amounting to nearly 400, there are many small groups consisting of eight to ten people. Eventually, the sanctuary became quieter. When the room was still (or, in some cases, after it had been silent for a few minutes), one of the lay ministers or the minister began to sing the closing hymn, either an "Alleluia" or "Old One Hundredth."

The meeting that began with boisterous singing, laughter, and clapping was concluded with a softly sung old hymn. At times, the minister will say a closing prayer, thanking God for the opportunity to have had the joy to be a part of the meeting and wishing the group good night. At other times, the meeting breaks up just after the hymn is sung. The silence is then broken by people wishing each other good night, speaking with friends and acquaintances whom they had not seen before the meeting. Soon they go home.

Some members leave immediately. However, for about twenty minutes following the close of the meeting, many members remain about and converse. Some get together with the groups they had been with at the start of the meeting and resume their interrupted conversations. Others wander about looking for certain friends. One is commonly asked: "Have you seen so-and-so?" Members seem to have a large circle of acquaintances within the group. Individuals are continually introducing themselves to new members and are always in the process of expanding their number of acquaintances.

In the end, after individuals have seen the persons they wanted, they find their rides home. People with cars give fellow members rides home, and most people leave in groups of four, five, or six.

From the foregoing description, it can be seen that the Sunday evening meeting of the Seekers consists of an elaborate series of rituals. These rituals — hymn singing, testimony through the discussion of a Bible passage, and sharing — have for the most part been drawn from a pre-existent corpus of ritual acts. The general outline of the meeting roughly follows that of the typical Congregational church service. Furthermore, this meeting very closely resembles a historical and contemporary form of Protestant worship known as the prayer meeting; although no member has ever, within my hearing, referred to the Seekers' meeting as a prayer meeting. Most members are not even aware of the historical background of the group. Their interest and knowledge extends back as far as their joining the Seekers. The only topic of historical interest is the growth of the group from the late 1960's, and their data on that are none too secure.

The rituals themselves are easily identifiable. In the context of the meeting, they are deliberately marked off from each other by the minister and lay minister, who are acting in a manner that an observer would be inclined to define as the role of a Master of Ceremonies. They keep the performance moving and intervene to conclude one ritual and initiate the next. The members themselves also refer to these rituals as discrete and separable units.

The lay minister initiates the first ritual, that of hymn singing, and continues through the second ritual, the identification of strangers to the group. The third and fourth rituals are led by the minister. These two rituals form structurally parallel units. In each, individuals first address the group as a whole, and second they address a segment of the group, which the members perceive to be an inferior kind of substitute for the group as a whole. This relative valuation of the small group *vis-à-vis* the whole is explicitly stated by the minister every so often. He expresses regret that the group is too large for everyone to have face-to-face communication, that for each individual to confront the group as a whole is impossible. In one sense, the small groups are negatively valued; they split up the whole group into dozens of tiny independent ones. The small groups are also perceived as having a positive aspect. The minister often expresses this positive aspect by saying that those who are too shy and reticent ever to stand up in front of 400 people will feel more at home and less uneasy in a group of 10 or less.

Whether this division into small groups is a function of the large size of the Seekers and is a technique that has been resorted to in order to ensure the participation of the maximum number of individuals or whether it has been used historically in similar kinds of meetings is unclear. There is little existing literature on prayer meetings, and what there is seems to presuppose a group of thirty or less (Luccock and Cook 1916; Wells 1896). Descriptions of Young Men's Christian Association (YMCA) prayer meetings also presuppose a small number of participants and make no mention of the use of small groups during the course of a meeting (Hopkins 1953; Connant 1858). The present minister, Reverend Hanson, said he was merely continuing the format of Seekers' meetings that existed at the time of his appointment. The pattern of organization, it has been remarked by persons outside the group who have read versions of the present paper, closely resembles that of T-Group dynamics. Within the group, however, the relationship between their meetings and T-Groups is not explicitly drawn. At this time, I would hesitate to make any interpretation of the relationships the group meeting may have to outside, secular sources.

Hymn singing is also the typical opening ritual of American Protestant meetings. All denominational churches, to my knowledge, open and close Sunday services with hymns, which are known, respectively as the processional and recessional. Singing an appropriate anthem or hymn appears to be an accepted way of opening many affairs in America — note the singing of the national anthem before football and baseball games.

For the Seekers, hymn singing is legitimated by past religious tradition, but hymns are not sung in an unthinking, unfeeling manner by the members, as if they were merely preparatory opening exercises. The hymns express their basic beliefs in salvation through Christ and commitment to the service of Christ as individuals and *as a group.*

Being part of the group, or the fellowship of Christ, as they call it, is an extremely important part of being a Seeker. In the prefatory remarks concerning the Seekers' system of belief, I commented that they perceive the salvation of the world and the second coming of Christ as consisting of two interrelated components. First, there is the salvation of each individual through belief in Christ as the Savior. The second component that I referred to is a social one. To the Seekers, it is not only the individual soul that must be saved but the social world of humans as well. When Jesus comes, he will rule not just individual souls for the millennium, but a society of souls. This social relationship is what is known to them as the fellowship, and participation in that fellowship is as important as individual salvation.

This explicit emphasis that the Seekers put on the social ideal of the fellowship may be a clue to an explanation of the intensity with which they attempt to involve and include all persons in the actions of the group. Strangers are introduced one by one to the group as a whole. They become known and are incorporated into the structure of the meeting. There are no outsiders. The strangers, who have no knowledge of the expectations of the group and who are not really expected to perform, are drawn into groups of members and are encouraged to participate, at least marginally in the sharing. Strangers are not allowed to collect along the sidelines. Seekers do not explicitly phrase their actions towards strangers in this manner. They term their behavior as being "friendly," "kind to strangers," and "Christian."

The structure of the Bible discussion and the sharing rituals also serve to implement this ideal of social interaction. The main demand implicit in these two rituals seems not so much to say something significant, but just to say something. The injunction to participate can override content.

The discussion tends to be past oriented. The individual states that, with the aid of the revelation granted him through reading the Bible passage, he or she was able to resolve a crisis. The use of the Bible passage may be a structure employed to break through embarrassment in talking about personal things.

In the sharing ritual, people are expected to discuss their current problems. The explicit purpose of this is to gain the spiritual aid of the rest of the community for the resolution of problems, comfort in sorrow, and the sharing of good tidings. If one rejects this means of problem solving by refusing to say something, one lets down the whole group. Not to share something is tantamount to rejecting fellowship. The kind of fellowship the Seekers perceive is not one of real political and economic interaction as a kind of commune, but rather, a fellowship on a spiritual plane that is demonstrated through sharing. When an established member has nothing to say, people are upset. They are disturbed that he or she will not share with them. It makes no difference to say: "I have nothing to share." Nobody has nothing to share. One should always be sharing one's faith and joy at being part of the perfect spiritual fellowship. As one fellow member said to me after the meeting at which I refused to say anything: "You should say something. Everyone has something to share."

Predictably, members are overjoyed when a newcomer starts participating in the sharing. When I first began to participate in the group, people were overjoyed that I "felt moved to say something." I was "becoming a member of the group."

The Seekers are a highly organized, unusually large youth group of an urban Protestant church. Unlike the popular conception of people involved in the Jesus movement, these people are very sober, middle-class persons, who are working for the salvation of the world and the millennium. Their concept of salvation, which is just as much social as it is individual, leads them to demand a high degree of individual participation in the rituals of the group.

REFERENCES

CONNANT, WILLIAM
    1858 *Narratives of remarkable conversions and revival incidents.* New York.
HOPKINS, C. H.
    1953 *History of the Y.M.C.A. in North America.* New York: Association Press.
LUCCOCK, H. E., W. F. COOK
    1916 *The midweek service.* New York: Methodist Book Concern.
WELLS, A. R.
    1896 *Prayer meeting methods.* Boston: United Society of Christian Endeavor.

The Country Place: An Intentional, Therapeutic Community

GEOFFREY NUSBAUM

R. D. Laing, a well-known radical speaker in the field of psychiatry and mental health, has written:

We are living in an age in which the ground is shifting and the foundations are shaking.... Perhaps it has always been so.... We know it is true today.... In these circumstances, we have every reason to be insecure.... When the ultimate basis of our world is in question, we run to different holes in the ground, we scurry into roles, statuses, identities, interpersonal relations.... We attempt to live in castles that can only be in the air because there is no firm ground in these social cosmos on which to build (Laing 1967:131).

Consistent with this psychosocial speculation of Laing, we are presently experiencing in the United States a tidal wave of social change, change of such far-reaching and fundamental dimensions that it may only be called revolutionary. We are no longer able to fall back unquestioning on the security of the old, traditional values, beliefs, and norms. Yet, without even knowing why, some persons are swept blindly forward in the cross-currents of alienation and meaningless change; others, equally alienated and lost, stand rigid and paralyzed, unable to move or grow in any direction.

I would like to address this inquiry to one particular aspect of the overall revolution in institutions and lifestyles, that is, the cropping up all over the United States of numerous small "intentional communities" or communes. These communes, though having ample historical precedent in nineteenth-century America, experienced their contemporary genesis in the late 1960's in the urban youth ghettos such as the Haight-Ashbury district in San Francisco and the East Village in New York City. As these so-called meccas of the new American youth culture grew, so unfortunately did their notoriety. The mass media took note, and soon these areas were swarming with tourists, weekend visitors, photographers, and reporters. Thanks to Herb Caen, columnist in the *San Francisco Chronicle,* these youth received the label "hippies," and the degeneration and dispersal of their community was virtually assured.

The still warm ashes of "over-media exposed" communities such as Haight-Ashbury proved to be fertile ground for the "new" communal movement. As early as the beginning months of 1967, certain groups in the Haight-Ashbury community had premonitions of what was to come, and they began to leave for the quieter, less publicized California countryside. One commune visited by this writer in Ben Lomond, California, seventy-five miles north of San Francisco, consisted predominantly of refugees from the Haight-Ashbury community. Today these refugees from the American middle-class number close to 500 (those who choose to identify themselves) and are springing up all over the country. Concentrated mainly on the West and East Coasts, they extend across the United States, with a substantial number concentrated in the Taos, New Mexico, area. They are organized, to some degree, around leaders and causes as varied as the persons who make them up. There are religious communes, political communes, work communes, all-female communes, free-love communes, extended family communes, and group-marriage communes. This new communal movement fits well within the traditionally pragmatic strain of American radicalism, dating back to the people who settled this country.

Kanter (1968: 499–518) has studied extensively the nineteenth- and twentieth-century communal movement from the perspective of commitment factors as a measure of the success and viability of a community. She found it useful to view the new communal movement as being roughly divided into two broad groups: small anarchistic communes and those formed around a growth-centered philosophy. This paper will be concerned with one growth-centered type community located in Litchfield, Connecticut.

In attempting to do an in-depth exploration of a growth-centered community, two problems immediately came to the fore. The first of these had to do with the following question: How was I to find an accessible community that fell under the general functional category that Kanter described as growth-centered? Second, what method among the myriad available, should I use in approaching this project? At this point in my thinking I became aware of Renee Nell and The Country Place. After hearing her speak about the community, I approached her about the possibility of doing research there. Her initial reaction was favorable, and she invited me to come to Litchfield, Connecticut, to acquaint myself in person with The Country Place. While there, I asked the residents if I could live in their community for a period of time. As it happened, those residents who were present thought well of the idea. Consequently I spent most of the month of January 1971, and part of February, as a participant-observer.

The decision to rely heavily on participant observation as a method of inquiry was based on two strong feelings. First I do not place as much validity in any instrument of evaluation of a human situation as I do on my own experience of that situation. Second, I am keenly aware of the risks involved for a community and a researcher in such a project. As many studies glaringly indicate it is all too easy for a researcher unknowingly to become little more than a condescending, prying, voyeuristic outsider (and in this case, decidedly untherapeutic), someone who, at best, can come to represent a barely tolerated nuisance in a community. This second feeling is based on my experiences in the commune in Ben Lomond. This commune was written about by a sociologist in what was to become a best-seller. The consequent onslaught of tourists and curiosity-seekers contributed greatly to the ultimate demise of this particular commune.

Since I was approaching this project as a concerned, utopian-minded seeker, as well as a researcher, I felt I needed a functionally oriented model from which to view the community. Aberle's functional prerequisites of a society (1950:100–111) proved to be useful in this respect. These include the following:

1. Provision for an adequate relationship to the environment and for sexual recruitment.
2. Role differentiation and role assignment.
3. Communication.
4. Shared cognitive orientation.
5. A shared, articulated set of goals.
6. The normative regulation of means.
7. The regulation of affective expression.
8. Socialization.
9. The effective control of disruptive behavior.

Not only do these nine points provide a viable theoretical framework for examining a growth-centered community, they also serve as an instrumental means of partially answering the inquiry underlying this entire effort. The central question becomes the following: Is there something functioning in an intentional (in this case) therapeutic community that does not function in society at large and that operates in such a way as to foster a greater feeling of well-being, belonging, integration, intimate involvement, and general good mental health on the part of its members? My hypothesis was that there probably *was* something functioning in this manner in The Country Place, that is, in the sense of its being somehow more generally therapeutic than society-at-large. The remainder of this paper, then, is devoted to exploring this issue, beginning with a brief, general history of The Country Place.

For this effort, I have utilized the observations of a month's residence at The Country Place as a participant observer, an hour-long taped interview with Renee Nell, numerous conversations with various members of the community, and selected research of available literature concerning therapeutic, utopian communities and general mental health.

THE COUNTRY PLACE — EARLY BEGINNINGS

Renee Nell, founder, director, and head psychotherapist at The Country Place, received her earliest psychological training in Zurich, Switzerland. Having originally come from Germany during World War II, she studied with Carl G. Jung, the founder of the analytic school of psychology. Upon arriving in the U.S., she studied for a B.A. at Clarement College, receiving it in 1943. She received an M.A. from the New School of Social Research and an Ed.D. from Teachers College of Columbia University in 1964. During this period of time, she had an active private practice as a Jungian psychotherapist.

The original impetus for The Country Place came during Renee Nell's early years in private practice. She decided that a number of her patients were borderline schizophrenics:

> They are not disturbed enough to benefit from a mental institution, and those who were in mental hospitals often complained that the institutional structure of the hospital made them more passive.... Nevertheless, they did not do well on their own.... They were just sitting around at home doing nothing.... Some had short-lived jobs that were meaningless to them, or they went to daycare centers as a stop-gap (Renee Nell, taped interview, February 18, 1971).

Since a large part of her original clientele were show business people, who were inclined to be unusually gifted — creatively, artistically, and intellectually — they were, for the most part, able to *survive* psychologically in the milieu of New York City, but survival was as far as it went. A number were confirmed alcoholics. Their marriages were suffering, and they were experiencing an unusual degree of difficulty in holding a job in their respective fields. They tended to be between thirty and forty years of age, and Nell has described them typically as:

> A person who, when pushed by another person *can* function in life and on the job, but the moment he has time on his hands that he has to structure, such as vacation, weekends, or evenings, he is incapable of mustering sufficient ego-strength to follow an insight to action (Renee Nell, taped interview, February 18, 1971).

The earliest prototype for The Country Place occurred when Nell took several private patients for an experimental weekend at a cottage that she owned in Connecticut. There, in a kind of work-therapy, they simply puttered around the cottage, doing such things as gardening, painting, and general repair on the cottage itself. She saw these weekends functioning theoretically as a highly structured time sequence, serving as a kind of functional alter-ego, whereby patients could literally borrow, or be infused with, the ego-strength that they lacked but needed to function in their assigned tasks.

The therapeutic results of these experimental weekends were so gratifying that she began to check with her colleagues to see if there were any functioning programs of this nature. Much to her surprise, she found a great deal of interest and support in the psychiatric world for this type of endeavor, but there were no existing programs. Consequently, she decided to begin her own. Nell managed to arrange adequate financing by 1966. She gathered a group of patients from her private practice and subsequently, the first Country Place was begun in New Preston, Connecticut. It was housed in a rented building, and the first few weeks were spent getting organized. Still commuting from New York City at this time, Nell hired a full-time psychologist to live on the premises of The Country Place. After she moved in, Ruth Fox, her friend and colleague in New York, provided the bulk of her first referrals to The Country Place. The majority of these first residents were alcoholics, between the ages of thirty and forty, and tended to come from show business backgrounds. The brochure of the first Country Place states:

We are able to accept adults over 18 years of age who have emotional or social problems and character disorders.... We can accept people who overindulge in food, drink, or nicotine, as well as the withdrawn and depressed personality.... We cannot accept anyone who is a mentally ill person within the purview of Section 17–176 of the Connecticut General Statutes, requiring hospitalization, shock treatment, or confinement.

As the reputation of The Country Place began to grow, however, the make-up of the residents changed. The burgeoning drug culture started to play a large part in referrals; by about 1969, the balance of residents were no longer predominantly alcoholics or between the ages of thirty and forty. Instead, most were between the ages of eighteen and twenty-five, often having experienced some difficulty with drug abuse, both hard (heroin, amphetamines, and barbituates) and soft (marijuana and its derivatives, LSD, and other hallucinogenic drugs). Some were there as an alternative to a drug-related jail sentence. The majority of the residents of The Country Place now tended to come from overwhelmingly white, middle to upper-middle class, and had high intelligence, a number of them being college dropouts. This trend continued until the present and has had a decided impact on the nature of the community.

The program for the residents is based on a weekly block of time, which Nell views as a basic principle of reality orientation in a therapeutic milieu.

> We think of The Country Place as a duplication of normal life situations and conditions on a smaller level, a kind of microcosm of society.... Life at The Country Place is determined largely by the residents with a semi-structured and essentially supportive atmosphere.... The rural isolation; the old colonial, rambling country house; the fact that each person has a private room with bath, furnished to his individual taste, gives The Country Place a homelike atmosphere representing a microcosm of the family (Nell 1968a:38).

A conscious effort has been made to structure the morning work program so it correlates closely with actual conditions in American society-at-large. The work is supervised and coordinated by two live-in work coordinators, who are paid a modest salary, but who function in every other respect as just another member of the community. Considerable role flexibility is built into the system with opportunities for men to try their hand in the kitchen and for women to work in the maintenance and repair of the house. From 2:30 P.M. to 8:30 P.M., time in the community is left relatively unstructured. During this time, the members of the community are encouraged to take advantage of the leisure opportunities provided by the community, such as art classes and seasonal sports. Some members of the community use this time to go to various local colleges or to work on a high-school equivalency diploma. Individual psychotherapy also occurs during the afternoon with one of the psychotherapists.

Evenings are devoted to a variety of activities. Group therapy, in which the residents are broken down into two groups of approximately twelve each, (Nell and her assistant each lead one) occurs on Monday, Wednesday, and Friday evenings. One of the three evenings is called a peer group session and consists of the regular group members without the leader. In this case, the group usually becomes more of a bull session than group therapy. Theoretically, however, it is designed to give the members of the group an opportunity to vent their feelings about the therapists who are not there. Since I left The Country Place, the groups have expanded to three, the third being led by a colleague of Renee Nell, due to a sudden influx of new residents. Tuesday night is devoted to art or music therapy. Participation is voluntary, and art therapy has a large, regular following. On Thursday, a house meeting is held at 8:30 P.M. During this time, practical considerations about The Country Place are discussed. The therapy groups being together presents an opportunity for feedback, encounter, and confrontation between residents who are in different groups. In many ways, the house meeting functions as a large group therapy session, with all members of The Country Place present and participating.

MILIEU THERAPY

When I was first able to question Nell about her view of the therapeutic process at The Country Place, I was laboring under one basically false assumption: I fully expected some form of hybrid exotica to emerge in the realm of theory, coupled with an unusual form of practice, both perhaps influenced by her Jungian training and/or her reading in milieu treatment theory. This simply was not the case, because she views The Country Place as functioning well within the realm of conventional, everyday, normative life. In fact, this conventionality represents a basic building block, theoretically and pragmatically, for her conception of The Country Place.

Originally, The Country Place was to be based on a work therapy program. She states, however, that:

All my American colleagues informed me that this "work therapy" is not a very liked word in America. You will not get a lot of people with that, but we know what you mean.... Maybe you can give it a less suspect name like "milieu therapy" (Renee Nell, taped interview, February 18, 1971).

She views the philosophy of The Country Place as expressing itself in three basic concepts: (1) socially useful work in teams, (2) individual responsibility, and (3) self-help and the exploration of existent reality. Each of these three concepts embodies a large part of the therapeutic process at The Country Place.

The "work" in the morning constitutes the most basic part of the process of therapy, since it provides the modality of self-presentation and interaction for the residents:

We introduced purposeful work in our milieu therapy because we are convinced that drug therapy and psychotherapy alone are not enough to achieve reconstruction of the kind of personality seeking our help.... Most of the residents feel a loss of identity; meeting the demands that are useful to the social functioning of our community is a first step towards the formulation of a new identity.... The teamwork in the morning promotes personal interaction, often friction, but even friction is better than emotional isolation.... The assigned work in the morning has another advantage: the team leader gains insight into the way a resident functions; does he disappear from his assigned task as soon as he can get away with it; does he get bogged down in an obsessive involvement with details? ... Is he helpful to others or does he tend to take advantage of them? ... More important than the abilities exhibited are the emotional characteristics that come to the fore in a work situation.... The therapist will use this information in the immediate situation and in a therapeutic encounter later on.... The way in which a person fulfills the assigned task in the morning becomes an indication of his mental health (Nell 1968a:38–39).

The work program functions then as a cooperative, but not competitive task-oriented attempt at getting for the resident a firm, functional foothold in objective reality. When a resident volunteers to take on an extra responsibility: "this step is generally a result of an increase in personal identity, a closer tie with the house" (Nell 1968a:39), and it culminates in a more integrated collective identity.

Nell views this work orientation of the therapeutic process as being nearly ideal for the type of residents that now compose a majority of the house. Many of these people come from very permissive, affluent homes; their parents are extremely successful in their respective fields. We are only now beginning to see that being reared in an atmosphere of permissive tolerance, with a large array of material things associated with the American ideal of the "good life" is not without its disadvantages. In fact, Slater suggests three basic human needs that are deeply and uniquely frustrated by this aspect of the American dream. They include the following:

The desire for *community*, the wish to live in trust and fraternal cooperation with one's fellows in a total and visible collective entity.... The desire for *engagement*, the wish to come directly to grips with social and interpersonal problems and to confront on equal terms an environment which is not composed of ego extensions.... The desire for *dependence*, the wish to share responsibility for the control of one's impulses and the direction of one's life (Slater 1970:5).

The end product of this basic frustration is the alienated, drug-abusing portion of the youth culture. The Country Place is composed mostly of this type of person. Nell views The Country Place as an environment in which its residents may attempt to get in touch with some of the simple, basic things in life that they were denied by their parents. Most of them had never worked at any kind of manual labor because a hired person was always called in to do that kind of work. The Country Place provides for these things in the work aspect of its program, but even more important, this work itself is an *integral* part of the functioning community. Every individual is dependent on and accountable to someone else. In sum, the work program was designed to provide a small model of society-at-large, and thus, a basic reality orientation, in which the residents are encouraged, via personal interaction among themselves and the work coordinators, coupled with individual and group therapy, to accept the responsibility and understand the importance of getting their work done and done well. The emphasis is on participation and responsible behavior, as opposed to irresponsibility and withdrawal, a dominant motif of the drug-abusing sector of the youth culture.

Springing directly from the work program are the two other concepts that make up Nell's conception of The Country Place. The concept of individual responsibility and self-help (The Country Place n.d.), enables the residents to pursue individual interests and avocations during the free time in the afternoons and evenings. Individual psychotherapy also plays an important role in the afternoon hours.

> The sessions are given more in terms of individual needs than by strict office schedule.... While one resident might wish to drop in for fifteen minutes every day just to make sure I still like him, another might not show up for ten or twelve days, [during which he is] working something out by himself, using sculpting as a means to do that.... When the sculpture is finished, we will look at it together, and it might develop into a two-hour session on two consecutive days.... Others like regularly scheduled sessions twice a week (Nell 1968a:37–42).

The concept of the exploration of existent reality is also linked to the basic work modality in the morning hours. The morning work is done in teams. The interaction of residents during these hours provides not only a form of reality testing, but material for the evening group therapy sessions as well. These group sessions are highly dependent on the emotional and intellectual makeup of their members and also on the orientation of their leaders.

Many interesting questions are raised within a therapeutic community such as The Country Place. One of them has to do with the way in which a resident is tangibly rewarded for growth towards better mental health.

> It is one of our problems that we have few tangible means of reward.... Being promoted to the staff fills that gap, and acts as incentive to exchange the gratifications of illness for those of health.... In order to qualify as a staff member, the resident has to do a great deal more than fulfill the hours of work in the morning.... He has to be well enough to stay with a task until it is finished, and to become aware of work that needs to be done without being told.... Next, the individual initiates assignments, and makes all the preparations necessary to carry them out.... He often guides a group of residents in carrying out the task.... As the work on this more advanced level involves effort and responsibility, it seems only fair to compensate it with a salary (Nell 1968a:37–42).

After residents have discharged their responsibilities as staff members for approximately two months, they are generally ready to go back to the outside world, returning weekends for therapy and to visit their friends.

A question also arises regarding how close The Country Place is to actual operation of the family and our society-at-large. Can it prepare residents for an eventual return to the real world with a consequent good adjustment? Nell feels that:

> The microcosm of society is not really a duplication of society in the "real" world.... The microcosm of the family is not a duplication of the family.... [She

evidently views The Country Place as a functioning family.] Our work situation, at least in the winter, includes a great deal of menial and domestic labor which often is not meaningful enough for the intelligent young person.... By necessity, attention then becomes focused on the manifest content of the task: Did John clean the window properly?... It is often difficult to understand that for the young intellectual, withdrawn from the world of objects, there is a relationship between his lack of consistency regarding window washing and his lack of consistency regarding homework.... Another kind of problem arises from the opposite type of behavior.... I am thinking of the person who defends himself against social relationships by always being busy with something.... Rather than coming to art therapy, he will choose to repair some equipment.... He likes to avoid group therapy by running an errand.... This kind of defense mechanism sometimes goes undetected for quite a while (Nell 1968a:37–42).

The role of psychotherapist then, in The Country Place, is as diversified as is the therapist's personality. Richard Beauvais, a co-worker with Nell, feels that each resident gets something different from the community and from each therapist, depending upon the varying moods of the therapist and the resident. Nell sums up her conceptions and feelings about the process of therapy at The Country Place, as well as the rewards she finds in the community for herself.

Many of the psychotherapists from the medical and psychological professions who have had doubts about our kind of milieu therapy have come to stay with us for a weekend.... They have become convinced that it can be done because our therapeutic staff is dedicated to the needs of our residents without regard to time or hours.... Beyond that, milieu therapy necessitates a willingness by the therapist to be seen and confronted as a person, which is always more difficult for the members of the profession than for the patient, who is conditioned to be "expensively humiliated."... In the past, we were accustomed to see such confrontation by patients, mainly as negative transference.... Those of us who have withstood the test have not regretted it, because it helped us to grow as therapists as well as individuals (The Country Place n.d.: 42).

IMPRESSIONS — OBSERVER TO PARTICIPATOR

Experiencing The Country Place as a participant-observer proved to be one of the most psychologically strenuous and rewarding aspects of the entire enterprise. Translating my feelings, ideas, and impressions of this month-long period into coherent words was a difficult task. I do feel that I received a broad exposure to the community, and I would like to attempt now to convey come impressions of my experience.

On the whole the residents were willing to spend long periods of time answering questions about their lives, their reasons for being at The Country Place, and their experiences. I received from people approximately the same degree of depth of feelings and knowledge that I was able to give in return, a fact that I found to be very different from the society-at-large. I also found that this phenomenon takes some getting used to, particularly for someone attempting to do research.

I definitely felt a strong sense of identification with the residents, for several reasons, but mainly, because they were young, hip, politically left-leaning members of the youth subculture, one to which I definitely owe allegiance. They dressed the way I do, used my vocabulary, and had a similar set of priorities and values.

This feeling of identification or inability to feel an objective distance between myself and the rest of the community is perhaps the dominant impression that I came away with: feedback and confrontation in my group therapy sessions indicated to me that I was transparent in my self-presentation, although I still was unable to achieve the objective distance I sought. With the passage of time, I became convinced more than ever that I was either a borderline schizophrenic or the whole psychiatric labeling scheme was essentially just a name game played for power stakes by one group of people (the psychiatric profession) against another (the mentally ill). The things I heard and saw in group therapy and in daily interaction at The Country Place were just not that different from what I have experienced, heard, or felt myself elsewhere. These feelings brought about a great deal of anxiety, insecurity, self-doubt, and depression. My difficulty in establishing a median between participating to the fullest extent in the community, on the one hand, and observing the community, on the other, only added to this burden. I was incapable of doing both simultaneously.

The community demanded that I participate in terms of self-revelation and participate as fully as possible. I could write this paper as a *participant*, but they would have no part of my *observing* them. I also received feedback in group therapy that some individuals thought I wanted special treatment. In my second week, I was delivered an ultimatum by the community during the Thursday night house meeting: Either participate fully, abandoning any pretense of observer-status, or leave. After discussing this with Nell, I decided to reveal to the community significant portions of my inner life and feelings. Many hours were devoted in various group therapy sessions to my problems as an individual, in relating to other people, and in marriage. This opening up was, and always has been, painful and difficult for me, and it is only in retrospect that I now see the essential validity of what the residents were trying to tell me. How were they to trust me with their thoughts and feelings if I was not able to trust them with mine? I found, eventually, with the help of the community, that by revealing myself as a person and participating fully, I was not only able to get a better idea of its functioning, but also to achieve significant insight and feedback about myself as well, both from the residents and from Nell and Beauvais.

As I look back over my stay at The Country Place, two themes stand out. First, I found the morning work sessions to be extremely satisfying. It was hard, dirty work at times, and yet, I have a good feeling about it. I found myself sleeping better and tightening up my sedentary body, something that made the various aches and pains well worth it. I also found that the work system operates loosely enough to allow plenty of talk while working. I found this to be a great opportunity to get to know the people with whom I was working. I am now convinced that relating to real, solid objects such as wood and tools in a regular fixed pattern is decidedly therapeutic, particularly for residents like myself, who have probably spent most of their lives relating to books, ideas, and abstractions. The drug-abusing sector of the American youth culture is particularly involved in ethereal, other-worldly, highly abstract reifications of their own particular drug mystique, and the work program at The Country Place provides an ideal counterbalance to this emphasis.

The second theme that emerged was concerned with the interaction among the residents of The Country Place. As just another resident, I found myself feeling closer to some individuals than to others, just as I would in any other community. I was able to discern two distinct patterns of social groupings or cliques. First, people who were in the same therapy group tended to be closer and friendlier to each other than to people in the others. This did not surprise me, having experienced many times the intense feelings that can be generated in the group process. Second, there was also a definite clustering around the charismatic figure of Nell. These tended to be people who knew her well, having seen her in individual therapy sessions, in group therapy, or who had been at The Country Place for long periods of time.

In summary, after I was able to get over the initial inability to reveal parts of myself to the community, I began to feel a sense of belonging comparable to any other resident. This, along with the gradual transformation in role emphasis (from *observer* to *participant*) greatly facilitated my ability to arrive at a better understanding of the functioning of the community.

QUESTIONNAIRE FEEDBACK

When I first arrived at The Country Place, I had a number of different methods in mind for obtaining the residents' views of their community. I had contemplated taped interviews, content analysis, collection of autobiographical materials, evaluation based on the Q-sort technique, and a thematic analysis of creative written work. As it happened, Nell expressed a strong desire that I work with some of the raw data that she had already gathered with a friend. After looking at this material, I decided that it would suit my purposes well and also function to broaden my perspective of the community by incorporating the views of past residents to whom I had not been personally exposed.

In the spring of 1970, Nell and a friend, Walter Lowney,[1] mailed a questionnaire, to a number of exresidents, that was designed to provide feedback about the experiences they had had after leaving The Country Place. This feedback was, in turn, designed to reflect indirectly back upon the nature of their experiences of The Country Place. Had the community been successful in its attempts to provide a therapeutic community for its residents? How did this success (or lack thereof) carry over into the exresident's life and interpersonal relationships? Although the data in these questionnaires was never tabulated, I have chosen to use it for the purposes of this paper.[2]

The actual number of responses to the Lowney questionnaire was thirty-two, approximately one-half being male and the other female. As it happened, there were also approximately thirty-two residents at The Country Place for the duration of my project. I selected at random 25 percent of each of these two populations, eight persons, consisting of four men and four women for my sampling. I then administered the questionnaire to eight randomly selected individuals (four men and four women) who are currently residents of The Country Place. They were asked to view the questionnaire as a projective instrument, filling it out as if they had been away from The Country Place for approximately one year; on the one hand, there were to be the projections (expectations) of the current residents, and on the other hand, the actual experience of the exresidents.

The questionnaire pointed out some definite trends among residents and exresidents.[3] For instance, there were variations between the projections of the current residents, and the experience of the exresidents. I have chosen to call this discrepancy in response the "projection versus reality-factor," it being rather uniformly distributed among the nineteen questions. This factor says two things: First, that there is a certain healthy degree of optimism on the part of the current residents. They feel that their experience in the community is definitely helping them. Although the experience of the exresidents bears this out, too, it is to a degree realistically tempered, which lends further weight to the validity of the current residents' projective optimism.

---

[1] Walter Lowney, a lawyer, was a work-coordinator at The Country Place in order to gain first-hand experience in the operation of a therapeutic milieu community. He eventually wanted to begin a similar community for exconvicts.
[2] This data appears in the appendix.
[3] From this writer's perspective, the Lowney questionnaire probably raises as many questions as it answers about the resident's perceptions of their community. It is certainly inadequate in terms of giving one a means for longitudinal comparison of the residents before they enter the community and after they leave.

Second, their lives after leaving the community are characterized by a stability, continuity, and responsibility that was definitely lacking previously, or they would not have been at The Country Place in the first place. From this perspective then, I would hold that The Country Place is undoubtedly experienced as a therapeutic community by its residents, this being well borne out by the current residents' projections and in dialogue about the experiences of the exresidents. In spite of the inadequacy of this questionnaire to measure this therapeutic phenomenon, it still has given a strong indication of its existence. Finally, I feel that I probably could have shown even more of this therapeutic effect had I possessed a means whereby the age and background differences of the two groups sampled could have been eliminated as a variable in the questionnaire, thereby enabling me to work in more *psychological* as opposed to *sociological* categories. I would like to elaborate, at this point, on my analysis and interpretation of the results of the questionnaire.

Fully 87.5 percent of the sampling of current residents projected that they would be living in essentially the same place, with the same people, for at least a year after leaving The Country Place. While this trend may lend itself to a certain degree of ambiguity in interpretation, I view it as a decidedly healthy trait, particularly in light of the demonstrable, destructive effects of the rootless, wandering lifestyle and background of so many of the current residents. While the actual experience of the exresidents does not demonstrate as high a degree of continuity in living arrangements (62.5 percent), a marked contrast does exist in another sphere. That is the fact that 75 percent of the exresidents lived alone, whereas 100 percent of the current residents projected a definite affinity for not living alone. This phenomenon may be interpreted as the difference between projection, on the one hand, and reality, on the other: I choose, however, to view it as an indication of the changed complexion of the residents who make up The Country Place. The new youth culture of the 1970's (the current majority of residents) is much more group and communally oriented than were the exresidents from which this sampling was taken, most of whom were residents from 1966–1967. To me, this accounts for the high percentage of the current resident projections toward living with one or more other persons.

Questions three through five dealt with the employment records of the residents after leaving The Country Place. The current resident projections indicate a high value placed on continuing education (50 percent), whereas the actual experience of the exresidents indicated an equal degree of propensity toward holding a paying job (50 percent). This phenomenon may be accounted for, I believe, by the differences in age between the residents of the two samplings: the current residents are predominantly between the ages of eighteen and twenty-five, whereas the exresident group was largely between thirty and forty. The exresidents had probably finished most of their education before coming to The Country Place, whereas a number of the current residents are college dropouts. Being of a younger age group, the current residents also probably have better access to some degree of parental, financial support than the exresidents did.

Questions seven through nine reflected the basic considerations vital to a good, viable, healthy life. Job satisfaction is moderately high in the projections of the current residents. (50–75 percent). Though somewhat lower in the actual experience of the exresidents (37.5–62.5 percent), the optimism inherent in the projections of the current residents impresses me with the fact that it is coming from a therapeutic milieu such as The Country Place. In terms of providing for one's own financial support, the relative age factor of the two samplings comes to the fore, once again, the older exresidents not having the access to parental money that the younger current residents tend to have. Chronology also plays a part in regard to the residents' marital status. Though neither of the two groups show any strong trends toward marital change, the relative youth of the current residents is evident, most of them having been single when they arrived at The Country Place.

Questions ten through twelve were, for my purposes, the most relevant in the questionnaire. The response to question ten indicated a strong trend on the part of both groups toward better relations with their own families. Full 100 percent of the current resident group said their family relationships would be satisfactory. I regard this as a positive sign, although I wish there had been a question to indicate the state of family relationships before they came to The Country Place. On the whole, I do not feel that The Country Place would tend to make for worse family relationships, though it is possible that some residents might have experienced this. The exresidents also had a high rate of response within the realm of "satisfactory" (75 percent). The age differential, in terms of the time period of previous estrangement from the family, might explain this difference. The current residents were young enough that there might still be a chance for reconciliation with the estranged portions of their families, whereas the exresidents may no longer be in a position to achieve this goal.

Fully 85.7 percent in each group indicated that the problem for which they came to The Country Place had improved to some degree. The amount of improvement in each group followed a standard bell-shaped distribution, indicating that The Country Place was indeed a therapeutic community in which to reside. I also found it interesting to note that current resident projections on this question matched exactly with the experience of the exresidents. This indicates to me a healthy streak of realism on the part of the current residents, something that I attribute to the basic reality orientation of the community.

Questions fourteen through sixteen dealt with the residents' therapy after leaving The Country Place. Fifty percent of each group continued in therapy of one type or another for a significant length of time after leaving. This factor, along with the high correlation between resident projections and exresident experience, indicates the strong reality orientation of The Country Place. The current residents have no illusions about there being a significant chance that they could still benefit from psychotherapy after leaving The Country Place, and this realistic assessment is borne out by the actual experience of the exresidents. In terms of frequency of therapy, the exresidents go more often than the current residents project they will go, which can be explained either as resident optimism or as exresident reality encroaching on the same.

Of the current residents, 87.5 percent project that they will not be using any medication to help them through their difficulties, whereas only 50 percent of the exresidents are not using medication. This could indicate either the optimism-reality dichotomy, which I noted earlier, or it could reflect the various types and ages of the people comprising the two groups. While I was at The Country Place, it was evident that most of the residents, having been through the entire drug scene, were extremely reluctant to put any unnatural chemical into their systems (marijuana excluded since it grows in a natural, organic form). The population from which the exresidents were drawn, however, were predominantly alcoholic and had no such compunctions. This is reflected in the fact that a large percentage of these exresidents are not using alcohol at all (62.5 percent), which is a fairly typical phenomenon among exalcoholics, whereas the current residents feel they are able to use natural alcohols (wine and beer) and natural drugs (marijuana and hashish) in moderation.

The general trends that have tended to emerge from this data represent a fairly distinct quantitative phenomenon. Qualitatively, however, the interpreted differences between the two sampling groups are ambiguous. Are these patterns of difference reflective of a multiplicity of response variations as the distinct life-styles of the two sampling groups? As mentioned earlier, the exresidents of The Country Place were largely alcoholic, between the ages of thirty and forty, and came from show business backgrounds. The current residents are predominantly from a drug-abuse background, and are for the most part between the ages of eighteen and twenty-five. Needless to say, the lifestyles of the two groups are very different.

CONCLUSIONS

There is no question in my mind that The Country Place functions as an essentially therapeutic community for its residents. The work program, with its basic reality orientation; the group-therapy sessions, with their opportunities for feedback and encounter among the residents; and individual therapy, with its potential for facilitating growth are all processes that play an important role in making the community lifestyle of the residents an essentially therapeutic experience.

I would like to delineate a more generalized conclusion about the basic functioning of the community. Returning for a moment to Slater's analysis of three basic human needs that are largely unmet in American culture, I am struck by the accuracy with which this analysis and these needs describe what is the essential, therapeutic function of the community. In meeting the resident's needs for a sense of community, a sense of engagement, and a feeling of dependence, The Country Place is functioning at a primary level as a milieu from which to develop better mental health. Slater summarizes his rationale behind these three needs:

In the past, as so many have pointed out, there were, in our society, many cases in which one could take refuge from the frenzied invidiousness of our economic system, institutions such as the extended family and the stable, local neighborhood in which one could take pleasure from something other than winning a symbolic victory over one of his fellows.... But these have disappeared one by one, leaving the individual more and more in a situation in which he must try to satisfy his affiliative and invidious needs in the same place.... This has made the balance a more brittle one, the appeal of cooperative living more seductive, and the need to suppress our longing for it more acute (Slater 1970:6).

We are faced with a situation then in which the resident is born into an invidious culture that not only emphasizes but in many instances demands intense competition among its members in every sphere of their lives. In order for one to get ahead or win at this competition, one or many others must lose. In the case of typical residents, their parents were eminently successful competitors, having in most instances finished the competition at the top of their respective heaps.

This orientation is projected by the parents and, in turn, introjected by their children (the residents), into every aspect of their lives: work, school, athletics, play, and, especially, popularity and peer-group acceptance. No residents were observed who did not give peer-group acceptance as one of the primary reasons for their having begun abusing various drugs. Slater's point is simply this: Given the society in which we live today, it is almost impossible to avoid a certain degree of frustration in the sphere of basic, human affiliative needs. I will take this contention one step further to state that a large amount of the mental illness in our culture is partially a product of this frustrated affiliative need. In the case of The Country Place residents, their problems represent both a response to this frustration and an inability to do anything about it, thereby adding a secondary source of frustration. This inability to fulfill their needs within the framework of existing institutions such as marriage, the extended family, the church, and the local neighborhood, forms the matrix from which springs the whole syndrome of symptoms that bring residents to The Country Place for help — drug abuse and borderline schizophrenia being the most notable of these.

I arrived at these conclusions about the therapeutic function of the community only after being singularly impressed with a number of things. In particular, I was impressed by the religious-like feelings of the majority of the residents toward Nell and the community. This phenomenon was especially evident to me as a new outsider in the group therapy sessions. Meeting three times a week, these sessions were permeated with an almost revivalist camp-meeting-like atmosphere. From the time dinner ended (6:30 P.M.) until the session actually began (8:30 P.M.), there was an air of expectation throughout the community. Many people assembled in their respective group's meeting place as much as an hour before their group was scheduled to begin. As the group began to function and as the spotlight turned on me, I felt at times an almost overwhelming demand to witness or to confess my sins. This feeling took the form of accepting group feedback and criticism (witnessing to the gospel of community via group infallibility) and acknowledging the validity or correctness of their criticism (confessing one's sins to the group). Having experienced this pressure in other groups before, I was somewhat wary of the tendency, feeling that it often functioned as a subtle form of community brainwashing. I was particularly impressed, however, by the ways in which Nell capitalized on her powerful, personal charisma and leadership position to work with the group. Time and time again, she skillfully used these group tendencies to drive home a therapeutic insight to a reluctant individual. My initial skepticism began to diminish as I felt more a part of the community, and in retrospect, I am convinced that this ability of The Country Place to socialize (convert) its new members is one of its most important therapeutic functions: I am also greatly respectful of Nell's ability to exploit these group tendencies within the therapeutic community and in the actual group therapy itself.

Mowrer (1964:iv) has stated that "a religious congregation worthy of the name ought to be a 'therapeutic community'." As time passed for me at The Country Place, I came to appreciate more and more the essential validity of Mowrer's statement in describing the therapeutic operation of the community, in terms of its basic functioning as a therapeutic milieu, in meeting the needs of its residents — needs that traditionally, for the most part, have been met by the close community matrix formed by the family and the church or synagogue. As these traditional structures have given way to the rapid onslaught of the change and evolution of the twentieth century, many groups and individuals have psychologically had the rug pulled out from under their feet. The drug-abusing sector of the youth culture is only a part of this casualty list, and in this case, they represent a majority of the residents at The Country Place.

In fulfilling this need to experience a warm, meaningful, secure, sense of belonging, community life at The Country Place provides an environment where, perhaps for the first time, residents feel free to develop themselves in their own way and at their own pace. The theory of a gradual process of personal growth has been described by Carl Rogers (1970:125–158). For the purposes of this paper, I have viewed this process from a more general and socio-psychological perspective, as opposed to Rogers, who deals primarily with individuals in therapy. The theory lends itself well, however, to an institution such as The Country Place and may be functionally described by again using Slater's three sociological concepts. As new residents begin to feel a greater sense of belonging in the community, they also start to experience a gradual sense of greater engagement, both in terms of their daily interactions with other residents and in terms of their daily work (which plays an integral part in the functioning of the community). As they come to feel a greater sense of dependency on the community to fulfill their previously frustrated affiliative needs, the community, in turn, begins to depend on them, both via their work and insofar as they are accepted and known. The time at which this resident-community transaction occurs represents the critical point in the therapeutic process at The Country Place. It is from this critical juncture that individual and group therapy may begin to function truly as growth-facilitating processes, enabling residents to begin to work through the problems that brought them to the community in the first place.

My original interest in The Country Place stems from my utopian search for a better way of life. I had a feeling, dating back to my earliest interest in collective living, that the community might be a viable model for an alternative lifestyle.

From my perspective, The Country Place fulfills the essential prerequisites for a functional community. It was originally created by adequate capital and is committed to sound financial policy. The residents pay a sufficient amount to guarantee more than just an adequate relationship to the environment. In fact, I found the physical plant moderately luxurious, and, in many instances, the food was excellent. Nell has more than enough referrals to keep the community running in sound financial condition.

Communication is perhaps a key modality in the community, the shared modes being the group therapy sessions and house meetings. From this basic communications matrix springs shared articulated sets of goals for the community, shared cognitive orientations, effective control of disruptive behavior, and the normative regulation of means. The socialization process negates the need for any regulation of affective expression per se, this being viewed instead as a component of the resident's overall presentation-of-self and treated accordingly by the community (Nell 1968d:303–312).

One has then a community that is indeed functional as well as therapeutic. Two basic questions remain to be answered. First, would anyone want to live in a community modeled after The Country Place? Second, how transferable is the model, from a functional standpoint?

Under the skillful, charismatic orchestration of Nell, the work program and the group therapy sessions foster a family-like feeling of acceptance and belonging among the residents. I observed this feeling actively at work in the community — in terms of commitment on the part of the residents to try and help themselves and in terms of their active participation in community affairs, coupled with a real desire to help make the community a functional, pleasant place to live. From this essential therapeutic matrix, it becomes possible for the individual resident to begin the slow, and often painful, process of personal growth back to better mental health and integration. The individual and group therapy sessions serve to meet this end, as does the work program; both keep the community functioning.

In terms of personal needs, I found the overall family-like feeling to be one of the more pleasing aspects of The Country Place. It represents something that is painfully missing in the majority of interpersonal relationships carried on in the outside world. Granted the strong interpersonal relations inherent in this way of life carry risks and responsibilities, but I feel strongly that this element of the community is worthy, viable, and transferable. I found that living twenty-four hours a day in a state of intimate, open involvement with the residents was a taxing experience, completely draining at times, physically and emotionally. Nell assured me, however, that after a while, a person begins to grow accustomed to the demands of the community for openness and usually comes to prefer this state to the impersonal and often phony modes of relating to other people that occur on the outside.

The functional needs for shared communication, cognitive orientations, and an articulated set of goals are perhaps the most basic determinants in the issue of transferability. Without the presence of these three factors, which are prominent in the organization of The Country Place, a community could not function. For these to transfer to another alternative community would require the same sense of commitment, coupled with the presence of the basic three functional prerequisites. Kanter has summarized the issue admirably:

In the light of history, the small anarchistic commune does not seem to be stable or enduring, while the growth-and-learning community appears to have much greater prospects.... Yet in today's world — a mobile, change-oriented society that is increasingly wary of long-range commitments — there may be room for both kinds of groups.... The small, dissolvable, unstructured commune may meet its members' needs for a temporary home and family.... The more permanent growth and learning center is a place for enduring commitment for those who want a rooted way of life in a community (1970:78).

For this writer then, The Country Place presents two distinct types of potential as a community. First, it is without question a therapeutic place. As stated earlier, 87.5 percent of the participants indicated that the problems for which they had first come to the community had improved to some degree. This was borne out by my experiencing of the community, both in terms of what I saw happening to other people and in what I felt happening to myself.

Second, The Country Place impresses me as having distinct potential as a model alternative community. Allport states in the preface of Frankl's *Man's search for meaning* that "Frankl is fond of quoting Nietzsche: 'He who has a why to live can bear with any how'" (1959:xiii).

A community such as The Country Place can provide the why that is so obviously missing in the lives of many contemporary Americans. This perhaps, more than anything else, has been the greatest contributing factor to the growth and flourishing throughout this country of myriad attempts to find a meaningful sense of community and a sense of belonging via shared or communal living.

APPENDIX

Questions	Resident projections		Ex-residents	
	Percentage	Number	Percentage	Number
1. When I first left The Country Place, I lived:				
a. alone	—	—	75	6
b. with friends	50	4	—	—
c. with spouse	25	2	—	—
d. common-law	12.5	1	—	—
e. with parents	12.5	1	12.5	1
f. other — (in a halfway house)	—	—	12.5	1
2. This living arrangement continued:				
a. temporarily	12.5	1	25	2
b. until the present time	87.5	7	75	6
3. My present living arrangement is:				
a. same as in number 1 above	87.5	7	62.5	5
b. other	12.5	1	37.5	3

Appendix (*continued*)

Questions	Resident projections Percentage	Number	Ex-residents Percentage	Number
4. When I first left The Country Place, I:				
a. continued my education	50	4	12.5	1
b. took a paying job	37.5	3	50	4
c. preferred not to accept a job or attend school	—	—	12.5	1
d. worked as a nonpaid volunteer	—	—	—	—
e. felt unable to work or attend classes	—	—	12.5	1
f. continued at a job in which I was working	12.5	1	12.5	1
5. Since leaving, I have held:				
a. one job	75	6	62.5	5
b. two jobs	—	—	25	2
c. three jobs	—	—	12.5	1
d. no job	25	2	—	—
Attended ——— schools:				
e. one school	75	6	25	2
f. no schools	25	2	75	6
6. My present position is:				
a. student	50	4	25	2
b. art therapist	12.5	1	—	—
c. magazine editor	12.5	1	—	—
d. laborer	12.5	1	—	—
e. teaching assistant	12.5	1	—	—
f. alcohol permit examiner	—	—	12.5	1
g. physical therapy aide	—	—	12.5	1
h. science research aide	—	—	12.5	1
i. writer	—	—	12.5	1
j. administrative assistant	—	—	12.5	1
k. museum job	—	—	12.5	1
7. With my present position, I am:				
a. very satisfied	12.5	1	37.5	3
b. satisfied	50	4	25	2
c. somewhat satisfied	25	2	25	2
d. somewhat dissatisfied	12.5	1	25	2
e. dissatisfied	—	—	12.5	1
f. very dissatisfied	—	—	—	—
8. I presently provide for my financial support:				
a. 100 percent	37.5	3	50	4
b. 95–75 percent	12.5	1	12.5	1
c. 74–50 percent	25	2	—	—
d. less than 50 percent	12.5	1	25	2
e. 0 percent	—	—	12.5	1
9. Since leaving The Country Place, I have:				
a. married	—	—	12.5	1
b. divorced	—	—	—	—
c. widowed	—	—	—	—

Appendix (*continued*)

Questions	Resident projections Percentage	Number	Ex-residents Percentage	Number
d. remarried	—	—	—	—
e. no change in marital status	100	8	87.5	7
10. My relationship with my own family is:				
a. very satisfactory	25	2	25	2
b. satisfactory	62.5	5	25	2
c. somewhat satisfactory	12.5	1	25	2
d. somewhat unsatisfactory	—	—	—	—
e. very unsatisfactory	—	—	12.5	1
f. no answer	—	—	37.5	3
11. My relationship with my primary family is:				
a. very satisfactory	—	—	12.5	1
b. satisfactory	37.5	3	12.5	1
c. somewhat satisfactory	37.5	3	12.5	1
d. somewhat unsatisfactory	12.5	1	12.5	1
e. very unsatisfactory	—	—	12.5	1
f. no answer	12.5	1	37.5	3
12. The problem for which I came to The Country Place for help is now:				
a. resolved	12.5	1	12.5	1
b. changed for the better	37.5	3	37.5	3
c. changed somewhat for the better	37.5	3	37.5	3
d. changed somewhat for the worse	—	—	—	—
e. changed for the worse	—	—	12.5	1
f. no answer	12.5	1	—	—
13. Since leaving The Country Place, I				
a. am lonely	25	2	12.5	1
b. have only acquaintances	—	—	—	—
c. have only group-therapy friends	—	—	—	—
d. have one good friend	25	2	37.5	3
e. have many good friends	50	4	37.5	3
f. no answer	—	—	12.5	1
14. After leaving The Country Place, I:				
a. continued therapy up to the present time	50	4	50	4
b. continued therapy for a limited time	12.5	1	12.5	1
c. did not continue therapy	37.5	3	37.5	3
15. The form of my therapy is:				
a. individual	37.5	3	37.5	3
b. group	—	—	37.5	3
c. both	25	2	—	—
d. no therapy	37.5	3	25	2
16. I am presently using prescribed medication for emotional difficulties:				
a. yes	12.5	1	50	4
b. no	87.5	7	50	4

Appendix (*continued*)

Questions	Resident projections		Ex-residents	
	Percentage	Number	Percentage	Number
17. I use drugs or alcoholic beverages:				
a. daily	—	—	—	—
b. more than once a week	50	4	25	2
c. more than once a month	25	2	12.5	1
d. other (No drugs or alcohol)	25	2	62.5	5
18. The drugs referred to in Question 17 are:				
a. marijuana	25	2	25	2
b. alcohol	25	2	25	2
c. oxalium	—	—	12.5	1
d. no answer	50	4	—	—
e. no drugs	—	—	37.5	3
19. Transition from The Country Place was:				
a. very easy	—	—	12.5	1
b. easy	25	2	37.5	3
c. somewhat easy	37.5	3	25	2
d. somewhat difficult	12.5	1	12.5	1
e. difficult	12.5	1	12.5	1
f. very difficult	12.5	1	—	—

REFERENCES

ABERLE, D. F., *et al.*
  1950 The functional prerequisites of a society. *Ethics* 60 (January 1950):100–112.

ALLPORT, GORDON W.
  1942 The use of personal documents in psychological science. *Social Science Research Council Bulletin* No. 49.

BERELSON, BERNARD
  1952 *Content analysis in communication research.* Glencoe, Ill.: Free Press.

BETTELHEIM, BRUNO
  1969 *The children of the dream.* New York: Macmillan.

COUNTRY PLACE, THE
  n.d. "Brochure of The Country Place." Privately printed.

DYMOND, ROSALIND F., CARL R. ROGERS
  1954 *Psychotherapy and personality change.* Chicago: University of Chicago Press.

FAIRWEATHER, GEORGE W., *et al.*
  1969 *Community life for the mentally ill: an alternative to institutional care.* Chicago: Aldine.

FRANKL, VIKTOR E.
  1959 *Man's search for meaning, an introduction to logotherapy.* New York: Washington Square Press.

GOFFMAN, ERVING
1961 *Asylums: essays on the social situation of mental patients and other inmates.* Garden City, N.Y.: Anchor Books, Doubleday.

GRALNICK, ALEXANDER, *editor*
1969 *The psychiatric hospital as a therapeutic instrument.* New York: Brunner Mazel.

HEDGEPETH, WILLIAM, DENNIS STOCK
1970 *The alternative.* New York: Macmillan.

HENRY, JULES
1963 *Culture against man.* New York: Random House.

HOLLOWAY, MARK
1966 *Heavens on earth's utopian communities in America 1680—1880.* New York: Dover.

HORNEY, KAREN
1964 *The neurotic personality of our time.* New York: W. W. Norton.

JOSEPHSON, ERIC, MARY JOSEPHSON, *editors*
1962 *Man alone: alienation in modern society.* New York: Dell.

JOURARD, SIDNEY M.
1964 *The transparent self.* Princeton, N. J.: D. Van Nostrand.

JUNG, CARL G.
1953 *The collected works of C. G. Jung.* New York: Bollington Foundation (Distributed by Pantheon Books, a division of Random House).

KANTER, ROSABETH M.
1968 Commitment and social organizations: a study of commitment mechanisms in utopian communities. *American Sociological Review* 33 (August 1968):499–518.
1970 Communes. *Psychology Today* (July 1970):53–57.

KRIYANANDA
1968 *Cooperative communities: how to start them, and why.* Nevada City, Calif: Ananda Publications.

LAING, R. D.
1967 *The politics of experience.* New York: Ballantine Books.

MOWRER, O. HOBART
1964 *The new group therapy.* Princeton, N. J.: D. Van Nostrand.

NEARING, HELEN, SCOTT NEARING
1966 *Living the good life.* New York: Schocken Books.

NELL, RENEE
1968a A new type of milieu therapy. *Journal of Contemporary Psychotherapy.* 1 (Fall 1968):4–6.
1968b Art and psychotherapy. *Voices, the Art and Science of Psychotherapy, A Journal Published by the American Academy of Psychotherapists* 4 (Winter 1968):4–6.
1968c Interpretation of dreams on the subjective level, its application in diagnosis, *Use of interpretation in treatment,* chapter 34. New York: Grune and Stratton.
1968d Sex in a mental institution. *Journal of Sex Research* 4 (November 1968):303–312.

NORDHOFF, CHARLES
1966 *The communistic societies of the United States.* New York: Schocken Books.

RIMMER, ROBERT H.
1966 *The Harrad experiment.* New York: Bantam Books.

ROGERS, CARL
　1970　*On becoming a person.* Boston: Houghton Mifflin.
ROSZAK, THEODORE
　1969　*The making of a counterculture.* New York: Doubleday.
SLATER, PHILLIP
　1970　*The pursuit of loneliness, American culture at the breaking point.* Boston: Beacon.
SPIRO, MELFORD E.
　1965　*The children of the kibbutz.* New York: Schocken Books.

Ethnography of Religious Factors in a Politically Oriented Communal Group of New England

RALEIGH E. BAILEY, JR.

This paper attempts to explore two distinct questions: first, there are the concepts and experiences of sacrality of six individuals, which show distinctions and common themes in their lives. These six individuals also constitute a group with a corporate identity in which there is a high degree of social interaction. Second, this paper explores the degree to which this group constitutes a religious community.

The subjects are a group of six persons who lived together in an urban setting and who identified themselves as a commune.[1] They had been living together in the same house for about eight months at the end of the research period in December 1971. Most of the group members were well acquainted with each other and had been for almost a year prior to the research. They lived in a house located in an integrated, transitional neighborhood of Springfield, Massachusetts, which bordered on a black ghetto near the core city.

At one point, there were eleven persons in the group, although the members[2] at the time of the study agreed that three of these persons were short term and peripheral. Two others, who were an integral part of the group, left after four or five months.

The last two persons to join the group did so in the summer of 1972. The membership was not closed. There were often visitors who stayed for a few days, and one person joined the group on a long-term basis after the research was completed.

---

[1] In order to preserve the anonymity of the group members, names and certain circumstances have been altered in the paper.

[2] Seven months after the research project was completed, the group members decided to disband, not because of any conflicts, but because of a feeling that individual needs were changing. Some moved on to more specialized communal situations, and others began living alone or with roommates. To varying degrees, everyone maintained his or her political activism. The communal group as such existed from May 1971 through July 1972.

The group characterized themselves as part of the counter-culture or "freak"[3] community. There were four males and two females. One of the males was black; the rest of the group were white, and there was a diversity in ethnic background and socioeconomic class. Age ranged from nineteen to twenty-six years. Formal education ranged from high school graduate to post-graduate degrees.

The group decided to organize collectively and live together communally shortly after the Jackson and Kent State campus shootings.[4] The shootings precipitated their decision to respond to problems of prejudice and oppression for minority people in a more organized way than they had in the past. The group had sponsored and cooperated with a number of projects that were social-action oriented, and they were recognized by most of the local counter-culture for their activities to unite counter-culture peoples.

METHODOLOGY

The researcher followed the group fairly closely for about six months and was involved in some of the communal activities as a participant-observer. Open-ended questionnaires were administered[5] and an in-depth interview was held with each subject after completion of the questionnaire.

The researcher met formally with the group as a whole after completion of the interviews. At this point, he shared the objective data from the questionnaires, and everyone discussed the issues of individual and group religiosity and their pertinence to the group as a whole. Particular ideas that had emerged in individual interviews were tested in the group context for confirmation or denial. This session, which was taped, lasted almost four hours.

The group became interested in the research project and the results. This session was used by the members to share personal experiences and make observations to one another about group identity and interaction. A number of members commented before and during this meeting that this was a good opportunity to share things with one another that had not

[3] The term "counter-culture" was popularized in a work by Theodore Roszak, *The making of the counterculture* (1968), which describes the phenomena that have influenced and characterized the counter-culture. A term that is more helpful from the view of theoretical sociologists is "contraculture." This was coined and interpreted by Milton Yinger in "Contraculture and subculture" (1960). "Freak" is a self-identifying term that is used warmly and affectionately within the counter-culture. Presumably, it is intended to embrace a word that has been used pejoratively by the dominant culture.

[4] In May 1971, a time of campus unrest across the U.S., two students were shot and killed by state troopers at Jackson State College in Mississippi, and four were killed by national guardsmen at Kent State University in Ohio.

[5] See Appendix, p. 277.

been shared before, and that it would help to raise group consciousness.

The questionnaire was intended to provide comparative data on various aspects of a given individual's life. The first section, on religious affiliation, provided data on an individual's formal religious ties in historical and contemporary contexts. The second section, on personal religious perspective, focused on individual religious experience and expression. The third section, on group perspective, provided data on the shared identity of the group and the individual's closeness to it. With this data, the researcher investigated the network of interacting relationships between sections 1 and 2, sections 2 and 3, and sections 1 and 3.

It was impossible to conduct the research without having an overall effect on the group. The nature of the group changed somewhat during this project. The group was aware of this and willing to accept it. There was a general feeling that the research might facilitate group communication and group awareness. This seemed to be the case.

Personal religious experiences are esoteric phenomena, and, in most cases, are very difficult to communicate to others. It becomes even more presumptuous for a person removed from an experience to attempt to record a description and make interpretive comments about it. This is precisely the situation in which the researcher found himself; he acknowledges the awkwardness of the situation. His first concern in this context was to attempt to represent the experience of the individuals; the second, to provide interpretive comments.

Methodologically, this approach is related to "the new ethnography" (Pelto 1970:68–76), a process with roots in Boas' historical particularism. An attempt is made to present the cultural system, or worldview, as it is understood by the experiencers themselves without artificially categorizing the data into the researcher's own framework. This is not to say that, after the data concerning the cultural system (or, in this case, a religious phenomena) has been collected, it cannot be cautiously evaluated from a theoretical or cross-cultural perspective. This, in fact, is the approach that has been used here.

Volumes have been written providing various theoretical frameworks for defining religion and religious experience. The purpose of this paper is neither to reiterate this discussion nor to make normative and exclusive claims about particular definitions. It is necessary, however, to indicate the concepts that are operative in the investigator's mind while conducting this particular research enterprise.

The concepts of sacrality and religious or mystical experience were treated largely in a subjective and personal manner. The experiences that the individual respondents regarded as sacred for them were accepted as sacred for purposes of this paper. The subjects were encouraged by the interviewer to respond on a personal level. The interviewer interpreted the term "sacred" to mean that which was of ultimate concern or of fundamental importance to the respondents. Three categories of sacrality were provided for the respondents: beliefs, practices, and images. These categories were not posed as normative, but rather, as a means by which sacrality might be expressed. The intent was to elicit as much response as possible by providing different perspectives to the problem.

The questions regarding religious or mystical experience seemed to be quite clear to the respondents, and in only one case did they evoke a conversation about definitions with the interviewer. At this point, the interviewer offered such interpretive statements as "feeling of transcendence" and "experiencing a radically new worldview." This respondent held firmly to the position that, even if he had experienced certain feelings and senses of awareness, they were not, and would not be, considered religious by him. The other respondents all indicated that they had had religious or mystical experiences.

The word "religion" generally evoked a negative response among the subjects. The term was perceived as referring exclusively to the religious institutions of establishment and was, therefore, deemed negative or even evil. The word "spiritual" was much more appropriate for the subjects in describing their own religious interests.

Clifford Geertz suggests that "for an anthropologist, the importance of religion lies in its capacity to serve, while for an individual or group, it acts as a source of general, yet distinctive, conceptions of the world, the self, and the relations between them" (Geertz 1966:40).[6] This is not a definition of religion; rather, it suggests the value of a functional understanding of religion for the anthropologist. This perspective with its multifaceted approach, both individual and group, is particularly appropriate for the subject matter of this research.

INDIVIDUALS AND THEIR SACRED EXPERIENCES

Design

Each subject was questioned with respect to formal religious background; attitudes towards religion; religious experiences and understanding of them; personal images, beliefs, rituals; and feelings about religious situations. In the following section, this data is used to draw composite pictures of each individual, with emphasis on each person's experience of

---

[6] The researcher was not operating from his own explicit definition of religion in the study, but was exploring, at least in part, the understandings of the subjects. It might be worthwhile to note Geertz's definition of religion, which is compatible with the researcher's perspective: "(1) a system of symbols which acts to (2) establish powerful, pervasive and long-lasting moods and motivations in men by (3) formulating conceptions of a general order of existence and (4) clothing these conceptions with such an aura of factuality that (5) the moods and motivations seem uniquely realistic" (1966:4).

sacrality. The subjects are arranged in an ascending order of chronological age. Much of the data is paraphrased from the subject's own words.

Subjects

JAN. Nineteen years old, Jan was an immigrant to the United States. Her parents were from Eastern Europe and of Byzantine Catholic background, although they had never been active in the church. She felt that her parents, particularly her mother, were hypocritical about this, because they claimed to have church ties, but did not attend. Jan was estranged from her parents and seldom saw them. Her parents lived in a lower-class immigrant community, and she felt that they were completely unsympathetic to her values and lifestyle. They did not know — or did not want to know — that she lived in a commune.

Jan went to college for a semester, dropped out, and took a secretarial job. She began going with Sam and lived with him prior to the formation of the group. No longer going together, they remained friends. They acknowledged some awkwardness in the relationship. She was no longer working and was then collecting unemployment compensation. She was considering leaving this group in a few months to join a women's collective.

Jan attended no formal religious activities, did not consider herself a church member, and was antagonistic toward organized religion. She described it as a "big capitalist lie; it tells oppressed people to suffer now so they can get a good place in heaven, while people like the Rockefellers have and control all the money."

Nevertheless, she was affirmative and clear about the role and importance of religion on a personal level, and was willing to relate this to the group. She described religion as a road moving toward goals of peace, happiness, and unity with the universe. She considered political and cultural activities as a means to religion, although she did not see them as being religious. She considered the process of sharing in interpersonal relations as religious, although the content of the sharing might not be. Sharing was related to trust for Jan, and building trust between herself and others was an important goal for her.

Jan claimed that she had had mystical experiences. Her two most significant experiences had occurred under the influence of LSD. Not all of her religious experiences had happened under the influence of psychedelic drugs, although her most significant ones had. She indulged frequently and was then the most active user of psychedelics in the group. She interpreted most of her tripping as strictly social and not mystical. She doubted that she would have other major mystical experiences with psychedelics, because two trips during the summer of 1971 had been so profound. A year and a half earlier, she had attended a couple of psychedelic services at the Church of the New Truth, a religious group in New York that used LSD as a sacrament. Her trips in that context were not particularly significant to her, and she did not continue a relationship with the group.

Jan was seeking other means for attaining mystical experiences. She was interested in the occult and witchcraft, and believed that she might have psychic powers. This was one channel she considered pursuing in the future; she was reluctant to do so at that time because she felt that she was manipulative with others, particularly men. She feared that, if she cultivated this psychic power in herself at present, she might use it against others.

Jan's most profound mystical experience occurred one night in September 1971 after ingesting six hits of "sunshine."[7] While she was out for a walk, she realized that she was having a very deep trip, so she went to a friend's apartment nearby. There were two major phases to her experience. The first was when she looked out of the window of her apartment and saw the whole world as if it were jigsaw pieces: it was a puzzle, and the pieces did not fit together. Related to this was a realization that the world was a mirror image: things were reversed and not what they appeared to be. Several times, she was sitting in a room with several other people watching a person play a guitar, when she became aware that the guitar syncronized with her own mind. A spiral image of energy appeared to be coming out of the guitar, encompassing her and others in the room, and then winding out of the room and moving into bigger spirals that gradually encompassed the entire cosmos. She realized that she had influence on the whole cosmos, and that everything was related through energy that transcended matter.

Jan said that the necessary component of a religious experience for her was a new or greater understanding of the workings of the universe. Of necessity, a part of that was a greater understanding of herself. She sought out religious experiences by exploring various means of attaining them. Implicit in her statement was the idea that the experience itself was beyond her control.

Jan thought of children as sacred images; for example, children playing and children smiling were sacred to her. There seemed to be at least a couple of reasons for this. One was that children were natural, that is, they were naive and not yet corrupted. Their joy and happiness was pure. Children were also the hope of the world. Jan wanted to be able to take

---

[7] "Sunshine" is a slang name for a form of LSD-25. A "hit" is a measure or pill. Jan had indicated that she had acquired a tolerance for LSD and required a strong dosage to "get off."

the children of "straight" people and protect and preserve them so that they would not be corrupted and taught to hate. Nothing was more delightful to her than a child raised in a "freak" family.

She did not identify any practices or rituals that were religious to her because they would merely be superficial means. Naturalness itself could be religious, but it could not be ritualized. Beliefs relating to peace and happiness were religious for her, and while she had very strong political views, she did not consider them religious as such because they were but a means to religious beliefs.

Jan definitely considered herself to be a religious person. This could not be measured quantitatively (she could not, by definition, be more or less religious); it was a direction, a path; and she was on the path of religion.

JOE. He was twenty-three years old, and his family background was Roman Catholic. His parents were occasional church attenders, but he was very regular in attendance when growing up. The church had been important to him. He attended parochial school for the first three grades, and felt he could talk to God until his midteens. He was active in the Catholic Youth Organization while in high school, and he felt that the experience was helpful to him. It had been his primary social activity. He had experienced considerable conflict in high school, not having been inclined toward academic studies.

After high school, he went to college, but he soon dropped out. He then became involved in the drug culture, particularly marijuana, and tried to stay high much of the time. Although he experimented with other psychedelic drugs, they did not interest him, and his preference was for marijuana. He no longer used drugs. During his drug period, he became more politically aware and active in social issues. He worked for a while, but he was presently collecting unemployment compensation. Sam and he were roommates just prior to the formation of this communal group. He was dating a girl who was to be a part of the initial group; however, she left at the end of the summer in 1971.

Joe was now seriously involved in macrobiotic foods, and his attitude toward organized religion was affected by this. Formal organized religion was of no importance to him. He said that traditional religion was not good for society. It tended to be "exclusive, prejudiced, and close-minded and has been responsible for lots of religious wars." He now felt himself to be part of a macrobiotic community that was a religious organization, even though he did not actually live in such a community and had relatively little contact with other persons who were committed to macrobiotic foods. It was of ultimate importance to him, insofar as macrobiotics could be considered an organized religion. Joe was considering moving into a macrobiotic communal group and working in a macrobiotic restaurant. In addition, the alternative of living in the wilderness by himself also held some attraction.

Joe claimed to have had mystical experiences that had occurred in two main contexts. Marijuana was, at one time, the primary context. After he gave up marijuana, macrobiotics took on a religious context for him. When he had first begun using marijuana, it had opened his senses, raised his level of consciousness, and stimulated new thoughts and perspectives. He did not cite specific instances of these new experiences, but rather, he indicated that a new level of consciousness was often available to him.

Religious experiences associated with macrobiotic food were somewhat different, but he saw some parallels. The food provided him with a feeling of well-being and happiness. In the process of eating, he became as one with nature. He actually felt high after some meals, felt himself moving toward a state of bliss and *nirvana*.

Joe referred to religious experience as a feeling of goodness, being high, and a sense of well-being. It was not something that could be sought, but as he grew to understand himself better, it could happen more. As he stated it: "When it happens, it happens."

Many images were sacred to Joe, among them, food symbols, especially brown rice, fresh bread, and food that he had prepared himself. Some long-term images that he had acquired before his macrobiotic interest, and which he still loved, included the ocean, forests, and all natural things.

The ritual of preparing meals, as well as eating them, was important to Joe. He prepared all of his own meals using his special utensils. The rest of the group did not have this commitment to macrobiotics, so his diet and foods were separated from that of the rest of the group. He often ate alone because there was not room in the kitchen to prepare different meals simultaneously.

Occasionally, he prepared a macrobiotic meal for the whole house. These were important occasions. Joe said that the ritual of smoking marijuana was never as significant for him religiously as food preparation and consumption had become. He now spent a great deal of time reading about nutrition, macrobiotics, and Eastern philosophy. Never before had he as much interest in reading.

Joe considered his beliefs in macrobiotic philosophy to be religious. He also pointed out that anything can be religious. Caring for people was religious to him, as was the principle of *yin-yang*.[8] Joe saw himself as a religious person; this he defined as living honestly, with respect to his feelings and philosophy. The concept of being more or less religious was

[8] This is related to macrobiotic philosophy. Foods are divided into *yin* and *yang*. There is a necessity to balance them in order to be in harmony with the balance of nature. Moreover, he viewed *yin-yang* in a perspective that is broader than the foods themselves. This stems from the Chinese philosophy showing the relatedness of apparent polar opposites.

not meaningful to him because "there was no measuring point." He said: "I am what I am, but nothing is constant. I am always changing. Things flow, it is not by will. I like things as they happen."

BONNIE. She was twenty-four years old. Bonnie's family was part of a close-knit Italian community, and the Roman Catholic church had always been a part of her family's life. She said that the church was important to her while growing up. "I got into it and really thought I could feel the presence of Jesus and the saints and all that." She did not now consider herself a part of the church and said it was of no importance to her, as she had not attended services for a number of years. As she grew older, she "realized that they lied. I found out 'the church' was not a rational set-up, but full of holes: money, pride, and prejudice." Her rejection of the church was modified somewhat by the statements she made offhandedly: "Once a Catholic, always a Catholic" and "They wouldn't want me back."

Bonnie described herself as being "a flower child" while in college and said this was "a beautiful time." She continued, "That period is gone because they [the Establishment] killed it." During college, she became estranged from her parents. She indicated that, though she still loved them, they could not accept her now. She became radical politically in college and was active in grassroots New Left politics. Bonnie was a major organizer in bringing this group together. She had a clear vision of its purpose as the promotion of radical political action. When the group was organized, she was dating one of the original group members, who had since left. She did not regard this relationship as significant in the formation of the group. Bonnie was an elementary school teacher for a short period after finishing college.

A sharp distinction existed for Bonnie between the spiritual world, which she saw as religious, and the temporal world, which she saw as political. She maintained this distinction even though she felt a strong commitment to both worlds.

Bonnie asserted that she had had a number of mystical experiences. When she was young, she reported mystical experiences associated with the consecration of the Host. When Jesus seemed to be there with her, she would feel ecstatic and loving. She stated, "Those feelings were an illusion, something created by the desires of my mind."

Although Bonnie was a moderate user of psychedelic drugs, she emphasized that they had not contributed to her religious experiences. She cited two particularly profound experiences. One experience occurred when she was having an intense conversation with a friend and discovered that she was really "getting into his head" and falling deeper and deeper. She had no control over the experience and did not know where it would end. She had a real sense of losing herself. This was a frightening experience, as well as a rare one, because she usually maintained tight control and distance in her social relations.

Another experience occurred at Cape Cod on a cliff overlooking the ocean. She was looking at the sky and ocean and was not thinking in her usual logical manner. She was having thoughts about death, whether there was life after death, and if so, what form it would take. She was more in touch with her feelings at this point than with her thoughts. She experienced a profound feeling of happiness, contentment, and joy, as peace and calm settled over her. She felt a loss of personality and acquired an awareness of love that had neither subject nor object.

Bonnie indicated that it was difficult for her to define or describe a religious experience. When it came, she knew it. It was a discovery, something she had not thought out for herself. She wanted very much to have religious experiences. She said that she wanted to find answers, wanted God and an afterlife to exist. Concerns about death were a major theme for Bonnie. She was interested in reincarnation and felt at times that she would return as the wind.

It was difficult for Bonnie to identify specific sacred images. Sometimes Krishna and Jesus served this purpose, but they posed problems, she said, "because organized religion has oppressed us so much." There were practices that had religious significance, such as Hare Krishna chanting and practicing yoga. She occasionally engaged in both of these activities, although she did not do either of them regularly. Practicing a discipline of nonattachment was religious for her at times. In this context, she tried not to think about sex, power, or being liked by others.

She did hold beliefs that she considered to be religious. At times, she believed in Jesus, and occasionally, she prayed to him when she was depressed. Right then, she said she was more influenced by Hinduism and Buddhism. She was then reading the *Gita* and found it deeply spiritual. She wanted to read the *New Testament*, but she did not believe she could accept it then "because of the lies in it." "The *Gita* is purely spiritual and does not make historical claims, but the *New Testament* is trying to be history, and it is not all true." Bonnie considered herself a religious person, but she also wanted to be much more religious than she was.

BOB. He was twenty-five years old. His mother was an active Roman Catholic, and his father had no religious affiliations. Bob went to church while growing up. He also attended parochial schools through high school. He elected to attend a Catholic high school, but he emphasized that the choice was a social one based on the fact that his friends attended the school.

While in high school, Bob began reacting strongly against his background and the role of the church. He said, "I decided in high school that the nuns and the church were fucking people over and that organized religion was anti-God." He had consistently followed this perspective since he finished high school and did not consider himself a member of a religious organization at the time of the interview. He could not remember when he had last attended religious services. The only religious services he could conceive of attending at present would be a funeral for the death of a relative.

Bob finished college and then went to law school, not because of clear career goals, but because of his interest in radical politics and a feeling that he should do something. He finished law school in the spring of 1970, and after an anxious summer spent wondering whether he would pass his bar exams and whether he would be licensed by the bar because of his activism, he was approved in late summer to practice law. He began practicing law independently, primarily serving the "freak" community, often without pay. With two other lawyers, he was considering the formation of a collective, particularly to serve college students.

Bob met other members of the house a little over a year prior to this research at a demonstration they were helping to organize. Shortly afterward, he was evicted from his apartment, whereupon he was invited to join the group because of his interest in political activism. He was completely estranged from his biological family, and he said of the group: "It is the only home I have."

Bob was the only person in the group who stated categorically that he had never had any religious or mystical experiences.[9] He said this was true because "I am very pragmatic; I think only in pragmatic terms." He stated that it would be impossible for him to define religious experience because the language was so different from his own. Bob did not seek to have religious experiences either, although he acknowledged that, late in his college years he had done some reading in Eastern religions. He said, "They were as oppressive as Christianity."

Certain images were important to Bob, but he chose not to use the term "sacred" to describe them. Most important were the image of freedom and the symbols related to freedom. He said that he would like to have a car as his one material object (he did not then have a car), primarily because it would give him such a feeling of freedom. He would be free to go wherever he wanted, whenever he wanted. He cited the summer of 1971, when he had access to a car and had driven to the West Coast just because he had wanted to.

Another important image to him was that of close friends. His two closest friends were not in this group, though they visited him and other group members.

There were no practices or rituals in which Bob participated that he

---

[9] Other members of the house argued this point with him, saying that some of his psychedelic drug experiences were religious. He denied this rigorously.

considered to be religious. He did not hold any religious belief, since he did not consider himself to be a religious person, and he had no desire to alter his own experience or relationship with religion. He commented, "I am happy the way I am."

PETER. He was twenty-six years old. His parents were of Lutheran background, but they were not active in the church; nor was Peter active in church activities, except for a short period in his early teens when he was institutionalized in a children's home. Methodist worship services were part of those institutional activities, but he did not see them as having a significant effect upon his life. He did not consider himself to be a member of a formal religious organization, and he said that organized religion was of no importance to him.

When Peter was nine years old, his mother died. He had never been close to his father. In the last few months, however, he had been attempting to reestablish a relationship with his father. His family was affluent, and he spent part of his childhood in private schools. He did not feel that he ever had a true home until he lived in the communal situation.

Peter had a master's degree in art, although his college career was a difficult and stormy one. He experienced a great deal of conflict with his professors because of his subjective approach to art and his appreciation of abstract art. His professors were wed to traditional concepts of form and order. In his post-school years, he believed that his work became even more creative and expressive. He did not have a formal job, but he painted when he felt like expressing himself or doing special projects for friends.

Peter was the last of the present members to join the group. In the summer of 1970, he had met a member of the group in a nearby park. He had been invited over and then had been asked to join the group. Because Peter was living by himself at the time and felt lonely, he decided to join the group.

Peter was critical of organized religion, particularly because he felt it left many questions unanswered. It conveyed to him a feeling of detachment, and it avoided certain issues, especially those involving the human body and sexuality. For Peter, organized religion was removed from more important concerns such as personal desires and happiness. He defined religion as "life itself, and living it."

Peter claimed to have had mystical experiences that frequently occurred in the context of his painting. The ability to convey personal feelings through his painting was a religious experience for him. Relating to other persons on a deep level was also religious. While this was usually experienced through his art, it could also be done through conversation.

He now remembers his primary religious experience as occurring when he was six years old. At that time, he had what he described as sexual relations with his mother. She was suffering from a brain tumor and was to die three years later. He could neither fully understand their sexual encounter at that time, nor could he comprehend her death when it occurred. He had been very close to her, and the memory of this sexual relationship became a way of keeping her memory alive and preserving her love. This memory had become a religious experience for Peter.

This fits closely with Peter's understanding of religious experience, which he described as "the interaction with another person so that there is a feeling of trust and oneness." He went on to explain, "Religious experiences are sought after every day by one's living; if one is to live religion, it must be a continual part of him." For Peter, religion and religious or mystical experiences are so closely related as to be almost inseparable. This is in keeping with his highly subjective and emotional perspective of religion.

He said there were many sacred images for him. While a very real one was his mother, in fact, any image was sacred at the point it evoked feeling in him.

Peter identified a particular ritual that had profound religious significance. He interpreted it in psychological terms, calling it a fetish that "creates a fantasy in that I am thrown back to the infantile stage of life." This ritual involved the touching and wearing of baby clothes. "In this paraphernalia, I repeat a scene where my mother is living and caring for me by treating me as a baby." Thus, the ritual served as a dramatic reenactment of a loving interpersonal relationship, that is, a religious experience.

Peter affirmed that he had religious beliefs, but these could not be stated directly in a conceptual way. They could more accurately be characterized as a process of awareness of self and others and the sense of meaning that evolves from this. Peter said that he is and he is not a religious person. He said he has some awareness of himself, but is not, and never can be, totally aware of himself. He wanted to be more religious, and he saw religious growth as completely integrated with personal growth, as an ongoing process throughout life.

SAM. He was twenty-six years old and the only black member of the group. Sam was reared in the North in an affluent suburban area, where his family were one of the few poor black families. His mother was Roman Catholic, but she was not active in the church. His parents separated when he was young, and he was unfamiliar with or uninfluenced by his father's religious orientation. While growing up, Sam was fairly active in the church and was a regular participant in the youth organization of his parish. He indicated, however, that the church was of little importance to him. It was strictly a social activity. Sam's parish priest was a member of the John Birch Society, and since Sam was a good student and interested in political philosophy, they had many discussions that quickly turned into heated arguments.

It was not until Sam was in college that he definitely decided to cut off his ties with organized religion. He went South for a racial demonstration, where he experienced his first real encounter with overt bigotry and discrimination. On the way home, he stopped in Maryland on Sunday morning to attend mass and found himself refused admission. That became a definite turning point for him. He did not consider himself to be a member of a religious organization after that, nor did he ever attend any more church activities. Sam stated quite strongly, "The church is the enemy. Organized religion, along with political systems, program man and choke off his creativity." He believed very strongly in personal freedom. He perceived the church as oppressive, both in its social structures and in its belief systems. At that point, he also affirmed Marx's analysis of religion as the opiate of the people. To a degree, Sam felt somewhat trapped by his Catholic background, and he said: "You can't leave your heritage" and "Once a Catholic, always a Catholic."[10]

While in college, Sam was active in politics and social action. He was one of the organizers of the black students union on his campus. He was also active in athletics. He took his time going through college and did not have specific vocational objectives. After college, he worked with an insurance company for a while, but he was strongly opposed to some of their practices. He was collecting unemployment compensation at the time of the study. Sam knew many members of the group well before they organized into a commune.

Sam affirmed that he had had a number of religious experiences. These seemed to occur in two major contexts. The first was in nature itself. The sky at night, sunrises, and sunsets were all conducive to religious experiences. One experience of major significance for Sam occurred at night in the late 1960's at Cape Cod. He met an old college friend, and after smoking hashish, they sat out and watched the stars for most of the night. They also took some LSD and then watched the sunrise. He said that this was one of the more profound experiences of his life. First, there were the stars and the feeling that he could see into the universe while traveling through space. This deep sense of insight and unity was coupled with the beauty and majesty of the sunrise. While this was his most profound mystical experience, these experiences did not need to be drug-related for Sam. He said that he often stopped what he was doing to watch a beautiful sunset, and this gave him joy beyond words.

Sam talked about the paradox between his appreciation of nature and the country, on one hand, and his desire for the people and excitement

---

[10] This statement was also made by Bonnie, but in her context, it seemed to indicate a ray of hope, while for Sam, it was more like a note of bitterness.

found in the urban situation, on the other. This related to another mode of his religious experience. Rallies and demonstrations were very important to Sam, and he attended them frequently. He found the charisma and excitement of the crowd conducive to religious experience. The rhetoric of the speakers and the accessibility of the objectives were not as important to him as was the dynamic of the demonstration itself.

Sam identified a strong sense of serenity and calmness, as well as a sense of "feeling high," as characteristics of a religious experience. One important dimension was a feeling of traveling through space. He cited the *Tibetan book of the dead* (Evan-Wentz 1957)[11] as being particularly influential in confirming and interpreting his own religious experiences. As a general rule, Sam said that he did not seek religious experiences, although he frequently searched for the contexts in which they occured. His general attitude was that when they happened, they happened. Occasionally, when feeling depressed, Sam sought religious experiences through contact with nature, but this was rare.

The main sacred images for Sam were related to outer space. Shooting stars in particular were very important to him, because he had always heard of them but had never actually seen one until he was seventeen. Stars, galaxies, and the sense of infiniteness that he associated with space, all had a sacred quality. He did not have any rituals or practices that he considered sacred, although at one time, smoking marijuana had served this function.

He considered just about all his beliefs to be religious, because he tried to live by them. His lifestyle was a reflection of his beliefs. He was more reluctant to say that he was himself religious. He said that it was possible, but that he was bothered by the semantics and the traditional concept of the word "religious." Sam wanted to integrate further his beliefs and his lifestyle, thus reducing some of the contradictions and paradoxes of his life. Finally, he emphasized, "Religion is to be practiced, not preached."

INTERPRETATION

The problem of interpretation is that it can easily lead to reductionism. One procedure for avoiding this pitfall has been suggested by Eliade (1960:13): "The surest method in the history of religions, as in all else, is still that of studying a phenomenon in its own frame of reference with freedom afterwards to integrate the results of this procedure in a wider perspective." Insofar as is practical, I am attempting to adhere to Eliade's point that sacred images must be understood on their own terms.

---

[11] This book, with a psychological commentary by C. G. Jung, is a presentation of Tibetan philosophy of reincarnation as developed through a Hindhu-Buddhist tradition.

An interesting aspect of sacred images is that they are neither myth nor dream; they fall somewhere in between. The myth, says Eliade (1960:14), is a characteristic of religion and is usually designated to the religious scholar for study, while the dream, a product of the unconscious mind, is studied by the psychologist. Sacrality is not easily identified with either camp to the exclusion of the other, and to opt for either would be seriously reductionistic. To attempt to provide a comprehensive integration of both would be too extensive for the purposes of this paper. Therefore, I choose to borrow selectively from both disciplines to highlight a few observations about the phenomena of sacrality as it has been experienced by the subjects cited in the preceding section.

A final word about the relationship of myth to dream is pertinent to our purposes: Eliade (1960:18) describes the religious experience as the crisis of existence and the solution of the crisis. This solution also serves as a measure of the distance that separates the universe of the unconscious and the universe of the religious. The study of religious experience and sacrality then also serves as a study of the integrating process in the individual. The religious experience is the attempt to merge the experience of existence with a desire for essence or meaning.

Relationship of Religion to Politics

All subjects in this study shared a marked antagonism toward organized religion. This antagonism was defined by the respondents primarily in terms of social and political issues; that is, religion was seen as exploiting people and supporting unjust social systems. Most of the subjects were of Catholic background, which is rich in imagery and symbolism. Yet, this rich Catholic imagery was not criticized by the informants.

The subjects shared a deep, common commitment to certain social and political principles. This shared commitment served as an integrating device for the group and was a channel for much of their activity. Still, most of them did not consider these activities to be religious. There tended to be a distinction between religion and politics on the personal level, a distinction that was sharper for some people than it was for others. Bonnie, for example, spoke of temporal versus spiritual realms. Jan spoke of religious experiences at rallies and demonstrations.

Religious and political realms overlapped most often for the subjects in the context of interpersonal relations on a one-to-one or a small group level. Peter enthusiastically stressed the importance of close personal relationships, but this was shared by all to varying degrees.[12]

---

[12] Even Bob, who claimed no personal religious awareness, said that close friends were an important image, that the most important thing about the group was living with people whom he liked.

Except for Bob, all discussed religious experience as a phenomenon that was part of their personal experiences and meaningful in that context. The experience of each individual was highly personalized, subjective, and rich in imagery.

It seems particularly significant that there was little sharing between the subjects regarding their own affirmative religious experiences on a personal level, though there was a considerable amount of exchange of negative images with respect to organized religion. One possible cause for this is the degree of intimacy within the group. The sharing of personal religious images among group members would reflect a higher degree of intimacy than was characteristic of the group. The sharing of negative experiences related to the organized church was more appropriate to the level of their group identity. Antagonisms toward the church function as a form of group affirmation.[13]

Religious Experience as "Numinous"

C. G. Jung (1958:7), borrowing a term from Rudolph Otto (1958), described religion as the observation of "the *numinosum*, that is, a dynamic agency or effect not caused by an arbitrary act of will." Thus, religious experience is the experience of a subject independent of his will. Such a perspective sets aside for the time being problems of creeds and organizations. It also speaks directly to the religious experience of the subjects of this study. Each subject who had these experiences acknowledged that they occurred independently of his or her own will. While the subjects could provide mind-sets and situations that were susceptible to religious experience, the experience itself was not determined by the subjects' own wills; it was the *numinous*. Three of the group members indicated they sought religious experiences, and three said they did not. In conversation with the respondents, the interviewer did not really sense a polarity in their positions; their positions were more a question of semantics. Seeking a religious experience is not necessarily contrary to Jung's description of the *numinous*. He cites various devices, such as yoga, meditation, and invocation, for encouraging the effect of *numinosum*, and he also points out the important distinction between seeking the *numinosum* and creating it (Jung 1958:7–8).

Nature of the Divine

The main imagery of the divine was clearly rooted in a naturalistic

---

[13] This same process of group affirmation also functions in respect to antagonism toward other social structures such as education and law, which are also seen as instruments of injustice and oppression.

experience. The divine was perceived as a part of the order of the universe, the beauty and wonder of nature, the image of cosmos, and man was seen as a part of that. Peace, love, and harmony (qualities of being) were central to the images. There was no sense of a being distinct from self or mankind. For most of the subjects, this imagery has been influenced by Eastern religions, especially Hinduism and Buddhism. Hindu/Buddhist traditions lend themselves easily to nontheistic approaches to religion through concepts such as *atman* and *nirvana* and also are easily linked with nature images. In the group interview, all the subjects indicated an inclination toward a doctrine of reincarnation.

Judeo-Christian theistic images of the divine seemed almost totally lacking in these subjects. The researcher recalls only one theistic reference to God in all of the interviews. This was made by Bonnie, who wanted to find out if there were a God. She is also the only one who indicated having had mystical experiences in the context of the organized church when she was growing up. Most of Otto's qualities (1958) of religious experience such as "creature feeling" and "wholly other" seemed inappropriate to the experiences of these subjects. While Otto (1958:30) occasionally made reference to Eastern and non-Christian religious experiences, his work is basically in reference to Christianity. Though this is part of the heritage of the subjects, it is clearly not the imagery they use in their experience of the *numinous*.

Psychedelic Drugs as a Medium

Psychedelic drugs have been part of the lifestyle of all of the subjects, and half of them cited situations in which they were using psychedelics to seek significant religious experiences. Much research has been done comparing drug-related psychedelic experiences of a religious nature with more orthodox mystical experiences. The evidence has indicated that, with controlled variables, the experiences were indistinguishable (Houston and Masters 1966:147).[14]

None of the subjects in this study believed that psychedelic drugs were necessary for their religious experiences. They were, in fact, aware of other means that made them susceptible to this experience. It is possible that the use of psychedelic drugs has opened up dimensions of experience for adherents that the dominant culture, with its emphasis on rationalism, scientific processes, and self-control, has all but thwarted. Once this realm of religious experience is actualized by some persons, they may be more readily open to it, even without the use of psychedelic drugs.

[14] See also Clark (1969) for an optimistic appraisal of the merits of psychedelic drugs for enhancing mystical experiences.

The frame of reference for the subjects was obviously more that of the counter-culture than of a traditional religious community. Therefore, the word symbols were closer to the counter-culture frame of reference. In the counter-culture, this means the use of drug-related images. Some of the subjects described personal religious experience as "feeling high," a term related to marijuana smoking. "Feeling high" might indicate the same phenomena that the traditionally religious person would call "being inspired" or "being close to God." Likewise, when individuals of the counter-culture say they are "tripping," this might be comparable to traditionally religious individuals saying that they "have the Spirit" or are "saved and sanctified and rejoiced in the Lord." Language, then, may be operating in such a way as to create false distinctions between cultural subgroups with respect to religious phenomena.

Self-Concept in Religious Experience

It is difficult to find clear patterns with respect to the self with these subjects. William James' categories (1958:18ff) of once-born and twice-born or healthy-minded and sick-souled do not seem appropriate. All subjects displayed an aversion to the conditions of this world, its evils, and the depravity of mankind, which is considered by James to be indicative of the twice-born or sick-souled type. Yet, all indicated a happiness with everyday life and a general appreciation for the beauty of the natural world, which would appear to represent a once-born model. Only Joe reflected a particular transforming experience of macrobiotics, and Bonnie indirectly related a desire for assurance of salvation. But everyone (except Bob, who rejected this terminology) experienced religion as an ongoing and a natural process.

James (1958:78) identified the religion of healthy-mindedness with both Catholicism and liberal-Unitarianism. James went on to acknowledge that the categories of once-born and twice-born are the extreme types, and that concrete human beings are usually intermediate mixtures. All people are involved in the process of unifying the divided self (James 1958:140).

While the self and its process of unification seemed visible in all the subjects, the style of the process varied with the individual. Jan spoke of the religious experience as a way of understanding herself. For Joe, self-understanding preceded the religious experience and helped it to occur. The religious experience then provided the self with a sense of well-being. Bonnie spoke of the religious experience as a way of losing herself, an act of discovery that provided a good feeling. Bob did not speak of religious experience, but he did refer to a drive within himself. Peter saw religious experience as a process of merging self with others. For Sam, it was a way of resolving the paradoxes within himself.

Some of the subjects thought in terms of losing themselves, and others, in terms of finding themselves, but all were speaking of a process of integration within the self. All the subjects visualized and/or experienced personal peace and happiness, both as a part and as a goal of this process.

GROUP EXPERIENCE

Identification

The group did not have a formal name with which they identified. When questioned by the interviewer about how they referred to themselves, a couple of subjects indicated that they referred to the group as "the house." This seemed to be the most accepted term, but it had not been formally agreed upon by the group and was used without symbolic value for simple purposes of identification within the group.

In a generic sense, group members referred to themselves as a commune or a collective. These terms have positive political and social connotations within the counter-culture, and the group liked this kind of reference. The group was particularly pleased when members of the counter-culture who were not members of "the house" referred to it as a commune or collective.

The group often were identified in the freak community by specific projects they sponsored or coordinated. For example, in publishing an underground newspaper called the *Free Voice*, they were identified by the freak community as the "free voice group." In fact, they did not like this type of identification, though it was commonly applied to them. They pointed out that they were more than any of their projects or even the sum of them. They wanted to be perceived in a broader sense than as only coordinators of particular programs or projects.

For purposes of relating to the business or the straight community, they adopted the name "volunteers." This name was not used as a means of identification within the freak community. Such an innocuous sounding name had special significance. It was supposed to sound innocent to the business groups for fund-raising purposes. The "volunteers" is also the name of a record album by the Jefferson Airplane that was popular with the group. It refers to a track on the record called "Volunteers," the theme of which is that the "volunteers of America" are calling for a revolution.

Shared Experiences

The subjects agreed independently and collectively that there were images and symbols that the group shared. Four of the six believed these symbols were of religious significance; two did not. In individual interviews, five of the group believed there were practices or rituals that the group shared. In the group interview, everyone agreed that there were group practices and rituals. Half saw these practices as having religious significance; one did not; and two did not know if there were religiously significant practices.

There was a great deal of variation among the subjects as to which phenomena were beliefs, practices, or images. In the group interview, there were no strong feelings expressed by any of the subjects regarding how the phenomena were categorized. For purposes of presentation, the researcher narrowed the categories to two: (1) beliefs and (2) images and practices. Some overlapping occurred between these categories. During the individual interviews, nearly everyone expressed some of the phenomena as shared-group perspectives. Other phenomena were suggested by only one or two subjects, and later, were confirmed through the group interview. For example, everyone suggested social-action projects as shared-group experiences, but only one suggested belief in reincarnation. In the group discussion, however, there was qualified acceptance of reincarnation as a shared-group belief.

Beliefs

The shared-group beliefs were expressed mainly in political terms. The beliefs might be paraphrased as follows: we live in a very oppressive society. The social structures and people in power exploit minority groups. These minority groups include blacks, chicanos, women, Native Americans, youth, and the freak community. The power structure and police of this society are particularly oppressive. If one could only get the oppressed peoples to work together and organize, one could make this a better world. We want freedom. We want to bring our brothers and sisters together in love.

While this value system was strong and fundamental to the group, the group was not highly ideological as a whole. Some members were reading Mao's works, and there was discussion of this, but the group did not spend much time discussing political theory. One of the subjects suggested socialism as a group belief, but others were not sure what she meant by it or how it would relate to the ideal communism. Other beliefs, such as reincarnation and vegetarianism, were discussed and shared to some degree by the group but not with the same vigor as were the political beliefs.

Practices and Images

A major interest that the group shared was its projects. Various activities that the group organized and promoted within the freak community absorbed a great deal of time and energy. The level of individual participation varied with different projects. It was assumed that each member would contribute his or her special skills (organizational, artistic, public relations, and so on) where needed. These practices related to the shared beliefs and to the stated purposes for the formation of the group.

The use of psychedelic drugs, particularly marijuana, was a shared practice. It was not done as a formal group activity and seldom involved everyone simultaneously, but it was a common unprogrammed activity that involved a portion of the group at any given time. The smoking of marijuana was a ritualistic procedure in itself when done in a group context, and this was recognized by members, although no one suggested that it was a shared religious activity. Some suggested that it had had that potential sacrality in the past, but at the time of the research, it was such a common social practice among young people that it had lost any religious or revolutionary mystique.

A number of situations when the group gathered were recognized as ritualistic. These were not highly structured or formalized. Instead, they were regular activities such as the weekly Monday night meetings. This activity was usually held for the ostensible purpose of planning projects and dealing with bills and other group business. There was no leader or prearranged agenda. This time occasionally was used for group enrichment activities, such as the discussion of a political philosopher. Another activity was dinner. Breakfast and lunch were individual responsibilities, but dinner was a group activity, with people sharing and taking turns in its preparation. Members of the group made an effort to be at dinner, unless they had plans that directly conflicted with it. This served as a regular but informal time to chat and visit together. The kitchen table also served as a gathering place for informal "raps". People gathered in the kitchen when they wanted to visit informally. Private conversations usually occurred in another room, but the kitchen table served as a community gathering place.

Various New Left or revolutionary images were shared by the group. For example, Angela Davis, the clenched fist salute, the killing of George Jackson, and the Viet Cong flag all served as integrative symbols for the group. Likewise, traditional, national symbols, such as the American flag or Boy Scouts, were negative symbols. Some more standaridized symbols of youth culture, such as peace signs and flowers were not part of the group symbolism. (Presumably, these had become commercialized and taken over by Madison Avenue. Thus, they were no longer politically appropriate.)

Illegal use of corporate goods and services or ripping off the Establishment was a symbolic activity that the group embraced. This was done more as a symbolic gesture of beating the oppressor at his own game than as an act to acquire material commodities. The art of falsifying telephone credit numbers was known and used to make free long distance calls. While these were sometimes made for personal reasons, the more significant purpose was making this knowledge available to others and using it, as in one case, to call a major oil company office in the South Pacific to complain of their destruction of the natural environment. Two other examples of ripping off relate to Christmas. Various group members shoplifted inexpensive items from major chain stores to exchange with one another. The group also had a Christmas tree in their living room, which was ornately decorated with commercial decorations. It was incongruent with the casual decor of the house; however, the tree and all its decorations had been ripped off from commercial establishments.

One person suggested that going to rallies and demonstrations was a shared-group practice. Others disagreed and expressed some disillusionment with rallies and demonstrations. The group however, had a role in organizing demonstrations, and members went to the major May Day demonstration in Washington in the spring of 1971, where most of them were arrested.

Images of country life, nature, peace, and harmony in the world were all suggested by individuals as shared-group symbols. When discussed within the group, no one voiced any objection to these as shared symbols, even though they were not highly visible. The group would, at times, participate in some shared activities beyond their projects and group life. For example, members might decide to go to the Saturday night horror movies at a drive-in. Since this was usually a spontaneous activity, the group did not consider this a group practice or ritual.

IMPORTANCE OF THE GROUP

Members all indicated that the value of the group had changed since they had joined. They referred specifically to the closeness that had developed within the group, which was described as an alternative family. Even shortcomings were measured in terms of family expectations. The subjects generally ranked the group as being very or extremely important in their lives. Five of the six subjects indicated that the closeness in personal relations was for them the most important aspect of the group. Only one indicated political action as most important, even though it was central to the group's formation.

It seems clear that for its members the value of the group was primarily in the closeness or potential for closeness among the group members. It provided a caring and supportive family for group members. For most of the group, these values were more important than the political activities of the group were, although these activities provided a sense of identification and group affirmation. The political activities provided a means of sharing via group experiences at a level that did not directly acknowledge the desire for interpersonal intimacy but which still met that need indirectly. This indirect approach to meeting group needs also generated some frustration because of hopes and expectations that were not fully or directly met, and this dilemma was expressed by some of the subjects. Everyone mentioned possible plans for themselves should this group dissolve. When the group was first formed, this apparently was not discussed much. There then appeared to be an implicit assumption that the group would have permanency. At that time, many of the group members were in couple relationships, and the group seemed to have the potential for a long-term commitment. At the time of the interviews, however, there was no longer a feeling about long-term commitment. There were higher expectations about what the group should be: the immediate worth of the group was important, even though nothing was said about staying together for a long time.

RELIGIOUS CHARACTER OF THE GROUP

At the beginning of the research project, the group members all had indicated that this community was not religious. At that point, the subjects were all thinking in terms of the concept of an orthodox and formal religious organization. At the end of the research, each subject was asked if he or she considered the group to be religious. At that point, half the subjects said "yes" and half said "no." A couple who said "no" did so because they considered the group to be social, and they felt that it did not share sufficiently in spiritual matters to be a religious community. The other subject said "no" because, with the possible exception of one, he did not consider the other members of the group to be religious. Those who considered it to be religious suggested the following reasons: "We believe in the brotherhood of man, and everybody is brother and sister"; "Man has the potential to be God"; and "The group as a whole has certain beliefs and feelings."

Each subject was asked if he would prefer the group to be more religious, less religious, or remain the way it was. Five indicated they wanted the group to be more religious. The strong preference for more religion indicates the expectations and hopes that the subjects have for the group. It is clear from the data that there were no other communities, formal or informal, that were functioning in a religious way for the subjects at this time. If any community was serving as a religious community for the subjects, it was, of necessity, the communal group in which the subjects lived.

CONCLUDING REMARKS

Individual Religion

It is clear from this evidence that the subjects all had experiences that were comparable to traditional religious ones. These experiences were highly personal, but all had common themes. The religious frameworks for these experiences, however, were dissimilar to much of traditional, organized Christianity. While this paper has not dealt critically with the subject, it may be hypothesized that the imagery and systems of belief have much in common with those of the counter-culture.[15]

All the subjects were reacting strongly against their religious backgrounds and formal, organized religion. Because of this, it was important for the subjects to distinguish their personal experiences from their cultural tradition. Their views varied in intensity, and for some, it was important to question or deny any experience that might be identified as religious or to deny the religious character of it. Nevertheless, most of the experiences are at least functionally equivalent to those that have traditionally been characterized as religious.

Group Religion

If one accepts a Durkheimian framework, it can be said that the religious framework of a society is at one with the social framework. For, "in a general way ... a society has all that is necessary to arouse the sensation of the Divine in minds, merely by the power that it has over them; for to its members, it is what a God is to its worshippers" (Durkheim 1915:206). Such a thesis may be highly reductionistic, and this writer does not embrace it in its totality. This thesis, however, can be used in part to emphasize the important relationship between the social and the spiritual. U.S. culture has attempted to distinguish between the sacred and the profane by developing such polar categories as church and state or temporal and spiritual spheres. The anthropology of religion has

---

[15] The researcher's fieldwork with other communal groups, including the "Healthy, Happy, Holy Organization," a communal organization of yoga ashrams that differ radically in structure and purpose from this group, still reflects an overlapping of belief systems, particularly with respect to interest in "Eastern" religious practices and symbols and an interest in a loosely defined "aspirituality," which emphasizes an intuitive, introspective approach to life.

served to document this integrative process of religion, not just within the individual human psyche, but also at the given community level. Religion functions as a means of integrating the individuals within a community. As Geertz (1966:40) suggested, it also helps the individual and community to clarify a model *of* the world and model *for* the world. The community examined here, with its strong social activism, has a clear sense of what the world is and should be.

When the traditional religious community no longer meets individual needs, it appears that an individual seeks new communities for affirmation and support. A major question considered here is: "Is this commune a religious community?" Does it meet the individual's needs?

The evidence clearly indicated that this communal group functioned as a religious community. The adequacy of the group as a religious community is another question. Some problems in communication and the indirect method of using political activities to meet some of the interpersonal, religious needs of the group members created frustration. This was particularly true for those holding high expectations for the community. The religious character of the group was not fully recognized by its members, and this may also have contributed to frustrations about the shortcomings of the community. There were many positive aspects of the group as a religious community, including numerous, informal shared beliefs and practices. There was a great deal of respect for individual differences, along with a recognition of the importance of the group and a high level of commitment to it.

It is understandable that the community was not as conscious as it might have been of the religious dimension. This was partly because everyone shared an antagonism toward institutionalized religion and thus had difficulty appreciating religious phenomena on a cognitive level within their own group. In addition, the culture has been particularly prone to the idea of segmenting and compartmentalizing various aspects of life, such as the spiritual, the social, and so on. This community had defined itself as a political group rather than as a spiritual one. It was difficult for the members to see the interrelationship between the two facets.

Interestingly, primitive societies remain prime examples of cultures that have maintained an integration of all aspects of life. Indeed, Malinowski (1948:24) stated: "... to a savage, all is religion ..." It can be theorized that the counter-culture in general, and the communal movement in particular, represents a return to primitivism and primitive religion. This group was clearly a *Gemeinschaft*[16] community, which would seem to be a step in the direction of primitive religion, at least within the confines of the group itself. While the group seemed to be moving toward

---

[16] The *Gemeinschaft-Gesellschaft* distinction in social relations is common. Weber (1947) provides a discussion of these concepts and their development.

Ethnography of Religious Factors

an integration of various aspects of life in a religious sense, the group consciousness seemed still to be closer to a dualistic conception of the world that does not recognize its functional value as a religious community.

APPENDIX: GROUP ATTITUDES SURVEY

This questionnaire is intended to provide some introductory materials concerning you and this group, especially with regard to religious experience and expression. (I am defining "religious" in a broad, open-ended sense. This could include anything that operates on a level that one might consider religious or that is comparable to a traditional understanding of religion.) After I get the questionnaire back from you, I would like to follow up by discussing some of the things in more detail. This data will be treated as strictly confidential, unless you indicate otherwise. If there is pertinent information that you do not want to write down or that this questionnaire does not include, I would welcome your telling me about it.

Please do not discuss your responses to the questionnaire with other group members before they have completed their responses.

Raleigh Bailey

I. *Religious Affiliation*

1. When you were growing up, did your parents belong to a religious organization?
   yes__4__no_____one parent belonged__2__.
   If yes, what religion or denomination?
   Roman Catholic__5__
   Lutheran__1__

2. When you were growing up, your parents' attendance at formal religious activities could best be characterized as:
   never_____seldom__3__occasionally__1__often_____regularly__2__

3. When you were growing up, did you belong to a formal religious organization?
   yes__5__no_____no response__1__
   If yes, what religion or denomination? Roman Catholic__5__
   Lutheran/Methodist__1__

4. When you were growing up, your attendance at formal religious activities could best be characterized as:
   never_____seldom__1__occasionally__1__often__1__regularly__3__

5. When you were growing up, how important was organized religion to you?
   extremely important__2__quite important__1__moderately important_____of little importance__3__not important_____
   Why?

6. Do you now consider yourself a member of a formal religious organization?
   yes_____no__5__no response__1__
   If yes, what?_____

7. When and where did you last attend a formal religious activity?
   _____

8. Your attendance now at formal religious activities could best be characterized as:
   never__6__seldom____occasional____often____regular____

9. Organized religion for you now could best be characterized as:
   extremely important____quite important____moderately important____
   of little importance____not important__5__no response__1__
   Why?_____

Please indicate below anything else you want to say about your formal religious affiliations.

II. *Personal Religious Perspective*

1. Have you ever had what you could consider a religious or mystical experience?
   yes__5__ no __1__
   If yes, when and in what setting did this occur?

2. What would you consider to be the necessary components of a religious experience for you, i.e., how would you know if you had one; could you define it?

3. Do you seek to have religious experiences?
   yes__3__ no __3__
   Why?

4. Are there certain images or phenomena that are sacred to you?
   yes__6__ no____
   Why? If yes, what?

5. Are there certain practices or rituals that have religious or symbolic value for you?
   yes__3__ no __3__
   Why? If yes, what?

6. Are there beliefs that you have that you consider to be religious?
   yes__5__ no __1__
   Why? If yes, can you briefly indicate the nature or content of these beliefs?

7. Do you consider yourself to be a religious person?
   yes__3__ no __1__ no response__2__
   Why?

8. Would you prefer to be more or less religious?
   more__3__ same__1__ less____ no response__2__
   Why?

9. Please indicate below anything else you want to say about your own religious perspective.

III. Group Perspective

1. Why did you join this group?
2. Has the meaning or value of the group changed for you since you joined?
   yes__6__ no_____
   If yes, how?
3. How important is this group to you in your own life?
   extremely important__2__ quite important__3__ moderately important__1__
   of little importance_____ not important_____
   Why?
4. What about this group is of the most importance to you?
5. What about this group is of the least importance to you?
6. Are there images or symbols that this group shares?
   yes__6__ no_____
   If yes, what?
   If yes, do any of these have religious significance for you?
   yes__4__ no__2__
   Why?
7. Are there practices or rituals that the group shares?
   yes__5__ no_____ no response__1__
   If yes, what?
   If yes, do any of these have religious significance for you?
   yes__3__ no__1__ no response__2__
8. Are there beliefs that the group shares?
   yes__6__ no_____
   If yes, what?
   If yes, do any of these have religious significance for you?
   yes__3__ no__1__ no response__2__
   Why?
9. Do you consider this group to be a religious community?
   yes__3__ no__3__
10. Would you prefer it to be more or less religious?
    more__5__ as is__1__ less_____
11. Please indicate below anything else you want to say about the group perspective.

REFERENCES

CLARK, WALTER HOUSTON
   1969 *Chemical ecstacy.* New York: Sheed & Ward.

DURKHEIM, EMILE
   1915 *The elementary forms of the religious life.* Translated by John Ward Swain. London: Allen & Unwin.

ELIADE, MIRCEA
   1960 *Myths, dreams and mysteries.* Translated by Philip Mairet. New York: Harper & Row.

EVAN-WENTZ, W. Y.
  1957   *The Tibetan book of the dead.* New York: Oxford University Press.
GEERTZ, CLIFFORD
  1966   "Religion as a cultural system," in *Anthropological approaches to the study of religion.* Edited by Michael Banton. A.S.A. Monographs 3. London: Tavistock.
HOUSTON, JEAN, R. E. L. MASTERS
  1966   *Varieties of psychedelic experience.* New York: Dell.
JAMES, WILLIAM
  1958   *The varieties of religious experience.* New York: New American Library.
JEFFERSON AIRPLANE
  1969   *Volunteers.* New York: R.C.A. Records.
JUNG, C. G.
  1958   *The collected works of C. G. Jung, Two: Psychology and religion.* Edited by Sir Herbert Mead *et al.* London: Routledge & Kegan Paul.
MALINOWSKI, BRONISLAW
  1948   *Magic, science and religion.* Garden City, N.Y.: Doubleday.
OTTO, RUDOLPH
  1958   *The idea of the holy.* Translated by John W. Harvey. New York: Oxford University Press.
PELTO, PERTTI
  1970   *Anthropological research.* New York: Harper & Row.
ROSZAK, THEODORE
  1968   *The making of the counterculture.* Garden City N.Y.: Doubleday
WEBER, MAX
  1947   *The theory of social and economic organization.* Translated by A. M. Henderson and Talcott Parsons. Glencoe, Ill.: Free Press.
YINGER, MILTON
  1960   "Contraculture and subculture." *American Sociological Review*, 25 (October): 625–635.

Aspects of Personality in a Communal Society

JOHN A. HOSTETLER

The Hutterian Brethren, who live exclusively in North America and number about 20,000 persons, demonstrate an impregnable sense of collective identity. They are conspicuous for their lack of identity problems. They neither share in the widespread symptoms of alienation and futility nor are they groping for meaning to ultimate questions. In a recent survey we discovered that the individual Hutterite thinks of him- or herself as having, on the average, slightly more than 100 close friends. By contrast, Rollo May has stated that the typical American has not a single close friend.

The Hutterites are known to us as an Anabaptist, Germanic sectarian communal group that has survived the Peasants War, the Thirty Years War, the totalitarian religions and nationalizing influences of several European empires, and the patriotism of the midwestern plains culture of North America. Specialized studies have called attention to their mental health (Eaton and Weil 1955), their prolific population growth (Eaton and Mayer 1954), their successful large-scale agriculture (Bennett 1967), and their effective training of the young (Hostetler and Huntington 1967). Hutterites do not regard themselves as a rationalized experiment in communal living. They are Christian believers equating the practice of communal living with the will of God, willing to be persecuted or die rather than compromise.

The general pattern of socialization in Hutterite society has been discussed in an earlier publication of the author (Hostetler and Huntington 1967). The life cycle is divided into clearly defined age and sex categories in keeping with the hierarchical values of the worldview. The individual is taught to be obedient, submissive, and dependent upon human support and contact. The goals for each stage of socialization are attainable by virtually all Hutterites. Roles are clearly defined. Individuals are rewarded by the smooth execution of their work and by the awareness that their contribution is needed by the colony. A certain amount of deviance is permitted within each of the age sets where individuals learn to relate positively to their own peer groups.

The thrust of this study is confined to one age stage, the "school children" in Hutterite society. Are there measurable differences between Hutterite and non-Hutterite personality patterns? From our anthropological fieldwork, we are convinced there are major differences. To ascertain differences that could be demonstrated, we gave simple inventory exercises to seventh- and eighth-grade pupils in the schools. The samples included seventy Hutterite pupils (from thirty-six colonies) from South Dakota and one hundred non-Hutterite children from rural South Dakota public schools. The exercises called for descriptive personal data, sentence completion, open-ended questions intended to discover attitudes toward parents, attitudes toward punishment, personal wishes, dreams, fears, and concept of self. We chose "tests" that were relatively free from clinical or psychopathic questions, since we wanted knowledge about normal personality profiles. The purpose was not only to discover what differences there were, but to see if our direct observations could be supported. The technical aspects of the analysis remain in an unpublished paper by Dennis Kleinsasser (1965), who assisted in the study. Some of the major findings follow.

ATTITUDE TOWARD PARENTS

Sentence-completion exercises designed to elicit attitudes toward parents were scored in terms of "positive," "neutral," and "negative" responses. The responses of Hutterite boys tended to be neutral, rather than positive or negative, while the boys and girls in the control group tended toward extremes in their attitudes toward their parents. These results are not astonishing in the light of our knowledge of the culture. Hutterite children are socialized to obey their parents and not necessarily to show affection. They are also not treated as equals. In both samples, girls tended to respond more positively toward their parents than did boys. There was, however, a significant difference between the response of boys and girls in the Hutterite group. Girls responded much more positively to their mother than to their father, while the response of the boys was primarily neutral toward both their father and mother. Negative response toward parents (mostly the father) was the highest among the control group. Among Hutterite boys and girls, there was little negative response toward parents. Kaplan and Plaut (1956:93) also observed a predominantly favorable attitude toward parents.

PUNISHMENT

To discover how children regarded punishment, whether they thought of *how* they were punished or in terms of *who* punished them, we asked this open-ended question: "Because Kathy (Dick) was bad, she (he) was punished by. . . ." The responses were grouped according to the presence or absence of a punitive figure or the method of punishment. The punitive figure response indicated a person who was carrying out the punishment, such as father, mother, or teacher. A response indicating the form of punishment contained statements such as "He got a spanking," or "He had to stay after school." The two groups of children responded very differently (see Table 1). Hutterite children mentioned the punitive

Table 1. Comparison of form of punishment and punitive figure responses among Hutterite and non-Hutterite children

Category	Hutterite (N = 70)	Control (N = 100)
Punitive figure	57	43
Form of punishment	6	54
(Nonclassifiable responses: Hutterite = 7; Control = 3)		
$\chi^2 = 32.5$ d.f. = 1	P 0.001	

figure in their responses with great frequency. (In Hutterite culture, it is important who punishes you, not how you are punished, for Hutterites learn to endure punishment.) The non-Hutterite children responded in terms of the form of punishment rather than the punitive figure. The differences are striking. The punitive figures mentioned by Hutterite children in order of frequency were father, teacher, and elder. In the control group, mother was mentioned as a punitive figure more frequently than among Hutterite children.

WISHES

To discover the cognitive pattern of aspirations, the two groups of children were asked: "If you had a wish and your wish could come true, what would you wish?" The purpose was to gain insight into the attitudes, thought processes, and values of the children. Again, there were striking differences in the responses. Hutterite children tended to wish for material possessions more frequently than did the pupils in the control group. The non-Hutterite children were more benevolent in their wishes in that they wished for things for their parents or friends more frequently than did the Hutterite children. The wishes of the Hutterites centered on things for themselves, rather than on direct benefits to others. They wished for adventure or travel more often than did the non-Hutterite children. (From the viewpoint of the culture, the elders are right: the children have a strong desire for property, material possessions, and the desire to be selfish. From the viewpoint of the elders, the age group still needs to achieve a mature Hutterite attitude toward material possessions.) An indirect method of discovering aspirations, through dreams, tended to substantiate the persistent wish for material possessions.

DREAMS

We asked school age children in three colonies to: (1) "write out on paper the best dream you ever had, that is, a dream you hope will come true," and (2) "write out on another page the worst dream you ever had, and one you hope will never come true. Write out as much as you can remember."

The responses were grouped according to content and were treated as observable behavior. No effort was made to emphasize the symbolic meaning of dreams. Our interest was in manifest content in light of the Hutterite socialization process. There was no control group for the dream analysis. The distribution of "best" dreams is shown in Table 2.

Most numerous were dreams in which the children received "material possessions and confections." Girls responded in this manner twice as much as did the boys. Toys and candy goodies were mentioned most frequently. Next highest in the number of responses were those involving

Table 2. Responses of 57 Hutterite children to "the best dream I ever had"

Category	Schmiedehof		Lehrerhof		Dariushof		Total respondents	
	Girls	Boys	Girls	Boys	Girls	Boys	No.	%
Wish for material possessions and candy	6		3	5	2	1	17	33
Positive social interaction (e.g. playing with friends, etc.)	4			1		1	6	11
Trips, visits, hikes	1		9			2	12	24
Going to heaven	1	1					2	4
Ending of a bad dream	1				2	2	5	10
Caught or trapped an animal				1		3	4	8
Hostility toward:								
interviewer	2						2	4
siblings					1		1	2
teacher						1	1	2
Lack of ability to feel pain						1	1	2
Total	15	1	12	6	6	11	51	100

"trips and visits." The trips were usually described as traveling to the home of relatives in other colonies. Trips to nearby cities were also frequent. A considerable number of girls reported dreams of trips to the nearest village post office. Some who dreamed of visiting other colonies wished never to return.

Examples of "best" dreams are these:

A boy and I went down the hill. I ran ahead of him, and I lifted up a plate and saw a big hole of money. The boy with me ran for a pail while I watched the hole. We carried it home to the preacher's house. (Boy age 11)

I once got a camera for a present. The camera was quite big and could develop pictures in two minutes. I was very glad, but then just as I was going to take a picture, I woke up, but I was happy anyway. (Girl age 14)

I dreamed we went to Saskatchewan. It took us a couple of years to get there. The dream was happy because I have a sister down there. (Girl age 12)

The predominance of responses in the category of material possessions must again be viewed in social context. Toys, money, and candy are not denied, but are strongly controlled. It is not uncommon for children to receive candy and gum from adults who return from nearby towns and cities. Our field observations indicate that, again and again, sweets are used as tokens of love and approval by the parent. Children strive desperately for any token of affection, and candy is such a token. It is occasionally withheld by parents when they are provoked. Sweets are also used as a substitute for personal attention. When children ask for candy, they often really want attention. Toys are given in recognition of work well done, so sweets and toys have social meaning in relation to superiors. Thus, the desire for hedonistic satisfactions and material possessions are by no means absent in the preadolescent Hutterite, but they are channelled into socially tolerated forms.

FEARS

To discover the pattern of fears among the children, a direct as well as an indirect method was used. The children were asked to write answers to the question: "What are some things that scare you, things that make you afraid?" The answers given by the two groups were very different, interesting, and significant (see Table 3). Hutterite children regarded animals as a source of fear far more than did the non-Hutterite children. The fears of non-Hutterite children were largely of other persons, including teachers, members of the opposite sex, and other adults. Hutterites were more afraid of supernatural phenomena than they were of other people. Children in the control group feared unpredictable happenings more than

Table 3. Response to fear: Hutterite and control subjects, by percent of category usage

Category	Hutterite (N = 70)	Control (N = 100)	Chi-square P value
Mediators of threat			
Animals	55.7	16	0.001
Other persons	4.3	29	0.001
Parents	0.0	0	
Teacher	0.0	8	0.05
Opposite sex	0.0	8	0.05
Peers	0.0	5	
Adults	0.0	3	
Siblings	1.4	0	
Other people	2.9	13	0.01
Natural phenomena	7.1	15	
Supernatural phenomena	10.0	2	0.05
Threats: psychological, social, and biological			
Loss of affiliation	0.0	2	
Exposure	4.3	5	
Punishment	1.4	1	
Unpredictable	1.4	10	0.05
Injury, illness and death	1.4	8	0.05
Dreams/fantasy	2.9	4	
Nonclassifiable	11.4	8	

Hutterites, and Hutterite children were less afraid of bodily injury than non-Hutterites.

These findings again substantiate what is known about the culture from observation. Hutterite children live in a colony environment that is secure and predictable. They know every person in the colony and have no apparent need to fear the adults in their immediate environment. Not knowing people well or intimately may make non-Hutterite children more afraid of adults and their environment less predictable. Children who attend public school in American society are taught from grade one to avoid contact with adults who are strangers.

The indirect method of discovering fears was to ask the Hutterite children to describe "the worst dream you ever had and one you hope will never come true." The response from children in three colonies are given in Table 4. The most frequent responses were in the category of "Threatening or strange animals." Snakes, bulls, and bears were the animals alluded to most frequently. Encounters with such animals were often quite vividly described and involved animals attempting to bite or devour the child or intending to attack the child when he was in bed. Threatening or strange people did not include any colony adults, but robbers and criminals.

Of the "worst" dreams, these are examples:

There was a ladder in our house. Some snakes were crawling up and down. Then they came to me and bit my foot. I couldn't sleep the whole night through. I was very frightened. (Girl age 12)

I dreamed that my mother and all my relatives died, and I was left alone and had nothing to eat or anything at all. Then I awoke. (Boy age 11)

We were playing behind the shed, and we heard a loud mooing sound. We went to the corral to see what happened. The wild bull was fighting with the other bulls. The wild bull looked up at us and chased us. He caught up to us and pushed us around on the ground. Finally we got into the cow barn. Then I awoke. (Boy age 11)

Table 4. Responses of 56 Hutterite children to "the worst dream I ever had"

Category	Schmiedehof		Lehrerhof		Dariushof		Total	
	Girls	Boys	Girls	Boys	Girls	Boys	No.	%
Threatening or strange animals	4	3	8	2	3	7	27	48
Threatening or strange people	5	1		1	1	1	9	16
Death or injury								
to subject			1	2		1	4	7
to siblings				1		1	1	2
to family (other than siblings)					1	1	2	4
Inflicted by the subject						1	1	2
Fire (burning buildings)	1	1	1	3			6	11
Fighting or maiming of bodies (general)		1	3				5	9
Good dream that failed to come true						1	1	2
Total	10	6	13	9	5	12	56	100

The predominance of threatening animals or threatening human figures in the Hutterite dream content may reflect two aspects of the Hutterite culture. First, parents often use threats as a coercive measure for the purpose of attaining conformity to Hutterite mores. Threats such as "a bear will eat you" are not uncommon in parent-child interactions. Another observation, with respect to the nature of this parental threat, is intimately related to the Hutterite worldview. Animals are often equated biblically with the instinctual or id components of the human personality. For the Hutterite, animals, in addition to the threat to physical wellbeing, also have a parallel threat of consummation by lusts and evils of the flesh. This association is most clearly seen in the use of the snake as a symbol, the referent being the id impulses of man depicted in the Genesis account of the Garden of Eden. Hence, the threat of animal attack carries with it the threat of expulsion from the community of the chosen people; the threatening aspect of attacking animals becomes dual in nature. Perhaps this explains why there is a general disregard for the welfare of birds and wild animals in the community.

A second reason for the preponderance of animal responses may be related to situational determinants; namely, animals are simply a part of this group's environment. Girls especially are threatened by animals. Our field data show that great differences are required between the behavior of boys and girls. Males are more assertive in relation to young girls. In one colony, girls have pronounced fears of strange people, perhaps directly related to the many outside visitors to the colony and the excessive cautioning the girls receive.

Hutterite culture has severe sanctions prohibiting aggressive behavior and affective expression, and there is a strong tendency toward socially patterned orderliness. The strong affective expression embodied in the dream content connotes a striking contrast. Such affective expression may merely be characteristic of the preadolescent developmental phase. On the other hand, these data may indicate aggressive and affective tendencies that are not permitted overt expression, and hence, they find expression in the dream content. The findings of Kaplan and Plaut (1956) support this notion. Their investigation revealed that Hutterite adults produced a great deal of aggressive fantasy material. In light of their findings, they felt that the general success of repressed aggression was quite remarkable within the culture.

To summarize, fears may be a reflection of the kinds of controls a culture has over various mediators of threat. Field observations indicate that in spite of the many fears involving animals, the culture has adequate control over the threat of animals. It is also interesting that Hutterite children do not frequently express fear of bodily injury, even though observations indicate that, with the constant movement of heavy machinery, hauling trucks, and other machinery, children are often in danger of being injured.

THE CONCEPT OF SELF

What conception does the communal personality have of him- or herself in contrast to the person who is reared in an individual-oriented culture? Most theories emphasize that the social self arises out of social interaction. We know that cultural and social interaction patterns are strikingly different in a Hutterite colony from those in the American population at large. The emergence of the social self in the process of socialization is essential in all cultures. To discover the concept of self, we gave the two groups the W-A-Y (Who Are You?) exercise (Bugental and Gunning 1955:41–46), with these instructions: "Ask this question of yourself, 'Who Are You?' Give three answers to this question that are different."

This method allowed individuals to structure their responses along the lines that are expressive of their needs and with virtually unrestricted freedom. The responses were tallied in twelve categories (see Table 5).

Table 5. "Who are you?" Response categories: Hutterite and non-Hutterite children, by percent and chi-square comparison

Category	Hutterite Percent (N = 70)	Control Percent (N = 100)	Chi-square P Value
Name	5.71	3.66	
Age	7.14	1.33	0.01
Sex	7.14	6.00	
Family	9.05	5.33	
Occupation	10.00	1.66	0.001
Group membership	(18.57)	(7.33)	0.001
Religious affiliation	4.76	1.60	0.05
General	13.81	5.66	0.001
Social	4.29	1.00	
Personal description	(18.81)	(48.33)	0.001
Positive affect	10.00	19.33	0.001
Negative affect	1.91	16.00	0.001
Physical attributes	4.76	2.66	
General	1.91	10.33	0.001
Unit	0.00	1.33	
Metaphysical	8.10	3.33	
Interests and special ability	10.48	14.00	
Nonclassifiable	10.48	6.33	

Hutterite children differed from other children in the frequency of their responses on these items: age, family, occupation, group membership, and personal description. Hutterites tended to respond according to their age category more significantly than did others. This supports empirically what we have observed, that age (within sex) is the single most important determinant of an individual's placement in the colony hierarchy. Age is a major means by which Hutterites identify with their place in the order of things.

Occupation is important to the self-image. Hutterite youngsters, in comparison to control subjects, chose to define themselves in terms of work responsibilities assigned to them by the colony. That this image of self is so strong in the adolescent period, while the youngsters are still in school and just prior to the assignment of adult responsibility, attests to very successful socialization. Most American young people of this age have minimal work responsibility and do not identify with an occupation.

Hutterite children identify with groups more readily than do non-Hutterite children. Being part of a group is important to them, and their answers indicate that a wide range of groups were included in their thinking. They thought not only of themselves as being a member of a religious group (Hutterite), but as a member of a family, of a state, and of a country. This way of thinking is essentially a nonindividualized identification, a response that tends to play down the uniqueness of the respondent.

In personal descriptions of themselves, such as height, dress, maturity, or happiness, Hutterite children tend to be neutral, rather than positive or negative. Non-Hutterites made more negative comments about themselves; they were more disparaging in their descriptions than the Hutterite children were. Responses that indicated an affirmation of belief or religious position (metaphysical) were greatest among Hutterite children.

Differences of the self-concept between Hutterite boys and girls showed the following features: boys thought more along occupational lines than did the girls. The cleavage between male-female subcultures is affirmed by our direct observations. Boys can associate with a farm job that might be retained for the better part of their life. A man's role in the colony is more clearly defined as a position of worth than is the role of a woman. Much of the work of women is done on a rotating basis. The response of Hutterite boys was higher in the categories of personal description, interests, and special abilities than for Hutterite girls.

To summarize, Hutterite children think of themselves as belonging to their colony group through the recognized social order, age and sex, and through work responsibility. To remain a Hutterite is a persistent undertone. Contentment with their reference groups is dominant. Hutterite children tend to think in nonindividualized terms among themselves and appear to lack the facility for individualized descriptions of themselves. The strong emphasis of the culture to control overt affective expression is reflected in the concept of the self. Self descriptions tend toward industriousness, in contrast to more hedonistic identifications among non-Hutterite children. In short, the evidence from these measures of personality underscore the general effectiveness of Hutterite socialization patterns.

These findings are suggestive, certainly not conclusive. The reliability of the generalizations, particularly of anyone doing psychological or educational research, depends greatly on the awareness of the fieldworkers and on the colony's acceptance of them. The young, like the adults in a Hutterite colony, are sensitive to the probing questions of the unwelcome visitors. Although they are often very free in talking with the outsiders, they also know when to withhold information or to confuse them.

REFERENCES

BENNETT, JOHN W
  1967 *Hutterian brethren: the agricultural economy and social organization of a communal people.* Stanford: Stanford University Press.

BUGENTAL, J. F. T., E. G. GUNNING
  1955 Investigations into self concept, part two: Stability of reported self-identifications. *Journal of Clinical Psychology* 11:41–46.

EATON, JOSEPH W., J. MAYER
  1954 *Man's capacity to reproduce: the demography of a unique population.* New York: Free Press.

EATON, JOSEPH W., R. J. WEIL
  1955 *Culture and mental disorders: a comparative study of Hutterites and other populations.* New York: Free Press.

HOSTETLER, JOHN A., G. E. HUNTINGTON
  1967 *The Hutterites in North America.* New York: Holt, Rinehart & Winston.
  1974 *Hutterite society.* Baltimore: Johns Hopkins University Press.

KAPLAN, BERT, T. F. A. PLAUT
  1956 *Personality in a communal society.* Lawrence: University of Kansas Publications.

KLEINSASSER, DENNIS
  1965 "A cross-cultural investigation of adolescence in the Hutterite communal society." Unpublished paper, Pennsylvania State University, University Park, Pa.

Communitarian Experiments and the Self

CARLOS C. DRAKE

> Strive therefore to know yourselves, and ye shall be aware that ye are in the city of God and ye are the city.
> *Oxyrhynchus saying of Jesus*

An obvious paradox of the commune movement is that many individuals who claim they are entering such experiments in order to gain a greater sense of personal fulfillment know that, in so doing, they necessarily will be obliged to sacrifice much of their individual freedom. Communal experiments vary, of course, and the extent of the sacrifice varies, too; nonetheless, most experiments surviving a year or more make considerable demands on the freedom of their members. It is somewhat surprising, then, to hear phrases such as "finding oneself," "attaining fulfillment," and "realizing one's being" when it is obvious that these individuals have involved themselves in a life plan that, on the surface, at least, would seem to have little to do with their individual goals. One cannot fail to be impressed with the sincerity and fervor of commitment of many members of communal experiments, yet I have not been able to resist wondering what it is that these people get out of it. Is this simply a philosophical stance? In the instance of religious experiments, is the belief system itself the basis for commitment? Since it is obvious that many members of communitarian experiments have been able to identify themselves with common goals, what is it that has bound them to the community in the first place? The question is not as banal as it might at first appear. The experiment may fail. What inspired those months or years of dedication? Is there something peculiar in the nature of communal experiments, as distinct from other kinds of group endeavors, that may evoke from their members a special kind of psychological response? I suggest that there is.

This paper is based on data derived from interviews at eight communal experiments and from numerous published accounts of others.[1] If, as one might suppose from Jungian theory, the archetype of the self is behind an individual's commitment to such a venture, how does this archetype work in practice? To put it another way, how are its projections evoked, and what mechanisms in the community sustain it?

Some qualifications need to be made. Urban experiments often have fewer problems maintaining themselves than do rural ones, and the extent of isolation and independence sought is usually much higher for the remote rural experiment than for one in an apartment whose members work at jobs in the city.[2] It does not follow that the degree of commitment is greater for the rural community, but it generally faces greater problems. The communities referred to here are ones that sought a high degree of self-sufficiency.

The universal existential problem for man is himself, and this is solved in various ways, usually in terms of the collective expectations of a given society. He defines himself in generally accepted terms, even negatively; for example, he may define himself as "a failure." For many people, this problem is central to their lives and causes great anxiety, especially when for one reason or another, they are unable to adjust themselves to the roles their society has provided. A role implies a life plan, and this is usually worked out chronologically, that is, different stages are anticipated and attained at different times. If, as in American society, these stages carry with them definite values, such as success or failure, then individuals will work out their life plans chronologically — perhaps their lives can be seen as an unbroken string of successes, or vice versa. In any event, individuals' progress is measured in time, and so time is an aspect of this anxiety.

A traditional escape from this dual tyranny used to be a religious vocation. Nuns and monks gave themselves completely to a religious ideal, and so were not obliged to accept other roles that could be measured in time. The price of such a choice has always been high, as in the case of celibacy, and thus has needed strong reinforcement: total devotion in a highly regulated environment. The religious vocation offered total security, for the most part, unless, as occasionally happened,

---

[1] The eight experiments were Celo Community, Burnsville, North Carolina; The Farm, Summertown, Tennessee; Padanaram, Silverville, Indiana; Rainbow People's Party, Ann Arbor, Michigan; Society for the Preservation of Early American Traditions (now known as The Christian Homesteading Movement), Oxford, New York; Twin Oaks, Louisa, Virginia; The Vale, Yellow Springs, Ohio; and, Word of God Community, Ann Arbor, Michigan.

[2] The members of some rural experiments have occasionally been obliged to live and work in the city so that their income could help the experiment and other members to survive. In each case that I have heard of, it was simply a question of time until the city workers could return (perhaps to be replaced, on a rotating basis, by other members).

missionary efforts were undertaken among hostile pagans; even then, one was assured of glory in the hereafter should an accident occur.

Many reasons are given today for joining communitarian experiments — from the desire to assure better schooling for children to wanting to avoid a nuclear disaster by going to a remote area — but a common theme along with these is that of individual fulfillment. What usually occurs in the highly organized communities is that individuals are submerged in the community life. If they are serious, they are encouraged to immerse themselves; a leveling process is worked through a variety of mechanisms, and they are brought eventually to the point where they must really choose (a choice that often is not made once and for all but again and again) between themselves and the community. What they may end up doing is so closely identifying with the community that they simply choose themselves in another guise.

Total identification with any group is rarely achieved, and in communal experiments, it may take considerable effort on the part of the individual. Nevertheless, the process is immeasurably aided by a controlled environment: the community often exists as an entity unto itself. Individuals must give themselves to this controlled environment in order to find release from the role playing of the external society; the extent to which they can do this likely will be the degree to which they are fulfilled as members. The community must be chosen to succeed or it will fail, as many have, for lack of commitment on the part of its members.

Obviously, this simplifies a rather complicated process. What is suggested is that the individual who is able to identify himself wholly with the community has at once solved the problem of himself, since success or failure in a particular role is usually not an attribute of membership — one is simply a member, equal to every other.

This is not a change that occurs at a cognitive level; it is emotional. Though I have rarely heard it described like this, it was obvious in some instances that such a change had occurred. Zablocki (1971:246–285) describes in detail the difficulties of the novice in the Bruderhof, a highly structured communal group. Here the process of becoming a member may even take several years, though usually it takes from six months to a year. Since the psychic level to be reached is beyond rational argument (and conscious control), simply telling oneself that one wants to be a member will not work; some sort of disciplined test, perhaps many, must be passed first.

Communitarian experiments do not gauge themselves in terms comparable, say, to businesses or corporations. They may make money in various ways, but these endeavors are never ends in themselves. They are not interested in bigness for its own sake; they do not mark their success in familiar business terms. The goal most often expressed is to be a model for other like-minded communities to follow and perhaps for outer society itself to eventually copy. These experiments do not place themselves in time, though obviously each has had a beginning; they exist. Existence in itself is all that is asked. An end is not contemplated. In other words, the time of the community is indefinite; it does not measure out its existence in five- or ten-year plans. (Though, as a practical matter, many experiments do have to meet deadlines, keep contracts, and otherwise behave like outside businesses to the extent that their business dealings with outer society necessitate it. Usually, however, certain individuals handle business details and the life of the community may go on as if such details did not exist.)

Within communal experiments, many mechanisms exist to reinforce the exclusive attention of the individual to the community itself.[3] One obvious threat to many communities has been the family unit, since a divided loyalty, at least potentially, is present when a couple have responsibilities to each other and perhaps to children.[4] This threat has been handled in various ways, some masked, some obvious, as for example, by advocating celibacy, misogyny, free love, or extended family arrangements. It is not posited that these are equivalents, but some one or combination of these is a factor in nearly every long-lived communal experiment, though, naturally, they are justified on other grounds.

The closer that members come to a deep commitment, the more likely it is that they will have something similar to the religious mystical experience of oneness — though there is a difference between this experience as it may occur when stimulated by drugs and as a stage in the individual's deeper identification with a community. The drug-related perception, as powerful as it may be, seems usually to be a separate and distinct experience not otherwise related to a stage of becoming within the framework provided by the community. This is a psychologically dangerous stage and is comparable to the *rite de passage* of many societies; the framework must be sufficiently resilient to allow individuals room to work out their problems and at the same time give them the necessary support to get through them.[5] This stage will be greatly aided if it happens that the community has a charismatic leader, since this individual may be able to

---

[3] A detailed discussion of reinforcement mechanisms may be found in Kanter (1972).
[4] A number of articles on family arrangements in communal experiments may be found in the October 1972 issue of *Family Coordinator*, whose theme is "Variant Marriage Styles and Family Forms." Another recent discussion may be found in Kanter, Jaffe, and Weisberg (1975). Although one might be tempted to suppose that a utopian novel would be a poor source of information on communal life, it happens that at least nine communitarian experiments today (1977) profess themselves to have been inspired by and to some degree to be based upon B. F. Skinner's *Walden two* (1948). Chapter 17 covers the family tie.
[5] This process has been well described, in a somewhat different manner, by Victor Turner (1969 and 1974).

supply or interpret the images in a way that makes sense of the emotional chaos the individual is likely experiencing. Communities with such leaders usually have a philosophical framework replete with motifs into which the members are gradually led as they are psychologically able. It is a matter of individual capacity; not everyone can move at the same speed. Motifs, long dormant or even unknown to an individual, are suddenly suffused with meaning, and a banality one day may become a matter of extreme urgency the next. Among these motifs, one often finds the notion of a sacred city, a special place where everyone lives forever in happiness and without worry, a jewel of surpassing value, a golden age, a secret garden.[6] The following is a quotation from an interview with the leader of a contemporary experiment in which he describes the process of screening new members:

He comes among us, a man would come among us. And each man will talk to him, each man will visit with him. And he'll come down to our meetings first, like on a Sunday, and if he enjoys the undenominational approach, if he's interested in the world problem, and he is a thinker, he's interested in various pursuits, and he has some particular trade that he loves to do which is not labor or work to him, and it is suitable to our need, why he'll just volunteer this information. He'll say, well, I'd like to live among you men. I'd like to be here. I like the idea. I like the concept of building a miniature city for the new world, an example of how men ought to live. If he has any nobility or altruistic motive, why, you can sense that. It isn't so much a curriculum or something he writes out like a dead letter questionnaire, but it's a human thing. (Recorded in March 1969.)

The motif of the sacred or special city (the city of God) is extremely old but nonetheless still powerful; in certain highly charged circumstances, it can trigger a powerful response in many people. An archetypal image, which the motif evokes and fills out, is projected on the source of the motif, that is, on the community itself. The individual experiences its power outside himself (generally, archetypal images are projected outside except in fantasies and dreams). Thus, the archetype of the self provides the emotional basis for one's identification with the community:

$$\text{Self} = \text{City}$$
$$\text{Self} = \text{City} = \text{Community}$$

When the community professes a particular religious belief, then the identification may be extended further, and naturally, may be enriched by particular religious imagery:

$$\text{Self} = \text{City} = \text{Community} = \text{Deity}$$

One can readily appreciate the power of such images, once evoked. It is not suggested, however, that many communities are able to sustain this level of projection. Those that apparently have, such as the Hutterites,

---

[6] Many such motifs are mentioned in Manuel and Manuel (1972). Ways in which some of these have been expressed in the architecture of communal experiments are described in Hayden (1976).

have done so only by a severe discipline and very limited contact with the outside world. The common danger in these endeavors, indeed, in any one-sided belief system, is that they will fall over into their opposites (how often the Devil has been cast in this role!), and so one must constantly seek to reinforce the original commitment — an unending task.

REFERENCES

HAYDEN, DOLORES
    1976 *Seven american utopias: the architecture of communitarian socialism. 1790–1975*. Cambridge: M.I.T.

KANTER, ROSABETH MOSS
    1972 *Commitment and community: communes and utopias in sociological perspective*. Cambridge: Harvard.

KANTER, ROSABETH MOSS, DENNIS JAFFE, D. KELLY WEISBERG
    1975 Coupling, parenting, and the presence of others: intimate relationships in communal households, *Family Coordinator* 24 (4) (October): 433–452.

MANUEL, FRANK E., FRITZIE P. MANUEL
    1972 Sketch for a natural history of paradise, *Daedalus* (Winter), 83–128.

SKINNER, B. F.
    1948 *Walden two*. New York: Macmillan.

TURNER, VICTOR
    1969 *The ritual process*. Chicago: Aldine.
    1974 *Dramas, fields, and metaphors: symbolic action in human society*. Ithaca: Cornell.

ZABLOCKI, BENJAMIN
    1971 *The joyful community*. Baltimore: Penguin.

Biographical Notes

Yu. V. ARUTYUNYAN. No biographical data available.

B. N. AZIZ (1940–   ) received her Ph.D. in social anthropology from the School of Oriental and African Studies in London. Her areas of advanced training and research include kinship, social structure, Buddhism, and Himalayan and Tibetan ethnography. In addition to numerous articles, Dr. Aziz has completed a monograph, *Tibetan frontier families* (1978). It marks the first ethnographic study of a Tibetan community. Presently, she is at the South Asian Institute, Columbia, working on a new project, the sociology of pilgrimage.

RALEIGH E. BAILEY JR. (1943–   ) received his Ph.D. from the Hartford Seminary Foundation in 1973. He has conducted research on various communal groups and religious organizations in the United States and Mexico. He is a LSD Research Training Fellow with the Maryland Psychiatric Research Center. He has taught anthropology and education at Guilford College and the University of North Carolina at Greensboro respectively. Currently he is Education Coordinator for Head Start in the State of North Carolina. He resides with his family in Greensboro, North Carolina.

DAVID BUCHDAHL (1946–   ) received a B.A. in Philosophy from the Johns Hopkins University and received his Ph.D. in Anthropology from the University of Chicago. He is presently teaching at Brown University, Providence, Rhode Island, and is conducting research on the spread of Vajrayana Buddhism in North America, and on the cultural constitution of time-consciousness. He is married and has two children.

B. D. DJAMGHERCHINOV. No biographical data available.

CARLOS C. DRAKE received his B.A. from the University of Chicago and M.A. from Columbia University. He did his doctoral work in folklore at Indiana University and also spent two years at the C. G. Jung Institute in Zurich studying mythology and Jungian psychology. He has written a number of articles for folklore journals. The paper here is part of a larger study entitled *The new folk community: mythology and tradition in contemporary communitarian experiments*.

JOHN A. HOSTETLER is Professor of Sociology and Anthropology at Temple University, Philadelphia, Pennsylvania. His teaching and research interests combine the areas of cultural anthropology and socialization. He is author of *Amish society, Children in Amish society, The Hutterites in North America*, and *Communitarian societies*.

M. K. KUDRYAVTSEV (1911–   ) was born in Russia. He received his doctorate from the Institute of Ethnography, Academy of Sciences, USSR. A specialist in the ethnography of India, he visited that country in 1957, 1964, 1966, 1974 and 1977. He is a Senior Scientific Worker at the Institute of Ethnography in Leningrad.

SEYMOUR B. LIEBMAN (1907–   ) was born in New York City. He received an Ll.B. from Saint Lawrence University 1929, and an M.A. in History from the University of the Americas 1963. He has been an adjunct Research Scholar at the University of Miami, Institute of Inter-American Studies since 1971. He has taught at the University of the Americas, Florida Atlantic University, Florida International University and was Visiting Lecturer at Columbia University, Brandeis University, New York University, Georgia State University, San José State, Jews College of London, and others. He is the author of *Jews in New Spain, The Inquisitors and the Jews in the New World, The enlightened, The writings of Luis de Carvajal*, and numerous articles in scholarly journals. His work on Sephardic ethnicity in the Spanish New World in articles is also to appear in vol. 2 of *The Sephardic heritage* (1978). *Exploring the Latin American Mind* is his most recent book.

L. K. MAHAPATRA. No biographical data available.

BHABAGRAHI MISRA (1934–   ) was born in Orissa, India and studied at the Universities of Utkal and Visva-Bharati in India, and Indiana University where he received his Ph.D. He has lectured in both India and the U.S.A. and was Associate Professor in Anthropology and Religion at the

Hartford Seminary Foundation, Connecticut from 1971–1973. He is now doing research work in Orissa, India.

JOHN H. MORGAN, a native of Texas, was educated in New England, receiving his B.A. Honors from Berkshire College and M.A. and Doctor of Philosophy degrees from the Hartford Seminary Foundation. Subsequently, he served as Postdoctoral Research Fellow at Yale University and as Postdoctoral Scholar at the University of Chicago. He has taught philosophy and anthropology at the University of Hartford and the University of Connecticut, and sociology at Earlham College and Grambling State University. Currently, he is Visiting Fellow at Princeton on-leave as Associate Professor from Newman College in Wichita, KS. Dr. Morgan is the author of *In search of meaning: from Freud to Teilhard de Chardin*, the editor of four research monographs on aging published by the I.M.E. Press, and has published in *The Journal of Religion*, *Social Science*, *Philosophy Today*, *Religion in Life*, *Journal of Religious Thought*, and *Encounter*. In 1973, he was elected to membership in the American Philosophical Association. In 1975, he was awarded the honorary Doctor of Divinity degree by The United Institute of Bethlehem, CT, for "original research and scholarly publication on the Shaker religious tradition." He is a regular contributor to the Shaker's own periodical, *The Shaker Quarterly*, and is a contributing editor for the *Communal Studies Newsletter* of Temple University as well as anthropological editor to the *International Journal of Cross-Cultural Studies*.

GEOFFREY NUSBAUM (1946–   ) was born in Berkeley, California. He received his Ph.D. from the Hartford Seminary Foundation. He is presently in private practice in the Greater Hartford area. Professional memberships include the American Association of Marriage and Family Counselors and the C. G. Jung Foundation for Analytical Psychology.

JAMES J. PRESTON (1941–   ) has advanced degrees in anthropology and religion. His special area of concern is religious change. Recently, Dr. Preston has completed a book entitled *Cult of the goddess*. This book is based on fieldwork conducted in a temple complex of Orissa, India. Presently Dr. Preston is chairman of the Anthropology Department at the State University of New York, College at Oneonta.

JOEL S. SAVISHINSKY was born and raised in New York City. He has a B.A. from the City College of New York and a Ph.D. in anthropology from Cornell University. Most of his fieldwork has been done in the Canadian Arctic, the results of which are reported in a recent book *The trail of the hare: life and stress in an Arctic community* (New York: Gordon and

Breach 1974). More recently, he has done research in the Bahamas and among American Jews of East European descent, with special emphasis upon religion, sex roles, and ethnic persistence. He currently teaches anthropology at Ithaca College, Ithaca, New York.

E. M. SCIOG. No biographical data available.

FRITS J. M. SELIER (1943–   ) was born in Amsterdam. He studied cultural anthropology at the University of Amsterdam, where he specialized in family sociology. He did fieldwork on the Israeli kibbutz, results of which were published in a M.A. thesis. A second research project, done in 1971 in several kibbutzim, was published in 1977 in his Ph.D. dissertation (Assen; van Gorcum, 1977). At present, he is engaged as a Senior Lecturer at the Free University of Amsterdam.

HOWARD WIMBERLEY received his graduate education in anthropology at the University of Texas in Austin and Cornell University where he earned his doctorate in 1967. He has done fieldwork in Japan and Mexico and currently teaches at Southwest Texas State University.

WALTER P. ZENNER studied anthropology at Northwestern University and Columbia University, where he received his Ph.D. in 1965. He has done fieldwork among Syrian Jews in New York City and Jerusalem, Arabs in the Galilee, and state workers in Upstate New York. He has taught at Lake Forest College (Ill.) and the University of Haifa and is currently Associate Professor of Anthropology at the State University of New York at Albany.

Index of Names

Aberle, D. F., 175n, 227
Adams, Robert McC., 168
Ahmed Shah Durrani, 41
Aiyar, C. P. Ramaswami, 28 and n
Alavi, Hamza, 60n, 72 and n, 73
Allen, M. Catherine, 175n
Allport, Gordon W., 245
Anderson, Robert T., 169
Andrews, W. Watson, 175n, 179 and n
Aniyankabhima III, King (Dera), 10–11, 12
Anselm, St., 190
Aries, Phillip, 204n
Aristotle, 189; *Metaphysics*, 189n
Arutyunyan, Yu. V., 79–85, 299
Aziz, B. N., 45–74, 299

Bailey, Raleigh E., Jr., 251–279, 299
Banfield, E. C., 135
Barber, Bernard, 97, 106
Barker, Sister Mildred, 184
Barkin, David, 136n
Barnes, J. A., 48
Barth, F., 48n, 72 and n, 161; *Ethnic groups and boundaries*, 161
Beauvais, Richard, 234, 235
Becker, Havard, 136n
Bellah, Robert, "Civil religion in America", 198n
Bell, Charles, 46n
Bell, Norman W., 144
Benedict, Ruth, 107
Bennett, John W., 135n, 136n, 281
Bernadette, M. J., 165
Bessac, F., 161
Bestor, A. E., 135n
Blanc, Haim, 166

Blom, Jan-Petter, 161
Blood, Robert O., 144, 146, 147
Boas, Franz, 107
Bose, N. K., 8, 12, 13
Bott, Elizabeth, 135n, 144 and n
Bouglé, C., 7
Boxer, C. R., 97
Brand, Steward, 201
Broderick, Carlfred B., 144
Buber, Martin, 206
Buchdal, David, 187–206, 299
Buck, H. A., 59 and n, 61n
Bugental, J. F. T., 288
Burke, Kenneth, 189, 190

Caen, Herb, 226
Campbell, Frederick L., 152, 153n
Campbell, J., 135n
Carrasco, P., 46n
Cassinelli, C. W., 46n
Cassirer, Ernest, 191n, 192
Castaneda, Carlos, 199n
Castro, Americo, 101, 103
Christian IV, King of Denmark, 108
Clark, Walter Houston, 268n
Cohen, Gerson D., 111
Cohn, Norman, 175n, 193
Colson, E., 64
Connant, William, 222
Cook, W. F., 222
Coser, L. A., 135n
Creel, H. G., 194
Cromwell, Thomas, 108

Darin-Drabkin, H., 139
Dash, S. N., 11
Dash, S. P., 11, 22

Index of Names

Datta, N. K., 8
Davis, Angela, 272
De Bocanegra, Mathias, 99, 100, 112
De Comarmond, P., 71
De Leon, Francisco, 106
De Leon Laramillo, Duarte, 104
De Medina Rico, Pedro, 109
Denison, N., 167
Diamond, S., 136n
Diaz, Nieto, Ruy, 102
Diaz-Plaja, Fernando, 103
Diderot, Denis, 192
Diez Nieto, Diego, 102
Djamgherchinov, B. D., 87–91, 300
Drake, Carlos C., 293–298, 300
Dube, S. C., 39
Dumont, Louis, 7, 27
Dunlavy, John, 181, 183 and n, 184
Durkheim, Emile, 189n, 275

Eaton, Joseph W., 281
Edwards, Johnathan, 192, 197
Ekvall, R. B., 46n
Eliade, Mircea, 265–266
Ellemers, J. E., 133n
Elwin, Verrier, 24
Ember, C. R., 170
Ember, M., 170
Enriquez, Beatrix, 101
Enriquez, Blanca, 101
Enriquez, Juana, 100, 105
Erikson, K., 197; *Wayward Puritans*, 197
Evans, Frederick W., 175n, 176, 177, 180
Evan-Wentz, W. Y.; *The Tibetan book of the dead*, 265 and n

Ford, J. Massingberd, 176n
Fox, Ruth, 229
Frankl, Viktor E., *Man's search for meaning*, 245
Fraser, Daniel, 179
Frazer, James George, 101
Freedman, Maurice, 115n
Friedman, Georges, 103
Fürer-Haimendorf, C. von, 45n, 46n, 48n, 66n

Ganzfried, Louis, 194
García de Proodian, Lucía, 97
Garcia, Genaro, 112
Geertz, Clifford, 203, 254 and n, 276
Gender, Rabbi Everett, 194n
Ghurye, G. S., 9
Gibson, Charles, 112
Gluckman, Max, 64, 135n
Goitein, S. D., 168, 170
Goldstein, M., 46
Gordon, Milton M., 161, 162n

Gorer, G., 46n
Gough, Kathleen, 27
Gould, H. A., 42
Graham, Billy, 188, 198
Granbois, Donald H., 149
Green, Calvin, 177–178, 181, 182
Greene, Arthur, 194n
Grotius, 191 and n
Gunning, E. G., 288

Hanson, Rev., 212, 216, 218, 222
Hartshorne, Charles, 189n
Hayden, Dolores, 297n
Heine-Geldern, R., 9
Heller, Peter L., 135
Henry, Jules, 204n
Herbst, P. G., 144, 145
Herskovits, Melville J., 95
Hertz, J. H., 98, 100
Herzog, Elizabeth, 120 and n, 121, 124, 125
Herzog, M. L., 164, 165, 167n
Hinds, W. A., 135n
Hobbes, Thomas, *Leviathan*, 191
Hobsbaum, E. J., 175n
Hocart, A. M., 7–8, 14, 17, 18–19, 20, 21, 23
Hoebel, A., 64
Hollenweger, W. J., 176n
Holloway, Mark, 135n
Hopkins, C. H., 222
Hostetler, John A., 135n, 136n, 281–290, 300
Houston, Jean, 268
Huguet, M., 146
Hu, Hsien Chin, 72
Huntington, C. R., 281
Hutchinson, Anne, 197
Hutton, J. H., 8
Hymes, Dell, 161, 166

Indradyumna, King, of N. India, 12, 23–24

Jackson, George, 272
Jaffe, Dennis, 296n
James, William, 269
Jäschke, H. A., 59n
Jimenez Rueda, Julio, 101
Jung, Carl G., 228, 265n, 267, 294

Kanter, Rosebeth Moss, 175n, 205, 226, 244–245, 296n
Kaplan, Bert, 282, 288
Kateb, George, 204
Keddie, N. R., 168
Kihara, H., 46n
Kirk, Jeffrey, 204n
Kleinsasser, Dennis, 282

Index of Names

Kohn, Hans, 97, 98
Komarovsky, M., 146, 152
Kropotkin, —., 205–206
Kudryavtsev, M. K., 37–44, 300
Kulke, Hermann, 10

Laing, R. D., 225
Lamm, Maurice, 116, 117, 119, 124, 127
Landes, Ruth, 116, 118
Leach, E. R., 161
Lea, Henry C., 100, 103, 112
Lebra, Takie Sugiyama, 130
Leon, Dan, 137, 140 and n
Leplae, Claire, 146, 147
Lévi-Strauss, Claude, 190n
Lewis, B., 164
Lewis, O., 39, 41, 42
Liebman, Seymour B., 95–112, 300
Locke, John, 191n
Longhurst, John E., 104
Lowney, Walter, 237 and n
Luccock, H. E., 222
Lutfiyya, Abdulla M., 135n

Mahapatra, L. K., 7–24, 300
Mahapatra, Manamohan, 13, 14, 27
Majumdar, D. N., 39
Malinowski, Bronislaw, 276
Malkiel, Yakov, 111
Mandelbaum, David G., 34–35, 37
Manuel, Frank E., 297n
Manuel, Fritzie P., 297n
Mao Tse-Tung, 271
Marriott, McKim, 7–8, 21, 39
Marx, Karl, 264
Masters, R. E. L., 268
Mauss, M., 60n
Mayer, A. C., 48n
Mayer, J., 281
Maynard, H. J., 8, 15, 23
May, Rollo, 281
McNemar, Richard, 178n
Mead, Margaret, 164
Medina, Jose Toribio, 99, 111–112
Meier-Cronemeyer, Hermann, 136n
Menasseh ben Israel, Rabbi, 108
Mendez, Justa, 103
Miller, B., 45 and n, 46, 48n, 69, 70
Miller, E. J., 41
Miller, Perry, 192; "From Edwards to Emerson," 197
Mishra, K. C., 10, 11, 12, 13, 14, 24
Misra, Bhabagrahi, 1–3, 176n, 187n, 300–301
Moerman, Michael, 161, 162
Morgan, John H., 175–184, 301
Moses, 105
Mowrer, O. Hobart, 242

Murdock, George P., 163

Naroll, Raoul, 161 and n, 162, 163–164, 165, 166, 167–168, 169, 170
Nash, Manning, 31, 34
Nell, Renee, 226, 228–237, 242, 243–244
Nichol, John, 176n
Nietzsche, Friedrich Wilhelm, 187, 188, 245
Nixon, Richard, 198
Nusbaum, Geoffrey, 225–248, 301
Nuttall, Jeff, 187n

Obregon, Luis Gonzalez, 112
Olson, David H., 144, 145
O'Malley, L. S. S., 24
Ooms, Herman, 129
Oppitz, M., 46n
Orenstein, H., 39
Ortner, Sherry Paul, 71–72
Otto, Rudolph, 267, 268

Pacheco de Leon, Juan (Salomon Machorro), 101
Panigrahi, K. C., 10, 12
Parsons, Talcott, 187n
Patai, Raphael, 95, 96
Patnaik, N., 9–10, 13, 17
Peale, Norman Vincent, 198
Pelto, Pertti, 253
Peter, Prince of Greece and Denmark, 46n
Phillip II, King of Spain, 99
Plath, David W., 115, 129
Plaut, T. F. A., 282, 288
Pocock, D. F., 7
Pollack, Herman, 117
Poll, Solomon, 163n, 167
Pradhan, M. C., 39, 41
Preston, James J., 1–3, 27–35, 301
Purushottama Deva, King, 11

Rabunsky, Carolyn, 144, 145
Radin, Paul, 190n
Ravid, W., 164, 167n
Read, Herbert, *Anarchy and order*, 202
Reese, William L., 189n
Ricoeur, Paul, 190
Ridgeway, Cecilia, 130n
Rieff, Philip, 204
Roberts, John M., 130n
Rodriguez de los Angeles, Juana, 99
Rogers, Carl, 243
Rosner, Menahem, 142, 151 and n, 152
Roszak, Theodore, *The making of the counterculture*, 252n
Roth, Cecil, 100, 112
Roy, S. C., 21, 22

Safilios-Rothschild, Constantia, 144
Sahlins, M. D., 48n
Samarin, W. J., 176n
Savishinsky, Joel S., 115–130, 301–302
Scanzoni, John, 149
Schmalenbach, Herman, 134
Schneider, David M., 187n, 192
Schwartz, Eli, 136n
Sciog, E. M., 209–224, 302
Selier, Frits J. M., 133–156, 302
Sender, Ramon, "Morning star open land," 199–200
Shankaracharya, Shri, 10, 24
Singer, Milton, 27, 187n
Sinha, S. C., 8, 22
Skinner, B. F., 201; *Walden two*, 296n
Slater, Phillip, 232, 241, 243
Slonsky, Abraham, 137n
Smith, M. W., 41
Smith, Robert J., 129
Snyder, Gary, 187n, 205
Soen, D., 71
Spiro, Melford E., 136 and n, 137, 138
Sprey, Jeste, 144
Srinivas, M. N., 8, 27, 39, 40
Stein, R. A., 46n
Stern, Boris, 137

Talmon-Garber, Yonina, 133n, 134, 135 and n, 136 and n, 142, 143, 148, 175n; "Pursuit of the millennium," 175n
Taylor, Leila Sarah, 179, 180–181
Tax, Sol, 3
Tejado Fernandez, Manuel, 97
Thompson, William Irwin, 187n
Tinoco, Juana, 104
Trachtenberg, Joshua, 103, 105, 117, 120n, 124, 125
Treviño de Sobremonte, Thomas, 102
Trueblood, D. Elton, 198
Turk, James L., 144
Turner, Victor W., 175n, 176 and n, 187n, 203, 296n

Tuveson, Ernest L., 195

Vidyarthi, L. P., 27, 33
Vinogradov, Amal, 168
Visvavasu, Savara Chief, 12
Viteles, Harry, 136n, 140n

Waterbury, John, 168
Watts, Alan, 190
Weber, Max, 194, 276n
Weil, R. J., 281
Weinrich, Max, 164
Weinrich, Uriel, 164, 167n
Weisberg, D. Kelly, 296n
Wells, A. R., 222
Wells, Seth Y., 177–178, 181, 182; *Millennial praises*, 176
White, Anna, 179, 180–181
Whitehead, Alfred North, 189 and n, 190–191
Willett, Ronald P., 149
Wilson, B. R., 175n
Wimberley, Howard, 115–130, 302
Wiser, W. H., 39, 42
Wolfe, Donald M., 144, 146, 147
Wordsworth, William, "Tintern Abbey," 191
Worley, Peter, 175n

Yamare, —., 135n
Yayati Keshari, Shaiva King, 12, 24
Yinger, Milton, "Contraculture and subculture," 252n
Youngs, Benjamin S., 177

Zablocki, Benjamin, 295
Zborowski, Mark, 116, 118, 120 and n, 121, 124, 125
Zenner, Walter P., 115, 116, 120, 122, 161–170, 302
Zevi, Sabbatai, 110

Index of Subjects

Aiyar Commission, *1960*, 28
Alcoholics, therapy for, 228–229, 240
America: colonial, Jews in, 95–96, 97–110, 195; causes for ethnic survival, 97; modification of rites, 103–107; decline and decadence, 107–110
American Indians: customs of, 101, 106; and Jews, 106–107
Anabaptists. *See* Hutterite Brethren, North American
Anarchy, in communes, 201–202
Anarchy and order (Read), 202
Ancestor worship: Japanese attitude to, 128, 129–130; compensates for family shortcomings, 129–130; harm attributed to, 130. *See also* Memorialism, Jewish
Andhra Pradesh, religious institutions of, 28n
Apocalypse, the, 195
Apology, Tibetan, 66
Arab world, Jews in, 165, 166, 168
Architecture, of Soviet Central Asian Republics, 89
Aristocrats, European, 169
Art, and American counter-culture, 262
Arts, of Soviet Central Asian Republics, 88–90
Ashkenazic Jews, memorialism among, 117, 120n, 127; in America today, 115, 119, 121, 128
Atheism, 187
Aymaran cultural type, 163, 165, 166, 167
Aztec cultural type, 162, 166, 167, 168

Babylonia, deities of, 9
Baghdad, dialects of, 166, 167
Bamilèkès, 71

Belgium, family organization in, 146, 147
Ben Lomond, California, commune in, 226, 227
Bible, the: and ancestor worship, 116; in colonial America, 99; discussion of passages from, by American youth group, 216–217, 223; Genesis, 98, 190, 192–193, 287; Jewish interpretation of, 98; Jewish Testament, 100; Jews in, 103; New English, 98n; Old Testament patriarchs, 115–116; perceived by American counter-culture, 260; Song of Solomon, 194n; translation of, 98n
Birth of children, celebration of: in Kirghizia, 91; Tibetan, 58, 60 and n, 62, 63
Brahman scholars, supreme council of, (*Pandit Sabha*), 15, 16
Brotherhood of the Free Spirit, 14th Century, 193
Bruderhof community: novice in, 295; prayers of, 199
Buddha, and cult of Lord Jagannath, 9
Buddhism; and American counter-culture, 260, 268; ancestor memorialism in, 128; Karmic law of, 59; at Orissa, 23; Zen-, 196
Buddhist societies, Tibetan, 46, 48n
Budgets: of families in kibbutzim, 139–142; and conjugal organization, 146–150, 155–156. *See also* Decision-making, in families; Marriage, in a Kibbutz
Bund, concept of, 134

Cambodia, ancient, God-King of, 9
Cameroon, Southwest, savings associations in, 71
Cape Cod, mystical experience at, 264

Caribbean Islands, in 17th Century, 108
Caste system: in India, 7-9, 37-44; attempts to abolish, 23; Brahmanism resurrected, 24; development of, 38; and family, 38, 40; and Hinduization of tribes, 21-24; and Kings, 7-9; and kinship ties, 38-39, 40, 43; and occupations, 38; origin of, 17, 18; in princedoms, 15-16, 19, 21, 23; and production relations, 42-43; and regions, 9; and ritual services, 7, 16-18, 22-23, 24; and social groupings, 38; and temple organization, 11-15, 27-29, 30-34; and village community, 18-21, 39, 40-43. *See also* Indian community; Ritual services in India; Temple servants
Catholic church: customs of, 105, 106; development of, 196; fasting by, 104; and Jews, in colonial Americas, 96-97, 98, 99, 111 (*see also* Inquisition, Spanish); and messianism, 98 and n; oppression by, 106-107 (*see also* Inquisition, Spanish); Papal Bull of Pardon, *1605*, 99; perceived by member of counter-culture, 259, 260-261, 266. *See also* Inquisition, Spanish
Ceremonies. *See* Rituals
Ceylon, temple organization in, 17
Charity, among Jews, 120 and n, 125
Children: birth of (*see* Birth of children); American counter-culture attitude to, 256-257; American rearing of, 232; in communes, 295; Hutterite, socialization of, 281-290 (*see also* Hutterite Brethren); Japanese, guilt feelings of, 128-129; Jewish, naming of, 117, 120-121, 124; Jewish, and parents, 121, 122-123, 126-127, 128-129; in kibbutz, 133n, 136, 137, 153 and n, 154; Tibetan, and *ga-nye*, 55-56. *See also* Education; Families and family life
China: "mourning circle" in, 72; reciprocation in, 69
Chinese philosophy, 258 and n; Taoism, 194-196
Christianity: and American counter-culture, 268, 269, 275; early, 196; and Messianism, 98; millenarianism, 209-210. *See also* Catholic church; Church and state; Religion; Shakers, the Christian settlements in India, 41
Church and state: American, 275; Indian, 8-15. *See also* Catholic church; Religion; Temples, in India
Church of the New Truth, New York, 256
City, the sacred, image of, 297
"Civil religion", the American, 198-202
Code. *See* Law

Communal group, *defined*, 134-135
Communes, of American counter-culture, 187, 203-206, 225-227, 294 and n; anarchy in, 201-202; and individual freedom, 293-298; rural, 203-206, 294n; screening new members, 297; therapeutic, 225-248. *See also* Ben Lomond, California; Litchfield, "The Country Place"; Springfield, Mass., commune at; Washington, commune in
Communism, American attitude to, 198; Russian, 135n; and Shakers, 175 and n
Communitarian experiments and the self, 293-298
Communitarianism, among Shakers, 175-184
Communities: as cultural units, *defined*, 161-164, 170; of developing societies, 2; functional prerequisites of, 227; Himalayan, 46; Indian temple, 27 (*see also* Temples, in India); Indian village, 39, 40-43; "intentional" American, 1-3, 225-226; "positive," 204; religious, 175 and n (*see also* Seekers, the; "Shakers", the); studies of, 1. *See also* Communes; Groups; Jewish communities; Kibbutzim
Community: Jewish sense of, 119-120, 127-128; and mysticism, 203-206; Shaker, 175-184; Tibetan, 46-64 (*see also* "Deling" village, Nepal). *See also* Hutterite Brethren; Indian community; Kibbutzim
Competitive society, modern American, 241
Confucianism, 194
Congregational Church. *See* "Seekers," the
"Contraculture," term, 252n
"Contraculture and subculture," (Yinger) 252n
Conversion, religious: Jews' attitude to, 96, 100-101; Shakers', 210
Conversos (New Christians), 97, 111
Counter-culture, modern American, 187-188; and the "civil religion," 198-202; religious orientation of, 187-206, 252-279; *term*, 252n. *See also* Springfield, Mass., counter-culture commune in
Covenanting, 178 and n
Crisis events, life: in Kirghizia, 91; and religious conversion, 210; and Tibetan *ga-nye*, 51, 60-63, 72. *See also* Birth of children; Death rites; Weddings
Crypto-Jews, 97, 111
Cultural interaction, in U.S.S.R., 79-85
Cultural systems, and conception of God, 192-197, 202-203. *See also* Counter-culture

Index of Subjects

Cultural types, Aymaran and Aztec, 163, 165, 166, 167, 168
Cultural units: definition of, 161–164, 170; applied to Jewish groups, 164–166; language and, 166–167; political boundaries of, 167–169; religion and ethnicity, 169–170
Culture: modern American competitive, 241. *See also* Counter-culture, modern American; "Youth culture," American
Cuttack, Chandi temple in: economy of, 29–32; and secularization, 33, 34

Dead: Japanese attitude to the, 115; Jewish dreams of the, 125. *See also* Ancestor worship; Funerals; Memorialism, Jewish
Death, Jewish attitude to, 122–124; as moral experience, 126–127
Death rites; Jewish, 101, 105, 106, 116–117, 119, 124–125. *See also* Funerals; Mourning
Decision-making, in families: concept and measurement of, 143–146; masculine and feminine perception of, 148–149; ideological and structural variables in, 149–154
"Deling" village, Nepal, Tibetan community in, 46–47; dispute settlement in, 64–69; *ga-nye* among, 48–58; and other cultures, 69–71; reciprocation among, 58–64
Denmark, Jews in, 17th Century, 107, 108
Developing nations, communities in, 2
Dispute settlement: in China, 72; Tibetan, *ga-nye* and, 64–69
Divine Kingship, 9. *See also* Kings, Indian
Divine, nature of the; perceived by counter-culture members, 267–268. *See also* God; Religious experience
Dogmatizers, in colonial America, 97, 111
Dreams, 266; "the American," 232; of the dead, among Jews, 125; of Hutterite children, 284–285, 286–288
Drugs, psychedelic: abuse of, 229, 232, 240, 241, 242, 243; in American counter-culture, 199, 200, 257, 259, 261n, 272; hashish, 264; L.S.D., 188, 200, 255–256, 264; marijuana, 240, 257, 258, 265, 269, 272; and religious experiences, 255–256, 258, 261n, 264, 265, 268–269, 296; therapeutic, 240
Duty. *See* Ritual services, in India

Economic systems; of Indian villages, 32–33; of Kibbutzim (*see* Kibbutzim); religious, 34 (*see also* Temples in India); savings associations, 71; of Soviet Central Asian Republics, 87; of Tibetan villagers, 70–71; of U.S.S.R., 81–82
Education: American youth and, 238–239, 267n; in Central Asia, 89; in communes, 295; in kibbutzim, 133n; in U.S.S.R., 82, 84
Egypt, ancient, dieties of, 9
Employment; of ex-residents of therapeutic community, 238–239. *See also* Work
England, 17th Century, Jews in, 107, 108

Families and family life: American, and material success, 232, 241; and communal group, 135–136, 273–274, 296 and n; compensated for by ancestor memorialism, 129–130; of counter-culture commune members, 255, 257, 259, 260, 262–263; decision-making in (*see* decision-making, in families); extended, 134n; investigation of, 145n; Jewish, 118–121, 122, 123, 126–127; in kibbutzim, 133–156 (*see also* Woman); "power" structure of, 143–148; of residents of therapeutic community, 239; size of, and organization, 153n; studies of, 204n; Tibetan, and *ga-nye*, 50, 55; variable functions, and organization of, 152–153. *See also* Children; Household, Tibetan; Kinship; Marriage; Mothers, Jewish
Familism, *defined*, 135
Family Coordinator, 296n
Farmers, in India; and caste, 18–21; and temples, 28, 32. *See also* Catholic church, fasting by; Jews, fasts by
"Flower children," 259
Flower concession, in Indian temples, 30
Food: fasting, 99, 104, 105; of Indian God-Kings, 10; of Indian gods, 29–30; Indian temple offerings and concessions, 29–30, 30–31, 32; Jewish, 101, 104–105; macrobiotic, 257–258; vegetarian, 10, 271; *Yin-yang*, 258 and n
France, family organization in, 146, 147
"Freak" community, American, 252 and n. *See also* Counter-culture, modern American
Freedom, individual, 200–201; and communes, 293–298; images of, 261
Free Voice (underground newspaper), 270
Friendship: in America, 281; Tibetan *trok*, 48 and n, 56n. *See also ga-nye* (Tibetan); Groups; "Sharing"; Social relationships.
Funerals: ancient Indian, 14; Jewish, 105; Kirghizian, 91; Tibetan, gifts at, 60 and n, 62. *See also* Death rites; Mourning

310   Index of Subjects

Ga-nye (Tibetan system of social bonds), 45, 46 and n, 47–74; as an action and moral system, 48–54; compared cross-culturally, 69–74; in dispute settlement, 64–69, 72; and reciprocation, 58–64, 72–73; recruitment of, 55–58
Germany, Jews in, 164, 165, 167 and n
Gifts, at life-crises, Tibetan, 60–62, 62–63
Gita, 260
God: change in conception of, 187–188; of Civil religion, 198–199; concept of, and cultural systems, 192–197, 203; definitions of, 190; perceived by U.S. counter-culture, 267–268; and reality, 188–192
Gods, Indian: hierarchy of Hindu, 21, 22, 24; and Kings, 8, 9–15; sacred meals of, 29–30; Lord Shiva, 9, 10; and villages, 20, 21; Vishnu, 9, 10, 15. See also Jagannath, Lord, cult of; Temples, in India
Greece, shepherds' community in, 135n
Group experience, of commune, 270–273
Group religion, 275–277
Groups: communal, *defined*, 134–135; division into small, 222; importance of, to members, 273–274; religious character of, 274–275; T-, 222. See also "Sharing"; Springfield, Mass., counter-culture commune in
Group therapy, at "The Country Place," 230–231, 235, 236, 242, 243
Guilt: of Japanese and Jewish children, 128–129; in Jewish families, 123–124

Haight-Ashbury district, San Francisco, 225–226
Hare Krishna, 260
"Healthy, Happy, Holy Organization," 275n
Himalayan, societies, 46
Hindu castes, and Kingship, 21–24. See also Caste system in India
Hindu gods, hierarchy of, 21, 22, 24
Hinduism: and commercialism, 33–34; 8th Century revival, 10; and Western counter-culture, 260, 268; spread among tribes, 21–24. See also Jagannath, Lord, cult of
Hindu Kings, and caste system, 8, 14, 15–16
Hindu Religious Endowment Commission, 31
Hindu state, building of, 14, 21–24
Hippies, American, 201; attitude to, 197; term applied, 225–226. See also Counter-culture, modern American
Holland, Jews in 17th Century, 107, 108
Household, Tibetan; disputes in, 64–69; and *ga-nye*, 55; and reciprocation, 60, 62
Hungarian Hasidim, in New York, 167

Hutterite Brethren, North American, 281–290, 297–298; children's attitudes towards parents, 282; children's concept of self, 288–290; children's dreams, 284–285, 286–288; children's fears, 285–288; children's wishes, 283–284; lack of sexual equality among, 134, 136n, 290; punishment among, 283
Hymn singing, 215, 218, 222–223

India: Cuttack, 29–32, 34; Deccan, 41; Delhi, 42; Doab, 41, 42; Gaya, 33; Kerala, 41; Mysore, 28; Punjab, 28, 41 42; Rajasthan, 28. See also Caste system, in India: Hinduism; Indian community; Jagannath, Lord, cult of; Kings, Indian; Land, in India; Orissa; Ritual services; Temples, in India; Villages, Indian
Indian community: characteristics of, 41–42; land control by, 42; production relations in, 42–43; social structure and, 7, 37–44; village, 39, 40–43; Temple, 27–35. See also Caste system, in India
Industrialization, in U.S.S.R., 81–82, 87
Inquisition, Spanish (Holy Office); established, *1478*, 97; in America, and Jews, 96–97, 99, 100, 101, 102, 103, 104, 107, 109, 110–111; and Protestantism, 109; surviving documents of, 111–112; tribunals of, 96
Institute of Ethnography of the U.S.S.R. Academy of Sciences, 80
Integration, cultural, 79
Iran, 168
Israel: Druze, 163; Jews migrating to, 109; kibbutzim in, 154 (*see also* Kibbutzim); state established, *1948*, 139
Italy, Jews of, 102

Jackson State College, shooting at, 252 and n
Jagannath, Lord, cult of in Orissa, India, 9–10, 15, 21, 31n; in hinterland, 24; and temple organization, 11–14, 16, 17
Jaina, island of, statue from, 106
Jainism, 23
Japanese: ancestor memorialism, 115, 116n, 128–130; children, 128–129; kibbutz, 135n; life compared with Jewish, 115
Jat communities, Indian, 41
Jefferson Airplane (music group), record by, 270
Jesus, code of, 196. See also Christianity; Messianism; Millenarialism
Jesus movement. See "Seekers," the
Jewish communities; as cultural units, 162–170; European, 164; isolated, 109;

Ladino-speaking, 165; rural *shtetls*, 116, 118–119, 120, 125, 128; Yiddish-speaking, 164, 165, 167 and n
Jewish women, 101–102, 106; mothers, 123, 129
Jews: Ashkenazic (*see* Ashkenazic Jews); Books of, 99, 100; in colonial America (*see* America, colonial, Jews in); compared with Japanese, 115; differences among, 96; as ethnic group, 95, 107; expelled from Spain, 97, 99, 103; fasts by, 99, 104, 105; food of, 101, 104–105; kinship among, 118–119, 121, 128; and land cultivation, 138n; sense of community among, 119–120. *See also* Jewish communities; Judaism
John Birch Society, 263
Judaism: Chasidism, 194n; circumcision, 100, 104; and conversion, 96, 100–101; decline of, in isolated groups, 109, decline of in New World, 107–110; *farda* (tax), 102; and Jewish groups, 95; and law, 193–194, 194n, 195, 196; and learning, 100; and marriage, 100–101, 102; and memorialism, 115–128; and Messianism, 97–99, 107, 110; opposition to, effect of, 103; practices of, 99–100; and prayer, 99–100, 104, 105; Sabbath observance, 100, 105–106. *See also* Jewish communities; Jews
Judaizars, 97; *defined*, 110–111

Kazakhstan: culture of, 87, 88, 89; labor system of, 90; writers of, 90
Kent State University, shooting at, 252 and n
"Kibbutz Artzi," 154; budget system in, 139–140; children in, 153n; sex differentiation in, 150; Alef, 150, 155; Beet, 150, 151, 155, 156
Kibbutz "Gan Siva," family finances in, 155
Kibbutz "Ichud," 154, 155; budget system, 140–142; children in, 153n; role differentiation, 150; Dalet, 150, 151, 155, 156; Gimmel, 150, 155, 156
Kibbutzim, Israeli, 154; budget system in, 139–142, 146–149; clothing in, 137, 138–139; collective consumption in, 136–139;
— conjugal organization in, 143–149; family finances, 133–156; and family variables, 152–154; and ideological variables, 149–152;
—family life in, 134–137; marriages in, 102, 136, 137; sexual equality in, 142–143; women in (*see* Women)
Kibbutzim, Japanese, 135n
Kibbutz Yod, 150, 153, 155

Ki-du (Tibetan association), 45n, 48n, 69, 70
Kings, Indian; and caste system, 7–8, 15–18; as gods, 8–10; and Hinduization of tribes, 21–24; palace of, ritual in, 8, 10, 14, 15, 16, 17, 18, 19; and princedoms, 15–16; ritual service of, 14, 15, 16, 17; rituals of spread to lower orders, 7–8; and temple organization, 10–15; vassal, 8, 11, 15, 23; and villages, 21
Kinship: Chinese, "mourning circle," 72; Indian and caste, 38–39, 40, 43; Japanese, 128; Jewish attitude to, 115–119, 121, 128; Tibetan, and *ga-nye*, 50–51, 57, 71. *See also* Ancestor worship; Families and family life; Household, Tibetan; Memorialism, Jewish
Kirghizia; celebrations in, 91; culture of, 87, 88, 89; hydropower project built, 88; labor system of, 90; poets of, 90
Kishan Garhi, India, households of, 8
Kishinev, Russian and Moldavian cultures of, 82, 83, 84
Konarak, Sun Temple of, 12

Lama, Tibetan, 52n
Land, in India: community control over, 42; ownership, 43–44; reform, and temple economy, 28, 32–34
Land, cultivation, Jews and, 138n
Language, 190n; categorization by, and God, 189–190; in Central Asia, 89–90; and cultural minorities, 166–167, 269; Hebrew, 166–167; in India, and caste, 9; of Jews, 95, 96, 164–167; in U.S.S.R., 84, 87, 88; Yiddish, 163n, 164, 165, 167 and n
Law: and "civil religion," 198–202; and conception of God, 192–197; and the counter-culture, 261, 267n; order of, 191
Lebanon, population of, 163
Leviathan, (Hobbes), 191
Litchfield, "The Country Place," commune in, 226–245; basic functioning of, 240–245; beginnings, 228–231; impressions of, 234–236; "milieu therapy," 231–234; questionnaire re, feedback from, 236–240, 245–248
Love, Shakers' view of, 183 and n

Macrobiotic food, 257–258, 269
Making of the counter-culture, The, (Roszak), 252n
Man's search for meaning, (Frankl), 245
Marranos, 97; *defined*, 111
Marriage: in communes, 205; of Jews, 100–101, 102. *See also* Marriage, in a kibbutz; Weddings

Marriage, in a kibbutz, 136; apartment for couple, 137; conjugal organization, 143–149; financial task division, 146–152, 155–156; variable family functions, 152–154. See also Decision-making, in families
Maryland, racialism in, 264
Massachusetts Bay, Quakers in, 197
Memorialism, Jewish, 115–128; compared with Japanese, 128–130; compensates for family shortcomings, 129–130; historical, 115–117; psychodynamics of, 121–128; in *shtetls*, 118, 125; structural features of, 118–121
Mental illness; in modern America, 228, 241–242. See also Psychotherapy
Messianism: among American Indians, 106; among Jews, 97–99; and pseudo-Messiahs of 17th Century, 107, 110; among Shakers, 175–184. See also Millennarialism
Metaphysics, (Aristotle), 189n
Methodist Church, 262
Mexico, colonial, Holy Office in, 96
Millennarialism, 175n, 209–210, 223
Millennial praises, (Wells), 176
Moldavia: culture of, 81, 82, 83, 84; local cultures in, 83–85; uniformity of, 81–83
Moral systems: Tibetan *ga-nye*, 48–54; in U.S.S.R., 82–83
Mothers, Jewish, guilt-inducing, 123, 129
"Mourning circle," Chinese, 72
Mourning, Jewish, 119, 124, 126. See also Death rites; Funerals
Muslim: dialects, 166; settlements in India, 41
Muslims; *farda* paid by, 102; in U.S.S.R., 82, 91
Mystical experience, of counter-culture members, 255–256, 258, 259, 262, 268–269, 296. See also Mysticism; Nature; Religious experience
Mysticism, 188; and community, 202–206; and the nature of the divine, 268. See also Religious experience
Myths, 190 and n, 266

Names, among Jews, 117, 120–121, 124
National culture; in Soviet Central Asian Republics, 87–91; in U.S.S.R., 80, 83, 84–85
Nature: and order, 191; and religion, 191, 257, 264; rural communities' experience of, 203–206
Needs, basic human, 232, 241–243
Nepal: law courts of, 66–67; Solu, 71–72; Tibetans settle in, 45 and n; tribes of, 47, 48n, 57. See also "Deling" village, Nepal, Tibetan community in
New Granada, Jews in, 17th Century, 107, 108, 109
New Spain: Inquisition tribunal in, 96; Jews in, 17th Century, 98–99, 102, 109; Jews arrested, *1642*, 107; See also America, colonial, Jews in
New York City: East Village, 225; Hungarian Hasidim, 167; Jewish communities in, 115, 119, 125; psychotherapy in, 228, 229
Numinous, the, 267

Observation, participant, 227, 234–236, 252, 253
Occult, the, 256
Oneida community, 205
Orissa, (Kalinga), India, 9; God-King in, 9–10; Hindu hierarchy in, 21; Hinduization of tribes in, 21–24; social structure of villages in, 19–21; state deity and temple organization, 10–18; temple community in, 27–34

Pakistan, West, *beraderi* system in, 72–73
Panda system, in India, 11
Panjab, West, reciprocation system in, 69
Peasants; European, culture of, 169; Indian, and castes, 20–21; Jewish, 194 and n
Peru: Holy Office in, 96; Jews in, in 17th Century, 109; Jews arrested in, *1634*, 107–108; Jews marry in, 102; Portuguese Jews in, 99. See also America, colonial, Jews in
Poland, Jews of, 164, 165, 167n
Political boundaries, and cultural units, 167–169
Political system, Soviet, 82
Politics: American New Left, 259; and religion, 266. See also State
Portugal: Jews expelled from, *1497*, 97; Jews move to, 99, 103; Spain dominates, *1580*, 99
"Portuguese Jews," 99, 111
Prayer meetings, 221, 222
Prayers: of American youth group, 218–219, 220–221; of Morning Star faith, 199–200
Prayers, Jewish, 99–100; *Amidah*, 99–100; for the dead, 116–117, 119, 122–123; posture during, 105, 106; private, 104; on the Sabbath, 100, 104
Priesthood, in India, 18; economics of, 28, 29–33; rights by inheritance of, 27–29. See also Temple servants
Primitive religion, 276

Index of Subjects

Production: collective, in kibbutz, 136; relations, in India, 42–43
Protestantism, in America, 109, 188; rituals of, 221, 222. *See also* "Seekers," the
Psychotherapy: at "The Country Place," Litchfield, 229–234, 235, 240–245; group-, 230–231, 235, 236, 242; and work, 231–234, 236, 243; after leaving community, 240; in New York City, 228, 229
Punishment, of children, 283
Puri, Shrikshetra; cult of Lord Jagannath at, 9, 10, 12, 24; Raja of, 9; temple of, 12, 14, 17, 24
Puritanism, in America, 195, 196–197

Quakers, 197

Racialism, in America, 264
Rajput, myth of, 22
Rallies and demonstrations, of counter-culture, 264, 265, 273
Reality, representation of, 188–193
Reciprocation: in India and Pakistan, 72–73: Tibetan concepts of, 58–64, 72–73; and attendance at life crises, 62; of gifts, 60–63; of information, 63–64
Reductionism, 265–266, 275
Reincarnation, and American counter-culture, 260, 265n, 268, 271
Religion: and caste, in India, 7–9 (*see also* Temple communities); civil, and the American counter-culture, 198–202; and cultural units, 169–170; group-, 275–277; organized, as perceived by counter-culture members, 254, 255, 257, 259–268 *passim*, 275, 276; and politics, 266–267; primitive, 276; significance of, 254 and n; in Soviet Central Asian nations, 90; study of, 265. *See also* Catholic church; Christianity; God; Gods, Indian; Judaism; Religious experience; Sacred images
Religious congregations, and therapeutic community, 242
Religious economic systems, 34. *See also* Temples, in India
Religious experience; of counter-culture members, 254–265, 275 (questionnaire re, 277, 279); *defining*, 253, 254; group, 270–271, 274–277; and nature of the divine, 268–269; as *"numinous,"* 267; and self-concept, 269–270; in Shaker community, 175–184; study of, 265–266. *See also* Religion; Sacred images
Religious orientation of members of counter-culture, 187–206, 252–279; re God and reality, 188–192; mysticism and community, 202–206; substance and code, 192–197
Religious vocation, 294–295
Religious youth group. *See* "Seekers," the
Rituals; and counter-culture members, 257, 262, 263, 272, 273; of life-crises, and Tibetan *ga-nye*, 51, 60–63; *rites de passage*, 296. *See also* Birth of children; Death rites; Funerals; Ritual services; Weddings
Ritual services, in India: and caste, 7, 16–18, 22–23, 24; in palaces, 14, 15, 16, 17, 18; in temples, 8, 9–10, 11–14, 16–18, 34; in villages, 19, 20
Roman Empire, 168
Rural communes, 203–206, 294n

Sabbath observance, by Jews, 100, 105–106
Sacred, the, and the secular, in India, 33
Sacred city, the, 297
Sacred images: of counter-culture members, 251, 253–260 *passim*, 263, 265; studying, 265–266
Sacred substances, 199–200
Sacrifice, and caste order, in India, 7, 17, 19
San Francisco Chronicle, 226
Sanskrit formula, 190
Savings associations, 71
Schizophrenics, 228
Science: the rise of modern, 190; in Soviet Central Asian nations, 90; in U.S.S.R., 79, 85
Secularization, in India, 33
"Seekers," the, American religious youth group, 209–224; fellowship of, 210, 223–224; leadership of, 212; meetings, 212–222; membership growth, 210–211; "sharing" in, 216–217, 218–220, 223–224
Self: archetype of the, 294, 297; and communitarian experiments, 293–298; concept of, in Hutterite children, 288–290; concept of, in religious experience, 269–270; search for the nature of, 2
Sephardic Jews (originally from Iberian peninsula), 95; memorialism among, 117; "Portuguese," 99, 111; Spanish, 99, 103. *See also* America, colonial, Jews in
Servants, in India: in palace, 14, 15, 16, 17, 18; of poor householders, 8; temple (*see* Temple servants); vassals, 7; in villages, 19–21
Sexual equality: in communal groups, 134, 136; in kibbutzim, 137, 142–143 (*see also* Marriage, in a kibbutz); in therapeutic community, 230. *See also* Women
Sexual intercourse, Jewish law re, 194
Shakers, the, community of, 175–184, 205

"Sharing": in American religious youth group, 216–217, 218–220; perceived by member of counter-culture, 255
Sherpa society, of Nepal, 47, 48n, 57; mutual aid among, 71–72; reciprocation among, 62–63
Shiva, Lord, worship of, 9, 10
Socialism; and American counter-culture, 271; in U.S.S.R., 87, 90
Social relationships: avoidance of, 234; in crowd rallies, 265; perceived by members of American counter-culture, 255, 262–263, 266 and n; *See also* Dispute settlement; Friendship; *ga-nye* (Tibetan); Groups; Group therapy; Marriage; "Sharing"
Soviet Central Asian Republics, national culture in, 87–91
Spain: *1492*, Jews expelled from, 97, 99, 103; *1580*, and Portugal, 99; 18th Century, Hapsburg dynasty ends in, 110. *See also* Catholic church; Inquisition, Spanish (Holy office)
Spanish America. *See* New Spain
Spanish Jews: in New World, 99; psyche of, 103. *See also* America, colonial, Jews in
Springfield, Mass., counter-culture commune in, 251–252; beliefs of members, shared, 271; group experience in, 270–273, 275–277; group identification of, 270; group importance in, 273–274; methodology and interpretation of research into, 252–254, 265–270 (questionnaire re group attitudes, 277–279); practices and images of, 272; religious character of group, 274–275; religious experience of members of, 255–265, 275–277; shared experiences, 270–271; symbols of, 272, 273; theft by members, 273; value system of members, 271
State: American, and church, 275; and cultural unit, 167–169; definition of, 167; Indian, and deity, 8, 9–10; and princedoms, 15–16; and temple organization, 10–15
Superstitions, Jewish, 103–104
Swat: Pathans of, 48n; reciprocation systems in, 69; *taltole*, neighborhood unit of, 72

Tajikistan, culture of, 87, 89
Taoism, 194–196, 202
Taos, New Mexico, communes in, 226
Tao Te Ching, 195, 202
Tatar Autonomous Soviet Socialist Republic, religion in, 82
Technical revolution, in U.S.S.R., 79, 85
Temples, in India: Bhubaneswar, 10, 12; Chandi, in Cuttack, 29–32, 33, 34; of Orissa, 27–34; of Puri, 12, 14, 17, 24; Sun, of Konarak, 12;
— economics of: 27–35: auctions, 29, 30–31; dispersal of offerings, 29–30; and land reform, 28, 32–34; rights by consignment in, 30–32, 33–34; rights by inheritance in, 27–29; rural, 28;
— organization of: ritual services in, 8, 9–10; and the state, 8–15; in villages, 20
Temple servants (*sevaks*) in India: rights by consignment of, 30–32, 33–34; rights by inheritance of, 27–29, 33–34; ritual duties of, 11–14, 16–18; wages for, 28
T-Group dynamics, 222
Theft, by counter-culture members, 273
Tibet, 45–46; "Gya-tri" village, 46 and n, 47, 56n
Tibetan book of the dead, (Evan-Wentz), 265 and n
Tibetans, in Nepal. *See* "Deling" village, Nepal, Tibetan community in
Traditions, developed in Soviet Central Asian Republics, 87–91
Tsok (Tibetan Saving association), 45n, 48 and n, 69–70
Turkmenia: carpets, of, 89; culture of, 87

Union of Soviet Socialist Republics: communism and the family in, 135n; cultural interaction in, 79–85; history of, 79–80; urbanization in, 81–82. *See also* Moldavia
United States of America: "civil religion" in, 198–202; communes in (*see* Ben Lomond, California; Communes, of American counter-culture; Litchfield, "The Country Place"; Springfield, Mass.); family organization in, 146, 147; Jews in modern, 115, 119, 125. *See also* Counter-culture, modern American; New York City
Urbanization, in U.S.S.R., 81–82
Utopianism, 204–205, 243; sacred city, the, 297
Uzbekistan, culture of, 87, 88, 89

Values, social and moral: of American counter-culture members, 271; in U.S.S.R., 82–83
Villagers, moving into towns, 70
Villages, Indian: caste system in, 7–8, 9, 18–21, 39; communities of, 39, 40–43; economy of, 32–33; temples of, 27
Vishnu, 9, 10, 15

Walden two, (Skinner), 296n
Washington: commune in, 187n, 203; demonstration in, *1971*, 273

Wayward Puritans, (Erikson), 197
Weddings: in a kibbutz, 136; Tibetan, gifts at, 60 and n, 61, 62–63; in U.S.S.R., 84, 91
"Who Are You?" exercise, (Bugental and Gunning), 288–290
Women: Congregationalist lay ministers, 214; in Hutterite community, 290;
— Jewish, 101–102, 106; in colonial America, and Messianism, 98–99; and marriage, 100–101; mothers, 123, 129; and Sabbath, 100, 105
— in kibbutzim: and clothing distribution, 138; and finances, 141, 146–153, 155–156; and marriage, 136, 137, 143–153, 155; and sexual equality, 137, 142–143; work of, 137, 142–143, 150
— Tibetan, at life-crisis rites, 62
— in U.S.S.R., work of, 83

Work: of Hutterite children, 289; of Indian castes, 38 (*see also* Ritual services, in India); in kibbutzim, 137, 142–143, 150; in therapeutic community, 231–234, 236, 243. *See also* Employment

Yiddish language, 163n, 164, 165, 167, 167n
Yin-yang, 258 and n
Yoga, 260, 267, 275n
Young Men's Christian Association, 222
"Youth culture," American, 2, 225–226, 232, 238; symbols of, 272; in therapeutic community, 235. *See also* Counter-culture, modern American
Youth group, American religious. *See* "Seekers," the

Zen Buddhism, 196